D0163715

AMERICAN COURTS AND THE JUDICIAL PROCESS

2 nd
Edition

9780190278892.

AMERICAN COURTS AND THE JUDICIAL PROCESS

G. LARRY MAYS
New Mexico State University

New York   Oxford
OXFORD UNIVERSITY PRESS

Oxford University Press, Inc., publishes works that further Oxford University's objective of excellence in research, scholarship, and education.

Oxford New York
Auckland Cape Town Dar es Salaam Hong Kong Karachi
Kuala Lumpur Madrid Melbourne Mexico City Nairobi
New Delhi Shanghai Taipei Toronto

With offices in
Argentina Austria Brazil Chile Czech Republic France Greece
Guatemala Hungary Italy Japan Poland Portugal Singapore
South Korea Switzerland Thailand Turkey Ukraine Vietnam

Copyright © 2012 by Oxford University Press, Inc.

For titles covered by Section 112 of the US Higher Education
Opportunity Act, please visit www.oup.com/us/he
for the latest information about pricing and alternate formats.

Published by Oxford University Press, Inc.
198 Madison Avenue, New York, New York 10016
http://www.oup.com

Oxford is a registered trademark of Oxford University Press

All rights reserved. No part of this publication may be reproduced, stored in a retrieval system, or transmitted, in any form or by any means, electronic, mechanical, photocopying, recording, or otherwise, without the prior permission of Oxford University Press.

Library of Congress Cataloging-in-Publication Data

Mays, G. Larry.
    American courts and the judicial process / by G. Larry Mays. – 1st ed.
        p. cm.
Includes index.
ISBN 978-0-19-973885-4 (alk. paper)
1. Criminal justice, Administration of–United States. I. Title.
KF9223.M29 2011
347.73′1—dc23
                            2011018568

Printing number: 9 8 7 6 5 4 3 2 1

Printed in the United States of America
on acid-free paper

This book is dedicated to the "wild bunch."
In order, they are Mina, Lucy, Oliver, Maggie, and Robby.

With special thanks to Gregory Mays.

CONTENTS

CHAPTER 2 – FOUNDATIONS AND FUNCTIONS OF LAW

II. COURT PARTICIPANTS: ROLES AND RELATIONSHIPS

CHAPTER 3 – THE COURTROOM WORK GROUP

CHAPTER 4 – JUDGES

CHAPTER 5 – LAWYERS AND LITIGANTS

III. TRIALS AND RELATED FUNCTIONS

CHAPTER 8 – SENTENCING

IV. COURT STRUCTURE

CHAPTER 11 – COURTS OF APPELLATE JURISDICTION

V. ISSUES FACING THE COURTS

CHAPTER 12 – ADDRESSING THE PROBLEMS AND CRAFTING SOLUTIONS

PREFACE

I had several purposes in mind when I started writing this book. First, I wanted to produce a student-friendly text that covered the essentials of the court systems in the United States without taking an encyclopedic approach that inundates students with too much information, much of which is extraneous.

Second, the court system in the United States presents a bewildering array of structures, functions, problems, and issues. Multiple actors are involved in the enterprise that we call the judicial process, and some are regular participants while others participate only occasionally. The average citizen, who may only attend court to pay a traffic ticket or who might be called for jury duty, can be perplexed at all of the activity and the use of unfamiliar legal terminology by attorneys and judges. If you have ever found yourself in this situation you are not alone. Therefore, another purpose of this text is to examine the many elements associated with courts and the judicial process, in a way that is concise and intellectually accessible.

Third, with the increasing prices of textbooks both in the United States and worldwide, it was especially important to me to produce a book that is affordable. Thanks to the editorial staff at Oxford University Press, we were able to do so.

The chapters in this book are laid out in a fashion that should take students through a logical progression of topics on courts and the judicial process. I begin with a brief overview of the legal system in the United States. This will provide an introduction to some of the terminology that appears in subsequent chapters. Concepts such as separation of powers, federalism, and adversarial justice are vital to understand how courts operate and why. Additionally, it is valuable to consider the foundations of the legal system in this country. It is especially important to examine the historical development of law that has led to the types of cases adjudicated and the courts and the judicial process we find within our contemporary legal system. Furthermore, distinctions are made between the broad areas of civil law and criminal law and their differing systems and participants. For some of you the initial material in the book will simply provide a review, especially if you have had an introduction to criminal justice class and/or a course on criminal law. Nevertheless, having clarity on the elements of a crime, various types of defenses, and different classifications of criminal offenses is worthwhile in setting the stage to consider the nature of the business that is transacted daily in our court systems.

Second, four chapters are devoted to examining the key actors typically found in the judicial process. I begin by delving into the concept of the courtroom work group. In some ways this notion is shorthand for the judges, prosecuting attorneys, and defense attorneys that daily participate in the various courts at all levels. Examining the courtroom work group helps us understand why a system that we typically characterize as adversarial actually is quite cooperative. This notion reveals that each member of the courtroom work group is dependent upon the others to help in one of the ultimate goals of the courts: disposing of cases. In addition to the core members of the court-room work group, you will be introduced to other actors in this process who operate largely behind the scenes, such as court administrators and judicial clerks. These individuals and groups also are addressed individually and in detail later in the text.

After considering the courtroom work group as a complete entity, I discuss the different members of the work group, focusing on who they are and what they do. The first chapter to undertake a more comprehensive view is Chapter 4 on judges. To more fully appreciate the office of judge it is crucial to understand the different ways in which judges are chosen for office. Along with judicial selection the issues of qualifications, concern over discipline for misconduct in office, and the functions performed by judges help us realize the complexity and importance of this office and the men and women who sit on the benches of courts at the local, state, and federal levels.

Chapter 5 takes us into the world of attorneys, including the way in which lawyers are trained in the United States and something about the way the practice of law is organized and stratified in this country. Particular attention is paid to the office of prosecuting attorney at various levels and the degree of control and power they may exercise. Also, I consider criminal defense attorneys, especially those that represent indigent defendants. Furthermore, the role of attorneys and litigants in civil cases is discussed.

In addition to the core members of the courtroom work group, there are other participants in court cases. Chapter 6 looks at ways in which citizens can be involved in the judicial process, primarily as either jurors or witnesses. Jury service is a civic obligation, one that some people look forward to and enjoy. However, not everyone is eligible for jury service, and some that are may not be particularly enthusiastic about serving on a jury. In fact, a few people actively try to avoid jury service. Witnesses do not have as much flexibility as potential jurors do in deciding whether to participate in a trial or not. When people who have witnessed a crime are subpoenaed to court they must report or face the possibility of being held in contempt of court and serving jail time.

The third section of the book is composed of two chapters, and one of these (Chapter 7) deals with trials and the various steps that transpire in preparing for and conducting trials. For most people a trial is the ultimate symbol of the American legal system and justice, even garnering the United States the description of being a "litigious society." However, the reality is that relatively few criminal cases go to trial (by some estimates around 20%); most are resolved through guilty pleas, with or without overt plea bargaining. Chapter 8 addresses one function of the courts—sentencing—that may be the most time-consuming of all. Each member of the courtroom work group plays a role in sentencing, but many of the sentencing options are decided by legislative bodies rather than the courts. Particular concerns in the sentencing process revolve around the impact that personal characteristics such as race, ethnicity, and gender have on the sentences handed down by judges.

The fourth section of the book discusses three different types of courts: the courts of limited or specialized jurisdiction, the courts of general trial jurisdiction, and the appellate courts. The limited jurisdiction courts in this country are very important because they process the bulk of the civil and criminal cases that are heard annually.

The limited jurisdiction courts truly are the workhorses of the judicial process, and they labor under heavy caseloads and, too often, extremely limited resources. The general jurisdiction trial courts are responsible for trying major civil disputes along with the most serious (felony) of the criminal cases. These are the courts that typically are shown in television and movie dramas about courts. In contrast with the trial courts, appellate courts are seldom seen or heard from by the general public, and most people have only vague ideas about what they do. In fact, juries are not present, and the vast majority of appellate decisions are made on paper in the form of written decisions. Nevertheless, appellate courts are responsible for correcting errors that have occurred in the trial courts, and they are also responsible for interpreting the constitutionality of statutes as well as the actions of representatives of the executive branch such as governors or the president. While they handle much smaller caseloads than the trial courts, the work of appellate courts is essential to the smooth functioning of governments and of our democracy, and they add a critical level of accountability to the judiciary.

Finally, the last chapter in the book considers some of the problems that continue to plague the operations of contemporary courts. Among these problems are the financial commitments we make to running all of our courts. Additionally, the question of judicial independence (addressed initially in Chapter 4) is revisited. Some of the most public concerns relative to the courts include the use of alternative dispute resolution (ADR) mechanisms in lieu of traditional litigation, the introduction of new types of scientific evidence (such as DNA testing) in criminal cases, the variety of reasons for wrongful convictions, and the emerging concern over adjudication and the rights of terrorism suspects. These are likely to be dilemmas facing the courts for decades to come.

In the end the goal of this book is to make each student a more informed individual. That should be the case whether you choose a career in criminal justice or some other governmental function. It should be equally true if you decide to work in the private sector. Understanding the courts and the judicial process should lead to each of you being not only more knowledgeable, but also a better citizen.

ACKNOWLEDGMENTS

There are a number of people who have contributed significantly to the writing and publication of this book. First, my sincere thanks go to my son, Greg Mays, who did a substantial amount of research, writing, and rewriting on the manuscript. In some ways he is an under-acknowledged coauthor. Second, my wife Brenda, as always, has been extremely patient with me as I have worked on this book (and a couple of others at the same time). Third, several individuals were gracious enough to review the manuscript at various stages and to make many helpful and constructive suggestions. These include M. Beth Bailey, University of North Florida; Jeremy D. Ball, Boise State University; Robin Cox-Lovett, St. Thomas University; Amy Craddock, Fayetteville State University; Mary Ann Eastep, University of Central Florida; Laura Fidelie, Midwestern State University; Lori A. Guevara, Fayetteville State University; Elizabeth Maier, Norwich University; Michelle Meloy, Rutgers University; Paul E. Meyer, Kent State University; Andrew A. Mickle, Georgia State University; Emmanuel C. Onyeozili, University of Maryland–Eastern Shore; Linda Robyn, Northern Arizona University; James J. Ross, SUNY–Brockport; and Jimmy J. Williams, University of Alabama. Fourth, the staff at Oxford University Press deserves a great deal of thanks. Although she bailed out on me mid-stream, Sherith Pankritz, who was my original editor when I signed the contract, is still one of my all-time favorite people. Her very capable replacement has been Sarah Calabi, who has had to put up with the often strange way I approach creating a book. Additionally, among those who have worked on the production processes have been Richard Beck, Paula Schlosser, David Bradley, and Debbie Ruel.

Finally, there is a legion of my former students over the past thirty-plus years who have lived through the trials and tribulations of studying about and doing research on the courts with me. It goes without saying that I cannot name them all, but they know who they are and they bear equal blame with me for this project as a result of their comments about "when are you going to write a book on courts?"

I welcome comments and questions from any of you about this book. Feel free to e-mail me at glmays@nmsu.edu.

PART ONE

PERSPECTIVES ON THE JUDICIAL PROCESS

1

An Overview of the American Legal System

Photo source: maXx images/SuperStock

CHAPTER OUTLINE

- Introduction
- The Criminal Justice System
- Separation of Powers
- Federalism
- Differences in Court Jurisdictions
- Adversarial Justice
- Summary
- Questions for Critical Thinking
- Recommended Readings
- Key Terms
- References
- Endnotes

INTRODUCTION

The system of justice in the United States is very complex. It involves a variety of actors from the three branches of government as well as from three levels (local, state, and federal) of government. Quite often there is duplication of effort in administering justice and, just as frequently, there are gaps in the network of agencies that are responsible for the administration of justice. Most of this book is dedicated to the exploration of courts and the judicial process in the United States. However, in this chapter we will examine some of the other agencies in the network of organizations that we call the criminal justice system in order to establish a framework of reference for the remainder of the book. Additionally, I discuss notions such as the separation of powers in our governmental system, the idea of federalism and the role it plays in distinguishing the jurisdiction of different courts, the various types of jurisdiction that courts typify, and the concept of adversarial justice.

Along the way—in this chapter and the chapters that follow—I discuss the operations of courts and related agencies in other nations. I also present boxed materials that are taken from current news stories, called "In the News." Additionally, we will hear from judges, attorneys, and others associated with the court system in a series of boxes that I call "In Their Own Words." Some of these boxes present original materials prepared especially for this book, while others include quotes from famous individuals who have been involved in the judicial process in one way or another. A final group of these boxes is taken from landmark court cases (typically decided by the United States

Supreme Court), and these highlight the opinions written by the justices on the Court as they reflect on critical legal, political, and social issues.

THE CRIMINAL JUSTICE SYSTEM

Many of you reading this book already have taken a course entitled "Introduction to Criminal Justice" or something similar. However, I do not make the assumption that this is universally true. Therefore, for the benefit of those who have not had such a course, and to jog the memories of those of you who have, I provide a very brief synopsis of the criminal justice system in the United States. Figure 1.1 illustrates the complexity of justice processes and procedures in the United States. As you can see, there are three major components of the criminal justice system (police, courts, and corrections), and each of these three components exists at three levels of government (local, state, and federal). I briefly examine each of these components and comment on the ways in which they play a role in the judicial process.

THE POLICE

The police play a variety of roles in the justice system and in our society. Within the criminal justice system the police account for nearly half (45 percent) of the total justice expenditures nationwide (Hughes 2006). Typically, we characterize the police role as encompassing three primary areas of responsibility: law enforcement, order maintenance, and public service.

Law Enforcement

Law enforcement is the function most often associated with the police. Law enforcement can involve actions ranging from writing traffic tickets to undertaking

FIGURE 1.1 THE CRIMINAL JUSTICE MATRIX

	Police	Courts	Corrections
Federal			
State			
Local*			

*Local agencies include those from cities, countries, townships, villages, and similar political entities.

complex criminal investigations and making felony arrests. Any activity that involves the criminal code of a particular jurisdiction falls within the category of law enforcement. One of the interesting pieces of information about the law enforcement function is that this is the aspect of the police job that is most interesting and appealing to new officers, and it is what we spend a lot of our effort training new police officers to do. However, it occupies a relatively small portion of the time for most officers.

1829 wrote all still app for today

BOX 1.1   In Their Own Words: Sir Robert Peel's Nine Principles of Policing

1. The basic mission for which the police exist is to prevent crime and ✓ disorder.

2. The ability of the police to perform their duties is dependent upon public ✓ approval of police actions.

3. Police must secure the willing co-operation of the public in voluntary ✓ observance of the law to be able to secure and maintain the respect of the public.

4. The degree of co-operation of the public that can be secured diminishes ✓ proportionately to the necessity of the use of physical force.

5. Police seek and preserve public favour not by catering to public opinion but ✓ by constantly demonstrating absolute impartial service to the law.

6. Police use physical force to the extent necessary to secure observance of ✓ the law or to restore order only when the exercise of persuasion, advice and warning is found to be insufficient.

7. Police, at all times, should maintain a relationship with the public that gives ✓ reality to the historic tradition that the police are the public and the public are the police; the police being only members of the public who are paid to give full-time attention to duties which are incumbent on every citizen in the interests of community welfare and existence

8. Police should always direct their action strictly towards their functions and ✓ never appear to usurp the powers of the judiciary.

9. The test of police efficiency is the absence of crime and disorder, not the ✓ visible evidence of police action in dealing with it.

Source: Magnacartaplus.org (2009).

Order Maintenance

By contrast, **order maintenance** was the reason many early police departments were created. For example, when British Home Secretary Sir Robert Peel established the London Metropolitan Police in 1829, much of their time was devoted to the maintenance of order (Thurman 2002). Peel recognized that there was much skepticism about a civilian police agency, so every effort was made to distinguish the police from the military. Box 1.1 presents the nine principles that traditionally have been associated with the Sir Robert Peel and Sir Richard Mayne, one of the first commissioners of the London Metropolitan Police (Roth 2002; see also Thurman 2002).

Even today, many state and local police officers devote a considerable amount of their on-duty hours to maintaining order. Order maintenance responsibilities include keeping the peace by controlling loud parties, providing traffic and crowd control at athletic events, and keeping a watchful eye at any location at which large crowds may gather (state fairs, concerts, protests, etc.). While sometimes not considered to be "real police work," order maintenance is directly related to issues that affect the quality of life of most citizens (Kelling and Wilson 1982).

Public Service

The final major area of police responsibility is **public service**. In some ways this is a catchall since the police are called on to do any number of things that at first would not seem to be their responsibility. For instance, public service might involve the proverbial cat-in-the-tree call. It also can involve other animal control types of situations. Additionally, the police are called on to deal with dented trash cans, unsightly neighborhood lots, abandoned cars, and a multitude of other situations. At the most basic level we might ask why the public calls on the police in such situations, and there seem to be two readily apparent answers. First, in some ways the police are the most visible manifestations of government for many people. The police are "the government." If people do not know who to call in a particular situation, they can always call the police. The second reason the police get called in so many non-law-enforcement situations is that if you call them they will come. The might not arrive very quickly, especially if the call appears to be one that lacks urgency, but they will come at some point. They will come to your home, your office, your school, or wherever you tell them to meet you to deal with the particular situation. These two points tend to perpetuate the public's tendency to call the police for all kinds of problems and difficulties.

To fully appreciate what the police do in this country, it is necessary to examine the three roles that we have outlined in the context of the different levels at which the police operate. This helps us understand more fully that when we talk about "the police," we are actually talking about a wide variety of different agencies with similar, but sometimes unique, functions.

LEVELS OF POLICE AGENCIES

In order to completely understand the police component of the criminal justice system, we also need to highlight the fact that police agencies exist at all three levels of government. While the inclination might be to start at the top and work our way down, it really makes more sense to begin with the agencies at the local level since they occupy the largest segment of the police responsibilities in the United States and account for over two-thirds of the expenditures for police services nationwide (Hughes 2006).

Local Police Departments

A report compiled by the Bureau of Justice Statistics found that in 2004 there were 12,766 local police departments in the United States. These departments ranged in size from the New York City Police Department with over 36,000 officers down to some of the smallest agencies with one or two officers. In total there were 573,152 sworn officers employed in these departments, or an average agency size of about 45 officers (Reaves 2007). Table 1.1 shows the number of full-time state and local law enforcement employees by the type and size of agency in 2004.

Sheriffs' Departments

In addition to municipal police departments there were 3,067 sheriffs' offices and another 513 agencies that included county constable offices in the State of Texas. The sheriffs' offices employed 326,531 sworn personnel, and the constable/marshal agencies employed 2,823. Thus, in 2004 the total number of local law enforcement officers (excluding the special jurisdiction agencies serving colleges and universities, parks and recreation, transportation, alcohol enforcement, etc.) was 902,506.

TABLE 1.1 Full-time Law Enforcement Personnel by Agency Type and Size, 2004		
Type of Agency	Number of Agencies	Full-time Sworn Employees
Local police	12,766	446,974
Sheriff	3,067	175,018
State	49	58,190
Special jurisdiction	1,481	49,398
Constable/marshal	513	2,323
Agency Size	Number of Agencies	Full-time Sworn Employees
1,000 or more	79	222,201
500–999	89	60,943
259–499	217	75,157
100–249	714	106,964
50–99	1,259	86,558
Under 50*	15,518	180,080

Note: This includes 2,202 agencies that are listed with 0–1 officers.
Source: Reaves (2007:2).

State Policing

We will consider state police agencies next, but it is important to note that these agencies represent the smallest segment of the overall police component: State police agencies employ only 8 percent of the state and local officer total, and fewer than 10 percent of the total national police employment numbers (Hughes 2006; Reaves 2006).

At the state level, there are forty-nine primary law enforcement agencies (the State of Hawaii—largely because of its unique geography—does not have a state police agency). They range in size from the California Highway Patrol with 7,085 sworn officers down to North Dakota with 135 officers and South Dakota with 154. In 2004 there were 58,190 sworn state police officers nationwide (Reaves 2007).

The state agencies vary in their responsibilities with some having exclusive assignments as highway patrols—dealing with traffic enforcement and accident investigations—on the state and interstate highways. Other state police agencies have general police powers, and they are responsible for enforcing all state law violations that they might encounter. As a practical matter, these departments often exercise their police powers in rural and remote areas that are not patrolled frequently by sheriffs' offices or municipal police departments. The names of these organizations vary from "highway patrol" to "state police" or "department of public safety." Interestingly, while the agency name might give a clue as to the department's overall mission (highway patrol versus general law enforcement), this is not universally true.

Most states also have one or more special jurisdiction law enforcement agencies. Many of these agencies are responsible for functions such as criminal investigations, gaming enforcement, drug and alcohol enforcement, agricultural law enforcement, and fish and wildlife enforcement. These state agencies employed about 8,700 sworn personnel in 2004.

Federal Law Enforcement

Finally, there are numerous federal law enforcement agencies dealing with a variety of specialized problems. As Table 1.2 shows, there were about 105,000 sworn federal law enforcement personnel in 2004. The largest federal law enforcement agencies were:

- U.S. Customs and Border Protection (including the Border Patrol) with 27,705 sworn officers;
- the Federal Bureau of Investigation with 12,242;
- U.S. Immigration and Customs Enforcement (ICE) with 10,399;
- U.S. Secret Service with 4,769;
- Drug Enforcement Administration with 4,400;
- U.S. Marshals Service, with 3,233;
- Postal Inspection Service with 2,976; and
- Bureau of Alcohol, Tobacco, Firearms, and Explosives with 2,373.

Unlike their state and local counterparts, federal law enforcement agencies typically have narrow jurisdictions that were defined when they were established

TABLE 1.2 Full-time Federal Law Enforcement Personnel, 2004	
Agency	**Full-time Sworn Employees**
U.S. Customs and Border Protection	27,705
Federal Bureau of Prisons	15,214
Federal Bureau of Investigation	12,242
U.S. Immigration and Customs Enforcement	10,399
U.S. Secret Service	4,769
Drug Enforcement Administration	4,400
Administrative Office of U.S. Courts	4,126
U.S. Marshals Service	3,233
U.S. Postal Inspection Service	2,976
Internal Revenue Service, Criminal Investigation	2,777
Veterans Health Administration	2,423
Bureau of Alcohol, Tobacco, Firearms, and Explosives	2,373
National Park Service	2,148
U.S. Capitol Police	1,535
Bureau of Diplomatic Security, Diplomatic Security Service	825
U.S. Fish and Wildlife Service, Law Enforcement Division	708
USDA Forest Service, Law Enforcement and Investigations	600

Source: Reaves (2006:2).

by Congress or the President (Reaves 2006).[1] In recent years, largely as the result of the major reorganization following the 9/11 attacks aimed at New York City and Washington, DC, many of the federal law enforcement agencies have had their jurisdictions redefined or expanded.

As I close out this section, it is important to note the role that different police agencies play in the judicial process. At the most basic level, law enforcement officers at all levels are responsible for investigating crimes and making arrests. The individuals that they arrest are then brought before the courts for initial appearances, arraignments, and trials. Thus, the police function as "gatekeepers," and they are responsible for providing the raw materials that will be processed, at least by the courts with criminal jurisdiction. The police will also be responsible for transporting prisoners to and from the courts, and often they will provide security for the courts and for courtroom personnel such as judges. Therefore, while they are not a part of the courts themselves, the police provide essential elements that assist in the smooth operations of the courts.

THE COURTS

Obviously, given the focus of this book, much will be said about the courts. However, at this point it is useful to note that we have courts performing a number of related functions all over the country at any given time. In large cities, such as New York, the courts may operate nearly around the clock. In small towns and rural locations the courts may meet only on a periodic or sporadic basis. Whichever is the case, as a society we look to the courts to protect us from criminal offenders and to resolve many of our interpersonal disputes (Calvi and Coleman 2008; Vago 2009).

LEVELS OF COURTS

In Chapters 9, 10, and 11 we will examine specialized courts and courts of limited, general trial, and appellate jurisdiction. As was the case with the police, these different types of courts operate at all three levels of government: local, state, and federal. There are many types of local courts in the United States, but the most common are municipal, magistrate, or county courts. For the most part, however, courts tend to be creations of the state, and even some "local" courts actually are state-funded and supervised tribunals. This is true for most of the magistrate and similar courts. If you look again at the matrix in Figure 1.1, the cell where "State" and "Courts" intersect represents the bulk of court activity in the United States.

As you will see throughout the remainder of the book, describing and sorting the court structure in the United States is no easy task. There are federal courts, courts for the District of Columbia, and unique state structures for each of the fifty states. Some of these courts handle a broad range of cases and issues, and others are very specialized in both their nature and functions.

CORRECTIONS AND CRIMINAL SANCTIONS

Once criminal defendants become convicted offenders, they become the responsibility of the corrections component of the criminal justice system. After holding sentencing hearings, the courts turn these offenders over to the custody and control of correctional agencies. These agencies are responsible for probation and parole, community corrections programs, and for institutional corrections. They have a number of areas of responsibility, and the purposes most often associated with corrections include: retribution (punishment), rehabilitation, deterrence (both general and specific), incapacitation, and reintegration (see Mays and Winfree 2009:5–11).[2] These purposes also may be considered justifications for sentencing or sanctioning on the part of the courts. Therefore, it is worthwhile to briefly consider each of these.

Retribution

Retribution is one of the oldest purposes behind criminal sanctions. In fact, we have examples of the notion of retribution dating back to the Code of Hammurabi king of Babylon and to the Law of Moses found in the Pentateuch, or the first five books of the Bible. These examples frequently are called the *lex talionis*, or literally the "law of the claw." Often this concept is expressed in the familiar phrase "an eye for an eye, and a tooth for a tooth," found in Hammurabi's Code. The meaning is that the injured party had the right to retaliate in-kind for the injury suffered. In a modern sense, we occasionally apply this concept in cases involving murders and imposition of the death penalty. However, as a society we do not usually employ the *lex talionis* for most crimes. For instance, when there has been a robbery, we do not say to the victim "you may now rob the person who robbed you." While the government still can utilize retributive punishments for crimes, today we mainly use incarceration as the punishment of choice.

Rehabilitation

While retribution is backward looking, providing punishment for what someone had done, rehabilitation was forward looking. It assumed that offenders could receive treatment and services that would make them productive members of society in the future. Rehabilitation was a sanctioning principle that emerged in the nineteenth century with correctional reformers such as Zebulon Brockway, superintendent of the Elmira Reformatory in New York. By the middle of the twentieth century, rehabilitation had been incorporated into many of the sentences imposed on both juveniles and adults convicted of crimes. The primary justification behind rehabilitation was the idea that there was some redeemable quality in each person, and the law was to provide a mechanism or setting where this redemption could occur. This notion was so significant that we got a word that we associate with prisons—penitentiary—from a place where convicted offenders were to do penance. Therefore, from the mid-nineteenth century up until about 1980, rehabilitation served as one of the major sanctioning philosophies in the United States and in many nations around the world.

Deterrence

Much like rehabilitation, deterrence is a forward-looking sanctioning philosophy. Deterrence still occupies a significant role in the creation of laws and is a principle behind many criminal sanctions. For example, many supporters of the death penalty believe that it serves as a deterrent for those who would commit murders. However, some of the research conducted over the past two or three decades has seriously called this assumption into question (Radelet and Akers 1996; but also see Decker and Kohfeld 1990 and Shephard 2005).

Traditionally, deterrence has been considered to have two dimensions: specific deterrence and general deterrence. Specific deterrence assumes that we punish the individual convicted of a crime for the benefit of that individual. While there might be a broader deterrence effect, none is assumed. By contrast, general deterrence (a key element in almost every criminal law statute) presumes that if you punish one law violator, others will be discouraged to violate the same law. As many states have learned through laws related to drunk driving, general deterrence has its limits. No matter how severe the sanctions seem to be, some people will continue to drive drunk.

Incapacitation

Incapacitation and reintegration seem to be sanctioning purposes that are less related to the courts than to correctional agencies themselves. Incapacitation might be characterized as the "rotten apple" theory of sanctioning. In simplest terms, incapacitation serves to remove criminals (the "rotten apples") from society and places them in a secure environment where they cannot cause physical harm or property damage or loss to other members of society. Individuals who support incapacitation are not particularly concerned about what type of person the offender will be in the future, as much as how much public safety can be provided now. In contrast, reintegration acknowledges that virtually all of the people who have been sentenced to jails and prisons will be released at some point. Therefore, one of the responsibilities of correctional agencies is to somehow try to prepare released offenders to reenter society with law-abiding attitudes and orientations.

LEVELS OF CORRECTIONS

In some ways, "local corrections" is misnomer. Most of the incarceration that is handled locally takes place in the roughly 3,400 city and county jails in the United States. In most of these facilities, very little correcting of deviant behavior goes on, but given the size of the inmate population they house, jails must be examined in order to get the full picture of corrections in the United States. For example, a recent report by the Bureau of Justice Statistics shows that in 2000 local jails housed 621,149 inmates and supervised another 65,884 outside of the jail facility (for a total of 687,033 people under jail supervision). In 2006 the total numbers had grown to 826,041 with 765,819 housed in the jails and 60,222 supervised outside of the facility. For 2007 and 2008 the total numbers were 848,419 (780,174 plus 68,245) and 858,407 (785,556 plus 72,851), respectively (Minton and Sabol 2009:8). These numbers are one-day counts of inmate populations and do not account for the several million admissions and releases that jails process every year.

To supervise these jail inmates, local governments had nearly 250,000 correctional employees on their payrolls. This is roughly one-third of the nation's correctional personnel, and local corrections is second only to the states in terms of the number of people on the payroll (Hughes 2006).

While many jails simply house inmates who are awaiting trial or those who have been sentenced but not transferred to prisons, some jails in the United States do operate treatment programs that could be classified as corrective in nature, and there are other local detention facilities such as workhouses, penal farms, and similar institutions that exist along with the jails. Additionally, a number of cities and counties operate their own probation departments for juveniles and/or adults, and all of these, plus other community corrections programs, can be considered local corrections.

State Corrections

The cell in Figure 1.1 where "State" and "Corrections" intersect is where the bulk of correctional activity occurs in the United States. There are 1,320 adult state correctional facilities, and states are responsible for supervising the vast majority of probationers and parolees around the nation; most of the institutional (prison) population in the United States (87.5 percent at mid-year 2007) is housed in state facilities. In fact, two states each have almost the same number of people in prison as the U.S. Bureau of

Prisons houses: At mid-year 2007 Texas had 172,626 inmates and California had 176,059 compared with 199,118 held by the U.S. Bureau of Prisons (Sabol and Couture 2008). There are also over four million state offenders on probation and another seven hundred thousand on parole (Glaze and Bonczar 2007).

Federal Corrections

Finally, the federal government employs 4,593 federal probation officers. These individuals (along with another 607 pretrial services officers) are responsible for the supervision of the nearly twenty-six thousand offenders under the jurisdiction of the federal courts (Glaze and Bonczar 2007).There are ninety-five federal court districts encompassing the fifty states along with the U.S. territories, and all but seven of these districts authorize some probation officers to carry firearms in the line of duty (Reaves 2006:3). Additionally, the United States Bureau of Prisons (USBOP) operates 115 facilities that range from minimum security prison camps through super-max (or administrative maximum) security around the country. Currently, the Bureau of Prisons supervises the nearly two hundred thousand federal offenders who are incarcerated in one of the Bureau's facilities. The USBOP now employs over 36,000 people, with 15,214 serving as correctional officers of various ranks (Reaves 2006; U.S. Bureau of Prisons 2009).

All of the figures on employment and payroll expenditures for justice agencies demonstrate one very important point: the justice system in the United States is big business. Box 1.2 further illustrates this.

BOX 1.2   In the News: Justice System Employment and Expenditures

The Bureau of Justice Statistics in the U.S. Department of Justice periodically collects data on justice expenditures and employment in the United States. The most recent report was published in 2006 for expenditures in 2003. The picture that emerges from the BJS publications is one of massive spending for operation of the multiple justice systems that exist in this country. For example, in 2003 total expenditures of police, courts, and correction services in the United States were $185 billion. This was an increase of 418 percent from nearly $36 billion spent in 1982. Nationwide there are almost 2.4 million people working in some justice-related function in the three components of the criminal justice system that exist at three levels of government. Nearly half (1.12 million) work in the various law enforcement agencies, and the remainder work in corrections (about 750,000) or in judicial/legal positions (500,000). The bottom line is that justice-related services constitute a major spending commitment for all governmental entities in this country.

Source: Hughes (2006).

SEPARATION OF POWERS

One of the distinguishing features of the system of government that we have in the United States is the notion of **separation of powers**. Simply put, this means that the different functions exercised by both federal and state governments are divided among three coequal branches: legislative, executive, and judicial. At the federal level, each of these branches has its own article or section within the U.S. Constitution. Article I deals with the powers and responsibilities of the legislative branch (Congress), Article II deals with the executive (the President), and Article III addresses the judiciary (the Supreme Court and inferior federal courts). Box 1.3 contains brief excerpts from the Constitution addressing each of the three branches of government.

Among the powers that the Constitution gives Congress are the authorities to:

- establish and collect taxes
- borrow money on credit
- coin money
- provide punishment for counterfeiting
- establish post offices
- create courts inferior to the Supreme Court
- declare war
- establish and support armies

BOX 1.3   The Constitution and Establishment of Three Branches of Government

Article I, Section 1 says that:
>   All legislative Powers herein granted shall be vested in a Congress of the United States, which shall consist of a Senate and House of Representatives.

Article II, Section 1 says that:
>   The executive Power shall be vested in a President of the United States of America. He shall hold his Office during the Term of four Years, and together with the Vice President, chosen for the same Term, be elected....

Finally, Article III, Section 1 provides that:
>   The judicial Power of the United States shall be vested in one supreme Court and in such inferior Courts as the Congress may from time to time ordain and establish.

Source: Constitution of the United States of America.

- provide for and maintain a navy
- make laws necessary for carrying out the powers that have been enumerated

THE LEGISLATIVE BRANCH

In relationship to the operations of justice agencies in the United States, Congress is responsible for the creation of a national court system, the establishment of laws and procedures for these courts, and the funding of justice-related agencies. The same holds true for the legislative bodies in each of the fifty states. All of these are substantial powers.

THE EXECUTIVE BRANCH

The executive power of government is carried out by the President for the national government, and by the governors for the states. This authority is demonstrated through the carrying out or enforcement of the laws that have been established by the legislative branch. The President serves as Commander-in-Chief of the armed forces of the United States, and he directs the civilian arm of the federal government through the appointment and supervision of secretaries who oversee the various cabinet-level executive departments (such as State, Defense, Treasury, Justice, Homeland Security, etc.). The President also holds the appointment power over a number of high-level government officials including the U.S. Marshals, U.S. Attorneys, and all of the so-called Article III federal court judges (we will examine this group in Chapter 4). The nominations from the President must be approved by the United States Senate, but in most instances the people nominated will be confirmed with little fanfare and without much controversy. Finally, the President prepares and presents a budget to Congress. Ultimately, Congress will have the final say on the budget, but the President possesses a great deal of symbolic and real power in the budget preparation process. It is the way he outlines and defines the priorities of his administration.

THE JUDICIAL BRANCH

The judicial branch of government (and especially the United States Supreme Court) was labeled by Alexander Hamilton in *Federalist Paper #78* as the "least dangerous" branch of the government. It was characterized this way because it was said that the courts wield neither the sword (executive authority to enforce the laws) nor the purse (legislative authority to appropriate funding). Nevertheless, since the case of *Marbury v. Madison*, 1 Cr. 137 (1803) the Supreme Court has been able to assert its authority to review the actions of state courts, and both the executive and legislative branches of the state and federal governments to determine their constitutionality. This power is known as **judicial review**, and while it has been exercised cautiously it still remains a potential curb to unbridled actions by the states, the president, and Congress.

In summary, we have three co-equal branches of government that exercise their own unique powers. However, because of the idea of **checks-and-balances**, the three branches of government must cooperate in order to achieve their individual goals. Therefore, instead of the three branches being independent, they really are much more interdependent.

FEDERALISM

Not only does the United States Constitution (and the various state constitutions as well) provide for three branches of government, it also recognizes that there are some functions that should be exercised by the national government and some that should be in the domain of the state governments. This separation of powers by levels of government is called **federalism**. The last amendment in the Bill of Rights (Amendment X) notes that "The powers not delegated to the United States by the Constitution, nor prohibited to it by the States, are reserved to the States respectively, or to the people." In simplest terms, this means that the Constitution recognizes that there are some responsibilities that are uniquely reserved for the national government (for example, the rights to coin money and declare war), but there are some functions that should be performed by the states (the creation of state laws, the provision of public education, and the maintenance of state highways, for instance).

However, it is very important to note that there are a good many gray areas where the interests of the federal government and those of the state governments intersect and overlap. There also can be jurisdictional intersections of interest between and among the states (over issues such as water rights and interstate commerce, for example). In those instances where there is potential legal conflict, one level of government (such as the federal government) may defer to the interests of another level (a state or a group of states). This "interjurisdictional judicial courtesy" is known as **comity** (Champion 2005:50). Another way to define comity is the "Recognition that one sovereignty allows within its territory to the legislative, executive, or judicial act of another sovereignty, having due regard to the rights of its own citizens" (*Black's Law Dictionary* 1991:183).

An example of comity involves the prosecution of Timothy McVeigh for the bombing of the Murrah Federal Building in Oklahoma City in 1995. When the truck bomb exploded in front of the federal building, 168 people were killed. Since this act occurred in Oklahoma City, the State of Oklahoma could have taken the lead in the prosecution of McVeigh and his co-conspirators. Instead, Oklahoma deferred to the federal government to allow for prosecution of the federal agents who were killed in the bombing. Nevertheless, Oklahoma reserved the right to try McVeigh for the other deaths and to execute him if he was convicted. The federal government beat Oklahoma to the punch, and McVeigh was sentenced to die by a federal court jury; he was executed in June of 2001 (see Reid 2007:346).

DIFFERENCES IN COURT JURISDICTIONS

The concept of **jurisdiction** is very important in the understanding of courts and the judicial process. At its most basic level, jurisdiction means the legal authority that a particular court has to decide or not decide a case. Champion (2005:139) says that jurisdiction is "The power of a court to hear and determine a particular type of case; also, the territory within which a court may exercise authority, such as a city, county, or state." While this meaning is relatively simple, the notion of jurisdiction is complex and can be divided into several subcategories. In the remainder of this section we will examine the concepts of subject matter jurisdiction, limited versus general trial jurisdiction, hierarchical jurisdiction, and law versus equity. Each of these will help us to gain greater understanding on the organization and operations of courts in the United States.

SUBJECT MATTER JURISDICTION

When it comes to **subject matter jurisdiction**, the major distinction that we make in courts is between those that hear civil cases only, criminal cases only, and those that can hear both kinds of cases. In some states, like Georgia (two counties), Tennessee, and Texas, there are courts that only hear civil cases (Rottman and Strickland 2006). These types of cases deal with matters such as torts, breaches of contract, personal injuries resulting from accidents, and the whole range of domestic relations issues (divorces, paternity, child support, and wills and inheritances). By contrast, courts that only hear criminal cases deal with murders, robberies, burglaries, assaults, and the many other acts that are defined as crimes by the states. Although only ten states have fully unified court systems, most states have eliminated courts that hear only civil or criminal matters (Langton and Cohen 2007).[3] Under the category of subject matter jurisdiction, other states have specialized courts that deal with a limited range of cases of particular types. Some of these types of courts are juvenile courts, probate courts, and family or domestic relations courts. I address some of these in the next section.

LIMITED VERSUS GENERAL TRIAL JURISDICTION

Legislatures in several states have created courts of **limited jurisdiction** (sometimes these are called specialized jurisdiction courts). Some people refer to these as **inferior courts** because they are not authorized to handle the full range of cases. For example, some states have what are called magistrate courts, which typically are only permitted to hear small claims or minor civil disputes up to a certain dollar amount ($5,000, for example). Often the limited jurisdiction courts do not conduct jury trials (or they have a limited number of six-person jury trials), they may not produce verbatim transcripts of proceedings, the judges may not be required to be licensed attorneys, and in some cases attorneys do not appear to represent either side. In a very real sense, these tribunals are "the people's court."

In many states, the limited jurisdiction courts do have initial processing responsibilities for felony cases. The judges in these courts may conduct initial appearances where the charges are read to the accused, the bond is set, and the question of appointment of counsel is addressed. Some states also empower these courts to conduct preliminary hearings where the state must establish probable cause in order for the case to be referred to the grand jury or trial court.

By contrast, **general jurisdiction courts** are *the* trial courts in the United States. They exhibit all of the trappings that people associate with the trial process in courts. Judges in general jurisdiction courts are required to be licensed attorneys (and many states require them to have practiced law for some specified length of time), there are court reporters who maintain verbatim transcripts of proceedings (making them "courts of record"), and jury trials are regularly scheduled. General jurisdiction courts are responsible for appeals from the limited jurisdiction courts on a process known as trial *de novo* (or a new trial, since there is no transcript on which to base an appeal). They also are the courts that hold hearings and trials related to major civil cases and for felonies on the criminal side of the docket. Later in the book I devote a chapter to each of these types of courts.

HIERARCHICAL JURISDICTION

The courts that first hear cases—whether they are limited jurisdiction or general jurisdiction courts—are called **courts of original jurisdiction**. Sometimes they are also called courts of first instance or simply trial courts. The idea behind these designations is that these courts are the first ones to receive cases from the prosecutor's office, and these are the courts where trials will be conducted for both civil and criminal matters.

Distinct from the courts of original jurisdiction are the **courts of appellate jurisdiction** or, simply, the appellate courts. The courts of appellate jurisdiction are those tribunals that receive appeals from the trial courts based on errors of law. Unlike the courts of original jurisdiction where there is one judge and a jury, the appellate courts hear cases in panels of three or more judges based on the review of trial transcripts and oral arguments by attorneys representing both sides of the case. The opinions of these appellate courts are published in a series of volumes called a *reporter* and they are available in law libraries as well as in some public or university libraries.

The federal courts, and many state systems, have a two-tiered appellate court structure. First, there are the **courts of intermediate appellate jurisdiction**. In states these are often called the state courts of appeals, and for the federal system they are called the Courts of Appeals for the various judicial circuits. There are eleven numbered circuit courts, plus Courts of Appeals for the District of Columbia and for the Federal Circuit (U.S. Courts 2009). Thirty-nine states have intermediate appellate courts, and a few have separate intermediate appellate courts for civil and criminal matters. Most of the cases that are appealed from trial courts never make it past these first-level appellate courts.

Additionally, all states have a **court of last resort**, and Oklahoma and Texas have two such courts—one for civil cases and one for criminal cases (Rottman and Strickland 2006). These courts vary in their titles, but most frequently they are called the state supreme court or some variation of that title.[4] At the federal level, the court of last resort is the United States Supreme Court, and it was created by Article III of the Constitution. As you will see in Chapter 11, the U.S. Supreme Court is composed of eight Associate Justices plus the Chief Justice, and when there is a vacancy these individuals are nominated by the President of the United States and confirmed by the Senate. Once approved the Supreme Court justices have lifetime tenure assuming good behavior. The Supreme Court has jurisdiction over civil and criminal matters, and it receives appeals from the federal intermediate appellate courts (the U.S. Courts of Appeals) as well as from state courts of last resort.

As we can see, then, state and federal courts differ in their exact configurations, but all fifty-one court systems (in addition to the courts for the District of Columbia) in the United States are hierarchically arranged with lower level trial courts (one or two levels) and higher level appellate courts (one or two levels).

LAW VERSUS EQUITY

The final element that we must consider in dealing with the issue of jurisdiction is the distinction between law and equity. Most of my focus in this book is on law, particularly on criminal law. You will see in the next chapter that there are different sources of law such as the common law, constitutions, statutes, case law (appellate court decisions), and administrative or regulatory law. However, my primary emphasis is on statutory law or those laws that are created by legislative enactments. As you will see, laws are a pervasive part of our justice system and of society in general. Laws of varying kinds touch all of our lives every day. However, at times the law is silent or inadequate to provide relief (and some might even say the law can be unjust), and in those cases **equity** is available.

Like many parts of our legal system, equity developed in England when the king would transfer certain legal responsibilities to his chancellors or assistants. Calvi and Coleman (2008:30) say that "Although the common law courts were initially creative and flexible, they soon petrified, adopting rigid, harsh procedures. In addition, the courts could provide only one remedy—damages." By contrast, equity can provide specific reliefs such as **injunctions**. Injunctions are court orders that some action be taken or completed; they also may require that some deed be halted. For instance, environmental groups might file for an injunction requiring that construction of a dam be halted because of the potential destruction of habitat for some types of fish or other aquatic animals. Also, construction of a building or housing development might be halted by injunction if the site is found to have historical significance.

As a result of the king shifting legal responsibilities to his chancellors in England, separate chancery (equity) and law courts developed and existed side-by-side for about four hundred years. However, in England in the late-1800s "the two were merged, and all courts were to apply the rules of both, with equity being dominant in case of conflict" (Calvi and Coleman 2008:31).

In the United States today, virtually all states have merged law and equity in their courts of original jurisdiction. However, the states of Delaware, Mississippi, and Tennessee still maintain separate chancery or equity courts (Rottman and Strickland 2006).

ADVERSARIAL JUSTICE

The final concept that we need to consider in this chapter is that of **adversarial justice**. To understand the adversarial system that we have in the United States, we need to contrast our system with procedures utilized in other nations. The primary point of contrast between the Anglo-American system of law and its adversarial nature is with the countries that employ accusatory or inquisitorial systems. Many of the countries in Europe and South America have utilized accusatory justice mechanisms, although the

BOX 1.4
Law Italian Style

The recent Italian trial of American college student Amanda Knox who was charged in Italy with killing her British roommate has highlighted the differences between an adversarial system of justice—such as the one we have in the United States—and an accusatory legal system like that of Italy. Although the advent of the European Union has brought Italy and most of Europe under a legal system similar to that of the United States, there are still important differences. Italy, like most of the rest of Europe, operates under a Roman/Napoleonic law (or code law) legal system in which the police, prosecutor, and judge all participate in the investigation and fact-finding processes in the early stages of investigating crimes. This type of system places a great deal of emphasis on finding the truth early in the process, and it may result in fewer people being charged with crimes. However, in those cases where criminal charges have been filed, the likely outcome of the case is that the defendant will be convicted. Legal observers in the United States and Amanda Knox's family expressed their dismay that she did not seem to get a fair trial and that the verdict seemed to be a foregone result. This type of conclusion is easy to reach when comparing continental European court systems with those of common law countries like the United States and England.

Sources: Rizzo and Falconi (2009); Walsh and Hemmens (2008).

advent of the European Union (EU) is causing a shift from this approach among some of its members.

In the United States, we say that each civil and criminal case has two sides that stand opposed to one another. Ideally, under an adversarial model only one side can "win" and, thus, the other side must "lose." In game theory this is called a **zero-sum game**, with one winner and one loser. The clearest manifestation of this ideal is the requirement in our legal system that the state must prove the defendant guilty, and the defendant is not required to prove anything.

In contrast to adversarial justice, countries that employ accusatory or **inquisitional justice** bring all of the government's power to bear against the defendant, and the judge and prosecutor both are responsible for gathering information relative to the defendant's guilt. This may result in fewer people being accused of crimes. However, for those who are charged, the court assumes that there already is sufficient evidence of the defendant's guilt that when the trial begins the defendant must prove that he or she is not guilty, which can be a monumental task.

BOX 1.5   Who has a Criminal Justice System Like the United States?

One of the questions frequently asked of professors who teach crime-related courses is: "Who has a criminal justice system like we have in the United States?" Of course, the easy answer to this question is "no one." Many countries have elements of their justice systems that are similar to ours, but no one has a system that exactly duplicates that of the United States. For instance, England has a decentralized policing system much like the one we have. By contrast, Ireland and many continental European countries (like France) have national police agencies.

The English legal system, which is the closest to being like ours, has a different method of training lawyers and judges (see Box 5.1 on the training of attorneys in Great Britain). Furthermore, in most European countries judges receive their training in law school, and none are chosen by popular elections like those in the United States.

Finally, the correctional systems around the world may be the element that most closely resembles correctional systems in the United States. Most countries have substantially smaller prison populations than we do, though, and the typical prison sentences are significantly shorter than the average sentence in this country.

All of this means that when we visit foreign countries we can find justice-related functions that would be somewhat similar to those with which we are familiar. Nevertheless, each nation has its own unique justice system, and those systems are reflections of history, culture, and the political regime of each nation.

Source: Bureau of Justice Statistics (2010).

SUMMARY

In order to understand the whole judicial process in the United States, we must understand the organizational and political context in which the courts operate. Courts are part of the civil and criminal justice systems, and they are organized at the local, state, and federal levels. The courts interact on a regular basis with the police at various levels of government, and the courts provide the corrections system with its basic raw product: convicted offenders. Additionally, the courts are the forums within which prosecuting and defense attorneys operate on a regular basis. The attorneys for the state and defense (on the criminal side) and for plaintiffs and defendants (on the civil side) operate within the courts, but they are not really a part of the courts.

In addition to the courts functioning as part of the justice system, they also represent one of the three branches of government in our political system. The federal government and the state governments all have legislative branches (represented by the U.S. Congress and by state legislatures or assemblies), executive branches (represented by the President of the United States and by state governors), and judicial branches (composed of different kinds and levels of courts).

Politically, the courts also are influenced by the concept of federalism. Federalism says that the different levels of government—especially state and federal—have unique roles and responsibilities. Each level should exercise its duties without interference from or without interfering with the other levels. However, inevitably there is overlap and duplication of jurisdiction, and at times one level of government will defer to another; this is the notion of comity.

It is also essential to comprehend the definition of jurisdiction and the way that various forms of jurisdiction will influence the manner in which courts discharge their duties. For instance, some states organize their courts around different types of subject matter; some states have unified civil and criminal courts, while others have separate courts for each type of case. A number of states also have specialized juvenile courts, as well as courts for domestic relations or family courts, and probate matters.

Most states also have courts of limited jurisdiction, and some states have more than one type of these courts. At times these tribunals are called magistrate courts, but they have a variety of different titles, including municipal courts and justice of the peace courts. In most instances the limited jurisdiction courts process minor civil matters as well as criminal cases involving misdemeanors. They also serve as the legal forum for initial appearances and preliminary hearings in felony cases. Above the courts of limited jurisdiction are the courts of general trial jurisdiction. These courts are responsible for trials in cases of major civil disputes (typically over $5,000 or $10,000), and for criminal cases involving felonies. These courts represent the pinnacle of procedural formality in our justice system.

Furthermore, all fifty-one court systems in the country are organized as hierarchies. Every system has trial courts (one or two levels) and appellate courts (again, one or two levels). The trial courts, or courts of original jurisdiction, are responsible for initially hearing and deciding the issues in dispute. Once they have disposed of a case—whether it is civil or criminal—unresolved issues can be taken to the appellate courts if there is an assertion of an error of law. Relatively few cases are appealed each year, but some of them make it to the state courts of last resort, or to the ultimate court of last resort: the U.S. Supreme Court. As I note at many junctures throughout this book, each state has its own unique court structure. Some are similar, but virtually all have distinctive features.

Finally, the idea of adversarial justice is at the core of the way courts are structured and how they operate. Each case has two distinct sides, and the interests of each side stand in opposition to the other side. As can be seen in the next chapter (and in some of the other chapters in the book), however, the textbook notion of an adversarial process and the reality of the interactions among the courtroom participants are sometimes substantially different. In other words, the law on the books frequently does not look the same as the law in action.

QUESTIONS FOR CRITICAL THINKING

1. In the chapter you were presented with a diagram of the criminal justice system called the "criminal justice matrix." When you look at this matrix, what might you learn about the inherent efficiency or inefficiency of criminal justice operations in the United States?

2. At what level of government do we find most police resources and activities? Why is this the case? What about for the courts and corrections? Explain.

3. The Founding Fathers created three coequal branches of government for our nation. What are the three branches of government? Are they really coequal? Why or why not?

4. What types of cases might arise in both the federal and state courts? Give examples of the types of cases that might cause a conflict in jurisdiction between the two systems.

5. Some people have described the courts, and particularly the federal courts, as inherently undemocratic. If this is true, what does this mean in terms of the practice of judicial review? Is this the most undemocratic action that can be taken by the courts?

6. Based on the notion of federalism, do federal courts and state courts exist one over the top of the other, or side-by-side? Justify your answer.

7. More than likely, your state court system has a website. If so, check out the information contained on the website, especially for a description of the number and types of courts in your state. How many levels are there in your state court system? How many levels of original jurisdiction courts? How many levels of appellate courts?

8. Find a dictionary of criminal justice or legal terms and look up the concept of equity. Is the definition relatively clear to you? How would you define equity to another student? How important is the concept of equity in our legal system?

9. In which system—adversarial or accusatory—would you rather stand accused of a crime? Why? Explain.

RECOMMENDED READINGS

Calvi, James V., and Susan Coleman (2008). *American Law and Legal Systems*, 6th ed. Upper Saddle River, NJ: Pearson/Prentice Hall. This book, written largely from a political science perspective, presents a very useful overview of the nature and history of law, and how the legal system in the United States developed. The authors provide separate chapters on constitutional law, criminal law, administrative law, environmental law, torts, contracts, property, and family law. While the focus of the book is not specifically on the courts, it provides a broad background for understanding the context in which the courts operate.

Mays, G. Larry, and Peter R. Gregware (2009). *Courts and Justice*, 4th ed. Long Grove, IL: Waveland Press. This book presents twenty-six readings (some original and some reprinted) that deal with a range of issues that confront the courts. In this edition some of the new additions include one on wrongful convictions (by Marvin Zalman) and another on gender in the courts (by Susan Lentz). Both of these issues are addressed in the final chapter of this book.

Melone, Albert P., and Allan Karnes (2008). *The American Legal System*, 2nd ed. Lanham, MD: Rowman & Littlefield Publishers. The authors of this book have compiled what easily could be characterized as an encyclopedic treatment of the development and nature of the legal system in the United States. Not only do they provide a very thorough treatment of the historical evolution of our legal system, but also they provide comprehensive chapters on alternative dispute resolution, tort law, property, family law, contracts, and governmental regulation of businesses. In some ways, while it is a textbook it really should be considered a reference work.

Vago, Steven (2009). *Law & Society*, 9th ed. Upper Saddle River, NJ: Pearson/Prentice Hall. Vago's book takes a sociological look at understanding the way law operates in our society. He focuses on the theoretical perspectives of how law has developed and the purposes law serves. Perhaps two of the most useful (and interesting to students) chapters in the book are the ones examining the legal profession (what it means to be a lawyer), and how to go about doing research on law and society.

KEY TERMS

adversarial justice

checks-and-balances

comity

court of last resort

courts of appellate
jurisdiction

courts of intermediate
appellate jurisdiction

courts of original
jurisdiction

equity

jurisdiction

federalism

general jurisdiction courts

inferior courts

injunctions

inquisitional justice

judicial review

law enforcement

lex talionis

limited jurisdiction

order maintenance

public service

separation of powers

subject matter jurisdiction

zero-sum game

REFERENCES

Black's Law Dictionary, 6th ed. (1991). St. Paul, MN: West Publishing Co.

Bureau of Justice Statistics (2010). *World Factbook of Criminal Justice Systems*. http://www.ojp.usdoj. gov/index.cfm?ty=pbdetail&iid=1435.

Calvi, James V., and Susan Coleman (2008). *American Law and Legal Systems*, 6th ed. Upper Saddle River, NJ: Pearson/Prentice Hall.

Champion, Dean J. (2005). *The American Dictionary of Criminal Justice*, 3rd ed. Los Angeles, CA: Roxbury Publishing Co.

Decker, Scott H., and Carol W. Kohfeld (1990). The Deterrent Effect of Capital Punishment in the Five Most Active Execution States. *Criminal Justice Review* 15:173–91.

Glaze, Lauren E., and Thomas P. Bonczar (2007). *Probation and Parole in the United States, 2006*. Washington, DC: Bureau of Justice Statistics, U.S. Department of Justice.

Hughes, Kristen A. (2006). *Justice Expenditure and Employment in the United States, 2003*. Washington, DC: Bureau of Justice Statistics, U.S. Department of Justice.

Kelling, George, and James. Q. Wilson (1982). Broken Windows: The Police and Neighborhood Safety. *Atlantic Monthly* 249:29–38.

Langton, Lynn, and Thomas H. Cohen (2007). *State Court Organization, 1987–2004*. Washington, DC: Bureau of Justice Statistics, U.S. Department of Justice.

Magnacartaplus.org (2009). A History of the Nine Principles of Policing. http://www.magnacartaplus. org/briefings/nine_police_principles.htm.

Mays, G. Larry, and L. Thomas Winfree, Jr. (2009). *Essentials of Corrections*, 4th ed. Belmont, CA: Wadsworth/Cengage.

Minton, Todd D., and William J. Sabol (2009). *Jail Inmates at Midyear 2008—Statistical Tables*. Washington, DC: Bureau of Justice Statistics, U.S. Department of Justice

Radelet, Michael, and Ronald L. Akers (1996). Deterrence and the Death Penalty: The Views of the Experts. *Journal of Criminal Law & Criminology* 87(1): 1–16.

Reaves, Brian A. (2006). *Federal Law Enforcement Officers, 2004*. Washington, DC: Bureau of Justice Statistics, U.S. Department of Justice.

Reaves, Brian A. (2007). *Census of State and Local Law Enforcement Agencies, 2004*. Washington, DC: Bureau of Justice Statistics, U.S. Department of Justice.

Reid, Sue Titus (2007). *Criminal Law*, 7th ed. Los Angeles, CA: Roxbury Publishing Co.

Rizzo, Alessandra, and Marta Falconi (2009). American Student Guilty: Italian Jury Gives Knox 26 Years. *Albuquerque Journal*, December 5, p. A3.

Roth, Mitchel P. (2002). History of American Criminal Justice. In *Encyclopedia of Crime and Punishment*, ed. David Levinson, 21–27. Thousand Oaks, CA: Sage Publications.

Rottman, David B., and Shauna M. Strickland (2006). *State Court Organization 2004*. Washington, DC: Bureau of Justice Statistics, U.S. Department of Justice.

Sabol, William J., and Heather Couture (2008). *Prison Inmates at Midyear 2007*. Washington, DC: Bureau of Justice Statistics, U.S. Department of Justice.

Shephard, Joanna (2005). Deterrence Versus Brutalization: Capital Punishment's Differing Impacts Among the States. *Michigan Law Review* 104:203–56.

Thurman, Quint C. (2002). Community Policing. In *Encyclopedia of Crime and Punishment*,. ed. David Levinson, 270–75. Thousand Oaks, CA: Sage Publications.

U.S. Bureau of Prisons (2009). About the Bureau of Prisons. http://www.bop.gov/about/index.jsp.

U.S. Courts (2009). Court Locator. http://www.uscourts.gov/courtlinks/.

Vago, Steven (2009). *Law & Society*, 9th ed. Upper Saddle River, NJ: Pearson/Prentice Hall.

Walsh, Anthony, and Craig Hemmens (2008). *Law, Justice, and Society*. New York: Oxford University Press.

ENDNOTES

[1] Every federal law enforcement agency maintains a home page on the Internet. You can check each of these websites to find a brief history of the agency and the particular laws for which each is responsible.

[2] Others include concepts such as restitution and restoration among the responsibilities that correctional agencies also may have.

[3] Langton and Cohen (2007:6) say that "Technically, a unified state court system has no limited jurisdiction courts, one type of general jurisdiction court with few jurisdictional divisions, and all trial court judges serving in a general jurisdictional capacity." While only a few states meet this definition, many states exemplify elements of it.

[4] Only Maryland (Court of Appeals) and New York (Court of Appeals) use a designation other than Supreme Court or some variation on that title, for their courts of last resort. In both Oklahoma and Texas the Supreme Court only hears appeals in civil matters and the Court of Criminal Appeals is the court of last resort for criminal cases. These two states have what some have called a two-headed court of last resort.

2

Foundations and Functions of Law

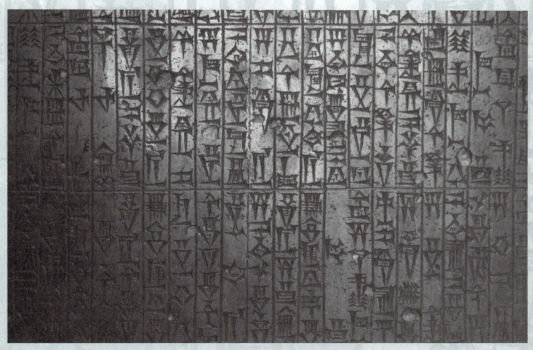

Photo source: Shutterstock

INTRODUCTION

When we talk about the criminal justice system we tend to focus on the three principal components of the system—police, courts, and corrections. However, the legislative branch of government is always a major player in the operations of criminal justice agencies in the United States. Legislatures are responsible for funding the operations of justice agencies in the United States, as well as creating criminal laws and deciding sentencing guidelines. In this chapter we will consider the historical development of courts and law (with a particular focus on criminal law), the distinctions between criminal law and civil law, the sources of law in the United States, the various degrees of seriousness, the elements of criminal offenses, incomplete (or inchoate) offenses, the defenses that may be employed in criminal trials, and the different ways we can classify crimes based on both the nature of the offense and the target of the criminal activity.

THE DEVELOPMENT OF LAW

In some ways it is appropriate to say that civilizations always have had laws, although the nature of these laws has not always been what we associate with criminal law today. In this section we will consider three periods relative to the development of law: (1) the pre-historical era, from earliest history until approximately 2000 BC, (2) the early historical era, from 2000 BC to 1000 AD, and (3) the modern era, from 1000 AD until the present. Steven Vago (2009) characterizes these three periods as having primitive, transitional, and modern legal systems.

THE PRE-HISTORICAL ERA

The most primitive societies that have existed in the world all have had what we would call laws. These societies (some of which still exist today) were based around clans, tribes, or kinship. Most of the laws within these groups could be characterized as **customary law**; that is, laws come about as a result of **norms**, **mores**, and **folkways** that develop over many generations. These three terms represent things like societal traditions, a group's historically accepted morals and values, even subtle social pressure to conform to these values. In fact, these laws become so ingrained in the society that often no one can remember where or when they originated. Typically they are passed down from "the elders," and normally they exist in unwritten form. Children are taught from the earliest times what is expected of them and the types of behavior that are acceptable and unacceptable.

Enforcement of norms in these types of societies is very informal, but effective. All the members of the clan or tribe become enforcers, and violations of the group's values may bring swift and occasionally severe sanctions. The "judges" within primitive societies are the tribal chieftains or a group of ruling elders who sit in judgment over controversies and dispense the appropriate sanctions (Vago 2009:43). Many of the penalties in such societies resemble what today we call **restitution** or even the seemingly modern concept of **restorative justice**. Stolen property may call for repayment two-, three-, or fourfold. Apologies before the entire group may be required. Most primitive societies seldom imposed the death penalty on members of their own group, since each member of the clan was essential to the group's survival in some way, and **banishment** often was the most severe sanction that could be imposed.

Max Weber (1954) characterizes one form of this type of legal system as **khadi justice**, and he says that it is informal, particularized, and irrational (his term for legal systems with no written rules or procedures). **Irrational justice systems** (like khadi justice) "rely on ethical or mystical considerations such as magic or faith in the supernatural... [they are] based on religious precepts and [are] so lacking in procedural rules as to seem almost completely arbitrary" (Vago 2009:52).

Does a legal system like this work? It depends on the context in which it is applied. In homogeneous societies based around tribes or kinship, this approach to law creation, enforcement, and adjudication seems to be very effective. However, as societies grow and become more complex, pluralistic, and heterogeneous, other legal mechanisms become necessary and emerge.

THE EARLY HISTORICAL PERIOD

In some ways it is difficult to pinpoint the development of law in this time period. For instance, the Egyptians, Babylonians, Hebrews and other groups in that part of the world had written legal codes 2000 to 3000 BC. Later, the Greeks and Romans developed systems of laws that would influence modern Europe and, by extension, the United States (Calvi and Coleman 2008:19–27). When you read English translations of some of

BOX 2.1   The Code of Hammurabi and the Law of Moses

When examining ancient legal codes, it is striking how similar some of these laws are to laws today, and how similar the codes are to each other. Consider how close the following two sections are that contain excerpts from the Code of Hammurabi, King of Babylon (modern-day Iraq), and the Law of Moses recorded in the Old Testament book of Exodus:

The Code of Hammurabi (about 1760 BC)

"If a man put out the eye of another man, his eye shall be put out. If he break another man's bone, his bone shall be broken. If a man knock out the teeth of his equal, his teeth shall be knocked out."

The Law of Moses (about 1300 BC)

"And if any mischief follow, then those shalt give life for life, eye for eye, tooth for tooth, hand for hand, foot for foot, burning for burning, wound for wound, stripe for stripe"

Sources: Hooker (2007); Exodus 21:23–25.

these early documents, they have a familiar ring to them. Some prescribed punishments that were monetary in nature, and others imposed **corporal punishments** (floggings, for example). Box 2.1 includes two ancient examples of written codes. Interestingly, Hammurabi's Babylonia code was very lengthy and included detailed procedural law too (Calvi and Coleman 2008).

The legal systems that emerged in the early historical period are important for a variety of reasons. Not only did they establish written codes, as we have indicated, but also different roles in the legal system started to emerge (Vago 2009). These societies distinguished between those who enacted the laws (today what we call legislative bodies), those who enforced the laws (our executive agencies), and those who advocated for or judged between the disputing parties (the judicial branch in modern times). Law enforcement remained the responsibility of military bodies. Eventually, in both Greece and Rome, the specialized function of lawyer (really an orator or accomplished public speaker) began to appear (see especially Vago 2009, Chapter 8).

These societies had a profound influence on the development of laws in both Europe and the United States, and that influence continues today. However, during this period another influence on legal systems began to become prominent: **canon law** (religious or church law). After the fall of the Roman Empire, the influence of the Roman Catholic Church was significant from Constantinople (modern Istanbul, Turkey) to what today is Great Britain. The church exerted a great deal of influence over what remained of the Roman Empire, and the church's laws often informally or formally became the law of the land. Thus, a number of behaviors were defined as criminal (adultery and suicide, for example) because the church considered them moral crimes.

THE MODERN ERA

The modern era in the development of criminal law is not really that contemporary. In fact, we have to date this period to the Renaissance (1300s to 1600s) and The Age of Enlightenment (1700s). During this period the notion of **natural law**, which had developed under Greek and Roman philosophers such as Cicero, began to reemerge. The key idea behind natural law was that there is a higher source of law (the Divine) than that of earthly governments or even the church. This law is fundamental, immutable, and unchangeable over time (Williams and Arrigo 2008:170–72). This is the type of law that is seen as governing the universe, and it applies to the lives of all citizens, no matter what country in which they live.

TYPOLOGIES OF LAW

One of the first things that becomes apparent when we study law and legal systems is that law can perform a variety of functions within any society. Donald Black (1976) says that law performs at least four functions in societies. These functions can be expressed as styles of social control or **typologies of law**. The categories provided by Black include penal law, compensatory law, therapeutic law, and conciliatory law. We will consider each of these in turn.

PENAL LAW

First, penal law is what most people think of when law is mentioned in a criminal justice context. Penal law describes those actions or behaviors that are prohibited by society (typically through criminal laws passed by legislative bodies) and can be punished by agents of the government. In this regard, "penal" denotes that there is some level of punishment prescribed for those individuals arrested and convicted of violating the law.

COMPENSATORY LAW

Second, as can be seen in the following sections, compensatory law fits within the framework of what we consider civil law or private disputes. In cases involving tort claims or breaches of contract, one party will sue the other to obtain compensation for the loss or damage suffered. There are no punishments such as imprisonment provided for under compensatory law, although most people would consider a large monetary judgment against them to be punishing. "Punishment" in such cases could then be defined as restitution or restoration.

THERAPEUTIC LAW

Third, therapeutic law seeks not to punish offending behavior, but to provide help for the offender. In Chapter 9 I discuss the movement toward specialized, problem-solving courts and the whole notion of therapeutic jurisprudence. Briefly, these courts are designed to confront social problems such as drunken driving, drug use, domestic violence, and mental illness. Rather than taking a penal or punitive approach with offenders in these situations, the judge and the attorneys, along with a treatment staff, will try to deal with the underlying problems that each offender possesses.

CONCILIATORY LAW

Finally, conciliatory law can be applied to a number of situations where it appears that there is no party that is all right or all wrong. For example, in organized labor and management disputes and in divorce cases it may be much more important to resolve the source of the conflict than it is to provide a winner and a loser. Later in the text I introduce you to the concept of a zero-sum game. As will become readily apparent, in many legal conflicts there can be only one winner and, thus, there is one loser. In some ways conciliatory law (as frequently exemplified by the processes of mediation and arbitration) rejects this concept and takes the approach that carefully structured situations can provide win–win outcomes.

As is true of many concepts in law, these four styles or typologies may not be found in absolutely pure forms. However, as we progress through the text you will see that each of these functions appears in many of the discussions that deal with law and legal processes.

DIFFERENCES IN CIVIL LAW AND CRIMINAL LAW

We have to be precise when we use the term **civil law**, because this phrase has different and distinct meanings in different parts of the world. In the following sections I distinguish between civil (primarily European) legal systems and common law systems, and also between civil and criminal law as these terms are defined in the United States.

CIVIL AND COMMON LAW LEGAL SYSTEMS

A civil law legal system—also called continental law or code law legal system—is distinct from a common law legal system, which is discussed in one of the following sections. Calvi and Coleman (2008:24–25) note that the civil law type of legal system is the dominant system in the world. In fact, the countries that compose Central and South America, many African nations that were former European colonies, some of the nations in Asia, and several of the former Soviet bloc countries operate under civil law legal systems. Additionally, all of the countries in Western Europe, except England and Wales, have civil law traditions where all infractions are carefully delineated in the criminal code and there is no notion such as that of judge-made law (see Walsh and Hemmens 2008:329–30). In the United States the State of Louisiana also employs the civil law or Napoleonic Code legal system.

There is a relatively long history in the development of civil law legal systems. Most historians trace the tradition back to early Roman legal codes such as the Twelve Tables (about 450 BC), later expanded into the *Corpus Juris Civilis* by the Roman Emperor Justinian (535 AD). This legal system remained in effect until the fall of Constantinople in 1453 AD (Mays and Winfree 2009:32–33). However, the modern roots of civil law legal systems can be found in the French Napoleonic Code of 1804 (Walsh and Hemmens 2008:330).

At least seven features distinguish code law systems from those of common law systems (such as those in the United States and England). First, common law, used primarily in the United States and England, relies on a broad set of ruling documents, such as the Constitution and criminal statutes, to provide a framework for judges on how to handle a case. Previous rulings by judges are treated as nearly equal to the written code when making decisions.

Second, in most common law systems there is a major emphasis on the rights of the accused. In fact, many of the provisions in the Bill of Rights are aimed at protecting those people accused of crimes from being unjustly treated by the government. Civil law systems (typified by France) focus instead on the "rights of the victimized community" rather than those of the suspected offender (Walsh and Hemmens 2008:331).

The third characteristic that distinguishes civil law systems from common law systems is the presence of written codes. Rather than developing through customary law—the common law tradition—code law is created when it is written (Walsh and Hemmens 2008:331). However, it is vital to note that today in most common law countries the development of statutory law (written codes) has largely supplanted the unwritten, customary law. Therefore, based on this factor it may be difficult to distinguish between modern civil law and common law systems.

Fourth, while previous cases can be acknowledged in code law systems, the notion of precedent plays a relatively minor role. Under the common law, the decisions in previous cases can serve as a guide to contemporary cases, with the understanding that precedent is never completely binding. This creates a much more flexible system of law than that of civil law nations, where once the legal code is written it is viewed as complete (Walsh and Hemmens 2008:331).

Fifth, civil law legal systems operate in an inquisitorial mode rather than the common law traditional of an adversarial system. It is on this point that the two systems seem the most divergent, and that one that gives common law due process advocates the greatest concern. Under an inquisitorial system, while there are legal protections for the person accused of a crime, the focus is much more on the procedures that must be followed in the process, and less on individual liberties of the accused. The police, prosecutors, and judges all participate in the process which thoroughly investigates the accusations against the suspect before any thought is given to a trial, so that as the evidence against a suspect mounts, the likelihood of a trial also increases. In some sense, therefore, trials are almost formalities in civil law countries (see Melone and Karnes 2008:250; Walsh and Hemmens 2008:332).

An illustration of the inquisitorial legal orientation relates to the right to remain silent during the investigation and the trial. Our common-law, adversarial system extends the right to remain silent to criminal suspects at all stages of the process. In fact, the famous *Miranda* warnings are designed to emphasize this fact to the accused before police interrogations begin. By contrast, in civil law legal systems the suspect is expected to cooperate in the investigation of the crime and "Remaining silent during civil law trial proceedings…may be legally considered as evidence of guilt, unlike in common law countries where jurors must not draw negative conclusions from a defendant's silence" (Walsh and Hemmens 2008:333).

The sixth major difference in the two legal systems is the traditional lack of reliance on juries in civil law countries. While it is difficult to make broad generalizations, given the variations from country to country, most civil law nations use multi-judge panels sometimes supplemented with lay jurors. The judges are allowed and even expected to ask questions, and the lay jurors may do so also. However, lay jurors generally play a more deferential role in respect to the professional judges (Walsh and Hemmens 2008:333). Civil law systems also frequently do not require unanimous verdicts.

Finally, the concept of **judicial review** is widely applied in common law countries (dating back to the beginning of the Supreme Court in the United States), but seldom so in code law countries. Reviewing legislative enactments and ruling them unconstitutional is viewed as undemocratic in civil law nations, thus there is a strongly held view that social issues should be decided by elected legislators and not by judges (Walsh and Hemmens 2008:334).

Now that we have briefly examined the operation of civil law legal systems around the world, it is time to turn our attention to the notion of civil (private) law and how it differs from criminal law in the United States.

CIVIL AND CRIMINAL LAW IN THE UNITED STATES

In countries with the common law legal tradition—such as Canada, England, and the United States—civil law is distinct from criminal law in that the former deals with disputes between private parties and the latter deals with offenses against society. In criminal law, the government serves as the party bringing the action on behalf of its citizens. I elaborate on this distinction in this section.

Examples of Differences

One way to understand the differences between civil law and criminal law is through the use of examples. For instance, divorces, breaches of contracts, and cases involving personal injuries resulting from traffic accidents are addressed by civil law (and procedures). By contrast, offenses that deal with assaults, robberies, and murder are criminal matters.

These examples seem to be fairly straightforward. However, it is important to note that many civil suits arise out of criminal matters. As a result, a traffic accident that results in a death might have criminal charges filed for driving under the influence (DUI)—or driving while intoxicated (DWI)—as well as a civil suit based on a wrongful death. An employee who embezzles from his or her place of employment might have criminal charges filed by the prosecuting attorney, and the employer might file a civil suit for damages caused by the employee's acts. Therefore, while we have the tendency to define civil law issues and criminal law issues as somewhat separate and distinct, it is important to remember that often the two are linked.

CIVIL LAW DISTINCTIVES

As we have mentioned, civil cases typically involve disputes between private parties. Divorces, breaches of contracts, and tenant–landlord disputes provide good examples. These are issues that arise out of the everyday interactions among individuals and groups, and for which no informal resolution seems possible. As a result, one of the parties (or possibly both of them) turns to the courts for dispute resolution. In such situations the government plays a relatively passive role. The issue is brought by an individual or group of people, and the government merely provides the forum and decision maker (the courtroom and judge) within which the dispute can be resolved.

In some states, there are separate civil courts and criminal courts. Texas is one example of a state that maintains this separation all the way through the highest level appellate courts. Other states—for example, Arizona, California, Colorado, and New Mexico—have unified judicial systems where courts can hear either civil cases or criminal cases (Rottman and Strickland 2006). Whatever the structural arrangement of the courts, the state legislature—and sometimes the courts themselves—will create civil procedures to govern the processes related to these disputes.

The labels given to the parties involved in a dispute are somewhat different for civil cases and criminal cases. In civil cases, the party who initiates a suit is called the **plaintiff**. The party against whom the suit is brought is called the **defendant**. As you will see in the next section, these labels are similar to, but vary slightly from, criminal law.

Another civil law distinctive deals with jury size. In virtually all states, criminal trials utilize twelve-member juries. By comparison, many states and the federal courts use six-member juries in a variety of civil matters.

One of the clearest areas of difference between civil procedures and criminal procedures has to do with the nature of jury verdicts and what is called the **weight of evidence**. In civil cases juries decide cases based on the **preponderance of the evidence**. In simplest terms, this means that the verdict should go in favor of the party that presents enough evidence to convince the jury slightly more than the other side. Some people would say that the winning party must be able to tip the scales of justice 51 percent, but judges and lawyers would resist any effort to provide such a precise quantification of the jury's decision-making process. Nevertheless, the key point here is that in civil law only a slight difference in the degree of persuasion is needed between the disputing parties in order to win a case.

Having made that statement, it is important to add that in civil law both parties may be at fault. For example, in a case involving an accident between two automobiles, the jury may find that one party ran a traffic light and the other party was speeding. Thus, both contributed in some way to the accident. This is the notion of **contributory negligence** (Calvi and Coleman 2008:255–56). In this situation, the jury may find that the plaintiff was speeding and the defendant ran the traffic light. If this is the case, they must decide what percentage of the blame belongs to each party. It is possible, in this example, for the defendant to be 60 percent to blame and the plaintiff to be 40 percent to blame. Thus, any award to the plaintiff will be reduced by 40 percent, or the plaintiff's contribution to the accident.

An additional difference between civil law and criminal law involves the appointment of attorneys. In civil law there is no constitutional guarantee of an attorney for people who cannot afford one. Therefore, many lawyers are willing to take civil cases on a **contingency fee** (or fee-contingent) basis. This is illustrated by the radio, television, and newspaper advertisements for lawyers that say "if you don't win, you don't pay." In these cases, the attorneys are betting on winning the case and recovering their usually substantially larger fees as a percentage (commonly one-third to one-half) of the monetary award received by their clients. This situation has the potential to create a conflict of interests between clients and their attorneys, however. For attorneys it may be preferable to settle out of court more often, resulting in a certain outcome, versus going to trial and facing an uncertain outcome and the potential not to be paid.

Finally, in civil cases there is no possibility of incarceration, meaning defendants in civil cases cannot be locked up if they lose their cases. Plaintiffs in civil cases seek monetary damages in most of their suits, but they also might seek **equitable relief** (such as filing injunctions to halt some action or to put circumstances back the way they were originally). For instance, environmental groups might seek an injunction against the Army Corps of Engineers to prevent the construction of a dam if the construction would destroy the habitat of certain fish or if it would spoil natural wilderness areas.

CRIMINAL LAW DISTINCTIVES

As we mentioned previously, some states maintain separate civil and criminal courts, although the trend for the past fifty years or so has been to move toward more unified court systems (Langton and Cohen 2007). Therefore, in states with separate courts, judges specialize in handling one type of case.

While the party that brings a civil case is called the plaintiff, in **criminal law** the case is initiated by the government and the party bringing the case is called the **prosecutor** (in Chapter 5 I address the different titles for prosecuting attorneys). The prosecuting attorney brings forward criminal charges on behalf of the citizens of a particular state, or for the United States government in federal criminal cases. In both civil and criminal cases, the person against whom the case is brought is called the defendant.

Criminal defendants can elect to have a **bench trial** before a judge with no jury. Some of them might choose to do so because of the inflammatory nature of the charges (an especially heinous murder or a crime involving a child victim, for example), or because of the extensive amount of pretrial publicity that might make a jury unsympathetic toward the defendant. However, the relatively small percentage of cases that go to trial in this country typically do so with a jury. In most states—by constitution, statute, or custom—criminal court juries are composed of twelve members. The Supreme Court has permitted smaller criminal trial juries, but twelve is the pervasive number nationwide.[1]

Just like there are rules of civil procedure, there are rules of criminal procedure as well. Two issues are of particular significance here. First, in terms of the weight of evidence in criminal cases, juries are charged with the responsibility of finding the defendant guilty employing the **beyond a reasonable doubt** standard. Again, it is difficult to quantify exactly what this means, but often judges explain to jurors that the evidence presented should clearly point to the defendant's guilt.[2]

The second procedural issue deals with the **burden of proof** or what some legal scholars call the burden of persuasion (Dressler 2009). In criminal cases the burden of proof rests with the prosecutor. In other words, it is the responsibility of the state to prove the defendant guilty, not the defendant's responsibility to prove himself or herself innocent. Given the enormous resources of the state in prosecuting crimes, this somewhat helps to level the playing field for the defendant. Box 2.3 discusses the type of legal system that was traditionally found in many European nations.

BOX 2.2

In Their Own Words: Alan Dershowitz

Harvard Law School professor and frequent news show commentator Alan Dershowitz has presented these comments on his perspective of the differences in the roles of the prosecutor and defense attorney in the trial process:

> "The prosecution wants to make sure the process by which the evidence was obtained is not truthfully presented, because, as often as not, that process will raise questions.
>
> The defendant wants to hide the truth because he's generally guilty. The defense attorney's job is to make sure the jury does not arrive at that truth."

Source: BrainyQuote (2009). http://www.brainyquote.com/quotes/authors/a/alan_dershowitz.html

BOX 2.3

Criminal Law in Italy

For most of the nineteenth and twentieth centuries, Continental European nations operated under an accusatory or inquisitional system of justice. Under such systems, judges play a very active role in gathering evidence and questioning suspects in court. Additionally, rather than the burden of proof resting with the government, the familiar "innocent until proven guilty," the accused must present a sufficient case to establish his or her innocence. Largely as a result of the emergence of the European Union (EU) as a political force, many nations that utilized inquisitional systems now have adopted models similar to the Anglo-American adversarial system. The following excerpt from the *World Factbook of Criminal Justice Systems* illustrates some of the changes that have occurred in Italy.

> The most important innovation of this new legislation [a change in the legal code in 1988] concerns the admission of evidence that, as a rule, can be obtained only during the course an oral and public trial, in front of the judge

Continued

BOX 2.3

Continued

(acting as a third party) on the basis of witnesses' cross-examination and other kinds of proof legally presented in the Court. The trial is conducted by the prosecution and defense on a parity basis.

The former inquisitorial procedure had allowed the admission of evidence obtained both in the course of the trial and in the preliminary investigation stage. The preliminary investigation was typically characterized by secrecy concerning documentation of the pre-trial investigation. An investigating judge was in charge of collecting criminal evidence as well as conducting direct examinations of the witnesses. During the trial, the examination of witnesses was conducted by the Chief Judge.

Although the new Italian Code of Penal Procedure is similar to the adversarial English and American systems, its system of written laws still retains important differences when compared with the Anglo-American system, such as the obligatoriness of penal action.

The obligatoriness of penal action is sanctioned by the Constitution (Art.112). According to this provision, the Public Prosecutor, when becoming acquainted with the commission of a crime, is legally bound to start the investigation and, if there is enough circumstantial evidence, to take penal action against the alleged culprit of that particular crime. The Italian Prosecutor is therefore without discretionary power to withhold prosecution. Prosecution is not simply a right, but a duty of the Italian Public Prosecutor.

Source: Marongiu and Biddau (2009).

Unlike civil cases, in criminal trials the defendants are entitled to the appointment of an attorney to assist in their defense. This is based on the **right to counsel** provision of the Sixth Amendment to the U.S. Constitution and is applied to the states through a series of U.S. Supreme Court decisions.[3] This right even extends to first-level appeals, but not beyond (see, for example, *Douglas v. California*, 372 U.S. 353 [1963]; *Ross v. Moffitt*, 417 U.S. 600 [1974]). Both state and federal governments utilize a variety of mechanisms to provide lawyers for the sizable number of criminal defendants who are indigent and, thus, cannot afford to hire an attorney. For individuals who can afford to retain an attorney, privately retained criminal defense attorneys may charge fees on an hourly basis or simply a flat fee for the entire process. This means that in virtually every situation, there is much more money to be made handling civil cases than criminal cases.

Finally, when criminal defendants are convicted they face a variety of sanctions. There can be fines, forfeitures, and other economic penalties (somewhat like civil cases). There also can be probation and other community-based sanctions and, potentially, jail or prison time. The possibility of incarceration is one way that civil cases and criminal cases truly can be distinguished.

SUBSTANTIVE LAW VERSUS PROCEDURAL LAW

Now that I have discussed the differences between civil law and criminal law, it is important to turn your attention to substantive law and procedural law (see Calvi and Coleman 2008:8) As you read the following section, keep in mind that most of what we call substantive law and procedural law today is legislatively enacted. However, some courts have rule-making authority over some of their own procedures as well.

SUBSTANTIVE LAW

In criminal law, the **substantive law** defines those acts that are crimes. For example, in a crime like first-degree murder the law typically will specify that there must have been an unlawful death, that it occurred with malice aforethought (or premeditation), and that other aggravating circumstances may exist. Simply said, the substantive law tells us what is illegal and what the penalties are for various offenses. For example, a man is accused of murder and is arrested. The laws that define murder and outline the accused killer's rights are substantive law.

PROCEDURAL LAW

By contrast, **procedural law** defines how a criminal case must be processed. This will include issues such as the appointment of attorneys for defendants that cannot afford them, the methods of selecting juries, and questions about the admissibility of evidence. Procedural law has been called the "rules of the game," since it defines how cases are handled from arrest through conviction or acquittal. In effect, procedural law provides the guidelines by which the government must abide in order to secure a *fundamentally fair* conviction. In the case of our previously mentioned accused murderer, his trial, rules of evidence presented against him, laws governing police conduct on arrest and investigation, and the sentencing process (if he is found guilty) are all examples of procedural law.

To simplify, substantive versus procedural law can be referred to as the laws versus the rules, the laws applying to accused criminals while the rules apply to those who process, try, and otherwise interact with them. A collection of procedural rules for the U.S. Federal Courts may be found online at http://www.uscourts.gov/RulesAndPolicies.aspx.

SOURCES OF LAW

In the United States today there are five primary sources of law. In this section we will examine common law, constitutional law, statutory law, case law, and administrative or regulatory law (see Calvi and Coleman 2008:8–15).

COMMON LAW

Common law is the fundamental basis for law in the United States. We inherited this tradition from England. There are a number of elements that characterize common law, and these distinguish this legal tradition from the civil (codified) legal system of most continental European countries.

Common law "originated during the period of English history when there were very few written laws" and "A rule of law become 'common' not in the sense of being ordinary, but in the sense of being common to all parts of England" (Calvi and Coleman 2008:14). It is based on the norms and values of the particular community. While it is unwritten, a certain consistency develops in common law that comes through the regular and routine application of legal principles. Today we call this concept **legal precedence** (the Latin phrase is *stare decisis*, or let the decision stand). This means that as judges decide cases over a long period of time they apply the same types of rulings to similar cases.

Community values are reflected in the common law as well, and community values as a result tend to shape common law. Therefore, changes in common law principles develop slowly over time, and they change slowly over time as well.

Common law is judge-made law and, in a sense, it is case law. However, unlike case law (which I will discuss in one of the following sections), which is based on the interpretation of constitutional provisions or statutes, common law is decided "in the absence of any positive law" (Calvi and Coleman 2008: 14). Since it is not enacted by legislative bodies—and, thus, it is unwritten—judges "make" law simply through the process of deciding cases. Over time citizens come to recognize what the legal principles are by virtue of the cases that have been decided previously. Today, as so-called "activist judges" decide cases, they often are accused of making law, though in some ways this is a part of the legacy of the common law tradition.

As we have previously mentioned, the United States (and many other former British colonies and parts of the Commonwealth) shares a common law tradition with England. Today states and the federal government have replaced much of the common law with written statutes, but it is still possible for authorities to make charges based on the common law. For instance, if groups of people running naked in public (the "streaking" fad popular in the 1970s) were to reappear on college campuses today, it might be possible to charge streakers with the offense of "common law lewdness." In other words, there might not be a specific statute on the books that prohibits running naked in public, but that doesn't mean that this behavior is socially acceptable.

BOX 2.4

In Their Own Words: Sir Edward Coke

Sir Edward Coke, who served as a jurist and member of the British Parliament, said of the common law: "Reason is the life of the law; nay, the common law itself is nothing else but reason. The law which is perfection of reason."

Source: Famous Quotes and Authors (2009). http://www.famousquotesandauthors.com/topics/law_quotes.html

CONSTITUTIONAL LAW

Aside from the common law, no source of law in the United States is more important than **constitutional law**. While this may seem like one source of law, in reality it is fifty-one sources. By that we mean that all laws ultimately must comport with the Constitution of the United States. Furthermore, each of the fifty states has its own constitution, and the laws of that state must be consistent with the state constitution *and* the Constitution of the United States.

The ultimate arbiters of constitutional law in the United States are the various state and federal appellate courts. These courts—typically sitting in multi-judge panels—review cases that are appealed to them and decide whether executive policies and the laws that have been enacted are consistent with the appropriate constitution. This also illustrates case law, which I discuss in a later section.

STATUTORY LAW

Under the common law tradition, there were no written laws on which violations were based. By contrast, criminal law in the United States is almost exclusively written law today. Legislative bodies at the local, state, and federal levels enact laws all the time. These written laws exemplify **statutory law**, and they typically are compiled (or codified) in volumes that are available in courthouses, law offices, and libraries. Statutory law is especially important today for two reasons. First, it illustrates the **legality principle** of criminal law, which says that people have the right to know what is against the law with a sufficient amount of specificity so they will know if they are breaking the law (see Fletcher 1998:207), legally referred to as "notice." Second, today there are so many offenses at every level of government that laws must be written so both citizens and agents of the criminal justice system know what is illegal at any particular time or place.

The extensive nature of statutory law is shown by the fact that every state has its own criminal code, and there is a federal criminal code as well (Title 18 of the United States Code [USC]). This means that a quick trip to a university or law school library or a Web search can turn up the criminal offenses that are contained in each jurisdiction's criminal code.

CASE LAW

In high school civics classes students are taught that the legislative branch makes the laws (statutes), the executive branch enforces the laws, and the judicial branch interprets the laws. This is true—to an extent. The reality is that all three branches of government "make" law. For instance, in the process known as judicial review, appellate courts examine the statutes enacted by legislative bodies and the actions of executive bodies to determine if they are constitutional. Judicial review was initially established in *Marbury v. Madison,* 5 U.S. 137 (1803), and is especially prevalent in First Amendment issues and civil liberties.

As one example, in recent years, the U.S. Supreme Court has heard a number of appeals based on the actions of the George W. Bush administration in the war against terrorism. These include the classification of detainees as "enemy combatants" and the use of military detention and military tribunals against individuals captured in Afghanistan, Iraq, and elsewhere and held at the military base at Guantanamo Bay, Cuba.

In concert with judicial review is the concept of judicial policymaking, or judicial activism, defined by *Black's Law Dictionary* (1991:590) as the "Judicial philosophy which motivates judges to depart from strict adherence to judicial precedent in favor of progressive and new social policies which are not always consistent with the restraint expected of appellate judges." Judicial policymaking is particularly relevant with the United States Supreme Court, as appointments of justices are made based on party affiliation and issue alignment with the sitting president. For example, when the Supreme Court decided the case of *Brown v. Board of Education of Topeka, Kansas*, 347 U.S. 483 (1954) banning government-approved school segregation, it struck down the case of *Plessy v. Ferguson*, 163 U.S. 537 (1896) that had allowed "separate, but equal" school systems to exist for blacks and whites. In this case, the Court acted in the absence of federal and state efforts to ban segregated educational facilities. Likewise, the Supreme Court demonstrated a policymaking orientation when it ordered states to provide state prison inmates with access to legal materials in the case of *Bounds v. Smith*, 430 U.S. 817 (1977). Any number of cases could be cited to show the Supreme Court's activity in areas where the executive and legislative branches have failed to address social problems, or where the actions by the political branches of government have brought about even greater conflicts and confusion.

Each time a state or federal appellate court decides a case, the decision is published in what are called "reporters." These volumes are available in many different types of libraries, and they allow people to read for themselves what the courts actually said in famous (or not so famous) cases like *Miranda v. Arizona*, 384 U.S. 436 (1966). Over time these volumes become the basis for case law, and like common law they represent a reliance on precedence. The text from these reporters can now be found online, of course, and nearly all research currently is done in this manner with subscription-based databases such as WestLaw and Lexis-Nexis.

ADMINISTRATIVE LAW

A final source of law, but one with which many individuals are unfamiliar, is **administrative law** (sometimes called regulatory law). Administrative law comes from a number of sources in the executive branch of government, even state regulatory agencies, but primarily it originates with the federal regulatory agencies. These agencies often are called the "alphabet soup" agencies of the federal government. Some common ones are: the Federal Aviation Administration (FAA), the Federal Communications Commission (FCC), the Food and Drug Administration (FDA), the Environmental Protection Agency (EPA), the Interstate Commerce Commission (ICC), and the Securities Exchange Commission (SEC), among others. What do these agencies have to do with law, you might be asking yourself? The answer is quite a lot. In fact, the actions of these agencies have a profound impact of the lives of every American on a daily basis.

Administrative agencies are constantly in the process of creating regulations, which essentially are laws. These agencies publish their regulations or proposed regulations in a document called *The Federal Register,* and after an appropriate period of notice and time for response, the regulations become laws. These laws remain in effect until modified by the agency or until someone goes to court to challenge the regulations. In fact, most of these agencies have their own in-house administrative law judges or hearing officers that serve as first-line reviewers of any legal challenges. Probably the most interesting aspect of administrative law is the fact that despite its pervasiveness, many citizens are largely unaware of its presence at all.

DEGREES OF SERIOUSNESS

Before I discuss the ways laws are legislatively classified in terms of their relative seriousness, it is useful to examine the degree of perceived evilness associated with specific acts, and how this then gets translated into offense seriousness.

EVILNESS

Not all laws are created equal, and in this section I address the different ways we can classify offenses based on their supposed evilness. Traditionally, actions that have been considered wrong have been labeled according to what might be considered the moral or social harm of the acts. Thus, some behaviors are categorized as *mala in se* and others as *mala prohibita*. We will examine each in turn.

Mala in se **offenses** are those that are considered evil or bad in-and-of themselves (the Latin phrase means "bad on its face"). These are actions or behaviors that would be considered inappropriate by virtually all members of society, even if there is no written proscription. Thus, these prohibitions are supported by a broad social consensus, and they convey a strong sense of morality or moral wrong. For instance, even in the most primitive societies, the taking of the life of another person in most cases is considered wrong. In modern societies, killing another person is considered a wrongful or evil act by almost everyone in almost any situation (obviously, there are exceptions), and this is supported by statutes prohibiting such behaviors. Virtually all "laws" in tribal groups would be considered *mala in se*, and many of the offenses (such as killing a person or the theft of property) that are included in our criminal codes typically would be considered *mala in se* as well.

By contrast, *mala prohibita* **offenses** are wrong because they are prohibited, and they are prohibited because we consider them bad. This is something of what logicians call a tautology: defining something by itself. *Mala prohibita* offenses may not be inherently evil, but for some reason legislative bodies have chosen to pass laws prohibiting these behaviors. Some examples, of *mala prohibita* crimes might be seat belt or motorcycle helmet law violations and vice offenses (gambling and prostitution). Also, drug offenses such as possession for personal use would fit in this category. Some people might consider these actions evil, while others would not. Thus, there is much less of a social consensus about these behaviors. In fact, social theorists call this lack of consensus a conflict perspective on the creation and enforcement of laws.

As you will see in the next section, the degree of evilness perceived by society can have practical implications as well. In fact, evilness can be translated into statutory categories differentiating the seriousness of offenses.

OFFENSE SERIOUSNESS

Another way to classify crimes is according to their seriousness as established by statute. Legislative bodies decide how serious each crime is, and the three most common statutory categories are: felonies, misdemeanors, and infractions (or petty misdemeanors).

FELONIES

By definition, **felonies** are the most serious criminal offenses, and two factors differentiate felonies from misdemeanors: (1) the place of possible incarceration, and (2) the potential length of incarceration. Convicted felons can be sentenced to serve time in federal or state prisons (depending on the type of law violated and the court that has jurisdiction). In most states felony sentences begin at one year. However, some states start felony sentences at higher levels; for instance, in New Mexico fourth-degree felonies call for sentences of eighteen months.

Different states have subcategories of felonies that are commonly labeled as first-, second-, or third degree felonies. In other words, not all felonies are considered to be of similar seriousness, and the penalties attached to each level will indicate the degree of seriousness. For example, in states that use the first-degree felony classification, sentences for these offenses may begin at twenty years, for example, and extend to life imprisonment or even death. By contrast, second-degree felonies might call for sentences beginning at ten years and extending to twenty years. At the lowest end, felony sentences might equal only one or two years' imprisonment.

MISDEMEANORS

In the case of **misdemeanors**, the place of potential incarceration typically will be some type of local facility like a jail, detention center, workhouse, or penal farm. In most instances, these facilities are operated by city or county governments, and just over two-thirds of the jails in the United States are managed by county sheriffs (Kerle and Ford 1982; Thompson and Mays 1991). Sentences for serious misdemeanors generally extend up to one year (364 days, or 11 months and 29 days in some states), and include a broad range of offenses such as simple assault, shoplifting, and most DWI offenses.

Petty Misdemeanors

States also can divide misdemeanors into different categories of seriousness, and both state and local governments may have what are called **petty misdemeanors** (in some instances violations of local ordinances are called **infractions**). Petty misdemeanors are different from more serious misdemeanors in that they may call for just fines—as is the case with most traffic offenses—or for jail terms less than 6 months.

ELEMENTS OF A CRIME

As I mentioned at the beginning of this chapter, the government bears the burden of proof in criminal cases, and the prosecutor must prove every element of a crime. The Latin phrase for the elements of a criminal offense is *corpus delicti* (literally, the body of the crime). The **corpus delicti** represents all of the factors that the state must prove to establish that a person has committed a crime, as well as which crime has been committed. At a minimum, three elements must be present: *mens rea*, *actus reus*, and concurrence (or nexus).

MENS REA

Mens rea involves the "guilty mind" of the person or persons suspected of having committed a crime (Garner 2000:435). Often *mens rea* is called by its more common name, **criminal intent**, and it deals with the motivation behind the crime. It is essential to understand two points when it comes to criminal intent. First, the criminal law does not hold people accountable for their thoughts (thank goodness!!) as long as these thoughts are not acted on, written down, or verbalized. Once some affirmative action has taken place they are no longer "thoughts," of course. Second, every crime requires some degree of thought or contemplation to be formed. In this regard, the most difficult job of the state may be analyzing the mind of the accused—the *why* of the offense. The state may have a difficult job or an easy one when it comes to establishing the *why* of the offense.

ACTUS REUS

In contrast to *mens rea*, or the guilty mind, the **actus reus** constitutes the wrongful act. For a crime to occur there must be some affirmative action toward completion of the offense. However, as you will see in one of the following sections, the offense does not have to be totally completed in order for a crime to have occurred.

CONCURRENCE

A crime exists at the point where the intent and the act come together. This might be called the fusion of the act plus the intent. Sometimes this has been called **concurrence**, nexus, or some similar term (Dressler 2009:199). At the time of a criminal trial the prosecuting attorney must establish to the satisfaction of the jury that the offender both had the intent necessary and acted on that intention in the commission of the crime. This is part of the proof beyond a reasonable doubt requirement.

INCHOATE OFFENSES

In the previous section I discussed the notion of *actus reus* as an element of a crime. It is important to note, however, that not all offenses are completed (for one reason or another), but this does not mean that no crime has occurred. In this section I discuss three types of **inchoate offenses** (acts that are incomplete): conspiracies, solicitations, and attempts.

CONSPIRACIES

A **conspiracy** exists when two or more people enter into an agreement to commit a crime (Mays 2004), and commit an overt act toward the commission of that crime, even if that act is innocent when considered apart from the conspiracy. Garner (2000:133) adds that a conspiracy "is a separate offense from the crime that is the object of the conspiracy" and that "A conspiracy ends when the unlawful act has been committed or (in some states) when the agreement has been abandoned." However, prosecutors—and this is especially true of federal prosecutors—often charge criminal defendants with the completed target offense as well as with conspiracy to commit the crime.

For instance, two college students who are struggling financially decide that robbing convenience stores is an easy way to solve their short-term financial difficulties. Once the two students agree to commit the robberies they have entered into a conspiracy.[4] In order to secure a conviction, the state may have to prove that the conspirators went beyond merely talking about the robbery to see whether they engaged in any affirmative actions or that they had taken "substantial steps" (purchasing a handgun, planning which stores to rob, mapping escape routes, etc.) toward committing the crime. However, in reality no action need be taken in order for a conspiracy to exist.

SOLICITATIONS

A **solicitation** occurs when one person tries to persuade another person to commit a crime on behalf of the solicitor (Garner 2000:632–33). Typically, this is an offer of some amount of money or other consideration to get the person to commit the crime. A brief example will illustrate this point. Mary decides that she no longer wants to be married to John, but she believes that she cannot afford a divorce and she does not want to go through the legal procedures necessary to obtain a divorce. One day in a discussion with her friend Elizabeth she mentions her desires and the fact that John has a sizeable life insurance policy. Elizabeth says she might have a solution to Mary's problem and has her brother-in-law, Fred, contact Mary. Mary discusses the possibility of Fred killing John and offers him $2,500 to do the job and another $2,500 once it is successfully completed. At this point there has been a solicitation to commit murder and, as with the case of conspiracies, all three parties may be guilty of one or more crimes.

ATTEMPTS

Attempts constitute a third type of inchoate offenses. Attempts occur when a person (or persons) moves toward the completion of a crime, but for some reason or another is unable to do so. For example, two men are sitting in an automobile in front of a liquor store at 10:00 pm. Both of them have on ski masks (and it is the middle of summer). Two policemen passing in a patrol car spot the two men and circle back around before the occupants of the car can get out. The officers order the two suspects to exit the car with their hands in plain sight, and on the front seat of the car they see a loaded handgun. In this case the police have intercepted the would-be robbers before they could enter the liquor store. While a robbery has not yet occurred, the officers could charge the suspects with attempted armed robbery. Once again, it can be a crime to engage in certain behaviors even if the contemplated offense is not fully accomplished.

DEFENSES

In the field of criminal law there can be a variety of defenses that can be utilized in court (or perhaps even before a case goes to court) that negate either the *mens rea* or the *actus reus*. In this section I address several of the most common defenses, particularly the affirmative defenses.

BURDEN OF PROOF

The burden of proof also may be considered the burden of persuasion or even the burden of production (also called the burden of going forward) (Dressler 2009:69–70; Fletcher 1998:14–15). It is different from the standard of proof, or what previously we called the weight of the evidence. As we begin a discussion of defenses, it is important to remember that under the common law tradition, the state bears the burden of proof (or persuasion) in criminal trials and, unlike accusatory or inquisitional legal systems, the defendant has nothing to prove in court.

For the most part, the burden of proof rests on the state. However, as I put forth in the following section, there are certain defenses to criminal acts that are known as affirmative defenses, and these may require some degree of proof (persuasion) on the part of the defendant.

AFFIRMATIVE DEFENSES

Affirmative defenses fit into one of two major categories: **justifications** and **excuses**. Joshua Dressler (2009:204–205) says that justification deals with those acts that are "right or, at least, not wrong," and he adds that "The justified actor [is] free of all legal impediments."

The most common example of a justification is in regards to self-defense. Normally, the law does not condone the killing of another person, but when someone acts in self-defense that act is justified and even expected. By contrast, in the case of excuses, the person who has committed the act acknowledges the wrongfulness of the deed but claims that there were extenuating circumstances that caused the behavior. In essence, the person "tries to show that [he] is not morally culpable for his wrongful conduct" (Dressler 2009:205).

Self-Defense

In the case of **self-defense** (and even in defense of others), a person is permitted to use necessary force to repel an attack for which they were not the initial aggressor. However, three elements must be present to justify the defense: (1) necessity, (2) proportionality, and (3) reasonable belief. Briefly, the necessity element means that the person must be facing an immediate threat of harm or evil to himself or another. Proportionality specifies that the degree of force used in self-defense must be equal to (but not greater than) the amount of force that has been threatened. And, finally, the person acting in self-defense must reasonably believe that he or she is the target of an attack (Dressler 2009:223–25).

Most affirmative defenses are excuses rather than justifications, and a small number may fit into the "failure to prove" category. I consider both of these in turn. First, some of the most common affirmative defenses are duress, entrapment, infancy, insanity, and intoxication. Most courts treat necessity as a justification (like self-defense) and distinguish it from duress.

Duress

Duress exists when a person is compelled to commit a crime by another, typically under the threat of bodily harm to the individual or to a family member. One definition of duress is that it is "An affirmative defense used by defendants to show lack of criminal intent, alleging force, psychological or physical, from others as the stimulus for otherwise criminal conduct" (Champion 2005: 85). Fletcher (1998: 83) says that the question each of must ask is: Would we have acted in the same way if we were found in similar circumstances?

Entrapment

Entrapment is a defense that alleges that the idea for a crime originated with someone else, especially with agents of law enforcement. It becomes an issue in situations where the police conduct undercover or "sting" operations related to crimes such as drug sales, prostitution, and the fencing of stolen merchandise. Essentially, jurors must decide whether the defendant was already inclined to commit the crime and the police merely provided the opportunity (in which case entrapment *does not* exist) or whether the police instigated a crime by an otherwise innocent person. The U.S. Supreme Court has sanctioned the use of informants and undercover agents by the police (see, for example, *Hoffa v. United States*, 385 U.S. 293, 1966), but they have emphasized that the police must not be impermissibly involved in the initiation or facilitation of the criminal activity (*United States v. Russell*, 411 U.S. 423, 1973).

Infancy

The criminal defense of **infancy** means that the person who committed an alleged offense was too young (as defined by law) to have formed criminal intent. States vary in their definitions of the minimum age for juvenile court jurisdiction, but many of them use the common law standard of seven as the age at which criminal intent can be formed (see Gardner 2009). This means that persons under the age specified in the statutes cannot be charged with a crime since they are deemed legally incapable of forming criminal intent.

Insanity

Insanity is perhaps the most controversial of the affirmative defenses. While it is not used often, when it is asserted it takes on great symbolic significance. Dressler (2009: 339) notes that "Since the time of Edward III in the fourteenth century when 'madness' became a complete defense to criminal charges, English and American courts and, more recently, legislatures have struggled to define 'insanity.'" Interestingly, unlike what most people would assume, insanity is a legal concept, not a medical one (Dressler 2009:340), though there are clear medical implications, and medical doctors may be involved in such cases through expert testimony. However, it blends legal notions such as *mens rea* with ideas that originate in psychology and psychiatry.

The insanity defense is based on the proposition that at the time the crime was committed, the person suspected of the offense was unable to adequately form criminal intent. This inability might spring from a chemical imbalance in the brain, mental illness, a psychological problem, or even blunt trauma injury to the head. Whatever the reason, the suspected offender alleges that he or she was incapable of possessing criminal intent.

Before leaving the topic of the insanity defense, a few summary points seem in order:

- Insanity is used in less that 1 percent of the criminal cases in the United States.

- The insanity defense typically is used in homicide cases (and even then not very often), and it is not always effective.

- Four states (Idaho, Kansas, Montana, and Utah) have completely eliminated the insanity defense.

- Largely as a result of the attempted assassination of President Ronald Reagan in 1980, thirteen states have retained the insanity defense, but they allow an additional plea or verdict of "guilty, but mentally ill" (Dressler 2009:365; Walker 2006).

Intoxication

Intoxication seems like the kind of defense that would be appealing to some college students; however, the nature of this defense and the circumstances under which it can be utilized are tightly defined by law and practice. First, it is very difficult to use *voluntary intoxication* as a defense to criminal behavior. If it were a legitimate defense, then we could not have crimes such as driving while intoxicated or driving under the influence (DWI/DUI). However, it might be used by the defense to refute the prosecution's case that the defendant had specific intent to commit a crime such as first-degree murder. Second, there are a few instances where a person might experience *involuntary* intoxication, and judges and juries must carefully weigh this appeal to lack of criminal intent. In most of these cases, the person was given an intoxicating substance without his or her knowledge. Involuntary intoxication also might result from an unanticipated reaction to a legal drug taken by someone.

Necessity

The defense of **necessity** is somewhat related to that of duress, but distinct from it. The principal difference is that duress arises from the interaction with, and compulsion from, another person. By contrast, necessity typically arises from forces of nature rather than human elements (Garner 2000:460–61). For example, two hikers get lost in a wilderness area during a snow storm. They stumble upon a cabin that has been inhabited, but no one is home and the doors and windows are locked. If they break into the cabin, this normally would be considered a crime (and potentially several crimes have occurred); however, if they are attempting to save their lives by seeking shelter from the storm, the law would treat this as necessity. Dressler (2009:289–90) says that necessity involves a choice between the "lesser of evils," and that it is "a defense of last resort" (see also Garner 2000).

Alibi

Finally, an **alibi** defense may be one of the most misunderstood of the affirmative defenses. Students often assume that having an alibi simply means having an excuse (such as, "my computer crashed," "my grandmother died [again]," or "the dog ate my homework"), but these are not alibis. The word alibi means "elsewhere." In such situations, the defendant is attacking the state's ability to prove guilt by saying "I could not have committed this crime because I was somewhere else." However, saying you were somewhere else and proving that to the satisfaction of a jury are two different things.

TYPES OF CRIMINAL OFFENSES

One of the most common ways of classifying crimes in the United States comes from the annual report compiled by the Federal Bureau of Investigation (FBI) called *Crime in the U.S.* or, more commonly, the Uniform Crime Reports (UCR). The Uniform Crime Reports have been assembled and published in the United States since 1930 (Federal Bureau of Investigation 2009). Reports are released on a quarterly basis, and the results often are reported by local and national news media outlets.

Unfortunately, there are several weaknesses associated with the Uniform Crime Reports. For instance, they only include crimes reported by the public to law enforcement agencies around the United States. As many victimization surveys have discovered over time, as much as half of the crime committed in this country is not reported to the police. Additionally, while there is nearly universal participation, a small number of police agencies do not report statistics to the FBI. Third, the FBI has tried diligently to promote uniformity in the reporting process, but states vary in their definitions of some offenses. Finally, as a result of the "hierarchy rule," the FBI counts only the most serious offense that occurred in any crime event. Thus, if a burglary, arson, and murder all occurred in connection with a crime, the UCRs would only include the murder in its count. Even with its flaws, the Uniform Crime Reporting system gives us the most consistent measure of crime in the United States, and the system has gotten progressively better in the past thirty years.

The crimes included in the Uniform Crime Reports can be classified in three major categories: (1) crimes against persons, (2) crimes against property, and (3) crimes against public order. Obviously, we could add a number of other categories or subcategories, but I focus on these three.

CRIMES AGAINST PERSONS

Crimes against persons (or simply personal crimes) are those offenses committed where there is a personal victim present. In the UCR Part I index crimes there are four offenses that are crimes against persons: aggravated assault, murder and nonnegligent manslaughter, forcible rape, and robbery.

Aggravated Assaults

A simple assault occurs when a person is put in fear for his or her life or safety. In many states simple assaults are misdemeanors and they are not counted in the UCR Part I index crimes (although they are counted elsewhere in the UCR). By contrast, **aggravated assaults** typically are felonies, and they are Part I index crimes. The Uniform Crime Reports define an aggravated assault as "an unlawful attack by one person upon another person for the purpose of inflicting severe or aggravated bodily injury." Furthermore, "this type of assault is usually accompanied by the use of a weapon or by other means likely to produce death or great bodily harm" (Federal Bureau of Investigation 2009).

So what changes a simple assault into an aggravated assault? The short answer is that some additional condition or circumstance must be present. For example, assault and battery, assault with a deadly weapon, and assault with intent to commit bodily harm all would be examples of aggravated assaults. Therefore, once the act goes from a fear-inducing threat (simple assault) to actual physical harm, an aggravated assault has occurred.

Murder and Nonnegligent Manslaughter

The categories of **murder** (or homicide) and **nonnegligent manslaughter** actually cover a variety of different offenses. For instance, states may have different categories of murder such as first-degree murder, second-degree murder, and so forth. There also may be varying degrees of manslaughter, such as voluntary manslaughter or involuntary manslaughter. However, at the most basic level murder and nonnegligent manslaughter involve "the willful (nonnegligent) killing of one human being by another" (Federal Bureau of Investigation 2009). In 2008 there were approximately 16,272 murders in the United States, and this was down 0.8 percent from 2004 but up about 4.8 percent from 1999.

Forcible Rape

Forcible rape is a unique offense among the UCR Part I index crimes for several reasons. First, as defined by the UCR, forcible rape "is the carnal knowledge of a female forcibly and against her will." By this definition, forcible rape can only occur against female victims. Second, largely because of the restrictiveness of this definition, a number of states have modified their laws to change rape to crimes such as "criminal sexual penetration" (or a similar designation) which allows for offenders and victims of either gender. Third, there is evidence to indicate that forcible rape is among the most under-reported of the Part I index crimes (Dressler 2009:579–80). Nevertheless, in 2008 there were estimated to be 89,000 forcible rapes reported to the police in the United States, the smallest number reported in the past 20 years. This number was down 6.4 percent from 2004 figures and 0.5 percent below 1999.

Robbery

The final crime against persons included in the UCR Part I index crimes is **robbery**. Robbery is a crime that sometimes gets confused with burglary (which I discuss in the next section). People will sometimes say that their house or car got robbed. However, as I have mentioned, robbery is a crime against the person. Thus, a carjacking or mugging would be robbery, but having your car broken into and your radio stolen would not be.

The FBI notes that a robbery is "the taking or attempting to take anything of value from the care, custody, or control of *a person or persons* by force or threat of force or violence and/or putting the victim in fear" [emphasis added] (Federal Bureau of Investigation 2009). In 2008 there were 441,855 robberies reported to law enforcement authorities nationwide. This number was down 0.7 percent from 2007, but up 10.1 percent from 2004.

CRIMES AGAINST PROPERTY

In the Uniform Crime Reports there are four personal crimes and four property crimes counted in the crime index. In this section we will examine the property crimes of: larceny/theft, burglary, motor vehicle theft, and arson.

Larceny/Theft

Larceny/theft by far is the most common Part I index crime. The FBI classifies larceny/theft as "the unlawful taking, carrying, leading or riding away of property from the possession or constructive possession of another." It is different from robbery in that it does not involve the taking directly from the person, and it is different from burglary in that it does not involve a breaking into a structure. It is the crime by which most people (including college students) are likely to be victimized, and the numbers are truly astounding. There were nearly 6.6 million larceny-thefts reported in the United States in 2008. Amazingly, this was down 5.3 percent from 1999.

Burglary

As I mentioned previously, burglary is a crime sometimes confused with larceny/theft or robbery. However, the UCR definition of **burglary** is "the unlawful entry of a structure to commit a felony or theft…the use of force need not have occurred" (Federal Bureau of Investigation 2009). In 2008 burglaries accounted for over one-fifth of the index crimes reported to the police: There were 2.22 million burglaries reported in the United States, and this was up 2.8 percent from 2004 and up 5.8 percent from 1999. Over two-thirds (70.3 percent) of the burglaries were of residences. Just over half (51.5 percent) of these were reported to have happened between 6:00 am and 6:00 pm. By contrast, about one-third (33.7 percent) of the non-residential burglaries occurred during the day. Non-residential burglaries involve structures such as schools, churches, businesses, and construction sites.

Motor Vehicle Theft

The category of **motor vehicle theft** can be complicated. Obviously, thefts of personal motor vehicles such as automobiles and pickup trucks are included. However, recreational vehicles, buses, motorcycles, snowmobiles, and other craft are also included in this category. Not included in this category are situations where there has been the taking and abandonment of a vehicle for temporary transportation. In many states this offense is labeled "joyriding" or some similar designation. There were 956,846 motor vehicle thefts in the United States in 2008 and, similar to most other index crimes, this was a decline (down 22.7 percent from 2004 and down 16.9 percent from 1999).

Arson

Finally, the last crime to be added to the crime index was arson (in the early 1980s). **Arson** involves "any willful or malicious burning or attempting to burn, with or without intent to defraud, a dwelling house, public building, motor vehicle or aircraft, personal property of another, etc." (Federal Bureau of Investigation 2009). In 2008 62,807 arsons were reported to law enforcement agencies nationwide. This number was down from the 67,504 arsons reported in 2005 and the 88,887 reported in 1996. Just over four in ten of these (43.4 percent) involved buildings.

PUBLIC ORDER OFFENSES

Public order offenses are not included in the Part I index crimes, but these offenses are tallied separately by the FBI as part of the nation's total crime picture. **Public order offenses** include crimes such as breach of the peace, fighting (sometimes called affray), disorderly conduct, public drunkenness, unlawful assembly, carrying weapons, obstructing traffic, and animal abuse (Reid 2007). Many of these crimes fit into the classification of *mala prohibita* offenses; they are not necessarily evil in-and-of themselves, but they are crimes because they have been classified as such.

OTHER CRIMES

Obviously, the previous sections do not include all of the possible crimes committed in the United States. Some offenses do not neatly fit into these categories. For instance, there are offenses that are sometimes called crimes against the public welfare. These include offenses such as "the manufacture or sale of impure food or drugs to the public, anti-pollution environmental laws, as well as traffic and motor-vehicle regulations" (Dressler 2009:147). There also are crimes against public morality such as prostitution, bigamy, and obscenity (Reid 2007: 304–15).

We also can classify crimes as white collar/occupational or corporate crimes. Although these are not necessarily separate legal categories, nevertheless some of the offenses with which the courts deal fall into these groupings. For the most part, white collar or occupational crimes are committed by individuals who work in positions of trust. The law says that they occupy positions of "fiduciary trust" (see, for example, Champion 2005:101). These are offenses committed against the company or corporate interest, and they include activities such as fraud, theft of property, and embezzlement. For reporting purposes, most of these crimes are included in other categories in the UCR, such as larceny/theft.

In addition to crimes committed by employees or agents, there also can be crimes committed by corporations themselves. These might include consumer fraud, the knowledgeable production of defective or harmful products, or predatory lending practices. Some of the most public cases of corporate crime have included the automobile industry (the Ford Pinto case), big tobacco companies, and the financial services industry (Enron and several others). Often with corporate crime, members of the public may not realize they have been victimized, and it frequently is very difficult to decide who really is to blame for the criminal activity (see Benson and Cullen 1998; Cullen, Maakestad, Cavender, and Benson 2006).

The justice system also is being confronted with a group of what we might consider more "modern" crimes. Some of these include intrusion into secure computer sites or data bases (so-called hacking), trafficking in humans (an updated form of slavery), stalking, cyberstalking, and others. In some instances law enforcement agencies have had to deal with these behaviors under the headings of traditional crimes. At other times, however, legislative bodies have been able to respond quickly to legally define these behaviors and make them illegal.

Finally, there are crimes against the government or related to the administration of justice. Some of the offenses against the government include treason and terrorism, while offenses related to the administration of justice involve perjury, bribery, misconduct by public officials, and obstruction of justice (Reid 2007: 315–20).

SUMMARY

The criminal law that we have in the United States today represents centuries of evolution and development. We can most directly trace American criminal law to the English common law tradition, which was further influenced by ancient codes such as those of Babylon and the Law of Moses, as well as the legal traditions of Greece and Rome. Contemporary European nations such as France and Germany also have influenced our notions of criminality and the development of the criminal law.

There are a number of features that distinguish civil law from criminal law, and these include the procedures legislatively defined for each type of court. The terminology employed in civil law and criminal law is distinct, but somewhat similar. Perhaps the major difference in the two types of law is the weight of evidence necessary to secure a verdict. In civil cases, proof is based on the preponderance of the evidence, while in criminal cases guilt must be proven beyond a reasonable doubt.

Contemporary law in the United States originates from a number of sources. The common law that we inherited from England still has some influence around the nation, but it largely has been replaced by statutory law. The ultimate source of law is the Constitution of the United States and the constitutions of the 50 states. Case law arises from constitutional challenges and appellate court interpretations, and some of the famous U.S. Supreme Court cases (like *Miranda v. Arizona*) illustrate the nature of case law. Federal regulatory agencies provide a final source of law, and administrative law has become a pervasive part of the legal system in the United States.

Crimes in the United States vary in their degree of perceived evilness and also in their legal seriousness and, as a result, we can classify them in several different ways. In terms of the degree of evilness we can distinguish between *mala in se* and *mala prohibita* offenses. Furthermore, legislatures define crimes according their degrees of seriousness, and we classify the two major categories as felonies and misdemeanors.

At the time of trial, the different elements of crimes become especially significant. Prosecutors must establish *mens rea* (criminal intent), *actus reus* (the wrongful act), and the convergence of the two. While *actus reus* implies that some wrongful act has occurred, it is important to remember that there can be inchoate crimes—such as conspiracies, solicitations, and attempts—that represent incomplete offenses.

The government bears the burden of proof or persuasion in criminal trials. However, in cases where affirmative defenses are asserted, some of the burden can shift to the defense.

Finally, crimes can be classified according to the target behavior. The major categories are crimes against the person, crimes against property, crimes against public order, and a variety of miscellaneous other offenses.

It is important to understand the criminal law, since this is what powers the engine of the criminal justice system. Each new law added to the statute books adds another group of potential offenders, and police officers, prosecuting attorneys, probation officers, and judges must constantly strive to stay current on the nature of potential offenses.

QUESTIONS FOR CRITICAL THINKING

1. What are the differences between customary law and modern criminal law? Which system of laws works best in which societal setting?

2. Even contemporary societies like Singapore still practice corporal punishments (like caning) for some offenses. Would you advocate that the United States return to the corporal punishments for certain crimes, instead of relying so heavily on incarceration? Why or why not?

3. Sometimes we talk about civil law and criminal law as if they are completely different entities. How different are civil law and criminal law? How much are they alike?

4. What are the advantages and disadvantages of having juries of twelve members? Would you be in favor of six-person juries for all trials? Would it

make a difference if the case was a criminal case instead of a civil case? What about for capital offenses?

5. Do the method of determining attorneys' fees and the method of payment have any effect on the type of law most attorneys are inclined to practice? What does the phrase "law follows the money" mean in this regard?

6. What are the primary sources of law in the United States? Based on your reading in this chapter, which source of law seems to dominate today?

7. Define and describe the differences between *mala in se* and *mala prohibita* offenses. Which would the public most likely consider true criminal activity? Why?

8. What do we mean by inchoate offenses? List and describe the most common types. Why are these activities considered criminal?

9. Which of the affirmative defenses would seem to have to best chance of succeeding? Why do you think so?

10. Describe the differences between robbery and burglary. Now, what are the differences between burglary and larceny-theft?

11. Should behaviors such as public drunkenness, prostitution, and drug use (not drug sales) be crimes? Why or why not?

RECOMMENDED READINGS

Katsh, M. Ethan (2010). *Clashing Views on Legal Issues*, 14th ed. New York: McGraw-Hill. Katsh produces this book annually, and it deals with many of the major issues facing the courts. He includes a number of carefully edited opinions from U.S. Supreme Court decisions, and the latest edition of the book has sections on the law and terrorism, the law and the individual, the law and the state, and the law and the community.

Reid, Sue Titus (2009). *Criminal Law: The Essentials*. New York: Oxford University Press. This is an abbreviated version of Reid's well-established and comprehensive criminal law text. This version is very useful as a quick-reference guide to the definition of law and the various types of offenses that the criminal justice system most frequently encounters.

Walsh, Anthony, and Craig Hemmens (2008). *Law, Justice, and Society*. New York: Oxford University Press. Walsh and Hemmens bring together the perspectives of a sociologist and a legal scholar to deal with the nature of law, particularly as an element of social control. This book gives an overview of the court system in the United States, and it has a separate chapter on the role of women in the justice system.

KEY TERMS

actus reus	bench trial	concurrence
administrative law	beyond a reasonable	conspiracy
affirmative defenses	doubt	constitutional law
aggravated assaults	burden of proof	contingency fee
alibi	burglary	contributory negligence
arson	canon law	corporal punishment
attempts	civil law	*corpus delicti*
banishment	common law	crimes against persons

criminal law

criminal intent

customary law

defendant

duress

entrapment

equitable relief

excuses

felonies

folkways

forcible rape

inchoate offenses

infancy

infractions

insanity

intoxication

irrational justice systems

judicial review

justifications

khadi justice

larceny-theft

legal precedence

legality principle

mala in se offenses

mala prohibita offenses

mens rea

misdemeanors

mores

motor vehicle theft

murder (homicide)

natural law

necessity

non-negligent manslaughter

norms

petty misdemeanors

plaintiff

preponderance of the
   evidence

procedural law

prosecutor

public order offenses

restitution

restorative justice

right to counsel

robbery

self-defense

solicitation

substantive law

statutory law

typologies of law

weight of evidence

REFERENCES

Benson, Michael L., and Francis T. Cullen (1998). *Combating Corporate Crime: Local Prosecutors at Work*. Boston, MA: Northeastern University Press.

Black, Donald (1976). *The Behavior of Law*. New York: Academic Press.

Black's Law Dictionary (1991). St. Paul, MN: West Publishing Co.

Bounds v. Smith, 430 U.S. 817 (1977).

Brown v. Board of Education of Topeka, Kansas, 347 U.S. 483 (1954).

Calvi, James V., and Susan Coleman (2008). *American Law and Legal Systems*, 6th ed. Upper Saddle River, NJ: Prentice Hall.

Champion, Dean J. (2005). *The American Dictionary of Criminal Justice*, 3rd ed. Los Angeles: Roxbury Publishing Co.

Cullen, Francis T., William J. Maakestad, Gray Cavender, and Michael L. Benson (2006). *Corporate Crime Under Attack: The Fight to Criminalize Business Violence*, 3rd ed. Newark, NJ: Matthew Bender/LexisNexis.

Douglas v. California, 372 U.S. 353 (1963).

Dressler, Joshua (2009). *Understanding criminal law*, 5th ed. Newark, NJ: Matthew Bender/LexisNexis.

Federal Bureau of Investigation (2009). *Crime in the United States*. Washington, DC: U.S. Department of Justice. www2.fbi.gov/ucr/cius2009/offenses/violent_crime/index.html.

Fletcher, George P. (1998). *Basic Concepts of Criminal Law*. New York: Oxford University Press.

Gardner, Martin R. (2009). *Understanding Juvenile Law*, 3rd ed. New York: Matthew Bender/ LexisNexis.

Garner, Bryan A., ed. (2000). *A Handbook of Criminal Law Terms*. St. Paul, MN: West Group.

Hoffa v. United States, 385 U.S. 293 (1966).

Hooker, Richard (2007). *World Civilizations—The Code of Hammurabi*. http://public.wsu.edu/~dee/ MESO/CODE.HTM.

Kerle, Kenneth E. and Francis R. Ford (1982). *The State of Our Nation's Jails*. Washington, DC: National Sheriffs' Association.

Langton, Lynn, and Thomas H. Cohen (2007). *State Court Organization, 1987–2004*. Washington, DC: Bureau of Justice Statistics, U.S. Department of Justice.

Marbury v. Madison, 5 U.S. 137 (1803).

Mays, G. Larry (2004). Conspiracy to commit a crime. In *Encyclopedia of criminology*, ed. Richard A. Wright and J. Mitchell Miller, 226–27. Hampshire, UK: Taylor & Francis.

Mays, G. Larry and L. Thomas Winfree, Jr. (2009). *Essentials of Corrections*, 4th edition. Belmont, CA: Wadsworth/Cengage.

Marongiu, Pietro, and Mario Biddau (2009). Italy. World Factbook of Criminal Justice Systems. http://bjs.ojp.usdoj.gov/content/pub/ascii/WFBCJITA.TXT

Melone, Albert P. and Allan Karnes (2008). *The American Legal System*, 2nd ed. Lanham, MD: Rowman & Littlefield Publishers.

Miranda v. Arizona, 384 U.S. 436 (1966).

Plessy v. Ferguson, 163 U.S. 537 (1896).

Reid, Sue Titus (2007). *Criminal Law*, 7th ed. Los Angeles: Roxbury Publishing Co.

Ross v. Moffitt, 417 U.S. 600 (1974).

Rottman, David B., and Shauna M. Strickland (2006). *State Court Organization, 2004*. Washington, DC: Office of Justice Programs, U.S. Department of Justice.

Thompson, Joel A., and G. Larry Mays (1991). *American Jails: Public Policy Issues*. Chicago: Nelson-Hall Publishers.

United States v. Russell, 411 U.S. 423 (1973).

Vago, Steven (2009). *Law and Society*, 9th ed. Upper Saddle River, NJ: Prentice Hall.

Walker, Samuel (2006). *Sense and Nonsense About Crime and Drugs*, 6th ed. Belmont, CA: Wadsworth.

Walsh, Anthony, and Craig Hemmens (2008). *Law, Justice, and Society*. New York: Oxford University Press.

Weber, Max (1954). *Law in Economy and Society*. Cambridge, MA: Harvard University Press.

Williams, Christopher R., and Bruce A. Arrigo (2008). *Ethics, Crime, and Criminal Justice*. Upper Saddle River, NJ: Prentice Hall.

ENDNOTES

[1] The United States Supreme Court ruled in the case of *Williams v. Florida,* 399 U.S. 78 (1970) that states may employ less than twelve-member juries in any criminal case except those involving the death penalty. Additionally, again in all but capital cases, states can allow twelve-member juries to decide with less than unanimous verdicts (*Apodaca v. Oregon,* 406 U.S. 404, 1972).

[2] Even the U.S. Supreme Court has struggled with defining or quantifying the notion of guilt beyond a reasonable doubt. However, the Court has ruled that "The beyond a reasonable doubt standard is a requirement of due process, but the Constitution neither prohibits trial courts from defining reasonable doubt nor requires them to do so as a matter of course" (*Victor v. Nebraska,* 511 U.S. 1, 1994).

[3] The Supreme Court has decided a long list of right-to-counsel cases. Among the most significant are *Powell v. Alabama,* 287 U.S. 45 (1932)—dealing with state-level capital cases; *Gideon v. Wainwright,* 372 U.S. 335 (1963)—all other state felonies; and *Argersinger v. Hamlin,* 407 U.S. 25 (1972)—misdemeanors that carry the potential of incarceration.

[4] Some people use the word "conspiracy" to describe both the conduct within a group contemplating a crime, as well as the group itself. Dressler (2009) does not approve of applying the term "conspiracy" to the group, and insists that it only should be applied to the contemplated action.

PART
TWO

COURT PARTICIPANTS:
ROLES AND
RELATIONSHIPS

3

The Courtroom Work Group

Photo source: AP Images

INTRODUCTION

Often when we think of court operations and the judicial process in the United States, we think of the people who serve in various positions within the courts. Instead of courts simply being majestic-looking buildings, or distinguished-looking rooms within those buildings, courts actually are dynamic institutions composed of many different types of individuals and groups who occupy mutually interdependent roles.

This chapter focuses on two particular groups of actors within the context of the trial courts. First we will consider judges, prosecuting attorneys, and defense attorneys, the individuals who comprise the core of what often is called the **courtroom work group**. The second group we will examine includes different individuals and groups that interact with the core group on a consistent basis.

Particular attention will be paid to who these people are, and the relationships they have with each other on an ongoing basis. It is important to note to begin with that given the somewhat unique nature of appellate courts (as I discuss in Chapter 11) there is much less routine interaction between the judges or justices and the attorneys who argue cases before them. Therefore, the work group dynamics are much different in these courts, and this is the reason for my focus on trial courts in this chapter.

THE ACTORS[1]

I examine each of the actors in the courtroom work group core in the two chapters that follow: judges in Chapter 4 and prosecutors and defense attorneys in Chapter 5. Additionally, other courtroom regulars are discussed in later chapters in the text. However, at this point it is important to briefly highlight the responsibilities of the three primary actors within the judicial process. At one level most people believe that they know what judges and attorneys do; at another level their jobs are complex and varied.

THE WORK GROUP CORE

One of the key concepts for understanding the operations of courts in the United States is that of the courtroom work group. Eisenstein and Jacob say that "Courts are not an occasional assemblage of strangers who resolve a particular conflict and then dissolve, never to work together again. Courts are permanent organizations." In simplest terms, this means that the core members within the judicial process have regular and ongoing relationships, and they interact with each other in a variety of settings within the courts. Therefore, "Viewing courtrooms as organized workgroups will enable us to unravel many of the mysteries of the judicial process" (1977: 20).[2] In the remainder of this section we will examine the principal individuals that comprise the courtroom work group. In the following sections we will examine some the different ways they interact with each other in the performance of their duties.

In previous discussions I have noted that the official perspective of the judicial process in the United States is that it is fundamentally adversarial. Attorneys for the two sides—prosecution and defense in criminal cases, and plaintiff and defense in civil cases—stand in opposition to one another. What one stands to gain, the other stands to lose. The image often used is that of a medieval jousting contest where two knights do battle with each other. The reality, however, is that in addition to the formal relationships demonstrated by trials, courtrooms represent something of an informal community that exists to expedite the processing of cases and, generally, to make the whole procedure as painless as possible for one another. As will be made clear, the core members of the courtroom work group typically all possess law degrees, they have been engaged in the private practice of law at different points in their careers and for different amounts of time, but they generally hold similar worldviews.

Judges

Before trials even begin, judges are responsible for discharging a number of duties. For example, in some courts judges have the day-to-day responsibility for interacting with the police through issuance of arrest and search warrants. They must decide whether sufficient probable cause exists to issue a warrant based on the affidavits presented to them by law enforcement officers. Additionally, after arrests have been made judges must decide whether the accused will be granted bail or detained, and if bail will be granted what the proper amount of the bail bond should be. In the lower level courts judges will preside over initial appearances as well as preliminary hearings to determine whether there is sufficient probable cause for the case to move forward.

Prior to a trial beginning, the judge may have to rule on pretrial motions and conduct hearings on motions such as the suppression of physical evidence or confessions. In civil cases, judges may place restrictions on the parties as to the types of issues that might be litigated, the degree to which issues can be discussed openly in the press, and the amount of time that each side may have to present its case. Such considerations may give rise to appeals later in the process, so judges must ensure that the rules are followed here and at trial.

The most visible role performed by judges is presiding over civil and criminal trials. It is in this capacity that the judge serves as the neutral referee between the two attorneys as they present their cases. During the course of a trial objections may be raised and motions may be offered on which the judge must rule. Ultimately, it is the responsibility of the judge to guarantee that both sides follow established rules and procedures. In most serious cases there will be a jury, but in some lower level courts jury trials are not conducted and the judge must decide on the issue of guilt or innocence in criminal cases and on liability in civil cases.

After the attorneys for both sides have concluded their cases, in jury trials the judge must read the instructions to the jury on the appropriate laws, the nature of the evidence presented and how it should be interpreted, as well as any special instructions that are necessary (for example, with specialized defenses such as duress, necessity, insanity, or entrapment).

Judges have other responsibilities as well, and many of these are discharged outside of the public view. Often judges are found in their private offices reviewing motions and researching various points of law or legal issues. They may be assisted by law clerks in the area of legal research. Some judges also are responsible for the daily administrative aspects of their courts such as supervising clerical staff and budgeting (Mays and Taggart 1986; Taggart, Mays, and Hamilton 1985).

Prosecuting Attorneys

The second key actor in the courtroom work group is the prosecuting attorney. Prosecutors may serve as the legal advisors to law enforcement agencies, and in this capacity they can help draft the affidavits for arrest and search warrants. They represent the state in criminal cases beginning with the initial appearances and preliminary hearings. Additionally, in most jurisdictions, someone from the prosecutor's office—an assistant district attorney—will serve as the legal advisor to each grand jury as that body hears and reviews the evidence from criminal cases.

Like judges, the most public functions performed by the prosecutor take place in the context of trials. However, before the trial begins the prosecutor has examined the evidence presented in preliminary hearings and by witnesses during grand jury testimony, as well as reviewed the list of potential witnesses for both sides. As the trial begins, the prosecuting attorney participates in the selection of a jury and in the presentation of opening arguments in the case. The prosecutor calls witnesses for the state and cross-examines defense witnesses. At the end of the trial the prosecutor also presents closing arguments to the jury. In these closing arguments the prosecutor reviews some of the key evidence presented and explains why the state believes that it has proven guilt beyond a reasonable doubt.

Defense Attorneys

The prosecutor's counterpart is the defense attorney. In some cases defense attorneys are privately retained by the people accused of a crime, and in other cases the court has appointed a defense attorney (such as a public defender). Unlike in England, where there are "office attorneys" (solicitors) and "trial attorneys" (barristers), in the United States most lawyers perform both functions of advisors and advocates. In criminal cases, defense attorneys work to ensure that the rights of their clients are protected throughout the process. While they are "officers of the court," they are expected to provide clients with a vigorous defense at every stage of the proceedings. In civil cases, defense attorneys may work for large businesses and corporations, or they may represent parties in a divorce, or defend automobile drivers who have caused accidents in personal injury cases.

In this and following chapters it is important to remember that in many jurisdictions throughout the United States judges, prosecutors, and defense attorneys have regular, routine, and ongoing relationships. They encounter each other in the courthouse and in courtrooms on a frequent basis. It is these ongoing interactions that provide the backdrop of what we call the courtroom work group.

OTHER WORK GROUP ACTORS

In addition to the core members of the courtroom work group, there are a number of individuals who support the functioning of the core group, or who interact with them on an occasional basis. In this section I discuss six such groups and individuals: law clerks, court clerks and other administrators, jurors, witnesses, police officers, and the news media.

Law Clerks

The work of law clerks frequently is discussed in the context of appellate courts such as the United States Supreme Court (see, for example, Rehnquist 2001). However, even many state and local trial court judges employ law clerks. In most instances, law clerks are recent law school graduates who either have just passed the bar exam or who are studying to take the bar exam.

Law clerks often have broadly defined duties, but one of their primary responsibilities is to do legal research for the judges who have little time to do it for themselves. They will examine recent relevant cases to determine what appellate courts have said on a particular issue and to summarize the statutory and case law of interest to the judge. Law clerks that work for appellate court justices may even be responsible for providing the first-round drafts of opinions which the justices then edit to suit their perspectives.

While they work behind the scenes in the judicial process, law clerks can be very influential in their interactions with the judges. Additionally, clerks—especially those that have worked for the justices of the United States Supreme Court—have been able to jumpstart their legal careers as a result of having this experience on their resumes. Clerking also provides an opportunity to establish networking ties that can help to boost one's career in the practice of law in both the short and long terms.

Court Clerks and Court Administrators

Often judges inherit administrative duties simply by virtue of the position they occupy. Nevertheless, not all of them are interested in administration, nor are they necessarily prepared to be administrators. Therefore, court clerks (elected in many jurisdictions in the United States) and court administrators or managers (typically appointed by judges) inherit many of the administrative duties that otherwise would fall to the lot of the judges.

Much like others in this realm, court clerks and administrators operate behind the scenes in the courthouse, but their duties ensure that the courts operate much more smoothly than they otherwise would. One area in particular—that of case docketing or calendaring—affects the way in which the core members of the courtroom work group discharge their duties. At times attorneys have been known to "judge shop," in order to find a judge who is more sympathetic to their case than some other judge might be. In these situations it may be helpful to have a good relationship with the office responsible for setting the court calendar. If the attorney wants a particular judge on his or her case, it is equally important not to alienate other judges before whom he or she might appear on another matter. Court clerks and administrators may be able to facilitate special requests from attorneys to have their cases set on certain dates or before certain judges.

Jurors

The fact that juries involve a rotating cast of characters prevents this body from being a part of the courtroom work group core. Most major civil and criminal cases will have a jury trial, and the jury experience allows the average citizen to play a key role in the judicial process. However, juries are formed to hear cases, and then they are dismissed after their particular cases are concluded. Nevertheless, the core members of the courtroom work group are keenly aware that juries introduce an element of unpredictability into the trial process. This means that while judges, prosecutors, and defense attorneys appreciate the work that jurors perform, they all have some degree of uneasiness over entrusting decision making into the hands of individuals who have no training in the law. As a result, much of what the core members of the courtroom work group strive to do is to minimize the need for juries by expeditiously disposing of cases without trials.

Witnesses

There is an old axiom among lawyers that is repeated by Frank Galvin, the attorney played by Paul Newman in the movie *The Verdict*: "Never ask a question that you don't know the answer to." Like jurors, witnesses introduce an element of uncertainty into trial procedures. Most attorneys carefully interview their own witnesses and, if possible, the witnesses for the other side as well to ascertain what their likely testimony will be. The idea is to minimize the likelihood of surprise at the time of trial, and a favorite tactic of some attorneys is to question opposing witnesses to determine whether they have been "coached" in their testimony.

Witnesses often feel that they are caught in a tug-of-war between the opposing attorneys, and this can be an uncomfortable feeling for most of them. Witnesses who are the victims of crimes, like rape, sometimes feel particularly set upon as they are questioned about their victimization. As a result of intense questioning, judges may have to come to the rescue of witnesses if they seemingly are being badgered by an attorney.

The courtroom work group may exert a great deal of effort into disposing of a case quickly, especially if it appears that there may be problems with the testimony of some witnesses. Like jurors, witnesses bring uncertainty into the process, and this may further facilitate plea bargaining.

Police Officers

Police officers occupy a unique place in the judicial process. In some instances they are witnesses in civil and criminal cases. They also interact with all members of the courtroom work group core on a regular basis, both in court and out of court. Some of them—especially detectives or investigators—may appear in court very frequently. However, they typically have different perspectives and hold different views than the work group core members. For instance, as I discuss in the following sections, one of the key values held by work group members is the smooth processing and disposal of cases. They often do this through the plea bargaining process. Police personnel, by contrast, are much more concerned about their own definition of a "successful" prosecution and case conclusion. While the prosecutor's office may be juggling hundreds or even thousands of cases, an individual police officer may be responsible for a handful of serious criminal investigations. Thus, the police are willing to risk going to trial in order to see a defendant receive a *severe* punishment, while the prosecutor (and the defense attorney, as well) is willing to take a guilty plea in order to ensure that the defendant receives *some* punishment. This often leaves police officers to question whether they and members of the courtroom work group are "on the same side" or not.

The News Media

At face value, it would seem that members of the news media are on the outside looking in when it comes to courts and the judicial process. However, after careful examination it becomes apparent that the work group members and the media have a relationship that can be mutually beneficial to all of them. As one example, prosecutors and judges (in some jurisdictions) are elected officials. This means that it can be advantageous for judges and prosecutors to grant access (and information) to reporters in high-profile cases. News reports that cast judges and prosecutors in an especially favorable light can be helpful at election time. Defense attorneys also can use the news media to their advantage. Often defense attorneys appear on camera outside of the courtroom explaining

FIGURE 3.1   ACTORS IN THE COURTROOM WORK GROUP

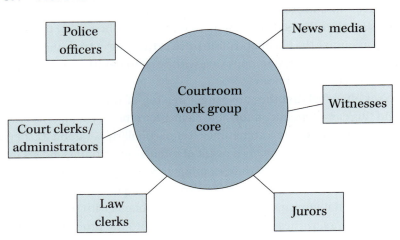

to reporters how their clients are victims of some misunderstanding or another and how the evidence that is presented will prove this. As a result of such efforts, judges may have to admonish the attorneys for both sides that the case must be tried in court, not in the news media.

All six of these groups and individuals operate in a realm just outside of the courtroom work group core, but each of them influences the manner in which the work group functions. These additional actors can facilitate the smooth operation of the work group, or they can complicate the process beyond its already complicated nature. We will more fully examine the members of the courtroom work group core and the additional actors that interact with them as we progress through the text. Figure 3.1 gives a visual depiction of these actors.

DEFINING THE COURTROOM WORK GROUP

Why do we consider judges, prosecutors, and defense attorneys a work group, and what are the features of courts that are similar to work groups found in other occupational settings? Eisenstein and Jacobs say there are seven characteristics:

1. They exhibit authority relationships.

2. They display influence relationships, which modify the authority relationships.

3. They are held together by common goals.

4. They have specialized roles.

5. They use a variety of work techniques.

6. They engage in a variety of tasks.

7. They have different degrees of stability and familiarity (1977: 20).

Each of these features will be examined in unraveling the complex network that comprises the courtroom work group.

First, as Figure 3.1 illustrates, it is possible to envision the courtroom work group as the hub of a wheel around which several spokes radiate out. Within the innermost circle are the core members of the workgroup: judges, prosecutors, and defense attorneys. These groups and individuals participate in the courtroom often, if not daily, and share common demographic characteristics and professional backgrounds. They also share common perspectives when it comes to the operation of courts. In the United States there are a few lower-level courts that have non-lawyer judges. However, in most instances the core members of the courtroom work group all have attended law school and they have some degree of experience in the practice of law (see Langton and Cohen 2007). Many judges and attorneys have come from upper middle class backgrounds, and they tend to be financially better off than a large percentage of the general population (Goldman, Slotnick, Gryski, and Schiavoni 2007). In a word, together they are members of an exclusive and somewhat elite profession.

Attached to the inner circle of core members of the courtroom work group are regular members within the judicial process who do not participate as frequently as the core members. This would include law enforcement personnel and certain types of witnesses (for example, expert witnesses), who may appear regularly in courtrooms but who do not participate daily. The news media also might be included among the groups that have regular interactions within the courts.

Finally, there are the occasional participants; groups or individuals who rarely appear in the courts. Here we would find citizens called for jury duty, as well as victims of crimes, or individuals appearing for a traffic ticket or to litigate a divorce. Importantly, the actors outside of the courtroom work group core typically do not share the same training, values, and orientations as the core members of the courtroom work group.

As we examine some of the other characteristics of the courtroom work group, the relationships among these core actors is explored further. Additionally, I will treat judges (Chapter 4) and prosecutors and defense attorneys (Chapter 5) more fully later in the text. For the time being we need to reexamine those seven defining features of the courtroom work group that I listed from Eisenstein and Jacob (1977).

AUTHORITY RELATIONSHIPS

The clearest authority patterns are exhibited by judges. As an illustration and reflection of our English legal heritage, the judge sits as the supreme ruler in the court, much as a king or queen would. Judges are intimately involved in virtually every aspect of case processing. At the very beginning, they are responsible for authorizing arrest and search warrants. They make decisions about the setting of bail, and they rule on pretrial motions submitted by the prosecuting and defense attorneys, as well as motions that may be made during the trial itself. They oversee the process of jury selection and determine when or if potential jurors will be excused. During the trial, judges sit as the neutral arbiters (some would call them referees) making sure that proceedings operate smoothly and that both attorneys adhere to proper procedures.

The judge's symbolically superior status is reflected in the manner of dress, the design of the courtroom, and the way in which participants address the judge. Unlike other members of the courtroom work group who wear normal business attire, judges wear black robes similar to those of ministers or college professors at graduation. When they are on the bench, judges sit in a position that is elevated above the rest of the courtroom. In effect, they preside from above the battle between the two opposing attorneys. Furthermore, the attorneys and others who participate in courtroom activities refer to the judge as "Your Honor," a title indicating an elevated position relative to others in the process.

However, the authority of the judge is not without limits. For instance, as I discuss at length later, only the prosecuting attorney can bring cases to court, and prosecutors can file motions for **nolle prosequi** (or no prosecution) even in cases that have been scheduled for trial (see Cole 2004). Also, while prosecutors and defense attorneys work *with* judges, and while judges hold an elevated position in the court, lawyers do not work *for* judges. In most jurisdictions in the United States, state and local prosecutors are chosen in partisan elections, and court-appointed defense attorneys may be part of an appointed counsel system or of a state or local public defender organization. The result is that while judges may exert symbolic authority over the attorneys, they really do not have operational control over them.

There are four other areas in which the authority of the judge may be limited: budgetary control, jurisdiction, sentencing guidelines, and appeals. In terms of budgets, judges are not the masters of their own fates. Funding for the courts typically comes from state governments, local (city or county) governments, or a combination of both. I return to this topic in the final chapter, but at this point it is important to note that the trend nationwide since the 1980s has been for states to assume an increasingly larger role in funding court personnel and operations (Langton and Cohen 2007). Therefore, although courts can submit budget requests, the final allocations result from negotiations between the executive and legislative branches. This means that judges inherit their budgets and they are provided funding to pay for supplies, operations, personnel, and travel expenses.

Courts and judges are also at the mercy of legislative bodies to define their jurisdictions. The United States Constitution (in Article I, Section 8 and Article III, Section 1) provides that Congress shall decide on the nature and number of courts below the level of the U.S. Supreme Court, and shall determine the jurisdictions of those courts. By the same token, state legislatures also have the authority to create, abolish, and define the jurisdictions of state courts. This legislative authority somewhat limits the power and prerogatives of judges within the respective jurisdictions.

Sentencing guidelines may also limit judicial authority by proscribing a suggested or mandated range of sanctions. These usually are varying lengths of time to which a judge may sentence a guilty party. It depends on the court system, but these guidelines may be mandatory and serve to reduce sentencing disparity from different judges and different jurisdictions. These guidelines are produced by the U.S. Sentencing Commission at the federal level and by various state sentencing commissions as well.

FIGURE 3.2   RELATIONSHIPS AMONG THE COURTROOM WORK GROUP

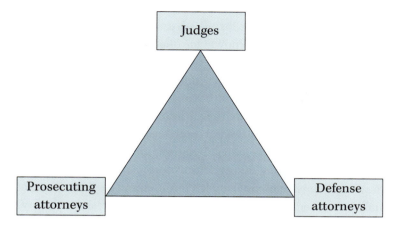

Finally, the authority of judges is limited by the process of appeals. Whenever a case has been concluded, the attorneys have the opportunity to file appeals in situations where they perceive there has been an error of law. As you will see in Chapter 10, when cases are appealed, both intermediate appellate courts and courts of last resort may modify or completely overturn the decisions made by the trial judges below them. The appellate process reduces the likelihood of arbitrary decisions and actions by judges, and it allows for the correction of errors that have been made in the trial process. Figure 3.2 depicts the relationships between judges and lawyers.

INFLUENCE RELATIONSHIPS

Each member of the courtroom work group influences the other members, and in turn each one is influenced by the others as well. For example, as a result of the authority possessed by the judges, they are able to influence the actions and relationships between themselves and the attorneys, and between the prosecutor and the defense attorney. While this would seem to put the judge in a superior position relative to the attorneys, that is not really the case. The formal authority of the judges is more than offset by the superior case knowledge of the prosecutors and, to a lesser extent, the defense attorneys. Once a trial has started, the judges exercise a great deal of control over the pace of proceedings, but even then the attorneys may have an influence over the process.

As I have mentioned previously in this chapter, since most local prosecutors are elected, they possess a base of power that is independent of the judges. Furthermore, prosecutors ultimately decide which cases they will actually take to trial (Jones-Brown 2002). They influence the process of police investigations, as well as the review process of the preliminary hearings and the grand jury. Thus, if the prosecutor believes that there is not sufficient evidence to bring a case to trial, there is very little anyone else can do to move the case forward. Obviously, this has an influence over judges and their potential workloads. If the saying that "knowledge is power" is true, then the greatest power the prosecutor possesses—and, thus, the greatest source of influence—is knowledge (Cole 2004; Koski and McCoy 2002; Walsh and Hemmens 2008). No one else in the entire process has more complete knowledge of a case than the prosecutor (see Eisenstein and Jacob 1977:23). Prosecutors have access to all of the police reports, any laboratory reports on forensic evidence, and the grand jury testimony of witnesses. This places them at the center of an information vortex relative to the trial.

By contrast, defense attorneys have less information, but they still are able to interview prosecution witnesses and to have access to the analysis of physical evidence through pretrial motions for **discovery**. Defense attorneys can increase the workload of judges through the process of filing pretrial motions, and by asking for certain types of pretrial hearings. They also can ask for continuances (to locate witnesses, to have evidence analyzed, or because of case scheduling conflicts) that may delay the trial. Additionally, they will challenge the testimony of prosecution witnesses through the procedure of cross-examination. Furthermore, they may be able to prevent the prosecutor from getting admitted physical evidence or admissions and confessions by the defendant by challenging the procedures under which these items were gathered. Therefore, defense attorneys can influence the pace of justice by prolonging the process of the trial for both strategic and tactical advantages.

BOX 3.1
The Courtroom Work Group in Germany

Like most of the nations of Western Europe, Germany has a criminal justice system that is substantially different from that of the United States. While the United States is composed of fifty states, Germany has a system of sixteen states, eleven from the former West Germany and five from the former East Germany. In Germany the administration of justice principally occurs at the state level. However, unlike the United States, Germany has only a single national criminal code, as well as one system of criminal procedure for the entire nation. There is also a more unified system of courts.

Some of the differences between the judicial systems of Germany and the United States can be seen in the organization and interactions among and between members of the courtroom work group. For instance, in the United States there are 2,344 prosecutors' offices responsible for prosecuting criminal cases in state courts. By contrast, in Germany there are only 116 prosecutors' offices, and the prosecutors are not elected like in the United States but instead are civil servants.

In the United States, once the police complete their investigation and make an arrest the case is referred to the prosecutor's office, and charges normally are filed within a few days. In Germany, the prosecutor is responsible for directing police investigations, and charges are not filed until later in the proceedings.

Continued

BOX 3.1

Continued

The pace of trials in the United States often is governed by the attorneys in the case, especially the prosecutor. In German trials there is no jury, and the case is presided over by an individual judge in minor cases and by one, two, or three judges plus two lay members in the increasingly more serious cases. The judges assemble the evidence and do most of the questioning of witnesses. The prosecutor and defense attorney may ask questions, but only after the judges have completed their questions. If the attorneys want to call additional witnesses, they must ask the judges for permission to do so.

Finally, one of the hallmarks of the courtroom work group in the United States is the amount of discretion possessed by the prosecuting attorney. By contrast, German prosecutors have much less discretion, especially in the most serious cases. The view typically is that German prosecutors are obligated to investigate and prosecute every case that comes to their attention, in contrast to U.S. prosecutors who are relatively free to pick and choose which cases they will accept from law enforcement agencies. Recently this has become somewhat less so, but still the prosecuting attorneys in Germany have significantly less discretion than their counterparts in the United States.

Sources: Aronowitz (2010); Feeney (1998); Kury and Smartt (2002); Perry (2006).

COMMON GOALS

While the differences in authority and the varied influence relationships would seem to put the members of the courtroom work group into a constant state of conflict, there is one fundamental point that we must remember: "Courtroom workgroups have a job to do. Like most people pressed for time, their members do not often pause to philosophize about their ultimate purpose or goals. It is difficult enough just to keep going" (Eisenstein and Jacob 1977:24). Even when it operates at its most ideal state, the judicial process often has been compared to an assembly line (Packer 1968), and like an assembly line all of the workers must do their part and cooperate to make sure the process continues to function and to flow smoothly.

Eisenstein and Jacob (1977:25) say that there are four goals that unite the courtroom work group:

1. Doing justice.
2. Maintaining group cohesion.
3. Disposing of the case load.
4. Reducing uncertainty.

I consider each of these in turn.

DOING JUSTICE

Doing justice is an *expressive goal* in that it is largely symbolic in nature. Additionally, it is externally imposed or expected of the members of the courtroom work group by groups and individuals outside of the justice system. In the United States, doing justice is a goal around which nearly everyone in society can rally. However, exactly what it means to "do justice" varies depending on one's perspective, or the position one holds within the judicial process. For instance, judges will believe that justice is done if the trial is fair and impartial to both sides, irrespective of the outcome. Prosecutors may feel that justice is done only when the trial results in a conviction of the defendant. By contrast, defense attorneys may only feel that justice is done if their client is acquitted or if the defendant receives a suitably lenient sentence. Thus, for the goal of doing justice there seems to be inherent conflict in the interactions between and among the members of the courtroom work group.

MAINTAINING GROUP COHESION

The second objective—maintaining group cohesion—like doing justice, is an expressive goal. However, unlike doing justice, maintaining group cohesion is an internally imposed goal. Members of the courtroom work group quickly learn that they can make each other's lives more comfortable or more complicated based on how they act or interact with one another. The underlying message seems to be that "to get along, one must go along," in order to make each day and each case as pleasant an experience as possible. To enforce cohesion, members of the courtroom work group have ways to informally sanction those who are overly aggressive or too obstructionist. To provide one example, Eisenstein and Jacob (1977:27) say that "the occasional defense attorney who violates routine cooperative norms may be punished by having to wait until the end of the day to argue his motion; he may be given less time than he wishes for a lunch break in the middle of a trial; [or] he may be kept beyond usual court hours for bench conferences." The routine and ongoing interactions among the members of the courtroom make the maintenance of group cohesion a highly prized goal.

DISPOSING OF THE CASE LOAD

The third goal for the courtroom work group is disposing of cases and, in some ways, this may be the most obvious goal of all. Disposing of cases is an *instrumental goal* in that it serves the function of getting the court's work done. Like "doing justice," disposing of cases is an externally imposed goal. Everyone, including members of the general public and various consumers of justice services, believes that cases should be disposed of in a prompt and efficient manner. Within the courtroom work group, judges want to move cases along to maintain a current and reasonable-size docket. None of them wants to suffer the scorn of other judges in their jurisdiction who may feel that there are slackers in their ranks. Prosecutors want to dispose of their cases as quickly as possible as well. Many of the cases do not have facts that are in dispute, so the prosecutors want to process these uncontested cases quickly so they can turn their attention to the more difficult (and usually higher profile) cases that will be going to trial. The motivations of defense attorneys may vary depending on whether they are privately retained or court-appointed attorneys. If they are public defenders, they typically have a huge stack of case files, and they need to dispose of the routine cases as rapidly as possible since new cases are arriving daily. Privately retained attorneys, by contrast, may be motivated by income considerations. The more cases they can handle in a short span of time, the more they will earn. All of these factors taken together provide a major incentive (along with the final goal) to plea bargain the vast majority of cases. I discuss plea bargaining at length in Chapter 7, but it is important to remember that irrespective of the caseload size, there always is pressure to move cases along (see Rosett and Cressy 1976).

REDUCING UNCERTAINTY

The fourth goal of the courtroom work group is to reduce uncertainty. This is an instrumental goal (that is, it serves a very real function), but it is one that is internally imposed. Students of the judicial process in the United States quickly recognize that the involvement of actors outside of the courtroom work group (this especially includes jurors and witnesses) greatly increases the amount of uncertainty in a trial. Therefore, when cases go to trial this produces uncertainty for all parties and particularly for the attorneys. This uncertainty, combined with the goal of disposing of cases, magnifies the pressure to plea bargain all but the most exceptional cases.

SPECIALIZED ROLES

One of the unifying characteristics of the members of the courtroom work group is that they are all trained in the law. They know each other's roles and responsibilities and have an appreciation for the work that the others do. However, while there are many similarities in functions, training, and backgrounds, the three primary roles—judge, prosecutor, and defense attorney—are not interchangeable. The judge must focus on responding to motions before, during, and after the trial by both sides. Judges also must demonstrate an attitude of impartiality in conducting every phase of the trial itself. There should never be an occasion where the judge favors one side over the other.

By contrast, the prosecuting attorney is charged with representing the people of the state in bringing charges against the defendant. Ultimately, attorneys for both sides in the case are responsible for seeing that justice is done (the first of the shared goals of the group), and they must not obstruct the efforts of the other side in pursuit of winning. For instance, prosecutors must not deliberately withhold evidence that would exonerate the defendant (this is called **exculpatory evidence**). However, just as the defense attorney is under no obligation to help the state with its case, the prosecutor is under no obligation to represent the defendant's interests.

Finally, the defense attorney has the narrowest focus of any of the primary members of the courtroom workgroup. The defense attorney is obligated to represent his/her client to the maximum extent possible. Every defense attorney carries the designation "officer of the court," but in the final analysis their real obligation is to make sure the defendant receives the best representation possible.

In summary, the core members of the courtroom work group share similar legal training, perhaps similar work histories, and a cluster of shared goals. Nevertheless, they approach the task of discharging their duties in distinctly different ways and, at times, with different motivations.

WORK TECHNIQUES

Knowledge is the basis of power and influence in the judicial process, and each member of the courtroom work group possesses different degrees and types of knowledge, and different ways to put that knowledge to use. In terms of discharging their duties, the courtroom work group members employ three sets of techniques in their interactions with one another. These techniques include: "(1) unilateral decisions, (2) adversarial proceedings, and (3) negotiations" (Eisenstein and Jacob 1977: 30). We will briefly examine each of these.

There are a variety of circumstances in which one member of the courtroom work group can make a unilateral decision with no consultation or permission from the other members. In exercising their duties and responsibilities, prosecutors and defense attorneys can take actions independently of one another. Such actions include the decision over what charges to file and how many different criminal counts to pursue (by the prosecutor), and whether to pursue certain charges. Prosecutors also can decide whether to file a motion for a *nolle prosequi* (no prosecution).

Defense attorneys make decisions over how many and which witnesses to call and whether to have the defendant take the stand in his/her own defense. Defense attorneys even must decide whether to put on a case at all, or whether just to ask the court for a directed verdict of acquittal after the state finishes its case.

Judges can decide whether certain potential jurors should be seated, or whether to allow one attorney or the other to ask that certain people not be allowed to serve on a jury because of potential bias (or some unspecified reason). Judges also unilaterally rule on a wide range of motions that might be filed by either one or both attorneys. In the final analysis, these decisions rest solely with the judge, although they may be subject to both sentencing guidelines and appeal.

Although many decisions can be made independently by members of the courtroom work group, much of what transpires during the courtroom proceedings comes about through the give-and-take of the adversarial process. The adversarial nature of proceedings resembles a jousting tournament between two medieval knights. In effect, the attorneys are the champions for their respective sides. They square off early in the process with attempts to establish probable cause in preliminary hearings, during pretrial proceedings, at the time jurors are questioned and selected, and especially during the trial itself. As I discuss further in Chapter 7, each side calls and questions its own witnesses with the prosecution presenting its case first. However, after a witness is first questioned on "direct," the other side has a chance to question the witness during the process of cross-examination. This give-and-take between the two sides is designed to produce the fullest information and the clearest picture for both the judge and the jury.

In anticipation of questioning the witnesses, most attorneys thoroughly question each of their own witnesses in order to have some idea about what the nature of their testimony will be. The purpose of this process is not so much to "coach" the witnesses on what to say but to eliminate uncertainty (one of the work group's shared goals) and to prevent surprise testimony that might be damaging to their own case.

The final work technique involves negotiation. The textbook model of court proceedings is that they are adversarial from beginning to end. The reality, however, is that there is much cooperation among the parties of the courtroom work group. A variety of decisions are reached by work group members through negotiation. These include the exchange of information, particularly between the opposing attorneys. Early in the process, there will be negotiations about whether the defendant is eligible for bail, the amount of bail, and what the conditions of pretrial release should be. The setting of trial dates and the granting of continuances also might be negotiated. However, the ultimate manifestation of the negotiation process is plea bargaining.

Judges may or may not be directly involved in plea bargaining, depending on the rules of procedure or local customs. However, if they are involved, they may meet with the attorneys in their chambers and encourage them to reach a suitable disposition on a certain case. During the plea bargaining process prosecutors and defense attorneys will meet—sometimes in an assistant district attorney's office, and sometimes over lunch or coffee—to discuss a particular case or group of cases. These negotiations will center on the final charge(s), the number of counts that will be accepted, and what the most appropriate sentence will be. Sentencing negotiations will include discussions about whether probation is acceptable to both parties. This often is called the "in-or-out" debate. Additionally, the attorneys will debate whether there will be local jail or prison time that must be served.

One point to recognize in the negotiation process is that the parties do not necessarily negotiate from equal positions of power. Between the attorneys there clearly is a power differential and, in most instances, the prosecuting attorney is at an advantage relative to the defense attorney. However, as we have noted previously, the shared goals of the work group members tend to level the playing field in whatever negotiations occur.

TASKS

Courts exist at a variety of levels in the United States, and they also process vastly different volumes of cases. Nevertheless, there is a pattern or routine of case processing that is fairly similar from one jurisdiction to the next. These tasks are illustrated in the flow diagram in Figure 3.3.

The tasks that must be accomplished in disposing of cases begin shortly after law enforcement agencies make an arrest. One of the first judicial functions will be the initial appearance, where the police will bring a suspect before a magistrate to deal with the issues of the formal charges, bail, and representation by counsel. Next, in some jurisdictions in the United States, there will be a preliminary hearing during which the prosecution will try to convince the judge that there is <u>sufficient probable cause</u> to bind the case over to the grand jury or schedule it for trial in a court of general trial jurisdiction.

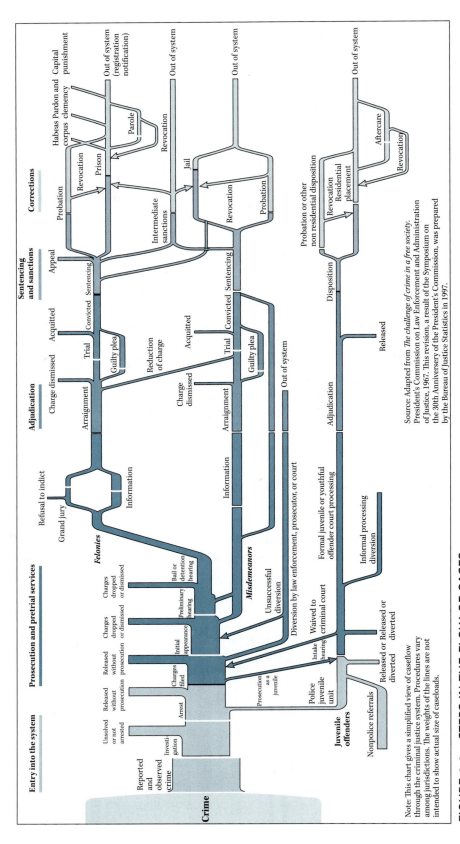

Entry into the system

Prosecution and pretrial services

Adjudication

Sentencing and sanctions

Corrections

Crime

Reported and observed crime

Investigation

Unsolved or not arrested

Arrest

Released without prosecution

Charges filed

Prosecution as a juvenile

Felonies

Misdemeanors

Grand jury

Refusal to indict

Information

Released without prosecution

Charges dropped or dismissed

Initial appearance

Preliminary hearing

Charges dropped or dismissed

Bail or detention hearing

Unsuccessful diversion

Diversion by law enforcement, prosecutor, or court

Arraignment

Charge dismissed

Trial

Acquitted

Guilty plea

Reduction of charge

Information

Arraignment

Charge dismissed

Trial

Acquitted

Guilty plea

Out of system

Convicted

Sentencing

Appeal

Probation

Revocation

Prison

Parole

Revocation

Habeas corpus

Pardon and clemency

Capital punishment

Out of system (registration notification)

Out of system

Intermediate sanctions

Jail

Probation

Revocation

Out of system

Convicted

Sentencing

Juvenile offenders

Nonpolice referrals

Police juvenile unit

Released or diverted

Intake hearing

Released or diverted

Formal juvenile or youthful offender court processing

Waived to criminal court

Informal processing diversion

Adjudication

Disposition

Released

Probation or other non residential disposition

Revocation

Residential placement

Revocation

Aftercare

Out of system

Note: This chart gives a simplified view of caseflow through the criminal justice system. Procedures vary among jurisdictions. The weights of the lines are not intended to show actual size of caseloads.

Source: Adapted from *The challenge of crime in a free society.* President's Commission on Law Enforcement and Administration of Justice, 1967. This revision, a result of the Symposium on the 30th Anniversary of the President's Commission, was prepared by the Bureau of Justice Statistics in 1997.

FIGURE 3.3   STEPS IN THE FLOW OF CASES

If the preliminary hearing establishes that there is probable cause, the case will be referred to the prosecutor's office for presentation to the grand jury, in those states that utilize grand juries. Grand juries will meet periodically to review the cases scheduled by the prosecutor's office, and they will typically only hear from witnesses for the prosecution. After the cases are presented, the grand jury members will vote (a unanimous decision is not required) on whether they too find probable cause for a trial. If they do, they will return a true bill, also called an indictment. In those states that do not require grand jury hearings, the prosecuting attorney will prepare a document known as a **criminal information** document. This is a formal document that outlines the accusations against the defendant and the specific provisions of the case related to the establishment of probable cause (Melone and Karnes 2008:248).

Following a grand jury indictment, the case will be set for arraignment in one of the general trial jurisdiction courts. At the arraignment the judge will make sure the defendant has legal counsel. After this, the judge will once again review the charges for the sake of the defendant and his/her attorney. If the defendant is being held in jail, the question of bail also will be addressed again. At this point the judge typically will ask for a plea from the defendant, and most plead innocent. This allows the judge—frequently with the assistance of the court clerk—to set a date for the trial.

Before the trial begins, the attorneys have the opportunity to file motions for the judge to consider. For example, if there has been an excessive amount of pretrial publicity because of the nature of the case, the defense attorney may ask for a **change of venue**. There may be motions to dismiss some or all of the charges, and there may be other motions related to the admission of physical evidence or admissions by the defendant. In most cases, just as a matter of routine, the defense attorney will file a motion for discovery. This is a request by defense counsel to have the opportunity to review all of the physical evidence held by the prosecutor and the list of potential witnesses.

At the beginning of the trial, the judge may have other motions to attend to (such as a request for a **continuance** to locate a missing witness or for additional time to prepare for the case), but in most instances the case is now ready for trial. One of the first orders of business is the selection of the jury. In most jurisdictions the court clerk is responsible for summoning people for jury service, but some courts utilize what are called jury commissioners.

Once the trial has started, there are several tasks that are ongoing. For example, if the defendant is still in custody, someone (a law enforcement agency like the sheriff's department or court bailiffs) will have to be responsible for maintaining control and custody over the defendant during proceedings. Additionally, the court clerks and court reporters will have to record all of the proceedings in order to produce the verbatim transcript of the trial, and items of evidence will have to be logged in and secured.

In small, rural jurisdictions, all of these tasks will be performed by one court and perhaps by one or two judges. However, in very large, urban jurisdictions, these functions typically are processed by specialized judges/courts and prosecutors. In those jurisdictions, instead of speaking of *the* courtroom work group, we really have a number of specialized work groups. In assembly line fashion, the scheduling and processing of each group has an effect on the workload and pace of all of the groups that follow.

STABILITY AND FAMILIARITY

The relationships that exist among the various members of the courtroom work group will be influenced by several factors. First, the more stable the membership of the work group, the more likely it is that the members will know each other well and develop long-term patterns of interaction. Second, the smaller the group of judges and attorneys, the more intimate the patterns of interaction will be. The result is that the stability and size of the work group will impact the familiarity of the members. Eisenstein and Jacob (1977:35) say that "The more the workgroup members are familiar with one another, the better they can negotiate; the more familiar, the less they need to rely on formalities and the more than can utilize informal arrangements."

Therefore, in small jurisdictions virtually all of the lawyers will know the judges and, likewise, the judges will know the lawyers. This will make for a very distinct, and somewhat closed, **local legal culture** (see Eisenstein, Flemming, and Nardulli 2004). Even in fairly large court districts like Los Angeles, California, some judges and attorneys work together fairly often, and others are known by their reputations within the legal community. In these cases, rather than familiarity breeding contempt, it provides the foundation for cooperative relationships.

GROUP INTERACTIONS

I have briefly touched upon some of the ways in which the courtroom work group members interact with one another, but in this section I examine more fully some of the group dynamics that are likely to manifest themselves. A simple way to examine the intra-group dynamics is to focus on the way each member of the group interacts with the other two members.

JUDGES

In many discussions of the judicial process in the United States, trial judges are presented as somewhat passive actors in proceedings. They seem to be dependent on the prosecuting attorneys to bring cases to court, and they respond to motions filed by both prosecutors and defense attorneys. However, the reality is that judges are far from passive participants. Furthermore, most judges come to the bench after some period of serving as a prosecuting attorney, or having been a public defender or an attorney in private civil and criminal practice. Therefore, judges understand the pressures under which the prosecution and defense operate.

In their interactions with prosecuting attorneys judges can encourage prosecutors to move matters along, especially when the cases seem weak and the charges are relatively minor. When new assistant prosecutors come to court full of zeal to vigorously prosecute each case, judges can privately counsel them (or their bosses) that each case does not involve the death penalty and that they should have a realistic view of the seriousness of the case. This assessment of the true seriousness of the case often is characterized as the **going rate**, and it becomes a mutually agreed upon value by the courtroom work group for each case that comes to court (see, for example, Walker 2006). Knowledge of the going rate by all parties helps facilitate the rapid processing of cases, particularly through plea bargaining. Prosecutors who do not cooperate in the collaborative process may find some of the charges or some of their cases dismissed by judges.

Interactions with defense attorneys may be somewhat different, since not all of the same defense attorneys are in court with the same regularity that prosecutors are. However, especially with public defenders and other court-appointed attorneys, they appear in court with enough frequency to develop a relationship with the judge. In many of the criminal cases with court-appointed attorneys there are two factors that encourage plea bargaining, and over which judges can exert some influence. First, public defenders typically carry heavy caseloads, and in most instances they do not have a lot of time to prepare for each case. Second, the facts of the case may not be contested by any of the parties. The underlying issue simply may be why the crime was committed and how the accused can receive leniency. Therefore, judges may encourage public defenders to try to "work out" something with the prosecutor's office in order to expedite the disposal of such cases. For privately retained attorneys, judges can encourage cooperation through the sentencing process. If a defense attorney has been especially uncooperative during the trial, the judge can impose a severe sentence on the defendant. This is an indirect way of punishing the attorney, since future clients may be reluctant to hire a lawyer who has the reputation of allowing defendants to receive long sentences or high fines.

PROSECUTING ATTORNEYS

Prosecutors operate from a position of power within the courtroom work group. They have the ultimate decision over which cases to take to court and which ones they may refuse to prosecute. They can be very selective in this process, or they can flood the courts (and judges' dockets) with multitudes of cases. In some ways judges recognize that the prosecutors control the flow of cases, and this creates something of a dynamic tension between the two offices.

If judges dismiss charges or an entire case, there is always the possibility that the prosecutor could reindict an individual and begin the prosecution all over again (unless a jury has returned a verdict of not guilty). Prosecutors also can appeal to the "court of public opinion." Very often prosecutors who are unhappy with the way in which cases have been dealt will hold a press conference and explain to the public the way in which they handled a particular case properly, but the judge dismissed it based on a "technicality" (usually with the investigating police officer standing nearby). While this does not mean that prosecutors have authority over judges, they do have an independent authority that accrues to them by virtue of their popularly elected position.

In dealing with defense attorneys (especially public defenders), prosecutors have a great deal of leverage. Prosecutors can offer plea deals—based on the going rate for a case—in which some of the charges are dropped or the level of the charges is reduced. Often the deal can be sweetened by offering little or no prison time, or even allowing for time-served for defendants who have been in jail awaiting trial. The ultimate threat possessed by the prosecutor (and one even they are reluctant to use for some cases) is that they will take the case to trial. This is a time-consuming process for all involved and is typically reserved for the most serious charges.

DEFENSE ATTORNEYS

Defense attorneys often find themselves in the position of having to "sell" a deal to their client. This can be done with veiled threats of the reputation of the judge ("she's a hanging judge") or of the assistant prosecutor on the case ("he's going for the maximum on this one"). In most instances this is sufficient to get the client to accept a plea deal.

When they deal with judges, defense attorneys can employ two tactics that impede the steady progress of cases. First, they can ask for continuances. This may be done in order to have more time to prepare for the case, or as a result of scheduling conflicts with other courts and other cases. Since many judges have been practicing attorneys themselves, they will be sympathetic to requests for continuances, up to a point. After long periods of delay, judges may lose their patience and set a firm date for trial. The second way attorneys can slow down the process is through the filing of motions. These may occur prior to the trial commencing, or during the course of the trial itself. Whether the motions have any validity or not, judges must respond to all of them.

Interactions between defense attorneys and prosecuting attorneys demonstrate the greatest divergence between the "official" adversarial model of courts and trials, and the cooperative system that operates on a daily basis. Public defenders (and other defense attorneys, as well) and prosecutors are often seen interacting informally before trials begin, on breaks in the trial, and after the trial is concluded. In fact, some defendants seem concerned about the cozy relationship that seems to exist between the two sides and wonder to themselves which side the defense attorney is really on. However, it is this ongoing relationship—especially between assistant public defenders and assistant district attorneys—that allows deals to be struck and cases to be disposed of quickly.

As I have noted throughout this chapter, the interactions and relationships that exist between the three parties in the core of the courtroom work group allow for the achievement of goals supported by all. Officially, all of the parties are committed to seeing that justice is done in each case. Informally, much of what occurs is designed to dispense of the heavy caseload experienced by each of the parties. However, as I elaborate in the next section, forces outside of the courtroom work group may alter the dynamics of the relationships.

DISRUPTIONS IN GROUP GOALS

Occasionally, factors are introduced that change the methods by which the courtroom work group does business. One of the clearest illustrations of this was the adoption of the "three strikes" law in California in 1994. This law was intended to punish second-time serious offenders with twice the penalty that normally would apply. For third-time offenders, the punishment would be 25 years to life in prison. Interestingly enough, the offenses that qualified as "strikes" involved not only felonies, but some serious misdemeanors that were termed "wobblers" (Benekos and Merlo 1995; Dodge, Harris, and Burke 2009).

In examining the effects of California's three strikes law, Harris and Jesilow (2000: 186) found that the law had "fundamentally changed the relationships and power among members of the courtroom work group, significantly disrupting the efficiency of their work and making the prediction of case outcomes difficult, if not impossible."

The disruptions caused by implementation of the three strikes law principally came from altering the nature of the going rate. Since second and third offenses potentially could be punished much more seriously than in the past, defendants were much more willing to go to trial in the hopes of receiving less serious penalties. Perhaps, in some cases, juries would even acquit—a concept known as **jury nullification**—if they felt that the punishment was grossly disproportionate to the offense (see Dodge et al. 2009; Harris and Jesilow 2000). Given the possibility of an increasing number of trials, in courts already with heavy dockets, the response was adaptive behaviors. For instance, Harris and Jesilow (2000:201) found that "judges . . . routinely offered second-strike defendants the lowest possible sentence, seemingly to encourage defendants to plead guilty."

Irrespective of the adaptive behaviors by members of the courtroom work group, it is obvious that external forces (such as changes in sentencing laws or structures) can affect the intra-group dynamics. As will be seen in Chapter 8 on sentencing, there are a number of potential changes that have had an impact on courtroom processes, and there likely will be more in the future.

SUMMARY

Courts in the United States are extremely complex social organizations. They certainly are more than just imposing buildings, and to understand them fully it is essential to comprehend the concept of the courtroom work group. At its most expansive, the courtroom work group involves lawyers, judges, security and support personnel, jurors, witnesses, and even the news media. However, at the core of this work group are the judges, prosecutors, and defense attorneys who interact with each other on a routine and ongoing basis.

Each member of the work group has the authority to act in a variety of situations. These actions can be taken independently of the other members of the work group. However, in fulfilling their tasks, work group members exert influence over one another, and they are bound together in a web of interdependent relationships.

Of particular significance for the work group are a cluster of common goals. Eisenstein and Jacob (1977) note that the four most important goals are: doing justice, maintaining group cohesion, disposing of the caseload, and reducing uncertainty. What we find when examining these goals is that while each member of the work group is an independent actor, the reality is that they must cooperate to a significant extent in order to fully discharge their responsibilities.

Once we understand the nature of the courtroom work group, the professional experiences shared by the members, and their orientations or worldviews, we can better appreciate why the courts operate the way that they do. The conclusion that we often reach is that the law that exists "on the books" is not necessarily the law that plays out every day in the judicial process in the United States.

QUESTIONS FOR CRITICAL THINKING

1. What do we mean by the term "courtroom work group?" Who are the "regular" members of this work group, and what do they have in common?

2. What individuals and groups routinely interact with members of the courtroom work group? How can these actors influence the ways in which the work group goes about disposing of cases?

3. Look at Figure 3.1. Are there groups or individuals that you would remove from this diagram? Are there any that you would add? Explain.

4. What do we mean when we say that the judge's authority is largely symbolic? Does that mean that judges really do not have power within the courtroom setting?

5. Who is the most powerful member of the courtroom work group, and why? Who would you classify as the least powerful member? Again, why?

6. Eisenstein and Jacob say that one feature that distinguishes a work group is the presence of common goals. List the four goals that they say unite the courtroom work group. Which of these four do you think is the most important one, and why?

7. What is the difference between an expressive goal and an instrumental goal? Explain.

8. Is there one characteristic of the members of the courtroom work group that might promote an "us versus them" mentality? What is it, and why might such a characteristic be influential?

9. Someone has suggested that their skill in negotiating makes attorneys like car salespersons. Would you agree with this assessment? How do you think attorneys would react to this comparison?

10. What do you think is meant by the notion of the "local legal culture?" Would this culture be significantly different in different parts of the country, or in small town courts versus big city courts?

11. When individuals graduate from law school and become assistant district attorneys or assistant public defenders, how vigorously do you think they initially approach doing their jobs? Does this orientation change over time? Why or why not? What influences the likelihood that an attorney is willing to "go to the mat" over a particular case?

12. How can forces outside the courtroom work group alter the group's normal operations? Give examples that you have encountered in other courses, or that may have been discussed in recent news stories about the kinds of factors that likely would upset the balance of work group dynamics.

RECOMMENDED READINGS

Connelly, Michael. *The Lincoln Lawyer*. New York: Little, Brown and Co. (2005). This is a fictional account of a criminal defense attorney from Los Angeles, California. Connelly is a former newspaper reporter, and he knows many of the types of characters that inhabit his books. In this book, he gives us an inside look at the world of the solo practitioner—lone wolf—attorney and how this lawyer interacts with others in the courtroom work group and how he is perceived by them.

Eisenstein, James, and Herbert Jacob. *Felony Justice: An Organizational Analysis of Criminal Courts*. Boston: Little, Brown and Co. (1977). This is the book around which most of this chapter is organized. Eisenstein and Jacob, perhaps more than any other authors, fully developed the notion of the courtroom work group. The core of the book is based on their studies of criminal courts in three locations: Baltimore, Maryland; Chicago, Illinois; and Detroit, Michigan. In the book they try to develop a theoretical framework from which to study and more fully understand felony dispositions in criminal courts.

Packer, Herbert. *The Limits of the Criminal Sanction*. Stanford, CA: Stanford University Press (1968). This book is one of the classics in the field of criminal justice. Of particular significance is Chapter 2 of this book where Packer examines two models of the criminal process: due process and crime control. The two ideal models help us to understand the case processing orientations that appear in various courts, and that understanding supplements our understanding of how the courtroom work group functions and why.

Rosett, Arthur I., and Donald R. Cressy (1976). *Justice by Consent: Plea Bargains in the American Courthouse*. Philadelphia: J. B. Lippincott. In this book, Rosett and Cressy undertake a very thorough study of the plea bargaining process. They examine the stakes held by the various actors and, notably, they find that factors more than caseload size influence the pressures to plea bargain in courts all over the United States.

KEY TERMS

change of venue	discovery	local legal culture
continuance	exculpatory evidence	*nolle prosequi*
courtroom work group	going rate	
criminal information	jury nullification	

REFERENCES

Aronowitz, Alexis A. (2010). Germany. In *World Factbook of Criminal Justice Systems*. Washington, DC: Bureau of Justice Statistics, U.S. Department of Justice.

Benekos, Peter J., and Alida V. Merlo (1995). Three Strikes and You're Out! The Political Sentencing Game. *Federal Probation* 59(1): 3–9.

Cole, George F. (2004). The Decision to Prosecute. In *The Criminal Justice System: Politics and Policies*, 9th ed., ed. George F. Cole, Marc G. Gertz, and Amy Bunger, 178–88. Belmont, CA: Wadsworth Publishing Co.

Dodge, Mary, John C. Harris, and Alison Burke (2009). Calling a Strike a Ball: Jury Nullification and "Three Strikes" Cases. In *Courts and Justice*, 4th ed., eds. G. Larry Mays and Peter R. Gregware, 393–403. Long Grove, IL: Waveland Press.

Eisenstein, James, Roy B. Flemming, and Peter F. Nardulli (2004). The Criminal Court Community in Erie County, Pennsylvania. In *The Criminal Justice System: Politics and Policies*, 9th ed., eds. George F. Cole, Marc G. Gertz, and Amy Bunger, 257–79. Belmont, CA: Wadsworth Publishing Co.

Eisenstein, James, and Herbert Jacob (1977). *Felony Justice: An Organizational Analysis of Criminal Courts*. Boston: Little, Brown and Co.

Feeney, Floyd (1998). *German and American Prosecutions: An Approach to Statistical Comparison*. Washington, DC: Bureau of Justice Statistics, U.S. Department of Justice.

Goldman, Sheldon, Elliot Slotnick, Gerard Gryski, and Sara Schiavoni (2007). W. Bush's Judiciary During the 109th Congress. *Judicature* 90(6): 252–283.

Harris, John C., and Paul Jesilow (2000). It's Not the Old Ball Game: Three Strikes and the Courtroom Workgroup. *Justice Quarterly* 17(1): 185–203.

Jones-Brown, Delores D. (2002). Prosecutorial Discretion. In *Encyclopedia of Crime and Punishment*, ed. David Levinson, 1279–84. Thousand Oaks, CA: Sage Publications.

Koski, Douglas D., and Candace McCoy (2002). Prosecutor. In *Encyclopedia of Crime and Punishment*, ed. David Levinson, 1273–78. Thousand Oaks, CA: Sage Publications.

Kury, Helmut, and Ursula Smartt (2002). Germany. In *Encyclopedia of Crime and Punishment*, ed. David Levinson, 784–91. Thousand Oaks, CA: Sage Publications.

Langton, Lynn, and Thomas H. Cohen (2007). *State Court Organization, 1987–2004*. Washington, DC: Bureau of Justice Statistics, U.S. Department of Justice.

Mays, G. Larry, and William A. Taggart (1986). Court Clerks, Court Administrators, and Judges: Conflict in Managing the Courts. *Journal of Criminal Justice* 14(1): 1–7.

Melone, Albert P., and Allan Karnes (2008). *The American Legal System*, 2nd ed. Lanham, MD: Rowman & Littlefield Publishers.

Packer, Herbert L (1968). *The Limits of the Criminal Sanction*. Stanford, CA: Stanford University Press.

Perry, Steven W. (2006). *Prosecutors in State Courts, 2005*. Washington, DC: Bureau of Justice Statistics, U.S. Department of Justice.

Rehnquist, William H. (2001). *The Supreme Court*. New York: Alfred A. Knopf.

Rosett, Arthur I., and Donald R. Cressy (1976). *Justice by Consent: Plea Bargains in the American Courthouse*. Philadelphia: J. B. Lippincott.

Taggart, William A., G. Larry Mays, and David Hamilton (1985). Caseflow Management Conflict in Non-appellate State Courts: Some Findings and Implications for Court Administration. *Justice System Journal* 10(1): 19–36.

U.S. Department of Labor Statistics (2011). *Occupational Outlook Handbook*. Washington, DC: U.S. Department of Labor.

Walker, Samuel (2006). *Sense and Nonsense about Crime and Drugs: A Policy Guide*, 6th ed. Belmont, CA: Wadsworth/Cengage.

Walsh, Anthony, and Craig Hemmens (2008). *Law, Justice, and Society*. New York: Oxford University Press.

ENDNOTES

[1] This section is based largely on the information provided by the U.S. Department of Labor Statistics (2011).

[2] Much of this chapter is built around the book entitled *Felony Justice* by James Eisenstein and Herbert Jacob, and this chapter owes a great debt of intellectual gratitude to this book and these scholars. While many people have discussed and elaborated on the concept of the courtroom work group since this book was first published, this text should be considered the seminal work on the topic.

4

Judges

Photo source: AP Images

INTRODUCTION

Courts in the United States employ a variety of different people to conduct the business of processing civil and criminal cases. However, for many people, the individual who most symbolizes the court and the courtroom work group is the judge. Courts could operate without some of the support personnel they employ, but the judge represents the essential function of adjudication performed by courts. In later chapters we will examine judges in the specific contexts of state and federal court systems, but at this point it is necessary to lay the foundation for those later discussions. Therefore, in this chapter I present the basics of what judges do, how judges are selected for office (and thus who becomes a judge), what the qualifications are for becoming a judge, and how judges are disciplined for official or unofficial misconduct. To set these issues in a broader context I discuss the notions of **judicial independence** and judicial accountability. These are concepts that provide a dynamic tension for members of the judicial branch of government and that frequently are debated by groups of lawyers, judges, and organizations like the **American Judicature Society**.

Also I discuss actors who might be considered quasi-judges—such as masters (or special masters), hearing officers, and referees—that are used in some court settings. Finally, I address the administrative roles judges must fill in the performance of their duties.

SELECTION OF JUDGES

One of the great scholarly and practical areas of debate concerning judges in the United States is over the various methods by which they are chosen (for thorough discussions of this topic see Brown 1998; Di Pietro, Carns, and Cotton 2000; Webster 1995). Judges come to office in a number of different ways, and most members of the general public are grossly uninformed on the topic of judicial selection. The type of selection system or systems utilized depends on whether we are examining federal or state courts. Furthermore, among and within the states there are variations and hybrid systems employed, sometimes depending on the level of the court we examine (Webster 1995).

Hundreds of articles and dozens of books have been written on the various methods of judicial selection, the kinds of judges the different methods select, and the impact this has on the quality of justice dispensed (see, for example, Levin 1998; Sheldon and Lovrich 1991). In this section I devote some space to explaining the different methods of judicial selection and the implications each method may have for the kinds of people chosen to be judges, but before I do so one very important point must be made: *to date there has been no conclusive research that indicates that any one method of judicial selection is superior to the others.* Perhaps Webster (1995:15) says it best when he notes that "Empirical work suggests that the method of selection has little, if any, effect upon the overall quality of judges."

As a follow-up to this observation we might ask: Is any one group or type of person a better judge than any other? Apparently not. Do different methods select different kinds of people? There is some evidence that indicates specific judicial selection methods choose certain kinds of people, so we can conclude that we must give careful consideration to the type of selection method utilized if we are looking for particular types of people to serve us as judges.

There are a number of variations on selection methods, but I consider the following four categories since they represent the most common systems (see American Judicature Society 2008; Vago 2009):

- *Partisan election*—In this method judges run for popular election on a ballot where their political party identification is clearly indicated.

- *Non-partisan election*—Candidates for judicial positions in some states (and many local jurisdictions) run in popular elections, but with no political party label indicated; this approach can be characterized as a "horse race"; all candidates run, and the one with the most votes (if a majority is not required) wins.

- *Appointment*—Two categories of judges are appointed: (1) federal judges, as you will see in later chapters, and (2) virtually every state has some provision for interim appointments when vacancies result from judges who die, retire, or resign suddenly from office.

- *Merit selection*—**Merit selection**, or the **Missouri Plan**, combines elements of election and appointment; this system is discussed more fully in the following paragraphs.

A fifth method, used only by South Carolina and Virginia, is legislative appointment (see Rottman and Strickland 2006; Meador 1991). In South Carolina the governor can make interim appointments, but full-term vacancies are filled by the state legislature. In Virginia the General Assembly makes both interim and full-term appointments.

PARTISAN ELECTION

A great deal of study has been done on the process of choosing judges through partisan elections (see, for example, Kiel, Funk, and Champagne 1994). In some ways, partisan political considerations are involved in every method of judicial selection. However, in a **partisan election**, political involvement is much more explicit since it entails the selection of judges by popular vote in which the judge runs for election or reelection on a ballot on which political party labels are attached to each candidate.

Most people associate judicial selection with the election of state and local judges. This method of judicial selection has a relatively long history in the United States, and for most of the twentieth century it was the primary way of selecting state court judges (see Rottman and Strickland 2006) However, this system of selecting judges did not become widely practiced until the period of Andrew Jackson's presidency (see especially Key 1958; Meador 1991; Plano and Greenberg 1967). As a result of Jackson's influence many states developed what has been called the **long ballot**. Under this process every office, from dog catcher to governor, was filled by popular election, and during this time most states began to elect judges as well.

TABLE 4.1	Methods of Judicial Selection for General Jurisdiction Judges by State, 2004*
Jurisdiction	Method
Alabama	
Circuit, district, and probate courts	Partisan election
Alaska	
Superior and district courts	Gubernatorial appointment from the judicial nominating commission
Arizona	
Superior court	Gubernatorial appointment from the judicial nominating commission (Maricopa and Pima counties, all others use non-partisan elections)
Arkansas	
Circuit and district courts	Non-partisan election
California	
Superior courts	Non-partisan election

Colorado	
District courts (plus some local courts)	Gubernatorial appointment from the judicial nominating commission
Connecticut	
Superior courts	Gubernatorial appointment from the judicial nominating commission with consent of legislature
Delaware	
Superior courts	Gubernatorial appointment from the judicial nominating commission with consent of legislature
Florida	
Circuit courts	Non-partisan election
Georgia	
Superior courts	Non-partisan election
Hawaii	
Circuit courts	Gubernatorial appointment from the judicial nominating commission with consent of legislature
Idaho	
District courts	Non-partisan election
Illinois	
Circuit courts	Partisan election
Indiana	
Tax Court	Gubernatorial appointment from the judicial nominating commission
Superior, circuit, and probate courts	Partisan election
Iowa	
District courts	Gubernatorial appointment from the judicial nominating commission
Kansas	
District courts	Gubernatorial appointment from the judicial nominating commission (seventeen districts) and partisan election (fourteen districts)
Kentucky	
Circuit courts	Non-partisan election
Louisiana	
District, juvenile, and family courts	Partisan election

Continued

TABLE 4.1	*Continued*
	Maine
Superior and district courts	Gubernatorial appointment with consent of the legislature
	Maryland
Circuit courts	Gubernatorial appointment from the judicial nominating commission with consent of legislature
	Massachusetts
Superior courts	Gubernatorial appointment from the judicial nominating commission with approval of executive council
	Michigan
Circuit and claims courts	Non-partisan election
	Minnesota
District courts	Non-partisan election
	Mississippi
Circuit courts	Non-partisan election
	Missouri
Circuit courts	Partisan election (forty circuits) and gubernatorial appointment from the judicial nominating commission (five circuits)
	Montana
District courts	Non-partisan election
	Nebraska
District courts	Gubernatorial appointment from the judicial nominating commission
	Nevada
District courts	Non-partisan election
	New Hampshire
Superior courts	Gubernatorial appointment with approval of executive council
	New Jersey
Superior courts	Gubernatorial appointment with consent of legislature
	New Mexico
District courts	Partisan election
	New York
Supreme and county courts	Partisan election

North Carolina	
Superior courts	Non-partisan election
North Dakota	
District courts	Non-partisan election
Ohio	
Common pleas courts	Partisan election
Oklahoma	
District courts	Non-partisan election
Oregon	
Circuit and tax courts	Non-partisan election
Pennsylvania	
Commonwealth Court	Partisan election
Common pleas courts	Partisan election
Rhode Island	
Superior courts	Gubernatorial appointment from the judicial nominating commission
South Carolina	
Circuit courts	Legislative appointment
South Dakota	
Circuit courts	Non-partisan election
Tennessee	
Circuit, chancery, criminal, and probate courts	Partisan election
Texas	
District courts	Partisan election
Utah	
District courts	Gubernatorial appointment from the judicial nominating commission with consent of legislature
Vermont	
Superior and district courts	Gubernatorial appointment from the judicial nominating commission with consent of legislature
Virginia	
Circuit courts	Legislative appointment
Washington	
Superior courts	Non-partisan election

Continued

TABLE 4.1	*Continued*
West Virginia	
Circuit courts	Partisan election
Wisconsin	
Circuit courts	Non-partisan election
Wyoming	
District courts	Gubernatorial appointment from the judicial nominating commission

Note: This information is only for full-term selection and does not include selection for unexpired terms. The numerous courts of limited jurisdiction, such as municipal and justice of the peace courts, are not included in this table.
Source: Rottman and Strickland (2006:25–37).

In partisan elections, local and state political organizations play a major role in determining who will be on the ballot for various offices. In most instances, the party faithful—those who have worked for, and contributed financially to, party causes over the years—are rewarded for their faithfulness by being chosen to run for office. This places the initial influence over the election process in the hands of the state and local party organizations and their officers.

One of the key assumptions of popular elections is that the voters have a say in who serves them and, ultimately, if a public servant is not performing adequately that person can be voted out of office in the next election. However, there are two very important factors that represent the reality of the election process: (1) most voters are pitifully uninformed about the education and professional experience of judicial candidates, and (2) relatively few judges are ever voted out of office (Webster 1995). As a result:

- Significant portions of voters do not cast votes for the office of judge at all; there is a substantial drop-off in the number of votes cast for offices like governor or state legislators and those cast for judges.
- Some voters primarily are influenced by factors such as an identifiable ethnic name.
- Some voters cast ballots along straight party lines.
- Many voters routinely reelect incumbent judges.

The American Judicature Society (2007) summarizes the difficulty of electing judges:

Democracy requires an informed choice, and with the large number of candidates in some areas, it is impossible for even the best-intentioned voter to be well informed. At the same time, in many jurisdictions, candidates run unopposed and the voter has no choice at all.

Low voter turnout in judicial elections can be attributed to a number of factors. First, many voters may have little contact with, and consequently little knowledge of, the candidates for judge. Second, as indicated by the American Judicature Society, in many races incumbent judges run unopposed. Third, even in hotly contested elections judges are constrained by canons of ethics from making specific campaign promises. They run on slogans like "firm, but fair." This ultimately makes most judicial campaigns "meaningless and uninformative" (American Judicature Society 2007; see also Meador 1991). Box 4.1 includes Canons 28 and 30 on partisan politics and candidacy for office taken from the American Bar Association's (2009) "Canons of Judicial Ethics."

BOX 4.1
Partisan Politics and Candidacy for Office

The American Bar Association has spoken to the issues of partisan politics and candidacy for office in its "Canons of Judicial Ethics." The following excerpts from the ABA demonstrate the kinds of restraint that should be exercised by judges and those who are candidates for the office of judge.

> While entitled to entertain his personal views or political questions, and while not required to surrender his rights or opinions as a citizen, it is inevitable that suspicion of being warped by political bias will attach to a judge who becomes the active promoter of the interests of one political party against another. He should avoid making political speeches, making or soliciting payment of assessments or contributions to party funds, the public endorsement of candidates for public office and participation in party conventions. (Canon 28)

> A candidate for judicial position should not make or suffer others to make for him, promises of conduct in office which appeal to the cupidity or prejudices of the appointing or electing power; he should not announce in advance his conclusions of law on disputed issues to secure class support, and he should do nothing while a candidate to create the impression that if chosen, he will administer his office with bias, partiality, or improper discrimination.

> While holding office he should decline nomination to any other place which might reasonably tend to create a suspicion or criticism that the proper performance of his judicial duties is prejudiced or prevented thereby.

> If a judge becomes a candidate for any office, he should refrain from all conduct which might tend to arouse reasonable suspicion that he is using the power or prestige of his judicial position to promote his candidacy or the success of his party.

> He should not permit others to do anything in behalf of his candidacy which would reasonably lead to such suspicion. (Canon 30)

Source: American Bar Association (2009).

BOX 4.2
Research In Brief: Electing Judges

Since the early 1900s reform advocates have steadfastly maintained that electing judges in the United States is a relatively poor way to fill judicial vacancies. Many times groups such as the American Bar Association and the American Judicature Society have championed methods other than elections to fill vacant judicial positions. Chris Bonneau and Melinda Gann Hall (2009) studied state supreme court elections in the United States, and they believe that judicial elections are very much justified. Their research supports a number of conclusions, including the following:

■ Elections strengthen democracy and establish a bond between the voters and the members of the judiciary they select.

■ Voters can distinguish the quality of the candidates for judge, and this is especially evident in state supreme court elections when challengers have prior judicial experience (versus those who do not).

■ There can be conspicuous voter turnout in cases where elections are contested and competitive.

■ There is relatively little evidence (other than assertions by some critics) that elections undermine the legitimacy of the judiciary.

■ There is no system of judicial selection that is apolitical; there is some form of politics (broad-based versus elite) in every method we use to choose judges.

Source: Bonneau and Hall (2009).

In contrast to the assertions of the so-called reform advocates, Bonneau and Hall (2009) have undertaken research on some of the actual effects of electing state supreme court judges in the United States. Box 4.2 summarizes their research.

As can be seen in the following sections, a crucial question for every method of judicial selection is: who gets chosen? With partisan elections the answer to this question somewhat depends on the political and cultural environment of the state or local jurisdiction (see Kiel et al. 1994; Sheldon 1994). For example, partisan elections tend to favor those candidates who have been most active in party politics at the state and local level.

Some evidence indicates that women and minorities are less likely to be selected as judges through partisan elections. As Brown (1998:324) asserts: "Without question, as matters stand today, minorities [and presumably women] are more likely to be appointed to state appellate courts than elected." In support of this, in a study of state supreme courts, Martin and Pyle (2002:50) found that "States that use nonpartisan elections are more likely to have courts with higher percentages of women, but nearly half of these women first came to the bench through interim appointments. Nearly 100% of the African-American justices in electoral states gained their initial term via gubernatorial appointment." In the following section I consider the process of non-partisan elections further.

BOX 4.3
In the News: Campaign Contributions and Judges

In 2009 the United States Supreme Court issued a ruling in the case of *Caperton v. A.T. Massey Coal Company*. This breach of contract case was originally brought by the Harman Mining Co. against Massey Coal, and a West Virginia trial jury found in favor of Harman and awarded a $50 million judgment. Massey Coal Co. appealed the judgment, and eventually the case reached the West Virginia Supreme Court of Appeals, which overturned the award in a 3–2 vote.

The problem in this case was that one of the three judges who voted in the majority had received a substantial campaign contribution (over $3 million dollars in various forms of donations) from Massey's C.E.O. in his bid to unseat an incumbent judge on the court. Brent Benjamin was the successful challenger, and when the case came before the West Virginia appellate court there was a motion requesting the newly elected judge to recuse himself from the case, which he refused to do.

Justice Anthony Kennedy, writing for a five-justice U.S. Supreme Court majority, said that the standard that must be applied in this case, and one the Supreme Court had proposed in the past, was that a judge must recuse himself whenever "the *probability* of actual bias on the part of the judge or decisionmaker is too high to be constitutionally tolerable" (emphasis added). In this case the majority of justices believed that there was a clear perception of conflict of interest on Brent Benjamin's part and that he should have removed himself from deciding this case.

The four dissenting justices in this case, led by Chief Justice Roberts, believed that by requiring that there be no "probability of bias" (as opposed to actual bias), the majority members were asserting a new rule. In the end, this case demonstrates some of the difficulties associated with campaign contributions and judicial elections in the United States.

NON-PARTISAN ELECTIONS

In the case of **non-partisan elections**, organizations such as the local bar association or other professional groups that can issue endorsements may play a major role in the selection of candidates and ultimately judges (Levin 1998). However, as Sheldon (1994:302) found, in states using non-partisan elections media coverage played a more prominent role than endorsements by the bar association.

Some observers have said that the non-partisan election system has the lowest level of accountability of any method of judicial selection (Bonneau and Hall 2009; Sheldon 1994). Webster (1995:26) maintains that "far from being an improvement upon partisan elections, nonpartisan elections are an inferior alternative to partisan elections because they possess all of the vices of partisan elections and none of the virtues." The states of Arizona, Arkansas, California, Florida, Georgia, Idaho, Kentucky, Michigan, Minnesota, Mississippi, Montana, Nevada, North Carolina, North Dakota, Ohio, Oklahoma, Oregon, South Dakota, Washington, and Wisconsin utilize non-partisan elections to choose some or all of their judges (Arkansas changed in 2000, and North Carolina made changes in 2000 and 2002). Non-partisan popular elections are most common for trial court judges, and in many states elections for positions such as municipal judge also may be non-partisan (Rottman and Strickland 2006:232–45).

Non-partisan elections may bring the same kinds of people to the bench as partisan elections. If women and minorities are less likely to be elected—and this is a point of contention—then it is probably irrelevant whether the elections are partisan or non-partisan.

APPOINTMENT

Some states have appointed judges—usually **interim appointments**—and all of the Article III federal judges are chosen for office by **executive appointment**. Both of these types of appointment are considered in this section.

Currently, twenty states—Alaska, Arizona (Maricopa and Pima Counties), Colorado, Connecticut, Delaware, Hawaii, Iowa, Kansas, Maine, Maryland, Massachusetts, Nebraska, New Hampshire, New Jersey, Rhode Island, South Carolina, Utah, Vermont, Virginia, and Wyoming—appoint judges to office for full terms (Rottman and Strickland 2006; see also Webster 1995:13). In some states the governor makes full-term appointments with the consent of the state legislature, while in others it is done in concert with the judicial nominating commission. Furthermore, virtually every state gives the governor the power to fill vacant offices, like that of judge, in cases where the incumbent has died, retired, resigned, or been removed from office before expiration of the term (Nase 1997; Rottman and Strickland 2006; Webster 1995). In these situations, state statutes or the state constitution allow the governor to fill vacancies on an interim or emergency basis, until the expiration of the original term of office or until the next general election.

Interim appointments serve a number of important practical and political purposes. First, interim appointments allow courts to continue to operate with the appointment of a replacement judge rather than leaving the office empty until the next scheduled election. These appointments also prevent having to call a costly special election to fill a position that may have been vacated suddenly and without warning.

Second, interim appointments allow governors to reward friends, political allies, and faithful party members with an appointment to political office. The terms "political patronage" and "cronyism" (rewarding friends and supporters) often are used in these types of situations, and good government movements and civil service laws in many states over the years have severely restricted the amount of patronage that can be dispensed by politicians. Nevertheless, interim judicial appointments are one way governors can allocate political favors without seeming overtly political. After all, these appointments are "emergency" hires that must later go through the normal channels of judicial selection.

While interim appointments appear to be stop-gap measures, in the end they give those appointed a powerful position from which to launch a bid for election. In effect, an interim appointment confers on the appointee instant incumbency status. Many observers comment that incumbency is a powerful element in states that have popularly elected judges because, as noted previously, incumbents often run unopposed, and voters routinely reelect them (see Nase 1997).

The so-called Article III federal judges all are appointed by the president of the United States. These include all of the federal district court judges, the judges in the courts of appeals, and the justices of the United States Supreme Court. Other federal judges also are appointed, but they do not enjoy the same tenure in office as the Article III judges. In the federal system one of the major exceptions to executive appointment are the **U.S. magistrate judges**, who serve eight-year terms (if they are full-time) and who are appointed by judges in the district courts (Cavanaugh 2008). In order to fully appreciate service in the federal judiciary it is necessary for us to explore the process of appointment to the federal bench.

First, vacancies for federal judgeships can occur in several different ways. Occasionally, the U.S. Congress may create new judicial positions to meet the growing or shifting workloads of the federal courts (Carp and Stidham 2001). When new positions are created the machinery for filling these positions goes into motion. Federal judicial vacancies also occur when judges die, retire, resign, or are removed from office. However, filling these vacancies is not always simple, and nearly all recent presidents have been criticized for not filling vacancies in a timely manner (see Jost 1998; Massie, Hansford, and Songer 2004; Smith, Stuckey, and Winkle 1998).

When a judgeship becomes available, the president's staff will begin the process of assembling a list of appropriate candidates for the position. In virtually every case nominees will be of the same political party as the president. However, since the president and his staff cannot possibly know all potential nominees in every state, they must rely on the U.S. senators, congressmen, and governors (particularly those from the president's party) to supply them with names. As with interim state appointments, federal judicial appointments often go to attorneys, judges, and occasionally law professors who have been faithful and active members of the president's political party and who may have been financial contributors in the previous campaigns. To help you fully understand the federal judicial selection process, I should include a step-by-step hypothetical examination of the road to a federal judgeship.

Let's say a federal district judge in Ohio suddenly dies in office. The president asks his chief legal counsel and the U.S. attorney general to begin the search for a suitable replacement. The attorney general's office contacts the senior U.S. senator from Ohio from the president's political party. This senator asks his staff to contact key party members in the state for names of judges or lawyers from the judicial district who would be good candidates for this position. The senator's staff comes up with the names of two state court judges and a county prosecuting attorney as potential nominees, and they forward these names to the U.S. attorney general's staff. At this time two activities are undertaken. The Federal Bureau of Investigation begins a background check on the potential nominees to determine if there is any illegal or unethical conduct that might prove embarrassing to either the nominee or the president. At the same time the American Bar Association—perhaps in concert with the state bar association of Ohio—is asked to rank the potential nominees as not qualified, qualified, well qualified, or exceptionally well qualified (Carp and Stidham 2001). Once this has been accomplished the president's staff, and often the president himself, will interview the individuals under consideration and make a selection.

After the choice of a nominee has been made, the person's name and supporting documentation are forwarded to the U.S. Senate, and the Senate Judiciary Committee schedules hearings to consider the nominations. The action is in fulfillment of the mandate stipulated in Article II, Section 2 of the United States Constitution that the president will fill judicial positions with the "advice and consent" of the Senate.

Historically, most judicial confirmation hearings were routine and uneventful. Over the past three decades this has been less and less the case. The Senate Judiciary Committee schedules hearings for a day or two during which most nominees are questioned about their "judicial temperament" and views on a variety of subjects of interest to different senators. There may be individuals and groups that request permission to testify on behalf of, or in opposition to, the nomination, and in a number of recent instances there have been more opponents than there have been supporters. A few nomination hearings are televised on C-SPAN or the Cable News Network (CNN), but this typically only occurs for Supreme Court nominations.

It is important to remember that, increasingly, federal court nominations at all levels have generated some degree of controversy. The nomination and eventual confirmation of Clarence Thomas (a George H. W. Bush nominee) to the High Court represents one of the most contentious in recent history, as there were questions about his legal competence and allegations of sexual harassment by a former female colleague. Likewise, Barack Obama's nomination of Sonia Sotomayor to be the third woman and first Latina to serve on the Court also was not without controversy and national attention. Most nominees for federal district judge positions and those on the courts of appeals are not that controversial, and relatively few garner the public and media attention of the two cases just mentioned.

Once nominees are confirmed they have a date chosen for swearing in, and they begin their term of office. As I illuminate later, federal judges appointed under Article III of the Constitution serve life terms during good behavior.

As Carp and Stidham (2001) note, the process for selecting federal judges produces a fairly select group of individuals. Most are male, and a substantial number of those appointed in recent years are from upper socio-economic backgrounds. Federal judges frequently have attended prestigious private colleges for their undergraduate and law degrees, and over two-thirds previously have been judges or prosecutors. Interestingly, recent federal appointees have come from families that have been politically active, including a number who have had judges as members of their families (Carp and Stidham 2001). Do these judges resemble a cross-section of American society? Hardly. Carp and Stidham (2001) characterize them as a most elite group of individuals within a very elite group.

MERIT SELECTION

Finally, the **merit selection** system has gained favor in a number of states since its introduction in Missouri in 1940, and many groups like state bar associations and the American Judicature Society (2009) have strongly endorsed this approach. This system combines elements of appointment with election (Carp, Stidham, and Manning 2007; Watson and Downing 1969). The American Judicature Society (2008:6) says that merit selection is "The process by which judicial applicants are evaluated by a nominating commission, which then sends the names of the best qualified candidates to the governor. The governor appoints one of the nominees submitted by the commission."

When a judicial vacancy occurs in a merit selection state, the district or statewide judicial nominating commission is convened. These commissions are composed of judges, lawyers, and citizens and they accept nominations and applications to fill vacant positions. From the list of potential candidates the nominating commission will send a short list (often three names) to the governor. In some states the nominees are ranked, but in most they are not.

The governor can appoint any of the persons on the short list to the vacancy without explanation or reject the list completely, stating why in writing and requesting another list of acceptable candidates. The person appointed by the governor serves in office until the next general election where, in most states, he/she must run for election against any candidates who are interested in the position. Once elected, the judges in these positions serve a full term in office (whatever length that might be), then at the next election they run on a retention (yes/no) ballot where voters can decide whether to retain these individuals in office. States vary in their percentages of votes required to be retained. Most require 50 percent plus one of the votes cast, and some require more. While requiring more than a majority might seem like a high standard, as with most selection systems, incumbent judges typically have little trouble being retained.

BOX 4.4   In Their Own Words: The Politics of Judicial Selection and Retention

Because most states involve judges in the electoral process, state court judges cannot be insulated completely from politics. The important question is whether that necessary involvement in the political process has an adverse impact on judicial decision-making that, in turn, undermines judicial independence.

From a practical viewpoint, judges must campaign in order to garner support in the form of votes and campaign contributions. This is true regardless of whether the state uses an election or retention system for judicial selection. Both systems demand that judicial candidates attract voters, which in turn demands that they raise money. In the not-too-distant past, most judicial elections were relatively low-key, low-dollar events, mainly involving newspaper announcements and editorials, a few advertisements, and a bounty of spaghetti suppers and pancake breakfasts. But in the last two decades judicial campaigns have changed dramatically in at least three significant ways: their cost, their tone, and their financiers. Rather than defining the exceptional campaign, the high-dollar campaign often defines the norm. The tenor has shifted from conversations about the candidate's backgrounds to discussions of his or her political beliefs, personal opinions, and social convictions. This shift is largely attributable to a decision of the United States Supreme Court in the case of *Republican Party of Minnesota v. White* (2002), which struck down an ethics provision that had previously prohibited judges from announcing their views during campaigns. Following *White* dozens of federal and state court decisions extended the holding to remove other barriers that had limited political activity by judicial candidates.

The post-*White* action has not only loosened the standards on judicial campaign speech, it has also broadened the scope of acceptable judicial political activity and has created a perfect climate for special-interest groups to attempt to exert control in judicial races. Because of the need to raise substantial campaign funds, candidates may turn to special-interest groups who have the resources to supply the funds. Those groups then expect judicial candidates to espouse their views on issues of importance to the groups and reward those candidates who share the views of the special-interest groups.

Thus, modern-day judicial elections are not only marred by the need to raise campaign funds, but they are also influenced by the views of those who supply the funds. The large purses that judicial candidates need to attract are usually held by organizations with precise social and political agendas, not by neutral voters motivated to elect fair and impartial judges. The judicial candidate's need to raise more and more money has coupled the judiciary with

Continued

BOX 4.4

Continued

well-financed special-interest groups. But establishing that special-interest groups are in a better position to influence judicial decision making does not necessarily mean that their influence has undermined judicial independence. In fact, given the wide variety of cases and the many factors that properly impact judicial decision making, establishing a nexus between political support and judicial outcomes is likely impossible. Nonetheless, most agree that even the appearance of political influence undermines the integrity and independence of the judiciary and diminishes the viability of the judiciary as a governmental institution.

Source: Penny J. White is Elvin E. Overton Distinguished Professor of Law at the University of Tennessee College of Law and former Associate Justice of the Tennessee Supreme Court.

BOX 4.5

Gifts and Favors

[A judge] "should not accept any presents or favors from litigants, or from lawyers practicing before him or from others whose interests are likely to be submitted to him for judgment."

Source: American Bar Association (2009).

An increasing number of states have gone, in whole or in part, to merit selection of judges. Apparently three major reasons explain this trend. First, judicial elections in some states have become incredibly expensive (see Aspin and Hall 1994; Brown 1998). For example, the American Judicature Society (2008) reports that in 2003–2004 candidates for judicial elections in the United States raised about $47 million in campaign contributions. Because they must run in contested and expensive elections, judges have to rely on contributions from organizations, groups, and individuals (corporations, law firms, and attorneys) who may appear before them as litigants in the future. As an illustration of this, "In 2005–2006 44% of the contributions to state high court candidates came from business groups, and 21% came from lawyers" (American Judicature Society 2008:5). Box 4.5 contains Canon 32 of the American Bar Association's Canons of Judicial Ethics that addresses the issue of gifts and favors.

Second, judicial elections in some states have become much more competitive and at times somewhat divisive (Kiel et al. 1994). This has caused some judges to feel their decisions will be scrutinized and called into question, even when they have acted properly (Aspin and Hall 1994). A study by the Annenberg Public Policy Center found that over two-thirds of the respondents to one study believed that "raising money for elections affects a judge's rulings to a moderate or great extent" (American Judicature Society 2008:5). Finally, attorneys in merit selection states feel that they have a significant input in the judicial selection process through service on judicial nominating commissions and as a result of bar polls (Sheldon 1994).

As noted with other methods of judicial selection, there is not universal agreement over which system is most likely to favor certain types of candidates. However, in its endorsement of the merit system, the American Judicature Society (2009) maintains that

> Conventional wisdom says that the only way to promote diversity on the bench is to use elections to choose judges. But, as is often the case, conventional wisdom is wrong. The best way to achieve diversity is by using a well-designed merit selection system. Even absent provisions that specifically aim to produce diversity on the bench, merit selection is as effective at producing greater numbers of women and minorities who serve on the bench as elections are. With provisions that specifically advocate diversity (for example, a merit selection system that specifies that members of the judicial nominating commission should represent the demographic makeup of the population), merit selection outperforms elections in achieving diversity on the bench. In fact, research has demonstrated that minority judges are significantly more likely to have been appointed than elected.

It is interesting to note, however, that politics still can play a significant role even in merit selection systems. As a result, two female state supreme court justices—Penny White (in Tennessee) and Rose Bird (in California)—both lost merit system elections as a result of concerted efforts by groups opposed to their retention.

JUDICIAL QUALIFICATIONS

Judges' qualifications vary from state to state and somewhat depend on the level of courts in which the judges serve. Early in our nation's history, before formal law school training became necessary to take the bar exam and practice law, it was not unusual to find non-lawyer judges in many state courts (see Abadinsky 2007; Mansfield 1999). Until the twentieth century law schools were relatively unique institutions, and many practicing attorneys learned the law the way Abraham Lincoln did, through "reading the law" or apprenticeship programs. During the last half of the twentieth century legal education became more formal, most attorneys possessed a law school degree (first the LLB, then the JD), and most judges likewise were educated in the law. When states began to modernize their court structures in the last quarter of the twentieth century some of the **lay judge** positions—those not requiring a law degree—were eliminated,

BOX 4.6

In the News: The End of Lay Judges?

For many years, cities in Washington State that had populations under five thousand were allowed to use "lay judges," or individuals who did not possess a law degree. However, in 2002 the Washington State legislature passed a law requiring all courts in the state to require judges to have law degrees. Tribal courts are exempt from this requirement, along with any lay judges serving at the time the law was passed. Currently, three communities—Zillah with a population of 2,600; North Bonneville with a population of about 600; and Uniontown with a population of just under 400—still have non-lawyer judges. But when these judges leave office (for whatever reason), the state law requires that their replacements will have to have a law degree. The movement to professionalize courts, in Washington and other states as well, causes changes in the lowest level trial courts. The result is that the last vestiges of the "people's courts" have now disappeared in many jurisdictions.

Source: Courtney (2009).

or the requirements were changed to mandate a law degree. This resulted in offices such as justice of the peace disappearing in most states.

Today many jurisdictions have gone even further. It is not uncommon to find states that require not only a law school education, but also admission to the bar and the requirement of a certain number of years of legal practice (see Rottman and Strickland 2006). In Part III, on court structure, I discuss federal courts and federal judges, and one of the unique contrasts between state judges and federal judges is that there is no formal written list of qualifications for the federal judiciary. This does not mean that no requirements exist; instead, they have developed informally between the U.S. Justice Department and members of Congress (Carp and Stidham 2001).

LOCAL AND STATE JUDGES

I already have dealt with local and state court judges to some degree. However, in this section I briefly examine some of the major issues related to these judges. First, in 2004 nationwide there were 10,282 state judges serving in courts of general trial jurisdiction, and this was up from 9,109 in 1998. Additionally, there were 16,275 judges serving in courts of limited jurisdiction (Langdon and Cohen 2007:6).

Second, as I have indicated, state judges are selected in four major ways: (1) partisan election, (2) non-partisan election, (3) merit selection, and (4) appointment. There is controversy over whether each of these systems brings different types of people to the bench

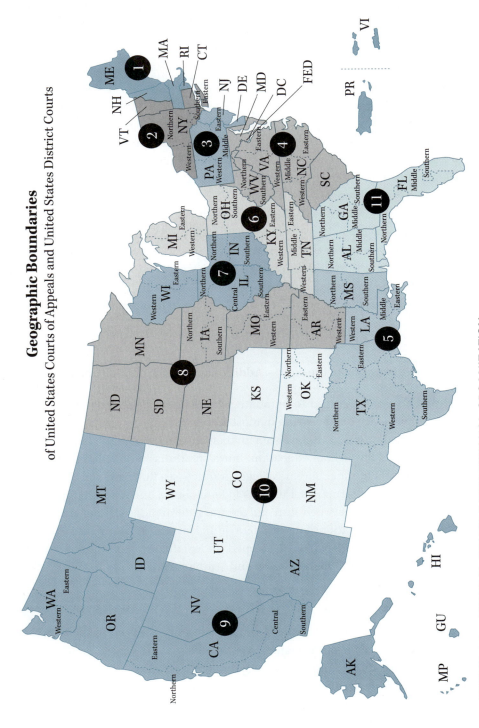

Geographic Boundaries
of United States Courts of Appeals and United States District Courts

FIGURE 4.1 FEDERAL COURT JURISDICTIONAL ORGANIZATION

and even greater controversy over whether one of these systems is superior to the others. In other words, does one system select "better" judges than the others? To date we would have to conclude that there are mixed results on the nature of the judges chosen by each system, and almost universal agreement that each system has strengths and weaknesses. We have not been able to conclusively prove that one selection system is the best.

Another issue that always will be of concern is the appropriate qualifications for state judges. As previously mentioned, judges in courts of general trial jurisdiction typically must be licensed attorneys, and most states require them to have practiced law for a certain number of years. However, twenty-nine states still allow non-lawyer judges in local courts or the courts of limited or inferior jurisdiction (see Mansfield 1999; Rottman and Strickland 2006). These judges may be known by a variety of titles, but the most common seem to be magistrate or justice of the peace.

Two very important points should be made about state court judges here. First, irrespective of the method of selection employed by different states, a significant number of individuals come to the bench through interim appointments. This power given to governors (or state legislatures) is substantial in that most of these interim appointments result in the incumbent being selected for a regular term of office. Second, again irrespective of the method of judicial selection, once an individual becomes a judge in most states that person is routinely reelected or retained in office. In fact, most judges leave the bench through voluntary acts such as resignation or retirement.

The role of judge is a significant one, and you will see in several other places throughout the text that judges can impact the quality of justice dispensed. They also influence the pace of litigation in the courts. Additionally, public opinion about courts, judges, and justice may be shaped by the actions of judges more than any other actors in the judicial process.

FEDERAL JUDGES

There are a variety of people who work in and for the United States courts. In later chapters we will examine federal appellate judges, but in this section let us briefly consider the different types of judges that serve the federal trial courts.

Three categories of individuals serve as judicial personnel in the federal district courts: district court judges, magistrate judges, and bankruptcy judges. District court judges' positions have existed since the Judiciary Act of 1789, and these judges serve as the front-line judicial officers for the entire federal judicial system. Figure 4.1 shows the jurisdictional configuration of the federal judicial system, with the outline of courts of appeals and district court boundaries. The judgeships for the ninety-four federal court districts are authorized by Congress, and their numbers have gone from 13 in 1789 to 678 in 2008 (see Administrative Office of U.S. Courts 2009). Unlike the time when the district courts were first created, today there are no single judge districts. The smallest districts have as few as two (Vermont) or three (Maine and Rhode Island) judges, and the largest districts have more than twenty judges (Carp and Stidham 2001).

One of the interesting contrasts between state and federal judges exists over their qualifications. In virtually every state today, trial court judges are required to possess law degrees, and some states even specify a particular number of years of experience as a practicing attorney (see, for example, Rottman and Strickland 2006). A few states still have courts of limited or inferior jurisdiction (municipal, magistrate, or justice of the peace, for example) where non-lawyer judges preside. By contrast, the Constitution of the United States does not specify the qualifications for federal judges (Carp and Stidham 2001). Nevertheless, "members of Congress, who typically recommend potential nominees, and the Department of Justice, which reviews nominees' qualifications, have developed their own informal criteria" (The Federal Judiciary 2009). The result of this process is that while it is theoretically possible for federal judges not to possess law degrees, at this point in our history it is highly unlikely.

The federal district judges are responsible for presiding over civil and criminal trials in their courts, and also supervising the work of federal grand juries. When a vacancy occurs—through death or resignation, creation of a new judgeship, or removal from office—these positions are filled by nominations from the President of the United States. In virtually all cases the president will receive recommendations for possible nominees for the vacancy from the senior U.S. senator from the president's political party, or from the senior member of the House of Representatives delegation from the president's party, or from the governor of the state (Abraham 1986). In this way an incredibly high percentage of the nominees will be from the political party of the current president.

The following list of characteristics illustrates the gender, race, and political party affiliations of district judgeship appointees from Lyndon Johnson's presidency (beginning in 1963) through the mid-point of George W. Bush's second term (2007; see Pastore and Maguire 2009):

- Gender—98.4 percent of Johnson's appointees were males, as were 99.4 percent of Nixon's, 98.1 percent of Ford's, 85.6 percent of Carter's, 91.7 percent of Reagan's (two terms), 80.4 percent of George H. W. Bush's, 71.5 percent of Clinton's (two terms), and 80.3 percent of George W. Bush's (first six years).

- Race—93.4 percent of Johnson's appointees were white, as were 95.5 percent of Nixon's, 88.5 percent of Ford's, 78.2 percent of Carter's, 92.4 percent of Reagan's, 89.2 percent of George H. W. Bush's, 75.1 percent of Clinton's, and 82.8 percent of George W. Bush's.

- Political party affiliation (percent Democrat)—Johnson (Democrat) 94.3 percent, Nixon (Republican) 7.3 percent, Ford (Republican) 21.2 percent, Carter (Democrat) 91.1 percent, Reagan (Republican) 4.8 percent, George H. W. Bush (Republican) 6.1 percent, Clinton (Democrat) 87.5 percent, and George W. Bush (Republican) 6.9 percent.

In general, Democratic presidents have appointed more females and minorities than Republicans, and presidents from both parties tend to appoint judges who are members of their political party.

Once the President receives the names of potential nominees, the U.S. Department of Justice conducts background investigations on the individuals to see if there are any criminal or ethical reasons not to nominate the person. Additionally, the American Bar Association rates the potential nominees as to their suitability for the federal bench (Abraham 1986). This process results in two items of note: (1) federal judicial nominees are subjected to a great deal of scrutiny before and after their names are submitted for confirmation, and (2) the process often is a protracted one even under the best of circumstances.

After a name has been agreed on by the President and his advisors, that person's nomination will be submitted to the United States Senate. The Senate Judiciary Committee will conduct hearings on the nominee and will interview the candidate as well as others who would like to speak on behalf of or against the nomination.

For some new district court judges, appointment comes in recognition of upwardly mobile legal and political careers. Others come to the federal bench after a long career at the state level as a local prosecutor, state attorney general, or state court judge. Since this is considered the crowning achievement for many involved in the judicial process, it is not uncommon for the people who become federal district court judges to retire from that position.

Federal judges operate under what often is called the "rule of 80." For instance, judges who have 15 years of service, and who have reached at least 65 years of age, have the option of electing senior status. **Senior judges** in the federal system can "continue to hear cases, deal with administrative matters, and serve on special commissions and committees," and in 2006 there were 311 judges on senior status (Administrative Office of U.S. Courts 2009). In effect, senior judges continue to receive their full-time salaries and they can pick-and-choose their workload (Abraham 1986; Administrative Office of U.S. Courts 2009). Before assuming this is a soft, semi-retirement system for federal judges, it is important to note two things:

- Federal judges who qualify for senior status simply can retire, draw a full salary in retirement, and not have any judicial responsibilities.
- The use of senior status judges helps in the management of federal court caseloads; these judges handle about 15 percent of federal cases (see Administrative Office of U.S. Courts 2009).

Federal judges must have their nominations confirmed by the Senate. Additionally, Congress defines the jurisdiction and provides the operating budget for the federal courts. However, there are three ways in which the federal courts are insulated from the political whims of the day and the independence of the judiciary is maintained.

First, the Administrative Office of U.S. Courts (2009) says that the courts can only exercise judicial powers. In other words, "The courts cannot be called upon to make laws, which is the function of the legislative branch, or be expected to enforce and execute laws, which is the function of the executive branch." The truth, however, is that in exercising their judicial functions, judges frequently find themselves in law-making roles. This is certainly evident in common law countries like the United States.

Second, federal judges are appointed for life terms. The Constitution provides that they only may be removed from office by "impeachment for, and conviction of, treason, bribery, or other high crimes and misdemeanors" (Administrative Office of U.S. Courts 2009). Impeachment proceedings against federal judges can be initiated by any member of the U.S. House of Representatives or by the Judicial Conference of the United States. Once an impeachment resolution has been drafted it will be referred to a House committee, typically the Judiciary Committee. This committee only needs to adopt the resolution by a simple majority for it to be referred to the full House for a vote. If the House of Representatives passes the resolution (again by a simple majority) it will be referred to the United States Senate, which acts as a hearing body (somewhat of a court) in deciding whether to convict or acquit. If the judge is convicted, he or she will immediately be removed from office. Obviously, this is a cumbersome process, and in the history of the United States only fifteen judges (including Associate Supreme Court Justice Samuel Chase) have had impeachment proceedings brought against them, and four of those were acquitted.

Third, the salaries of current federal judges may not be reduced by the President or Congress. Article III, Section 1 of the Constitution says that judges' compensation "shall not be diminished during their continuation in office."

In every federal court district, the judge with the longest tenure, who is under the age of sixty-five, is designated as **chief judge**. Chief judges are responsible for district court administration in addition to handling a trial and hearing caseload.

Many of the federal district courts nationwide also have magistrate judges in addition to district judges (see Cavanaugh 2008; Smith 2009). The position of U.S. magistrate was created in 1968 to replace "the system of U.S. Commissioners—dating back to a 1793 statute authorizing circuit courts to appoint persons to take bail" (Wheeler and Harrison 1994:23). The U.S. commissioners were not required to be licensed attorneys, and about one-third were not. Rather than paying commissioners a salary they operated on a fee system—where they were paid a set amount per case or task completed—with a maximum limit (Wasby 1988:49).

The magistrates were given responsibilities to assist the federal courts with their growing workload. However, there was some confusion over the tasks to be assigned to the U.S. magistrates and the status they were to hold within the district courts. For example, was it appropriate to address magistrates as "judge"? As a result of some of this confusion, Congress changed the title for this position to U.S. magistrate judge in the 1990 Judicial Improvement Act (Smith 2009). Currently there are 505 full-time and 45 part-time U.S. magistrate judges assigned to assist the district courts with matters that are defined by statute or delegated by the judges (Administrative Office of U.S. Courts 2009). These functions range from issuing warrants; conducting certain types of routine proceedings like bond hearings, preliminary hearings, and handling pre-trial motions; civil consent cases; and disposing of misdemeanor cases, such as traffic citations for infractions occurring on federal land (see Administrative Office of U.S. Courts 2009; The Federal Judiciary 2009). To illustrate something of their workload, in 2005 the U.S. magistrate judges participated in over 941,000 cases. This included conducting 92,900 trials for misdemeanors and petty offenses. Additionally, they held 321,164 preliminary proceedings, such as initial appearances, detention hearings, bail reviews, arraignments, and attorney appointment hearings (Pastore and Maguire 2009).

The U.S. magistrate judges are appointed by the district court judges in their respective districts, and unlike the district judges these positions can be part-time or full-time appointments. Magistrate judges also do not have life tenure like the district court and other so-called Article III judges. Part-time federal magistrates have four-year terms, and the full-time magistrates serve for eight years.

BOX 4.7

In the News: U.S. Magistrate Judges

The federal district court judges in the District of New Mexico handle the second highest number of criminal cases per judge in the country. In 2009, these judges averaged 384 cases each, while the national average was ninety-one cases. As a result of such a heavy caseload—largely because of drug trafficking and immigration cases—the district court judges increasingly have relied on the state's eleven U.S. Magistrate Judges. The magistrate judges preside over many of the minor felony cases, and they are responsible for a large proportion of the civil docket as well. In fact, they can serve as the trial judges in civil cases unless the parties demand that the trial be presided over by a district court judge. The U.S. Magistrates, in New Mexico and other federal districts as well, provide a relief to federal district judges who otherwise would not be able to process all of the cases being brought to them.

Source: "New Chief Magistrate Judge Is Named" (2009).

The final group of judicial officers operating in the district courts includes the bankruptcy judges. Prior to 1973 these individuals were known as bankruptcy referees, and before 1946 (like the U.S. commissioners) they worked on a fee system (Wasby 1988:51). There are 352 of these judges authorized nationwide (with 337 active), and they are selected for office by "a majority of the active judges of the court of appeals encompassing their judicial districts" (Administrative Office of U.S. Courts 2009). These judges handle the district courts' specialized federal bankruptcy caseload, and they serve terms of fourteen years.

JUDICIAL DISCIPLINE AND REMOVAL FROM OFFICE

Aside from judicial selection and qualifications for judges, another major point of concern deals with judicial discipline and/or removal from office. Although these two items are related, for our purposes let us consider **judicial discipline** first, and removal from office second. Most states now have **judicial conduct commissions**. The first of these was created in California in 1960 to deal with complaints of illegal or unethical conduct on the part of judges (Frankel 1991). Judicial conduct commissions (also called judicial discipline committees, judicial qualifications committees, judicial performance committees, or similar titles) may be appointed, run by independent state boards, or they may operate under the auspices of the state supreme court (see Rottman and Strickland 2006:56–59).

When complaints are filed against judges, a staff person typically is assigned to investigate the allegations and to report the findings to the appropriate supervisory authority. If the complaint is founded, then disciplinary action can be taken against the judge. Forms of discipline can involve a verbal warning, written reprimand, censure, temporary suspension of duties or, in extreme cases, removal from office. As the following discussion makes clear, there are a number of ways judges can be removed from office, but this typically occurs in only the most extreme circumstances.

Removal from office could simply result from electoral defeat or a failure to retain vote. Some states also have provisions where a certain percentage of voters can file a petition with the election commission for a recall election. As noted previously, relatively few judges ever get voted out of office by whatever system, and when they do it typically is as a result of a concentrated effort resulting from a highly publicized decision or series of cases. Occasionally, interest groups mount extensive campaigns to defeat judges they feel are hostile to their causes. In the past decade, this has happened in California and Tennessee (Reid 1999) (see also Box 4.4 in this chapter). Few of these cases involve crimes committed by judges, but some of them may involve unpopular decisions or allegations of unethical behavior.

Other than voting judges out of office, two other methods dominate discussions in the area of removal from office. First, as I have mentioned, some state judicial conduct commissions may be empowered to remove judges from the bench temporarily or permanently as a result of sustained charges of ethical violations or crimes. Second, for federal judges the primary method of removal from office is through **impeachment**. This is true for some state judicial systems as well.

Impeachment requires that formal charges be brought against a judge and then a trial is conducted to see if the charges can be proved and, if so, what the appropriate punishment might be if necessary. In most instances—and this particularly has been demonstrated in federal courts—the process of impeachment is expensive, difficult, and time-consuming. Therefore, in the history of the United States only fourteen federal judges at any level have been impeached, much fewer than those removed by vote or state conduct commission (Federal Judicial Center 2009).

JUDICIAL INDEPENDENCE AND ACCOUNTABILITY

When we consider the role of judges in a democracy, two competing concepts inevitably become the focus of our discussions. On one hand, we are concerned about judicial independence; on the other hand, we equally are concerned with judicial accountability (see, especially, Griffen 1998 and Lubet 1998). In this section I discuss the definitions and importance of each of these notions.

First, from the founding of the United States, our national government and our state governments were created with three distinct branches: legislative, executive, and judicial. The Constitution of the United States spells out the separate and unique responsibilities, but equal status, of each branch of government. However, from the beginning it was apparent that the judicial branch was the least powerful of the three branches. The courts are dependent on the legislative branch to make laws and to appropriate funds for governmental operations (including the budgets of the courts). Legislatures can define the jurisdiction of the courts and add to or take away from them specific areas of responsibility. Legislatures also can create new courts and add judges and support personnel to staff those courts. Therefore, the judiciary clearly is dependent upon the legislative branch for its funding and in defining its jurisdictional parameters.

The judiciary also is dependent on the executive branch to enforce the laws and to carry out the mandates of the courts. This particularly has been apparent in situations where the courts have ordered schools and other public accommodations (such as restaurants and public transportation) to be racially integrated. The courts are also dependent on the executive branch to carry out orders related to the improvement of conditions in state mental hospitals and prisons. Obviously, there are any number of examples of this.

While the judiciary is to be a co-equal branch of government along with the legislative and executive branches, much of its authority is symbolic. People obey the rulings of the courts simply because they represent the authority and legitimacy of the law. However, because of their smaller and somewhat dependent status, courts always are concerned about judicial independence. Meador (1991:59–60) says that judicial independence "means that in deciding cases judges are free from control by the executive and legislative branches of government as well as from control by the popular will of the moment. In other words, judges act free of extrajudicial controls in determining the facts, ascertaining and enunciating the law, and applying the law to the facts to arrive at decisions in cases." However, as Meador (1991:60) is quick to add, "this has never meant, an absolute and complete independence of the judiciary." In some sense he is recognizing that the judiciary is influenced by the other branches of government, and judges (as human beings) are influenced by the factors and forces that surround them.

The issue of judicial independence often arises in the context of how judges are selected as well as how they make their decisions. For example, a great debate has been raging for decades over whether requiring judges to stand for popular election or re-election impedes their independence. In its advocacy of the merit selection process, the American Judicature Society (2009) has taken the stand that "Judicial independence is critical; it is the only way to guarantee fair and impartial justice for all Americans. In order to be sure that every American receives fair and equal justice in the court system, we need to ensure that judges are able to do their job without undue political pressure from parties, political leaders, and private citizens. By limiting the role of politics in selecting judges, we can limit the political influences that may hinder fair and impartial justice."

Nevertheless, judicial independence is a consideration under appointment and merit selection systems as well. Brown (1998:322) summarizes this point by saying that "Judicial independence flows from the makeup of the judge—not from the method of selection." Therefore, by whatever method judges may be chosen, they always are wary of efforts by the executive and legislative branches, as well as by the general public and lobbying groups to encroach into territory they define as being within their domain (Lubet 1998).

Standing in contrast to judicial independence is the notion of **judicial accountability**. Judicial accountability implies that judges, as public servants, ultimately must answer to the citizens they serve in a democracy. Herein resides the dynamic tension. How can they be both independent and accountable? For most judges it involves

walking a fine line balancing public opinion, canons of judicial ethics, political involvement, and their own personal consciences. This, rather than deciding difficult cases,
may be the greatest challenge for most judges (for an extended discussion of this issue
see both Meador 1991 and Webster 1995).

QUASI-JUDICIAL OFFICERS

In addition to the judges who serve in the state and federal courts throughout the
United States, we also have a group of court officers responsible for decision-making
"in the shadows" (Mays and Gregware 2009). Meador (1991) calls these individuals
judicial adjuncts. They may be known by a number of different titles and they assist,
while being subservient to, judges. The most common names are **masters**, **referees**,
mediators, and **hearing officers**.

The position of master is one that has been part of courts in the United States for much
of our nation's history. These individuals "are often practicing lawyers appointed to assist
the court in particularly complicated or protracted matters" (Meador 1991:65). Since the
early 1970s masters have been used in a number of states to oversee court orders such
as those involving state mental hospitals and prison litigation cases (see, for example,
Mays and Taggart 1985b, 1988; Nathan 1979, 1985). Masters serve as adjuncts to judges
through ad hoc appointments. They have responsibilities to oversee specific matters, and
when these matters are completed their assignments normally are terminated.

In the federal district courts the U.S. magistrate judges serve as permanent
judicial adjuncts. As previously stated, these positions initially were created as U.S.
Commissioners, and they performed some of the routine tasks such as issuing warrants
and conducting certain pre-trial procedures. However, in the past two decades, federal
magistrate judges have taken on increasing judicial responsibilities as the workloads
of the federal district courts have grown (Cavanaugh 2008; Smith 2009). These court
officers now routinely hear civil cases and misdemeanor criminal cases.

Referees, like masters, are designated to perform certain specific tasks on behalf of
the courts. In fact, one definition of the office of referee is any "Person who is appointed
by [the] court to exercise certain judicial powers, to take testimony, to hear parties,
and report his findings" (*Black's Law Dictionary* 1991:886). This office is similar to that
of master, and historically in some states referees, who were required to be licensed
attorneys, performed functions for inferior court judges (like those in juvenile courts)
who were not licensed attorneys. In many states this office has been replaced by magistrates or other judicial officials.

Mediators are increasingly more popular and prevalent in the court system, especially in the case of divorces. The process of mediation is defined as "a private, informal
dispute resolution process in which a neutral third party, the mediator, helps disputing
parties to reach an agreement" (*Black's Law Dictionary* 1991:678). The goal of mediation is to settle disputes through compromise instead of litigation and to avoid the time
and expense of a trial. Parties involved have a comparatively larger amount of personal
control over most facets of the mediation, including who the mediator is and what the
settlement will be—which ultimately gives them more control over the outcome of the
case. If mediation does not reach a satisfactory solution, a lawsuit may still be pursued.

BOX 4.8
In the News: A Bar Fight?

For the past several years neighbors living near two bars in El Paso, Texas, have complained about the noise, fights, and generally obnoxious behavior exhibited by bar patrons. Part of the problem stems from the fact that the bars are located on land leased from the city airport. Rather than terminating the leases of the two bars, the El Paso City Council unanimously voted to hire a mediator to try to bring some resolution to the dispute. City officials estimate that mediation will cost between $2,500 and $4,000, whereas if the case went to court it would cost the city over $2,000 per day. El Paso's mayor, Jonathan Cook, said that he believed the mediation process would be substantially less costly than an all-out court fight.

However, one of the lingering issues in cases involving mediation is: What are the perceptions of justice by the participants? Mediation certainly can speed the process of conflict resolution along, but because it is usually not binding the parties still may end up in court. Additionally, in some cases there may be a tradeoff in terms of the quality of justice dispensed and the speed with which a resolution is reached.

Source: Burge (2009).

Hearing officers also may be known as hearing examiners or administrative law judges. These individuals usually do not work in (or for) the courts, but they act as quasi-judicial officials nonetheless. Their responsibilities are to preside "at an administrative hearing, with power to administer oaths, take testimony, rule on questions of evidence, regulate [the] course of proceedings and make agency determinations of fact" (*Black's Law Dictionary* 1991:29). Frequently they are required to be licensed attorneys.

Hearing officers can be found in a number of state and federal administrative agencies, and they rule on matters such as veterans' benefits and Social Security claims. Appeals from these agencies find their way into either specialized courts created to deal with these matters or into courts of general trial jurisdiction.

Quasi-judicial officers, or judicial adjuncts, have been used in a variety of courts throughout the history of the United States. However, the clear trend in most states is to institutionalize these positions—when the workloads warrant it—and to make them full-fledged judicial officers. This means that some judges may appoint adjuncts to help the courts manage their caseloads, and eventually some of these positions may be expanded by the legislature.

FUNCTIONS PERFORMED BY JUDGES

Judges are responsible for a wide range of activities, and many of these functions are dealt with elsewhere in the book. However, in order for you to understand the variety of matters over which judges must preside, it is useful to group these responsibilities into (1) pretrial, (2) trial, (3) post-trial, and (4) appellate responsibilities.

PRETRIAL FUNCTIONS

Most of the responsibilities we associate with judges occur at the time of trial. However, a significant amount of activity also must be completed before a case ever goes to trial. Among the pretrial functions performed by judges (often in conjunction with the court clerks) are:

1. Issuing arrest and search warrants to be executed by law enforcement agencies.
2. Issuing summonses, and subpoenas for witnesses in trials.
3. Holding initial appearances for those individuals who have been arrested to make sure they understand the charges against them and to determine whether they are represented by counsel.
4. Deciding whether the accused are eligible for bail and, if so, setting bail and conducting bail-reduction hearings.
5. Conducting pretrial hearings including those dealing with changes of venue.
6. Ruling on pretrial motions such as suppression of evidence, severance of defendants, and dismissal of changes.
7. Responding to the requests of attorneys to settle a civil case without a trial or approving plea agreements between the two sides in criminal cases.
8. Establishing a docket by which cases are scheduled for adjudication in a timely manner (see Abadinsky and Winfree 1992:383; Eisenstein and Jacob 1977; Spohn and Hemmens 2009).

Not all of these roles are performed by the same judges or same courts, but trial court judges will conduct all of these functions at some point in their judicial careers.

TRIAL FUNCTIONS

During trials judges are kept busy interacting with the parties involved in the case and dealing with technical issues such as rules of procedure and the admissibility of evidence. Judges are to be neutral referees in order to guarantee a fair trial to all sides.

As the trial begins the judge must preside over the jury selection process. Jurors and the jury process are examined more fully in Chapter 6. However, at this point it is essential to provide a brief overview in order to more completely understand the judge's role. Jury selection is known in most courts as the *voir dire*—which means to speak the truth (Champion 2005:264)—and it is the method by which an impartial jury is chosen. Often the public assumes that attorneys are trying to pick a neutral jury. In fact, both sides want to have a jury that is favorable to their cause. Therefore, in the process of questioning and eliminating the obviously biased jurors, a reasonably neutral jury is selected. In some jurisdictions the attorneys question prospective jurors (so-called veniremen) based on biographical information forms provided to them by the court. Other jurisdictions require lawyers to submit lists of questions to the judge, then the judge questions potential jurors.

After the voir dire process is completed, the attorneys and the judge announce those individuals who will be excused from jury duty. In some jurisdictions all of the deliberations and discussions are done in open court, and in others the judge and attorneys will adjourn to the judge's chambers to consider which members of the jury pool will be excused. Attorneys are allowed to ask that some veniremen be excused "for cause." In reality there is one cause: prejudice, or prejudging the case. If the judge can be convinced that the prospective juror is biased, that individual is dismissed. There is no limit on the number of "strikes" attorneys have for cause. However, they must be able to convince the judge—not an easy task at times—that the person truly is prejudiced. By contrast, each side is given a limited number (sometimes six or eight) of discretionary strikes. These are called **peremptory challenges**. Attorneys can exercise peremptory challenges if they feel uneasy about a prospective juror's answers, or if there is some suspicion or hunch that makes them feel uncomfortable, but which really does not rise to the level of overt prejudice. However, there are limits on the ways that peremptory challenges can be exercised, and the United States Supreme Court has ruled that they cannot be used in a way that discriminates against persons of a certain race or gender (see *Batson v. Kentucky* 476 U.S. 79 [1986] and *J.E.B. v. Alabama ex rel. T.B.* 511 U.S. 127 [1994]).

After the jury is selected, the trial begins. Most judges set time limits for the prosecutor and defense attorney to give their opening statements. After each side presents its opening statement, then the state begins the presentation of its case. Following the state's case the defense *may* (with emphasis on the word "may") present its case. Since the burden of proof rests with the state, the defense is not required to call any witnesses or present any evidence.

During the direct examination and cross-examination of witnesses, one attorney or the other may object to a specific question or line of questioning, and the judge must rule on the objection. The judge also must rule on motions to introduce or exclude from introduction any piece of physical evidence or admissions and confessions. The objections or motions made by attorneys during trial can provide the basis for appeals from a guilty verdict.

As the trial comes to a close, the judge is responsible for giving the jury instructions (or the charge) that must guide their deliberations. These instructions include issues such as the elements of the offense, the notion of guilt beyond a reasonable doubt (or the preponderance of the evidence in civil cases), the weight and credibility that should be given to different witnesses, consideration of lesser included offenses, and how to consider affirmative defenses such as insanity, duress, alibi, and entrapment. During jury deliberations the judge may need to answer questions or explain points of law further to jury inquiries.

Once the jury has delivered a verdict of guilty, the judge will instruct the probation department to prepare a **presentence investigation report** (PSI) and set a date for sentencing the defendant. Some people believe that sentencing is one of the most difficult and complex tasks that judges must perform (Benavides 2002). There are a variety of reasons for this. First, the judge must make the in-or-out decision: will the defendant be placed on probation, or will he/she be incarcerated for some period of time? Second, there is the question of whether multiple sentences will be served concurrently or consecutively. Third, since states vary in their sentencing mechanisms, judges must decide on the exact term of either probation or incarceration. For example, some states use indeterminate sentencing, and the sentence imposed will have a minimum and a maximum number of months or years to be served. Other states employ determinate sentencing, and individuals who are found guilty are given a specific term of months or years to serve (Mays and Winfree 2009).

In most jurisdictions, all but the most extreme crimes may be eligible for probation. The probation department can recommend a sentence composed of conditional community supervision, and the judge can agree or disagree with that recommendation. Studies nationwide have shown that there is a remarkable degree of agreement between the recommendations of probation officers and judges (Abadinsky 2011). In states that use indeterminate sentencing schemes, judges may have wide latitude in ordering offenders to serve probation or to incarcerate them for a range of time (for example, from one to ten years, or twenty years to life). For states with determinate sentencing systems, the sentencing discretion of judges is much more constrained, and for the few states with presumptive sentencing the state sentencing guidelines are even more prescriptive. Over the past thirty years, both states and the federal government have gone toward determinate sentencing schemes (illustrated by sentencing guidelines), and judges have been given less discretion in sentencing (see Champion 1989; Steen 2002). No matter which sentencing system is employed, in virtually every case, except those imposing capital punishment, the judge will decide what the appropriate sentence will be. I return to the issue of sentencing and some of the problems associated with this function in Chapters 7 and 8.

POST-TRIAL FUNCTIONS

Following imposition of the sentence, the judge will entertain motions from the attorneys (usually just the defense) in regard to unsettled issues. The attorneys may ask the judge to reconsider the sentence, especially if it appears too severe given the facts of the case. The defense attorney also may ask for a lower bond or release-on-recognizance pending an appeal. At this point, notice of appeal, stating the grounds upon which the appeal is based, also are filed.

Revocation of probation also constitutes a post-trial function performed by judges. Since judges sentence offenders to terms of probation, they must conduct probation revocation hearings to determine whether probation should be ended and the offender incarcerated.

APPELLATE FUNCTIONS

If they believe there were errors of law (as opposed to errors of fact), criminal defendants may file an appeal. As you will see in a much more extensive discussion in Chapter 10, appellate courts will review criminal cases to see if errors were made in the trial process or in sentencing (if appealable). Also in civil cases, appellate courts may review and overturn or modify judgments awarded to either plaintiffs or defendants. Judges in appellate courts sit in panels—typically three or more judges—to decide cases, instead of alone as they do in trial courts.

JUDGES AS ADMINISTRATORS

One of the touchy subjects in courts is the role judges do play, or should play, in the day-to-day administration of court business (see McConnell 1991). Chapter 12 covers something of the administrative environments of various courts. However, it is essential to emphasize at this point that ultimately judges are responsible for the smooth and effective administration of justice within their domains. Therefore, we must ask: (1) How well are judges prepared to be administrators? (2) What are the functions over which they must exercise administrative control? and (3) If judges do not serve as administrators, who will?

Very little in the way of their educational background prepares judges to be administrators. A few have undergraduate or graduate degrees in business or public administration, but virtually nothing in their law school training equips them to be administrators. Furthermore, some judges are not prepared to be administrators as a result of their professional backgrounds and experience. The very nature of legal education is to look at the individual cases and to pay attention to individual factors shaping cases and the law. By contrast, the administration of courts requires judges to develop routine procedures for handling court business and to deal with a term from which many of them recoil: *bureaucracy*.

Wheeler and Whitcomb (1977:18), in a relatively early reflection on the field of judicial administration, said that the administrative responsibilities often fall on a group of people—judges trained as lawyers—who are "not necessarily well suited for management, either by training or professional behavior." This means that many judges are neither educationally prepared nor do they have the personal inclinations toward administrative roles. A situation like this leaves the courts often caught on the horns of a dilemma. Either judges delegate administrative tasks to others, with potentially little to no follow-up, or they ignore the administrative dimension of courts altogether.

To handle some of these problems courts at all levels have developed several solutions. For example, over the past three decades there has been a clear movement toward employing professional **court administrators**. These individuals are trained in law, public administration, business administration, or similar disciplines. Their purpose is to oversee the non-adjudicative functions of the courts, such as budgeting, personnel administration, scheduling potential jurors and, at times, managing court calendars or dockets (see, for example, Mays and Taggart 1985a; Taggart and Mays 1983/84).

Another option is the creation of positions known as **chief judge** or presiding judge in multi-judge jurisdictions (Bureau of Justice Statistics 1981). These individuals typically have a reduced caseload, and they become responsible for administering the courts' day-to-day functions. The position of chief judge may be determined by seniority, through a vote by the body of judges, or by one judge volunteering to be the chief administrative officer for the courts (Rottman and Strickland 2006).

Perhaps the most conspicuous position for the judge-as-administrator is the Chief Justice of the United States. In this role, the Chief Justice not only presides over the Supreme Court, but also he is head of the federal judicial branch. He also presides over the Judicial Conference of the United States, and this group serves as the rule-making body for the federal courts. Like the President of the United States in the delivery of the State of the Union address, the Chief Justice of the United States annually submits a letter to Congress on the state of the judiciary in which he discusses the various challenges facing the federal courts, including providing an adequate number of judges and appropriate salaries for members of the federal judiciary.

BOX 4.9
Judges in Other Countries: Egypt

It is easy to overlook the fact that judges in other countries are chosen in ways that differ from the ways we choose judges in the United States. For example, in the nation of Egypt, individuals who hold the position of judge are considered very high-ranking government officials. The candidates for judge are selected by the Supreme Judiciary Council, which consists of seven experienced judges and is presided over by the president of the Egyptian Court of Cassation. Once the candidates are chosen, the list is sent to the Minister of Justice who then forwards it to the President of Egypt. Once the President has decided whom to appoint as judges, these individuals will serve as public prosecutors until they reach the age of thirty.

Since the position of judge in Egypt is such a high-ranking one, the government expects a high level of qualifications. For instance, judges must have a law degree (there are no judges in Egypt without law degrees). The candidate must be Egyptian and have Egyptian parents as well. Generally speaking, the candidate must be a man, but recently the Egyptian government has accepted women for the position of judge; both men and women must be at least thirty years old. The candidate must pass all exams for the judge position. The exams include a personal interview, oral exam, and investigations about the candidate's family. All members of the family are subject to investigation to determine if anyone in the family has committed any crime, even in the distant past, which could prevent the candidate from being chosen as a judge. This part is the most important and difficult part. Many institutions undertake different investigations, with all the outcome and reports going in the candidate's file.

Source: This information was provided by Hamdy Selouma, an Egyptian judge who has been studying criminal justice in the United States.

SUMMARY

Judges occupy the dominant role in the adjudicative function of courts. They are the most conspicuous people in the judicial process, and they are responsible for a variety of functions before, during, and after trials. In this chapter we have examined the processes by which judges in state and federal courts are chosen. The methods differ from jurisdiction to jurisdiction, and the various methods of judicial selection may choose different types of people to sit on the benches of courts around the nation. From a public policy standpoint the chief question remains: Does any one system pick the best judges? Perhaps the opposite question is more appropriate: Does one system pick the fewest bad judges? For decades, a great debate has been raging over this topic, but no conclusive evidence has emerged that any one system is superior (or inferior) to the others. Each system has its own strengths, and each has its own weaknesses as well.

Along with the issue of methods of judicial selection comes the question of the qualifications for judges. The general trend over the past fifty years or so has been to require most judges to be trained in the law and furthermore to require them to have a certain number of years of legal experience. Nevertheless, the use of lay (or non-lawyer) judges continues throughout the United States, particularly in the courts of limited or inferior jurisdiction.

Since no selection system can guarantee that good judges are chosen and bad judges are avoided, both state and federal court systems have had to develop methods to handle complaints against judges once in office. States have created judicial conduct commissions to investigate complaints of impropriety and to recommend appropriate sanctions. Eventually every state court system and the federal courts will have to deal with the removal of unfit judges from office. This is a traumatic experience for most of the people involved, so this step is not taken quickly, and the potential consequences are considered very serious. Unfortunately, on occasion a judge will have to be removed from office through some method other than electoral defeat.

Any action taken against judges—for appropriate or inappropriate behavior—raises the specter of encroachment into the domain of judicial independence. In a democracy judges must be free to make decisions in cases based on their consciences and their understanding of the law. By the same token, as a society we feel that all public officials, including judges, ultimately must answer to the citizenry. This creates a dynamic tension that is not easily avoided, and one that is not likely to be resolved in the foreseeable future.

One of the unique features of some courts in the United States is the use of quasi-judicial officers or judicial adjuncts. These court officials may hold regular full-time or part-time positions, or they may be appointed by judges on an ad hoc basis to fulfill certain limited functions at which time their responsibilities would be discharged. Common names for judicial adjuncts are commissioners, masters (or special masters), referees, mediators, hearing officers, or magistrates. As a result of mounting workloads, some of these positions now have become institutionalized parts of court systems. If legislative bodies do not add a sufficient number of judges and support staff personnel, court systems increasingly may turn to these positions over which they have appointment power and control.

Finally, a lingering issue facing courts is the degree to which we expect judges to be administrators. Judges primarily are trained to guide the adjudication of civil and criminal cases. They are expected to know the law and to apply the appropriate substantive and procedural laws to the cases that come before them. Few are schooled in the current principles and practices of administration. Judges often have personalities that make them good judges but poor administrators. This means that some are ambivalent toward what they perceive as bureaucratization of the courts and others are openly hostile toward such a movement. However, whether they want to be immersed in the day-to-day operations of the courts or not, judges are responsible for the way cases are processed and the impact this has on the administration of justice. Perhaps the next decade will resolve this dilemma and judges will become more administratively inclined—or trained—or they will shift the responsibility for judicial administration to professional court administrators.

QUESTIONS FOR CRITICAL THINKING

1. At what point in the criminal process would a judge's responsibilities begin? When would they end?

2. Consider the *voir dire* process. What are the defense attorney and the prosecutor trying to achieve? What is the judge attempting to accomplish during this process? Are all members of the courtroom work group working toward the same goal?

3. What are the two methods by which potential jurors can be excluded? Do attorneys hope to achieve the same goal with both types of exclusions?

4. Put yourself in the judge's position. What one area of responsibility would be most difficult for the average person to accomplish?

5. Does it really make any difference how we choose judges? Could we draw names out of a hat? What if different methods choose different kinds of people? Is this a problem or not? Why?

6. Should judges be accountable to the public? If so, how can we hold them accountable?

7. Choose a pro or con position to the following proposition: Governors should be able to appoint anyone they want, including their friends and political allies, to positions such as judge whenever vacancies occur.

8. If you graduated from law school and chose to become a judge (and there was no difference in salary), would you rather serve in a federal court or state court? Why?

9. How well informed are most members of the general public about the qualifications and records of judges? How could the public be better informed?

10. Should all judges possess a law degree, or can non-lawyer judges serve effectively in limited jurisdiction courts? Which courts do most people have contact with?

11. Choose one of the following positions and list the reasons you believe it is true:

    (a) the judicial branch is the *least* powerful branch of government; or

    (b) the judicial branch is the *most* powerful branch of government.

RECOMMENDED READINGS

Bonneau, Chris W., and Melinda Gann Hall (2009). *In Defense of Judicial Elections*. New York: Routledge. When you examine the nearly century-old judicial reform movement, it seems that Bonneau and Hall are swimming upstream. However, they empirically test a number of the assertions made by reform advocates and find that electing judges in the United States is an effective system and one that has certainly not outlived its usefulness.

Carp, Robert A., and Ronald Stidham. *Judicial Process in America,* 7th ed. Washington, DC: CQ Press (2007). Carp and Stidham present an overview of federal and state court processes in the United States. In one chapter they deal with several of the issues we have touched upon here including backgrounds, selection, qualifications, and removal of judges.

Sheldon, Charles H., and Linda S. Maule (1998). *Choosing Justice: The Recruitment of State and Federal Judges*. Pullman, WA: Washington State University Press. Sheldon and Maule examine the history of judicial selection in the United States from the days of legislative appointments through the use of partisan and non-partisan elections and merit selection. They discuss the differences in the ways state and federal judges are chosen and the types of candidates that emerge from the different methods of judicial selection.

Spohn, Cassia, and Craig Hemmens (2009). *Courts*. Thousand Oaks, CA: Sage Publications. Spohn and Hemmens provide a unique approach to the topics of courts. They have prepared a text with seven major sections dealing with a variety of court-related topics. Relative to this chapter they provide a section on judges, and this is followed by a series of readings that have been gleaned from a number of the leading scholarly journals in the field. The approach is designed to provide a context for the topic that is being discussed along with some of the recent scholarship dealing with that particular topic.

KEY TERMS

American Judicature Society

chief judge

court administrators

executive appointment

hearing officers

impeachment

interim appointments

judicial accountability

judicial adjuncts

judicial conduct commissions

judicial discipline

judicial independence

lay judge

long ballot

masters (special masters)

mediators

merit selection/Missouri Plan

non-partisan elections

partisan election

peremptory challenges

presentence investigation report

referees

senior judges

U.S. magistrate judges

voir dire

REFERENCES

Abadinsky, Howard (2007). *Law and Justice: An Introduction to the American Legal System*. Upper Saddle River, NJ: Prentice Hall.

Abadinsky, Howard (2011). *Probation and Parole: Theory and Practice*, 11th ed. Upper Saddle River, NJ: Prentice Hall.

Abadinsky, Howard, and L. Thomas Winfree, Jr. (1992). *Crime & Justice*, 2nd ed. Chicago: Nelson-Hall Publishers.

Abraham, Henry J. (1986). *The Judicial Process*, 5th ed. New York: Oxford University Press.

Administrative Office of U.S. Courts (2009). *Understanding the federal courts*. http://www.uscourts.gov/ FederalCourts/UnderstandingtheFederalCourts/FederalCourtsinAmericanGovernment.aspx.

American Bar Association (2009). Canons of Judicial Ethics. http://wwwamericanbar.org/content/ dam/aba/migrated/cpr/pic/1924_canons.authcheckdam.pdf.

American Judicature Society (2007). http://www.ajs.org/selection.index.asp.

American Judicature Society (2008). *Judicial Selection in the States: How It Works, Why It Matters*. Denver, CO: Institute for the Advancement of the American Legal System.

American Judicature Society (2009). Judicial Selection: Frequently Asked Questions. http://www.ajs. org/selection/sel_faqs.asp.

Aspin, Larry T., and William K. Hall (1994). Retention Elections and Judicial Behavior. *Judicature* 77(6): 306–15.

Batson v. Kentucky, 476 U.S. 79 (1986).

Benavides, Amy J. (2002). Indeterminate Sentences. In *Encyclopedia of Crime and Punishment*, ed. David Levinson, 875–78. Thousand Oaks, CA: Sage Publications.

Black's Law Dictionary (1991). St. Paul, MN: West Publishing Co.

Bonneau, Chris W., and Melinda Gann Hall (2009). *In Defense of Judicial Elections*. New York: Routledge.

Brown, Robert L. (1998). From Whence Cometh Our State Appellate Judges: Popular Election Versus the Missouri Plan. *University of Arkansas at Little Rock Law Journal* 20 (Winter): 313–25.

Bureau of Justice Statistics (1981). *Dictionary of Criminal Justice Data Terminology*, 2nd ed. Washington, DC: U.S. Department of Justice.

Burge, David (2009). Bar Dispute Goes to Mediation. *Elpasotimes.com*, November 18. http://www. elpasotimes.com/ci_13811589?source=most_viewed.

Caperton v. A.T. Massey Coal Co., 556 U.S. ___ (2009).

Carp, Robert A., and Ronald Stidham (2001). *The Federal Courts*, 4th ed. Washington, DC: CQ Press.

Carp, Robert A., Ronald Stidham, and Kenneth L. Manning (2007). *Judicial Process in America*, 7th ed. Washington, DC: CQ Press.

Cavanaugh, Dennis (2008). Magistrate Judges are Effective, Flexible Judiciary Resource. *The Third Branch*, Vol. 40, No. 10. http://www.uscourts.gov/News/TheThirdBranch/08–10–01/Magistrate_ Judges_Are_Effective_Flexible_Judiciary_Resource.aspx.

Champion, Dean J., ed. (1989). *The U.S. Sentencing Guidelines: Implications for Criminal Justice*. New York: Praeger Publishers.

Champion, Dean J. (2005). *The American Dictionary of Criminal Justice*, 3rd edition. Los Angeles, CA: Roxbury Publishing Co.

Courtney, Ross (2009). After Change in Law, Few "Lay Judges" Remain. *Yakima Herald-Republic*, November 27. http://seattletimes.nwsource.com/html.localnews/2010369833_apwasmall-townjudges1stldwritethru.html.

Di Pietro, Susanne, Teresa W. Carns, and William T. Cotton (2000). Judicial Qualifications and Judicial Performance: Is There a Relationship? *Judicature* 83(4): 196–204.

Eisenstein, James, and Herbert Jacob (1977). *Felony Justice: An Organizational Analysis of Criminal Courts*. Boston: Little, Brown and Co.

Federal Judicial Center (2009). Federal Judicial History. http://www.fjc.gov/history/home.nsf/page/index.html.

The Federal Judiciary (2009). Home page. http://www.uscourts.gov/faq.html.

Frankel, Jack E. (1991). Looking Back and Looking Forward. *Judicature* 75(2): 83–85, 113.

Griffen, Wendell L. (1998). Comment: Judicial Accountability and Discipline. *Law and Contemporary Problems* 61(3): 75–77.

J. E. B. v. Alabama ex rel. T. B., 511 U.S. 127 (1994).

Jost, Kenneth (1998). The Federal Judiciary: Are the Attacks on U.S. Courts Justified? *CQ Researcher* 8(10): 217–40.

Key, V. O. (1958). *Politics, Parties, and Pressure Groups*, 4th ed. New York: Thomas Y. Crowell Co.

Kiel, L. Douglas, Carole Funk, and Anthony Champagne (1994). Two-party Competition and Trial Court Elections in Texas. *Judicature* 77(6): 290–93.

Langdon, Lynn, and Thomas H. Cohen (2007). *State Court Organization, 1987–2004*. Washington, DC: Bureau of Justice Statistics, U.S. Department of Justice.

Levin, Martin A. (1998). Urban Politics and Policy Outcomes. In *The Criminal Justice System: Politics and Policies*, 7th ed., ed. George F. Cole and Marc G. Gertz, 331–51. Belmont, CA: West/Wadsworth Publishing Co.

Lubet, Steven (1998). Judicial Discipline and Judicial Independence. *Law and Contemporary Problems* 61(3): 59–74.

Mansfield, Cathy Lesser (1999). Disorder in the People's Court: Rethinking the Role of Non-lawyer Judges in Limited Jurisdiction Court Civil Cases. *New Mexico Law Review* 29 (Winter): 119–200.

Martin, Elaine, and Barry Pyle (2002). Gender and Racial Diversification of State Supreme Courts. *Women & Politics* 24(2): 35–52.

Massie, Tajuana D., Thomas G. Hansford, and Donald Songer (2004). The Timing of Presidential Nominations to the Lower Federal Courts. *Political Research Quarterly* 57(2): 145–54.

Mays, G. Larry, and Peter R. Gregware, eds. (2009). *Courts and Justice*, 4th ed. Long Grove, IL: Waveland Press.

Mays, G. Larry, and William A. Taggart (1985a). Local Court Administration: Findings from a Survey of Court Managers. *Judicature* 69(1): 29–35.

Mays, G. Larry, and William A. Taggart (1985b). The Impact of Litigation on Changing New Mexico Prison Conditions. *The Prison Journal* 65:38–53.

Mays, G. Larry, and William A. Taggart (1988). The Implementation of Court-Ordered Prison Reform. In *Research in Law and Policy Studies*, Vol. 2, ed. Stuart S. Nagel, 181–98. Greenwich, CT: JAI Press.

Mays, G. Larry, and L. Thomas Winfree, Jr. (2009). *Essentials of Corrections*, 4th ed. Belmont, CA: Wadsworth/Cengage.

McConnell, Edward B. (1991). Court Management: The Judge's Role and Responsibility. *The Justice System Journal* 15(2): 710–21.

Meador, Daniel J. (1991). *American Courts*. St. Paul, MN: West Publishing Co.

Nase, Jonathan P. (1997). Election Cycles and the Appointment of State Judges: A National Research Agenda Based on the Pennsylvania Experience. *The Justice System Journal* 19(1): 37–49.

Nathan, Vincent (1979). The Use of Masters in Institutional Reform Litigation. *University of Toledo Law Review* 10:419–64.

Nathan, Vincent (1985). Correctional Health Care: The Perspective of a Special Master. *The Prison Journal* 65:73–82.

New Chief Magistrate Judge Is Named (2009). *Albuquerque Journal*, December 28: A4.

Pastore, Ann L., and Kathleen Maguire, eds. (2009). *Sourcebook of Criminal Justice Statistics* [Online]. Available at http://www.albany.edu/sourcebook/.

Plano, Jack C., and Milton Greenberg (1967). *The American Political Dictionary*, 2nd ed. New York: Holt, Rinehart, and Winston.

Reid, Traciel V. (1999). The Politicization of Retention Elections. *Judicature* 83(2): 68–77.

Republican Party of Minnesota v. White, 536 U.S. 765 (2002).

Rottman, David B., and Shauna M. Strickland (2006). *State Court Organization, 2004*. Washington, DC: Office of Justice Programs, U.S. Department of Justice.

Sheldon, Charles H. (1994). The Role of State Bar Associations in Judicial Selection. *Judicature* 77(6): 300–305.

Sheldon, Charles H. and Nicholas P. Lovrich, Jr. (1991). State Judicial Recruitment, pp. 161–88 in *The American Courts*, eds. John B. Gates and Charles A. Johnson. Washington, DC: CQ Press.

Smith, Charles E., Jr., Mary E. Stuckey, and John W. Winkle III (1998). Executive–Legislative Conflict and the Nomination–Confirmation Controversy in the Lower Federal Judiciary. *Presidential Studies Quarterly* 28(4):832.

Smith, Christopher E. (2009). From U.S. Magistrates to U.S. Magistrate Judges: Developments Affecting the Federal District Courts' Lower Tier of Judicial Officers. In *Courts and Justice*, 4th ed., ed. G. Larry Mays and Peter R. Gregware, 95–108. Long Grove, IL: Waveland Press.

Spohn, Cassia, and Craig Hemmens (2009). *Courts*. Thousand Oaks, CA: Sage Publications.

Steen, Sara (2002). Determinate Sentences. In *Encyclopedia of Crime and Punishment*, ed. David Levinson, 509–11. Thousand Oaks, CA: Sage Publications.

Taggart, William A., and G. Larry Mays (1983/84). Preparing to Manage the Courts: The Educational Backgrounds of Court Administrators. *Judicature* 67(6): 284–91.

Vago, Steven (2009). *Law and Society*, 9th ed. Upper Saddle River, NJ: Prentice Hall.

Wasby, Stephen L. (1988). *The Supreme Court in the Federal Judicial System*, 3rd ed. Chicago: Nelson-Hall Publishers.

Watson, Richard, and Randal G. Downing (1969). *The Politics of the Bench and Bar*. New York: John Wiley.

Webster, Peter D. (1995). Selection and Retention of Judges: Is There One "Best" Method? *Florida State University Law Review* 23(Summer): 1–42.

Wheeler, Russell R., and Cynthia Harrison (1994). *Creating the Federal Judicial System*, 2nd ed. Washington, DC: Federal Judicial Center.

Wheeler, Russell R., and Howard R. Whitcomb (1977). *Judicial Administration: Text and Readings*. Englewood Cliffs, NJ: Prentice-Hall.

5

Lawyers and Litigants

Photo source: AP Images

INTRODUCTION

In this chapter we will examine the functions performed by prosecuting attorneys and defense attorneys in criminal cases, as well as the groups and individuals they represent. Additionally, I will briefly discuss plaintiffs' attorneys, defense attorneys, and their respective clients in civil proceedings. As you will see, in the United States many privately retained attorneys handle both criminal and civil cases, although the bulk of private legal representation is civil in nature. Therefore, these attorneys often have to change their roles or orientations quickly as they shift from one type of case to another.

LEGAL EDUCATION IN THE UNITED STATES

In order to fully understand the roles that attorneys play in the judicial process, it is important first to consider the nature of legal education in the United States. As will become evident, while law schools may differ somewhat in their admissions requirements and the quality of their faculty, as a result of American Bar Association accreditation the curriculum of most law schools looks very similar.

To begin this section it is essential to trace the historical roots of the practice of law and how this has affected legal education in the United States. The legal profession today largely is a function of the evolving ways in which we have trained lawyers.

In discussing the development of the practice of law, we can think of legal systems evolving through three phases of development. These systems change as societies grow in size and complexity and change in their composition. The three phases are (1) primitive legal systems, (2) transitional legal systems, and (3) modern legal systems.

PRIMITIVE LEGAL SYSTEMS

In primitive legal systems, laws were created and administered by tribal leaders or elders (Vago 2009:42–43). These systems were largely informal, and decision making was ad hoc. Court systems, as we know them today, did not exist, and most such legal systems did not have what could be identified as lawyers working within them. Instead, when a dispute arose among members of the tribe, clan, or family an informal tribunal or council was convened to decide between the disputants. Instead of employing lawyers, each side might have a respected member of the group present their case as a spokesperson. Even in the early days of advanced societies such as Greece and Rome there were not specially trained lawyers who served within the legal system. Instead persons known as "orators"—skillful public speakers—became the de facto attorneys of their day. These orators spoke for their clients not based on a special knowledge of the law, but because of their skillfulness in speaking and debating. Cases were won, then, as a result of presenting the most compelling argument to the judge or judges.

TRANSITIONAL LEGAL SYSTEMS

Transitional legal systems occur in advanced agrarian and early industrial societies (Vago 2009:43–44). When these systems appear, the roles of police, judges, and attorneys also start to emerge. If we look back to the early days of legal training in England, we can see the preparation of attorneys being treated as something of a skilled trade. Lawyers learned their craft in a system built around tutelage and apprenticeship more than what we would consider formal education. For example, in England, training in the law came from the Inns of Court where lawyers taught others who wanted to be lawyers. In the Inns "lawyers lived together during the terms of court, and for them, the Inns represented law school, a professional organization, and a tightly knit social club, all in one" (Vago 2009:374).

In colonial America, and following the American Revolution, virtually all of the lawyers in this country had been trained in England. The American system, as it started to evolve, copied the English system including a distinction between barristers (or in-court lawyers) and solicitors (lawyers who handled legal business outside of court; see Box 5.1.) After the American Revolution, though, this distinction within the legal profession disappeared, but the system of training lawyers through apprenticeship continued for some time. In fact, one of our nation's most famous lawyers (Abraham Lincoln) did not attend school to learn to be an attorney but instead "read the law" by studying books and records of court cases. Not until the late 1700s and the early 1800s did law schools start to emerge, and in 1870 Harvard University pioneered use of the now-common casebook method of teaching and learning the law (Vago 2009:376–77).

MODERN LEGAL SYSTEMS

Finally, in modern legal systems we see training for the practice of law becoming more institutionalized and formal. A university education, both at the undergraduate level and in law school, is required. Furthermore, once the period of formal education is completed the aspiring attorneys must also pass one or more bar exams in order to be licensed to practice law. The American Bar Association (ABA) prescribes the nature of legal education for the two hundred institutions that are ABA-approved. Of this group 199 confer the JD degree or the first degree in law. The other school is the U.S. Army Judge Advocate General's School, which offers a specialized advanced law degree program beyond the first degree in law (American Bar Association 2010a). In the 2007–08 academic year there were 141,719 students enrolled in JD programs around the United States (American Bar Association 2010b).

In addition to the ABA-approved schools, there are thirty-eight non–ABA-approved law schools operating around the United States (Law School Admission Council 2010). Most of these schools are independent entities not affiliated with any college or university. Unlike the ABA-approved schools, the non-approved schools may have more liberal admissions requirements and they often operate evening or part-time educational programs geared to individuals who work full-time jobs. The non-approved schools may have agreements with the bar associations in the states in which they operate that allow their graduates to take the state bar exam. However, attorneys with these types of degrees may not be eligible to take the bar exams in other states. Therefore, there may be drawbacks to having a degree from a non-approved school.

Once the legal education has been completed and the bar exam passed, the newly minted attorneys are ready to begin their careers. If they graduated from one of the nation's prestigious law schools (Harvard, Yale, or Stanford, for example), they may get immediate offers to join a high-status law firm as a junior member or associate. If they graduated from a less prestigious school, such as a state university law school or from one of the small university law schools, they may go to work for a medium- to small-size firm. Some new attorneys, by choice or by chance, will end up in small firms or as solo practitioners. As you will see, a disproportionate number of the privately retained criminal defense attorneys in the United States work in the small firms or solo practices. Later in this chapter I discuss what has been called the stratification of the urban bar, and much of this stratification is based on the perceived status of the law school from which attorneys are graduated, and the status of the firm in which they practice.

In addition to working in private law firms upon graduation from law school, a number of other recent law school graduates will find their way into work as government attorneys. These positions include lawyers who work for the various state or federal government agencies, along with those who serve as assistant prosecutors and public defenders. For the remainder of this chapter I focus on these last two roles, as well as those individuals who act as privately retained attorneys in both criminal and civil cases.

BOX 5.1

Legal Practice in Great Britain

While the legal profession in the United States is comprised of attorneys, the legal profession in Great Britain is made up of two different groups, **barristers** and **solicitors**. Barristers are usually legal specialists in a particular area of the law and act as advocates for their clients before a court. Solicitors are general legal practitioners and primarily serve their clients as legal advisors.

In order to become an attorney in the United States, one must obtain an undergraduate degree, followed by a three-year law degree. An attorney must also pass the bar examination for the state in which he or she will practice law. By contrast, in order to become a barrister, one must either obtain a law degree or take the Bar Professional Training Course and pass the Common Professional Exam. Unlike U.S. attorneys, barristers are also required to complete a pupilage, where they are supervised by experienced barristers before being permitted to practice law independently.

While many U.S. attorneys practice as part of a law firm, partnerships among barristers is prohibited. However, barristers are required to join a set of chambers, in which office space and administrative staff are shared with other barristers. In the United States, each attorney belongs to a state bar association; barristers, on the other hand, are required to become members of one of the Inns of Court. Like a bar association, the four Inns of Court (Gray's Inn, Lincoln's Inn, Inner Temple, and Middle Temple) provide both social and educational opportunities for barristers. While U.S. attorneys generally wear business suits when appearing in court, barristers wear black robes and wigs. To become a solicitor, one must possess an undergraduate law degree or pass the Common Professional Exam and take a one-year Legal Practice Course. All prospective solicitors must then complete two years of clerkship with practicing solicitors. Unlike barristers, solicitors may either form partnerships or practice as solo practitioners. Solicitors are not required to join a professional organization and do not wear robes and wigs when fulfilling their professional duties.

Source: Laura Woods Fidelie is an assistant professor in the Criminal Justice Department at Midwestern State University in Wichita Falls, Texas. She has taught comparative criminal justice systems in the summer British Studies Program for Midwestern State.

LAWYERS AND THE PRACTICE OF LAW

The exact number of practicing attorneys in the United States is somewhat uncertain. For example, the Bureau of Labor Statistics (2010) said that in 2007 the American Bar

Association reported 1,143,358 attorneys in the United States, and in 2008 the American Bar Association (2010b) reported that this number had grown to 1,180,386. By contrast, the Bureau of Labor Statistics (2010) reported that there were 759,200 attorneys in 2008. Part of the discrepancy in numbers may be between those individuals who are licensed to practice law and those who actually are in a legal practice of some type.

Of the licensed attorneys in the United States, 74 percent are in private practice; the remainder work for a governmental agency, in private industry, as judges or legal educators (college or law school professors), or they work for a legal aid or public defender organization (American Bar Association 2010b).

The trend nationwide is for lawyers to work in larger and larger law firms. In fact, some firms have expanded nationwide and have offices in a number of large cities. As evidence of this trend, Heinz and Laumann (1982: xviii) note that "In 1948, about 61 percent of all lawyers in the United States were in solo practice, but by 1970 this had declined to 37 percent." The American Bar Association (2010b) has published statistics that indicate that in 2000, 48 percent of attorneys in the United States were solo practitioners. Interestingly, while there has been some movement toward a corporate model for law firms, still 76 percent of the lawyers in the United States work in firms that have fewer than twenty attorneys.

Part of the appeal of the practice of law for some individuals is the earning potential in this career field. Obviously, the salaries earned by lawyers will vary based upon the sizes of cities in which they live, the sizes of the firms in which they practice, and the particular fields of law in which they specialize (Heinz and Laumann 1982: xvii–xviii). The Bureau of Labor Statistics (2010) notes that in May of 2008 the median wages for lawyers was $110,590. The range was from $78,540 for those who worked in state government to $145,770 for those managing companies. Nine months after they had graduated from law school, the median salary for new attorneys was $68,500, and this varied from $48,000 for those in academic positions or judicial clerkships to $108,500 for those in private practice.

Even with the significant number of attorneys in this country, there will continue to be a demand for lawyers and their services. The following sections discuss some of the positions that attorneys may fill within the criminal and civil justice systems in the United States.

PROSECUTING ATTORNEYS

In 2005 in the United States there were 2,344 prosecuting attorneys' offices handling criminal cases in state trial courts. These offices employed about 78,000 individuals as assistant prosecutors, investigators, victims' advocates, and support personnel. On average, between one-third and one-fourth of these people are attorneys (Perry 2006). These numbers are in addition to some city and county attorneys who handle misdemeanor cases only, states' attorneys general, United States attorneys and their assistants in ninety-four federal court districts, and federal prosecutors serving in the United States Department of Justice.

Prosecutors may be present in some misdemeanor cases, and they are in court on behalf of the people in all felony cases. In state courts the prosecuting attorneys may be known by a number of different titles, and they are selected in several different ways. There also are two levels of prosecutors in the federal system.

LOCAL AND STATE PROSECUTORS

The most generic title we can employ for local and state prosecutors is **prosecuting attorney**. This is more of a job description than the name of the office, although in some states (for example, Arkansas, Hawaii, and Michigan) it is the title utilized. For instance, as Table 5.1 shows, the most common designation (nineteen states) for local prosecutors is district attorney (DA), and in nine states the office is simply called prosecuting attorney. In Kentucky and Virginia the position is known as commonwealth attorney, in South Carolina it is the solicitor, and in ten other states the chief prosecutors are called county attorneys/county prosecutors (Perry 2006). The point I am trying to make is that the title can vary from one state to the next and even from county to county within a given state. As a result of the local legal culture, the job responsibilities may differ as well. However, at the most basic level the prosecutors ultimately are

TABLE 5.1	Chief Prosecutors Who Handle Felony Cases in State Courts, 2005	
State*	Title	Method of Selection
Alabama (42)	District Attorney	Elected
Alaska (1)	Attorney General	Appointed
Arizona (15)	County Attorney	Elected
Arkansas (28)	Prosecuting Attorney	Elected
California (58)	District Attorney	Elected
Colorado (22)	District Attorney	Elected
Connecticut (13)	State's Attorney	Appointed
Delaware (1)	Attorney General	Elected
Florida (20)	State's Attorney	Elected
Georgia (49)	District Attorney	Elected
Hawaii (4)	Prosecuting Attorney	Elected
Idaho (44)	Prosecuting Attorney	Elected
Illinois (102)	State's Attorney	Elected
Indiana (90)	Prosecuting Attorney	Elected
Iowa (99)	County Attorney	Elected
Kansas (105)	County Attorney	Elected
Kentucky (57)	Commonwealth Attorney	Elected
Louisiana (41)	District Attorney	Elected
Maine (8)	District Attorney	Elected
Maryland (24)	State's Attorney	Elected

Continued

TABLE 5.1	Continued	
Massachusetts (11)	District Attorney	Elected
Michigan (83)	Prosecuting Attorney	Elected
Minnesota (87)	County Attorney	Elected
Mississippi (22)	District Attorney	Elected
Missouri (115)	Prosecuting Attorney (City Attorney in St. Louis)	Elected
Montana (55)	County Attorney	Elected
Nebraska (93)	County Attorney	Elected
Nevada (17)	District Attorney	Elected
New Hampshire (10)	County Attorney	Elected
New Jersey (21)	County Prosecutor	Appointed
New Mexico (14)	District Attorney	Elected
New York (62)	District Attorney	Elected
North Carolina (39)	District Attorney	Elected
North Dakota (53)	State's Attorney	Elected
Ohio (88)	Prosecuting Attorney	Elected
Oklahoma (27)	District Attorney	Elected
Oregon (36)	District Attorney	Elected
Pennsylvania (67)	District Attorney	Elected
Rhode Island (1)	Attorney General	Elected
South Carolina (16)	Solicitors	Elected
South Dakota (66)	State's Attorney	Elected
Tennessee (31)	District Attorney General	Elected
Texas (155)	District Attorney (and other variations on that title)	Elected
Utah (29)	County Attorney (District Attorney in Salt Lake County)	Elected
Vermont (14)	State's Attorney	Elected
Virginia (120)	Commonwealth Attorney	Elected
Washington (39)	Prosecuting Attorney	Elected
West Virginia (55)	Prosecuting Attorney	Elected
Wisconsin (71)	District Attorney	Elected
Wyoming (23)	District Attorney (also County and Prosecuting Attorney)	Elected

*Note: The numbers in parentheses indicate the total of chief prosecutors in each state.
Source: Perry (2006:11).

responsible for representing the people of the state in bringing charges against criminal defendants.

At the most basic level, we can say that the prosecuting attorney performs a twofold duty: to represent the state in criminal cases and to ensure that justice is done in each case. The office of prosecuting attorney actually exists at two levels in most states. As a statewide office, all states have an attorney general. There can be various ways of selecting these individuals (including appointment), but the most common way of choosing the **state attorney general** is in a partisan election (Carp, Stidham, and Manning 2007). These individuals and their assistants represent the state in both civil and criminal matters and in trials and appeals that impact state government or the citizens of the state.

BOX 5.2   In Their Own Words: Kari Brandenburg, District Attorney

I knew at a young age what I wanted to do. My father was a prosecutor, eventually serving as the elected district attorney. I was fortunate to spend my summers in the courtroom, sitting behind him, watching with enthusiasm. When he came home after a long day in court, I would often sneak away with his briefcase, reading police reports and viewing crime scene photos. After I saw the movie *To Kill A Mockingbird*, what began as a curious desire gave way to a passion that has driven me ever since.

I began practicing law in the Public Defender's office. Within months, I had my first homicide case. The pace was frantic; there weren't many days off, but the opportunities to learn and grow as a trial attorney were exhilarating. I learned the value of the law and its importance to any moral, civilized society. I also learned how critical personal integrity was in all the battles to do justice.

Several years later, I went into private criminal defense practice with my father. We practiced in both state and federal courts. Although our clientele was different, the lessons I learned as a public defender served me well. While in private practice, between trials and once during a trial, I was blessed with five children. Despite the numerous demands on my time, I found my family enhanced my ability to connect with and understand others; something essential for any trial attorney.

I appreciate that serving as district attorney is about much more than prosecuting cases. I have had three goals that have helped guide me. The first is to support the employees in the office so they can achieve their full potential. Second has been to increase the office's effectiveness in prosecuting cases. Third, we must operate in a manner that maintains the public's faith in the integrity of the criminal justice system.

Our office is the largest law firm in the state, and it is severely underfunded. A constant challenge is meeting all the demands with limited resources. We handle approximately 30,000 cases each year. Each defendant and crime is unique, and each requires individualized attention to balance the desires of the victim to see justice done and the state's responsibility to seek justice.

Continued

BOX 5.2
Continued

As district attorney I set the tone for the office, determining which cases to prosecute, establishing appropriate plea guidelines, deciding how to best train and direct our employees, and ensuring that programs such as those regarding victim support are providing the services that we promise our community. Accountability is a big part of my job, as well, answering the hard questions and explaining why we do what we do. Being district attorney requires tireless effort, conviction, integrity, patience, humility, and a good sense of humor. Whether I am prosecuting a high-profile case or meeting with judges and legislators to construct new rules of procedure or laws, I am always mindful that I am the public's servant, working to see they get our best efforts.

Source: Kari Brandenburg is the first elected female district attorney in the Second Judicial District (Bernalillo County) of New Mexico. She is currently in her third term and has served in this capacity since 2001.

There also are local prosecutors who are elected from single counties (in very populous areas) or multi-county jurisdictions. States often divide the total number of counties into a smaller number of judicial districts of roughly equal size or population. Most local prosecutors in the United States are elected locally—primarily through partisan elections—in all states except Alaska, Connecticut, and New Jersey where they are appointed—and most serve four-year terms (Perry 2006).

In 2005, local prosecutors and their staffs totaled 78,000, and more than half of the 2,344 offices disposed of over 250 felony cases, or slightly more than one per working day. Nationwide, in total, state prosecutors closed over 2.4 million felony cases and an additional 7.5 million misdemeanor cases in 2005 (Perry 2006:1,6).

Prosecuting attorneys receive case referrals from various law enforcement agencies within their jurisdictions and review them for legal sufficiency. Time and personnel resource constraints prevent prosecutors from pursuing every case investigated by the police. Therefore, it has become common practice to employ **case screening** procedures to weed out the weakest or least important cases. If a case does not seem to meet the test of legal sufficiency (there is not sufficient probable cause, or there are problems with witnesses or physical evidence), it may be sent back to the police agency with instructions to continue the investigation. This approach typically results in ill feelings between the prosecutor's office and law enforcement agencies. The police generally feel that a case is complete when they forward it to the district attorney, but the DA may feel differently.

It is also important to recognize that prosecutors work with law enforcement agencies in a variety of capacities. The prosecutor's office may serve as formal or informal legal advisor to the police in obtaining arrest or search warrants. Prosecutors also can assist the police and other local government officials in drafting ordinances that are aimed at specific, recurring crime problems such as gangs and graffiti.

The prosecuting attorney's office functions as legal advisor to grand juries in roughly half of the states that still use the grand jury system. It is common to assign one of the assistant prosecutors as the grand jury liaison, and this individual is responsible for seeing that witnesses are contacted and cases are presented to the grand jury for review. While the assistant prosecutor cannot be present when the grand jury actually votes for indictments, the presence of an assistant DA obviously places the prosecutor in a position of great influence over grand jury decisions.

Finally, the prosecuting attorney is responsible for trying criminal cases in court. This extends from the period of the arrest, preliminary hearing (where utilized), grand jury indictment, arraignment, through pre-trial motions, to jury selection and the trial itself. In reality, as I discuss in Chapter 7, a relatively small percentage of criminal cases actually go to trial. Nevertheless, when a criminal defendant insists on a trial, the prosecutor must be prepared to present the case to the judge and jury. In many large jurisdictions, the assistant prosecutors are specialized by function. Some handle misdemeanors and preliminary hearings, some work with the grand jury, and others process arraignments and pretrial motions. In the largest offices and ones that are highly specialized, only the most experienced assistant DAs will be assigned to handle the major felony trials.

BOX 5.3

In the News: Suing Prosecutors

For most of our nation's history, the courts have taken the position that prosecutors are virtually immune to lawsuits challenging the ways in which they choose to process their cases. However, in the 2009–10 session of the United States Supreme Court the justices were asked to consider whether there is an absolute ban against civil rights lawsuits for prosecutors who are alleged to have misused their authority in a criminal prosecution.

In the case of *Pottawattamie County, Iowa et al. v. McGhee et al.*, 129 S.Ct. 2002, 173 L.Ed. 2d 1083 (2009) "Two Pottawattamie County, Iowa prosecutors allegedly obtained false testimony from a man who became the key witness against Curtis McGhee and Terry Harrington in the 1977 shotgun murder of an auto dealership security guard in Council Bluffs. They were sentenced to life in prison. Two decades later, after a friend of Harrington's sought the police record, it emerged that prosecutors Joseph Hvrol and David Richter had failed to turn over evidence about a leading suspect and allegedly coached the key witness" (Biskupic 2009). If the Supreme Court rules in favor of the plaintiffs in this case, they will be affirming their decisions in previous cases such as *Miller v. Pate*, 386 U.S. 1 (1967) dealing with prosecutorial misconduct, but the case now under consideration will take matters one step further. It will provide potential civil remedies against prosecutors who misconduct themselves.

Source: Biskupic (2009).

FEDERAL PROSECUTORS

Like state-level prosecutors, the prosecutorial responsibilities within the federal system operate at two levels. At the national level, the United States Department of Justice and the staff attorneys that assist the attorney general handle some of the federal cases that come forward for prosecution. This is particularly true of cases originating in the District of Columbia and cases coming out of the Office of Civil Rights (OCR) that may involve civil rights violations by state and local criminal justice officials and others.

Most of the prosecutorial work done in the federal district courts, however, is handled by the offices of the **United States attorneys**. This position, like so many others in the federal judicial system, was created by the Judiciary Act of 1789 and, thus, it predates the establishment of the U.S. Department of Justice. In fact, until the Justice Department was established in 1870, the U.S. attorneys operated independently of the United States attorney general.

Like the U.S. Marshals, there is a chief U.S. attorney appointed by the president and confirmed by the Senate. There are ninety-four U.S. attorneys serving the United States and its territories, with one U.S. attorney in each of ninety-three federal court districts and one serving over the territories of Guam and the Mariana Islands (U.S. Department of Justice 2009).

The U.S. attorneys (often abbreviated as USAs) have three principal areas of responsibility. First, they handle the prosecution of criminal cases brought by the United States government. Second, they also have responsibilities relating to civil cases in which the federal government is a party either as the plaintiff or as a defendant. Third, they have the statutory responsibility to try to collect the debts to the U.S. government that have been classified as "administratively uncollectable" (U.S. Department of Justice 2009).

In effect, the U.S. attorneys have administrative oversight for federal civil and criminal cases within their jurisdictions, and they coordinate the activities of their offices with those of federal law enforcement agencies like the Secret Service; Immigration and Customs Enforcement; Drug Enforcement Administration; Bureau of Alcohol, Tobacco, Firearms, and Explosives; and the Federal Bureau of Investigation.

Most of the day-to-day adjudicative business of the USA's office is handled by the assistant U.S. attorneys (AUSAs). In some districts, these individuals may be new lawyers who have just passed the bar exam, or they may have gained legal experience as state or local prosecutors. Some also may have served exclusively in private legal practice. A few individuals seek federal prosecutorial experience as a long-term career field, while others take one of these positions for just a few years and then move on to something else. Like many other prosecutorial positions, the office of U.S. attorney or assistant U.S. attorney frequently is a stepping-stone to other elected or appointed offices.

The types of criminal cases typically handled by the offices of the U.S. attorneys include those involving the Racketeer Influenced Corrupt Organizations (RICO) statutes, bank robberies, crimes that involve crossing state lines (such as kidnapping and auto theft), tax evasion, fraud, drug trafficking, political corruption, and civil rights violations. On the civil side, their cases frequently involve damages and tort claims against the federal government and litigation dealing with federal environmental laws. Fair housing, employment discrimination, and voters' rights cases also fall within their domain (Longley 2007).

BOX 5.4

In Their Own Words: David Iglesias

Early in 2006, two United States attorneys were ordered to resign from their positions, and this was followed on December 7, 2006, by a directive from senior Bush Administration Department of Justice officials to seven other U.S. attorneys requesting that they tender their resignations. This was out of a total of more than twenty-six U.S. attorneys that had been targeted for replacement. One of the individuals dismissed was David Iglesias, the U.S. attorney for the District of New Mexico.

As a result of the furor over these apparently politically motivated firings, Congress began hearings, and the U.S. Department of Justice's Office of the Inspector General and the Office of Professional Responsibility conducted an investigation that resulted in a nearly four-hundred-page report (U.S. Department of Justice 2008).

The Department of Justice (2008) in its report of the investigation noted a lack of cooperation by key White House officials, but the report did say "we believe the evidence we uncovered showed that Iglesias was removed because of complaints to the Department of Justice and the White House by New Mexico's Republican members of Congress and party activists about Iglesias's handling of voter fraud and public corruption cases. We concluded that the other reasons proffered by the Department after his removal [relating to his performance and management style, and his absence for military reserve duties] were after-the-fact rationalizations that did not actually contribute to Iglesias's removal" (U.S. Department of Justice 2008:187).

After he left office, David Iglesias responded to the allegations against him in a *New York Times* editorial entitled "Why I Was Fired." In his editorial, and subsequent book, Iglesias said, among other things: "[I]t seems clear that politics played a role in the ousters." He added: "Although we [U.S. attorneys] receive our appointments through the political process (I am a Republican who was recommended by Senator Pete Domenici), we are expected to be apolitical once we are in office. I will never forget John Ashcroft, then the attorney general, telling me during the summer of 2001 that politics should play no role during my tenure. I took that message to heart. Little did I know that I could be fired for not being political." He concluded: "What the critics, who don't have any experience as prosecutors have asserted is reprehensible—namely, that I should have proceeded without proof beyond a reasonable doubt [of voter fraud]. The public has the right to believe that prosecution decisions are based on legal, not political, grounds" (Iglesias 2007).

Sources: Iglesias (2007); U.S. Department of Justice (2008).

As I have mentioned, the U.S. attorneys are appointed by the president and confirmed by the Senate. However, unlike Article III judges, the USAs serve at the pleasure of the president and the attorney general. This means that when an administration of a different political party or even a new president of the same party takes office, all of the USAs submit their resignations, which are generally accepted by the new president. Once appointed, the USAs are thought of as somewhat insulated from partisan politics. Occasionally, however, political considerations are injected into the process, and USAs might be removed from office. As Box 5.4 shows, in 2006 the George W. Bush Administration chose to remove a group of "low performing" USAs in mid-term. It is interesting to note that all of these U.S. attorneys originally had been appointed by President Bush, but this move generated a political firestorm that eventually led to the downfall of then Attorney General Alberto Gonzales.

DEFENSE ATTORNEYS

As I noted in Chapter 1, in many ways defense attorneys may be in the least advantageous position relative to others in the courtroom work group. This does not mean that they are completely without leverage when dealing with judges and prosecutors, but often they do not have the finances, access to information, investigative personnel, and other resources equivalent to their prosecutorial counterparts. While prosecutors will eventually handle all criminal cases that go forward, privately retained defense attorneys will have considerably fewer cases each. The bulk of criminal defense work will fall on the court-appointed attorneys, such as public defenders, who are responsible for representing those individuals who cannot afford to hire their own lawyers.

As we begin to consider the functions performed by defense attorneys, the following topics will be of particular concern: (1) the various roles played by defense attorneys, (2) the constitutional right to counsel, (3) methods for selecting attorneys, and (4) the issues surrounding attorney competence. Each of these issues is significant because each one impacts the availability of legal representation and the quality of that representation received by the people accused of crimes.

THE ROLES PLAYED BY DEFENSE ATTORNEYS

To the average person, the role of the criminal defense attorney is fairly simple: to get the client off. However, interactions with, and observations of, defense attorneys quickly illustrate that there are a variety of additional responsibilities associated with this position. For example, defense attorneys spend a considerable amount of time counseling their clients. This may involve developing a legal strategy for defending the case, or it may involve getting the client—and, at times, the client's family—to develop a realistic view of his or her prospects if the case goes to trial (and perhaps results in a conviction). In this role the defense attorney is something of a mixture of a minister, teacher, and counselor as well as a legal advisor.

A second role played by defense attorneys is that of mediator or negotiator (Uphoff 2009; see also Blumberg 2004; Subin 2002). There are many audiences to which criminal defense attorneys must respond. They must try to please their clients (this, in and of itself, may be an impossible task), judges, and the prosecuting attorneys. The difficulty is that each one of these groups has different, and typically conflicting, goals in the criminal process. In some cases these differences result in the client's interests being placed in a subordinate position to the interests of the courtroom work group. I discuss plea bargaining at length in Chapter 7, but it is important to recognize that the role of mediator-negotiator is most apparent in the plea bargaining process. There the attorney must give the client an accurate appraisal of the likely outcome of the case based on the "going rate" (Walker 2006:47–67). This role blends elements of a service broker with those of an automobile salesperson.

Finally, the defense attorney is an officer of the court. Affirmatively, this means that defense attorneys are obligated to promote justice; negatively, they must not do things that impede the administration of justice. Again, this places the defense attorney in something of a difficult position in that the client's interests and "doing justice" may be on a collision course in some cases. When we consider all of these factors, it is easy to understand something of the difficulty of the defense attorney's role.

ATTORNEY STATUS

Based on movie and television portrayals, most students—and perhaps most Americans—believe that the practice of criminal law is exciting and filled with major challenges. That is true to a point. However, there are other features about the practice of criminal law that make it less than appealing to a lot of attorneys. To begin with, the clientele is not one with whom most attorneys normally would choose to socialize. These people are, after all, "criminals." Quite often criminal defense attorneys develop unsavory reputations based on the company they keep (see Connelly 2005). Occasionally these reputations are deserved, but in most instances they are not.

Aside from the criminal defense attorney's clientele, there is the issue of pay. If the attorney is a public defender, pay is based on a salary; thus, handling one case or one hundred cases results in the same size paycheck. For other court-appointed or assigned counsels, courts typically have fee schedules by which these attorneys are paid. They may be allotted a certain hourly rate and a maximum number of hours, based on the severity of the case. In some jurisdictions attorneys may be paid a flat fee of, for example, $250 for misdemeanor cases and $500 for felonies. This makes hard work and exceptionally difficult cases not only time-consuming but also financially unrewarding.

Even privately retained defense attorneys are not compensated for criminal cases in the same way they would be for civil litigation. A hypothetical case will serve as an illustration. A defendant hires an attorney to defend him for possession of 10 kilos (slightly over 20 pounds) of marijuana. The attorney could be hired at an hourly rate, but she tells the client she will take the case for $2,000 to be paid half immediately and half before the case is scheduled for trial. If this case is plea bargained and the attorney devotes ten hours to it, she makes $200 per hour. If it goes to trial and the attorney spends 100 hours on the case, she makes $20 per hour. This causes many attorneys to repeat the often quoted phrase: "I can't make any money in court; I make my money in the office."

At the beginning of the chapter I mentioned the notion of the stratification of the urban bar that was developed by Heinz and Laumann (1982). In order to fully appreciate the way lawyers are organized and how they go about performing their functions, we need to examine the level of stratification in greater detail.

In order to understand perceptions of prestige within the practice of law in the United States, Heinz and Laumann (1982) undertook a survey of 777 practicing attorneys randomly selected from among all of those practicing law in Chicago. This was supplemented by asking for the prestige rankings of thirty different fields of legal practice by law school professors and a group of lawyer-researchers who worked for the American Bar Association. The four highest prestige level clusters included:

1. Big business—here were legal fields that included securities, tax, antitrust (defendants), banking, general corporate, public utilities, and municipal.
2. Classic specialties—these included patents and admiralty.
3. Property—probate and real estate law fell into this category.
4. Labor—including both attorneys that worked for management and those that worked for labor unions.

There were three clusters of legal practice that were ranked among those with lower prestige than the four just mentioned. These three fields of practice were:

1. Small business/commercial—including commercial, consumer (creditor), consumer (debtor), and condemnations.
2. Public interest and litigation—the specific fields of law here were civil litigation, environmental (defendant), environmental (plaintiff), civil rights, family law (paying clients), landlord–tenant, and family law (poverty-level clients).
3. Personal litigation—the types of legal practice here were personal injury (defendant), criminal prosecution, criminal defense, personal injury (plaintiff), and divorce. (Heinz and Laumann (1982: 66)

As Heinz and Laumann (1982:70) note, prestige is a complex and multifaceted concept within the practice of law. Some of a field's perceived prestige comes from dealing with federal laws and federal courts as opposed to state courts. Furthermore, the earning potential is related to, but not the exclusive factor influencing, prestige within the legal profession.

While this research is somewhat dated now, and the perspectives can change over time, it is interesting to see the results of their survey of practicing attorneys and others involved in the legal profession. Table 5.2 shows the prestige rankings for the five highest ranked and the five lowest ranked fields within the practice of law on the four dimensions of intellectual challenge, rapidity of change, public service orientation, and ethical conduct.

Another way to understand the stratification of the legal profession is to think of lawyers operating in the domains of three concentric circles. In the innermost circle are the high-status lawyers who practice law in the most prestigious private law firms. Most

TABLE 5.2	Five Highest and Five Lowest Fields of Law by Prestige		
Intellectual Challenge	Rapidity of Change	Public Service	Ethical Conduct
Five Highest			
Tax	Tax	Civil Rights	Civil Rights
Antitrust (Plaintiffs)	3-Way Tie: Environmental (Plaintiffs), Environmental (Defendants), Civil Rights	Family (Poverty)	Admiralty
Antitrust (Defendants)	Securities	Environmental (Plaintiffs)	Patents
Securities	Consumer (Creditor)	Consumer (Debtor)	Family (Poverty)
3-Way Tie: Environmental (Plaintiffs), Environmental (Defendants), Civil Rights		Criminal Defense	General Corporate
Five Lowest			
Divorce	Probate	Antitrust (Defendants)	Personal Injury (Plaintiffs)
Personal Injury (Defendants)	Admiralty	2-Way Tie: Banking, Admiralty	Divorce
2-Way Tie: Personal Injury (Plaintiffs), Condemnations	Condemnations	3-Way Tie: Real Estate, Personal Injury (Defendants), Personal Injury (Plaintiffs)	Criminal Defense
2-Way Tie: Family (Paying), Family (Poverty)	Real Estate		Personal Injury (Defendants)
	Municipal		Condemnations

Source: Heinz and Laumann (1982:68).

of these attorneys have attended the most highly respected law schools and they have graduated at or near the top of their classes. These firms typically represent high-status clients such as major corporations, financial institutions, and wealthy individuals. The work of these firms has been described as keeping their clients out of court, so the attorneys that work in this domain spend relatively little time in the courtroom setting.

The next circle is composed of attorneys who work in medium-to-large law firms, and who represent clients who have legal interests that challenge the inner circle. These may be businesses that act as suppliers to the major corporations or people who have some type of contractual relationship with large commercial enterprises. Since the attorneys in the innermost circle strive to stay out of court, the attorneys in the middle circle often do not go to court either. When conflicts arise between these two groups, both groups often see a trial as a lose–lose proposition, so significant effort is expended to resolve the conflicts through some type of negotiated solution such as mediation or arbitration.

The outermost circle is comprised of lawyers who work in small law firms (typically with ten or fewer attorneys) and those who are solo practitioners. Many of these individuals have graduated from the less-prestigious law schools, or they graduated far down in their classes. Virtually all of them operate mixed civil and criminal practices, and among all of the attorneys described in this section they are the ones most likely to provide representation for people accused of crimes. They sometimes occupy small offices near the courthouses and bail bonding agencies and they are the most likely of all attorneys to advertise their services on television, radio, in the newspapers, and on bus benches. As a result of their perceived status, the lawyers that function in this outer ring may be looked down upon by many other attorneys. Michael Connelly (2005) has written a novel called *The Lincoln Lawyer* where he chronicles the life of a fictitious Los Angeles attorney by the name of Mickey Haller. Haller is a solo practitioner who operates with an answering service, but uses his Lincoln Town Car as his primary place of business. He even has a former client serve as his driver while he transacts business on his cell phone in the backseat of the car while he goes from appointment to appointment and courthouse to courthouse.

This characterization of the way attorneys are stratified or segmented based on their backgrounds and the context in which they work helps us recognize that not all attorneys in the U.S. are on par with the perceptions of one another. Some hold a much higher perceived status than others, and that is reflected in their incomes and the types of clients they choose to represent.

THE CONSTITUTIONAL RIGHT TO COUNSEL

When we talk about legal representation in criminal cases, we must return to the basis for the **right to counsel**: the Sixth Amendment of the Constitution. The Sixth Amendment provides in part that "In all criminal prosecutions the accused shall enjoy the right to…have the assistance of counsel for his defense." Three very important points must be considered when examining the constitutional right to counsel. First, the Sixth Amendment extends the right to counsel to criminal cases, but there is no civil case guarantee. Second, when the Bill of Rights was ratified the primary concern was over abuses of power by a strong national government. Therefore, for a substantial period of time the Supreme Court interpreted the Bill of Rights as applying to the federal courts and federal cases. Third, many legal observers originally understood the right to counsel to mean that any person who could afford a lawyer was entitled to have one (for the basis of this conclusion see *Betts v. Brady*, 316 U.S. 455 [1942], overruled by *Gideon v. Wainwright*, 372 U.S. 335 [1963]). Starting with a series of cases in the early part of the twentieth century, however, the Supreme Court began to extend the right to counsel to state criminal defendants (see, for example, Melone and Karnes 2008; Orvis 2002).

In the early 1930s the United States Supreme Court decided the case of *Powell v. Alabama*, 287 U.S. 45 (1932). With this decision, for the first time the Sixth Amendment right to counsel was extended to the states by way of the Fourteenth Amendment. However, the Supreme Court's decision in this case applied the right only to state death penalty cases. The issue of whether the right to counsel extended to all state felony prosecutions was not addressed until the case of *Betts v. Brady*, 316 U.S. 455 (1942). However, in *Betts* the Supreme Court refused to expand the right to counsel to include all state felony cases as an essential part of due process.

The true landmark case regarding the right to counsel was *Gideon v. Wainwright*, 372 U.S. 335 (1963). In *Gideon* the Supreme Court decided that *Betts v. Brady* should be over-ruled and that the Sixth Amendment right to counsel was a fundamental due process right for state criminal defendants charged with felonies. Once *Gideon* was decided, the primary question that was remaining was in regards to misdemeanors. A decade after *Gideon,* the Supreme Court resolved this issue in *Argersinger v. Hamlin*, 407 U.S. 25 (1972).

Unlike *Gideon*, which applied the right to counsel to all state felony cases, *Argersinger* did not provide the right to counsel in all misdemeanor cases. In *Argersinger* the Supreme Court drew a line, although not a particularly distinct one, by saying that attorneys must be provided in any case where the *possibility of incarceration* exists. This might cover serious misdemeanor cases like drunk driving or simple assault, but it might not apply to what traditionally have been called infractions or petty offenses (such as most traffic offenses). Therefore, today we can say that criminal defendants are granted the right to an attorney for all felonies and for a great many misdemeanors. Additionally, following *Gideon* but before *Argersinger* was decided, the Supreme Court added that accused suspects also have the right to counsel at any "critical stage" of the proceedings or pretrial confrontations by the prosecution in a case; this included police lineups (*United States v. Wade*, 388 U.S. 218 [1968]).

Now that I have addressed the issue of the right to counsel, it is important to consider the methods available for securing this right. In most instances the question of the right to counsel is most critical for indigent defendants.

METHODS FOR SELECTING ATTORNEYS

In this section we will turn our attention to the various ways legal services can be obtained. Of course, for those people who have the financial resources to do so there is the option of privately retaining an attorney. These expenses will be paid out-of-pocket, or some companies and organizations in the United States offer prepaid legal services as a form of insurance. However, the real issue involves **indigent defendants,** or those individuals who cannot afford to hire their own attorneys. Estimates of this population have ranged from 48 percent to 90 percent of criminal defendants nationwide (see, for example, Worden 2009:385, fn. 1). However, the Bureau of Justice Statistics found that in 1996 and 1998, 66 percent of the felony defendants in federal courts and 82 percent of the felony defendants in state courts were represented by some type of publicly funded attorney (Harlow 2000:1).

BOX 5.5

In the News: The Right to Counsel

The background story for the landmark United States Supreme Court case of *Gideon v. Wainwright*, 372 U.S. 335 (1963) is told in the book by Anthony Lewis entitled *Gideon's Trumpet* (1964). In the U.S. Supreme Court opinion in that case, Associate Supreme Court Justice Hugo Black, writing for a unanimous Court, asserted that "reason and reflection require us to recognize that in our adversary system of criminal justice, any person haled into court, who is too poor to hire a lawyer, cannot be assured a fair trial unless counsel is provided for him. This seems to us to be an obvious truth. Governments, both state and federal, quite properly spend vast sums of money to establish machinery to try defendants accused of crime. Lawyers to prosecute are everywhere deemed essential to protect the public's interest in an orderly society. Similarly, there are few defendants charged with crime, few indeed, who fail to hire the best lawyers they can get to prepare and present their defenses. That government hires lawyers to prosecute and defendants who have the money hire lawyers to defend are the strongest indications of the widespread belief that lawyers in criminal courts are necessities, not luxuries. The right of one charged with crime to counsel may not be deemed fundamental and essential to fair trials in some countries, but it is in ours" (372 U.S. 345).

Justice Black continued by saying that "From the very beginning, our state and national constitutions and laws have laid great emphasis on procedural and substantive safeguards designed to assure fair trials before impartial tribunals in which every defendant stands equal before the law. This noble ideal cannot be realized if the poor man charged with crime has to face his accusers without a lawyer to assist him" (372 U.S. 345).

In summary, the Court found that the right to counsel by state felony, noncapital defendants was a fundamental constitutional right. Therefore, individuals who could not afford to hire their own attorneys had to be furnished one by the courts.

Sources: Gideon v. Wainwright, 372 U.S. 335 (1963); Lewis (1964).

Public Defenders

Today in the United States there are quite a few ways of providing legal assistance to indigent defendants. The systems employed vary from state to state, and in some instances they even may differ from county to county. Therefore, in this section I consider some of the more common forms of legal defense for indigent defendants.

One of the most easily recognized forms of indigent defense—largely because of television and movies—is that of the **public defender**. The Bureau of Justice Statistics defines a public defender system as one in which there is "A salaried staff of full-time or part-time attorneys that render criminal indigent defense through a public or private nonprofit organization, or as direct government paid employees" (DeFrances and Litras 2000: 2; see also, Langton and Farole 2009:2).

The public defender system first began in Los Angeles County, California, in 1914 (Cole, Gertz, and Bunger 2004:175). Public defenders are the governmentally paid counterparts to the prosecuting attorney. As of 2007 there were 964 public defender offices in forty-nine states. Maine is the only state that does not have some type of public defender apparatus (Langton and Farole 2009:2).

Twenty-two of the states have state-operated public defender systems, and these states provide the funding for indigent defense services.[1] These state systems employed 4,321 full-time-equivalent attorneys and an additional 2,964 support personnel including investigators, paralegals, and other administrative and clerical staff members. In 2007, state-based public defender systems received nearly 1.5 millions cases, and on average each attorney handled 88 felony (non-capital) cases, 147 misdemeanor cases, and 3 appeals (Langton and Farole 2009:2,5).

By contrast, sixteen states have public defender offices that are completely funded at the county level, and the remaining eleven states have public defender offices that have a mixture of state and county funding.[2] These offices employed 12,827 full-time-equivalent attorneys and another 7,945 support personnel. In 2007 county-based public defender offices received nearly 4.3 million cases, and on average each attorney processed 106 felony (non-capital) cases, 164 misdemeanor cases, and 2 appeals (Langton and Farole 2009:2,5).

In order to determine client eligibility for legal services, public defender offices utilize a number of different criteria. Among the most common are: income level, the receipt of public assistance, a sworn application by the defendant, the amount of debt owed, residence in a mental institution or correctional facility, the ability to post bond, federal poverty guidelines, and in some jurisdictions the judge's discretion. Other factors also may be taken into account. These include consideration of: the defendant's family status, the number of dependents, the amount of monthly expenses, whether the person receives worker's compensation or disability payments, bankruptcy, the individual's personal assets, and letters from employers (Langton and Farole 2009:8).

Today public defenders serve 1,144 or slightly over one-third of the counties in the United States, but these counties contain 70 percent of the country's population. This means that public defender systems primarily are located in the most heavily populated, urban counties, and of the one hundred most populous counties in the United States ninety have public defender systems (DeFrances and Litras 2000; DeFrances 2001).

In addition to state public defender systems, the various federal court districts around the country also have a federal public defender's office assigned to them. The size of this office will depend on the population and the criminal caseload of the district, and in 1998 there were sixty-three federal public defender organizations serving in seventy-four of the ninety-four federal court districts (Harlow 2000:2).

Federal public defenders are responsible for providing criminal defense for indigent defendants as prescribed by the Sixth Amendment to the Constitution. As is the case with assistant U.S. attorneys, some federal public defenders are career employees and some are gaining experience prior to moving on to more financially rewarding and perhaps less stressful private practice positions.

A few features are common to many public defender systems in the United States. First, PDs almost always have smaller staffs than the prosecuting attorneys. For example, in 1999 the indigent criminal defense budgets for eighty-one of the country's most populous counties was $1.1 billion, while the budgets for the prosecutors' offices in these same counties was $1.9 billion. Although this difference may not seem great, it can translate into relatively large caseloads, less investigative or clerical help, less funding for crime lab analysis and expert witnesses, and less victim support for public defenders' offices (DeFrances and Litras 2000:3).

Second, many of the assistant public defenders are recent law school graduates who are looking for ways to gain legal experience and earn a living. By contrast, there are a few "true believers," or career public defenders who have dedicated their professional careers to helping those financially unable to help themselves (see Box 5.6).

Third, because of the high percentage of young attorneys, typically there is a high rate of turnover among the assistant PDs. Once they gain some experience, quite a few assistant public defenders begin looking for better paying "real jobs" with private law firms.

BOX 5.6 In Their Own Words: Public Defenders and Private Attorneys

Rory L. Rank is the Supervisor of the Juvenile Division of the New Mexico Public Defender's Office for the Third Judicial District:

> As a practicing attorney for over 30 years; I believe what Aristotle wrote: "We are what we repeatedly do. Excellence, then, is not an act, but a habit." As a New Mexico Public Defender since 1992, my mission is to ensure excellence in juvenile defense and promote justice for all God's Children.
>
> My mission is to help heal a broken heart, provide hope to children in despair and ensure the effective legal representation of our children. This is a noble cause: to do like Christ does, to be responsive and serve without being judgmental, and to represent the child's expressed interests. My wonderful dad and mom taught me to be of something or of nothing, to love what you do, and do it with passion, principles, and a Christ-Centered purpose.
>
> On June 5, 2009, I received the New Mexico Criminal Defense Association's highest honor, the Charles Driscoll Memorial Award. It states: "Attorney for the defense for his commitment to protection of life, liberty and constitutional rights. We are honored to stand beside you in carrying on the work of our late friend and mentor, Charles Driscoll, who inspired a generation of New Mexico defense lawyers with his courage, dedication, and his love."

Continued

BOX 5.6

Continued

I believe a commitment to protection of life, liberty, and constitutional rights are a noble habit and cherished thought. I believe a commitment to ensure excellence in juvenile defense of the impoverished and disenfranchised children is a noble cause and cherished thought. I believe promoting human welfare and social reform/justice is a noble cause and cherished thought.

As a defense attorney I believe in excellence—and carefully heed what Harold Clarke, Chief Justice of the Georgia Supreme Court, wrote: "We set our sights on the embarrassing target of mediocrity. I guess that means about halfway. And that raises a question. Are we willing to put up with halfway justice? To my way of thinking, one-half justice must mean one-half injustice, and one-half injustice is no justice at all."

As a defense attorney I believe we are required to react to cases with zealous advocacy and effective representation, but we must also be pro-active by creating preventive and intervention programs to divert our youths out of juvenile justice system. We can and must teach our children to be successful.

I believe we are entrusted to care for, protect, teach and restore a child to a sober, healthy, productive citizen, with a meaningful life. In conclusion, many have asked me: "Why are you a juvenile defense lawyer?" I could respond:

On the street I saw a small girl, cold and shivering in a thin dress, with little hope of a decent meal. I became angry and said to God: "Why did you permit this? Why don't you do something about it?" God said nothing that night. Then He replied suddenly: "I certainly did something about it. I made you." *Covenant House*

*****

Ryan Villa is a graduate of the University of New Mexico School of Law, and he has been in private legal practice for five years:

Private criminal defense practice is extremely rewarding and exciting. Every case has its own unique story, and many of the cases are more entertaining than any novel or television show. Unlike a public defender, who in most offices would be limited to certain jurisdictions, such as state court only, and limited to certain types of cases, a private lawyer can practice in different courts and can take on a variety of cases. The diversity of practice brings in a diversity of stories, and this keeps the work exciting and prevents the burnout that can come with doing the same thing over and over.

Continued

BOX 5.6

Continued

Where a public defender often is assigned a case after an arrest or indictment, as a private lawyer, I often see clients before the authorities even know a crime has been committed or while a crime is still being investigated. These cases are often very interesting, but can present difficult legal and ethical issues. For instance, should the client turn him or herself in? What if the client wants to give me evidence relating to the crime? These cases also allow time to start investigating and preparing a defense, even before the police make an arrest, which gives me a sense of control over the case.

Private practice also involves being a businessperson, which is often the most challenging part of the job. Being able to help your clients and ensuring that the proper financial arrangements are made in order to represent them do not always go hand-in-hand. Oftentimes clients do not always meet their financial obligations, but a lawyer has an ethical obligation not to withdraw from a case if it will be detrimental to the client. It can also be difficult to turn away a really interesting case because the client does not have the financial ability to hire you. That means that some interesting cases must be sacrificed for the sake of income.

Overall, being a criminal defense attorney in private practice, while challenging, is extremely entertaining. I get up every morning eager to get to work.

Research in the past few decades has demonstrated that, unlike the image that most people hold of them, public defenders and other types of indigent defenders are capable attorneys who are adequately able to represent their clients (see, for example, Hanson and Ostrom 2004). Interestingly, the Bureau of Justice Statistics has found that in federal courts about nine out of ten defendants were found guilty, and in state courts three out of four defendants were found guilty, no matter whether they had a privately retained or a court-appointed attorney (Harlow 2000). In a later section in this chapter I return to the issue of the type of representation and attorney competence.

Irrespective of their effectiveness, public defenders continue to suffer from low estimations of their legal ability by the clients they serve. In some ways this perception—which becomes a reality—results from associating cost and value: If indigent defendants pay nothing for their attorneys, then these attorneys must not be worth very much. Part of the perception problem also may result from the conclusion reached by some criminal defendants that if the state pays judges, prosecutors, and public defenders, this places all of these individuals on the same side.

Voucher Systems

To get around the problems of perception associated with public defenders, some jurisdictions have gone to a **voucher system** (Smith 1991). Indigent defendants are issued a voucher or "chit" worth a certain amount of money—commensurate with the serious-ness of the offense with which the defendant is charged—and this allows the accused to shop for a lawyer who is willing to accept the voucher. The quality of defense pro-vided may not be substantially different with vouchers than might be the case with public defenders, but with vouchers the defendants may feel more like they have had the opportunity to pick their own lawyer.

Assigned Counsel

Nationwide the most pervasive system of legal defense for those who cannot afford to pay is the **assigned counsel system**, sometimes simply called appointed counsel. The Bureau of Justice Statistics says that an assigned counsel system is one in which there is "appointment from a list of private bar members who accept cases on a judge-by-judge, court-by-court, or case-by-base basis" (DeFrances and Litras 2000: 2).

This type of indigent defense is found in nineteen states (about 60 percent of the counties throughout the nation), and some states rely on this system exclusively (Abadinsky 2007; DeFrances 2001). Assigned counsel systems pay attorneys a flat fee to handle a case. For example, an attorney might receive $250 to $500 to represent a serious misdemeanant or $500 to $1,000 to represent a felon. This compares with the 1999 nationwide average for public defenders of $490 per case (DeFrances 2001). As an alternative, attorneys might be paid for a prescribed number of "billable hours."

Jurisdictions that rely on appointed counsel frequently establish an annual list of attorneys available for assignment in one of two ways. First, judges, public defenders' offices, or court clerks may maintain alphabetical lists of all attorneys in the county bar association and assignments are taken in rotation. For the criminal defend-ants this means that they could be appointed the best criminal defense attorney in the jurisdiction, or they could receive an attorney whose specialty is real estate law. Second, judges may ask for volunteers to be appointed to cases. The volunteers often are young attorneys on their way up in their legal careers, or older solo-practitioner attorneys who may have declining practices for various reasons. Some of these vol-unteers regularly hang around the courthouse hoping to be appointed to cases on a frequent basis.

In addition to assigned counsel systems in state courts, there also are **panel attor-neys** in federal courts. Panel attorneys are "appointed by the court from a list of pri-vate attorneys on a case-by-base basis" (Harlow 2000: 2). In 1998 all ninety-four federal court districts used panel attorneys, and in twenty districts this was the only way indi-gent defense was provided for federal criminal defendants.

Contract Systems

A fourth system of indigent defense involves **contract defenders**. Contract legal sys-tems are provided by "Nonsalaried private attorneys, bar associations, law firms, con-sortiums or groups of attorneys, or nonprofit corporations that contract with a funding source to provide court-appointed representation in a jurisdiction" (DeFrances 2001:3). These programs can be stand-alone indigent defense systems, or they can operate in conjunction with public defender programs. Where they exist with public defender pro-grams they typically are responsible for overflow cases that the public defender's office cannot handle, or they may be called upon in situations where the public defender represents one co-defendant in a criminal case and someone outside of the public defender's office would be needed to represent another co-defendant.

Eleven states fund contract defense attorney programs (DeFrances 2001:1,3). In effect, court systems can put indigent defense out for bids on a yearly basis. For instance, based on previous experience a jurisdiction could anticipate needing one thousand hours of indigent defense work in the coming year. Individual attorneys, law firms, and other organizations could bid on this contract, and normally the lowest bidder would receive the award. To protect themselves, firms might build contingencies into their bids. Thus, the bid might be for $100 per hour for the thousand hours stipulated, but $150 per hour above that. Small law firms might be very anxious to receive such an award because it could mean $100,000 or more of guaranteed income for a year (see Worden 2009).

Legal Clinics

A fifth system of providing attorneys for indigent defendants is through use of **legal clinics**. Cities that have one or more law schools have a ready supply of law students who are anxious to get started on their legal careers. Normally through arrangements with the state supreme court and the state bar association, second- and third-year law students are able to take a legal clinic course and to represent clients in small civil cases and in some misdemeanor criminal cases. Some observers have likened this process to doctors having internship and residency opportunities before they are free to practice without supervision.

Legal Aid Societies

Finally, a number of large cities like Boston and New York City have active **legal aid societies**. Most legal aid societies handle only civil cases, and they do so based on a sliding scale by the ability to pay. Thus, indigent clients may pay nothing. These organizations coordinate time donated by lawyers as part of their community service. This type of representation often is called **pro bono** legal assistance, from the Latin phrase *pro bono publico*, or for the public good. Attorneys might donate forty hours of legal assistance per year, for which they receive a tax deduction as a charitable gift. The concern always with such systems is whether lawyers providing free legal assistance are undermining the earnings of lawyers who are being paid for their services. However, in virtually every instance the people who take advantage of such services otherwise would not be able to pay for them, irrespective of the cost.

As we conclude this section, what can we say about indigent defense in the United States? Several comments are worthy of note. First, practically every jurisdiction in the country is experiencing greater demands for indigent defense than they can meet. The twenty-one states that have state-funded indigent defense systems (whatever the type) spent $251 million for indigent defense in 1982. By 1999 this amount had increased to $662 million (DeFrances 2001:2).

In some states and individual counties, indigent defense funds have been exhausted long before the fiscal year is completed. In fact, a number of states currently have experienced crises over funding their indigent defense systems. Therefore, indigent defenders are likely to face a resource crunch for some time to come.

Second, the indigent defense systems described in this section can be found in a variety of locations in the United States, but there are some hybrids of these systems operating as well (DeFrances 2001; see also Hanson and Ostrom 2004). Finally, no system is perfect, and no system is completely inadequate. Each approach that is used does a reasonable job of representing the individuals who cannot afford an attorney, but none provide what might be characterized as the very best representation either. Personnel resource scarcity, the quality of the cases they inherit, financial considerations, and high caseloads prevent most indigent defenders from doing the kind of job they might like to do.

While being represented by an attorney is important for most criminal defendants, the real issue may be in relation to attorney competence. It is not very helpful to have a lawyer if he or she cannot adequately represent the client's interests. Therefore, let us briefly consider the issues related to attorney competence.

ISSUES SURROUNDING ATTORNEY COMPETENCE

First, I need to reinforce a point that was made previously: No one method of attorney selection (including privately retained attorneys) is necessarily superior to any other. To say it another way, any method of attorney selection can choose competent or incompetent attorneys.

Second, in discussing attorney competence it is essential to note that there is no single agreed-upon standard defining what constitutes competent action by attorneys. In other words, attorneys of equal ability may choose different courses of action in handling the same criminal case. Nevertheless, in several cases the U.S. Supreme Court has addressed this issue. One case in particular stands out. In *United States v. Cronic*, 466 U.S. 648 (1984) the defendant's privately retained attorney withdrew from the case just before the beginning of the trial. The trial court then appointed a young lawyer who had a real estate practice to represent Cronic. Cronic was convicted of the check "kiting" charges, but the Court of Appeals overturned the conviction by focusing on five factors: (1) the amount of time (25 days) the defense attorney had been given to investigate and prepare for the case (the government had spent over four years in its investigation), (2) the defense attorney's experience in cases like this, (3) the seriousness of the charges, (4) the complex nature of the charges and the possible defenses that could be employed, and (5) access to defense witnesses.

In viewing Cronic's claim of ineffective representation of counsel the Supreme Court noted that the lawyer's background did not necessarily justify a presumption of ineffectiveness. In a footnote, the majority opinion concluded: "If counsel is a reasonably effective advocate, he meets constitutional standards irrespective of his client's evaluation of his performance."

This means that two factors must be considered in assessing attorney competence. They are:

1. The defendant must be able to point to something specific the attorney did (or failed to do) that would be recognized as a procedural error.

2. The action or failure to act must prejudice the outcome of the case (see *Strickland v. Washington*, 466 U.S. 668 [1984]).

In effect, on appeal the convicted individual must demonstrate that any errors made by the attorney would have made a difference in the outcome of the case.

The Supreme Court has emphasized that the burden of establishing a constitutional deficiency of action (or inaction) rests with the accused. This is an incredibly high bar to reach, and the likelihood of establishing both of these factors, and especially that the attorney's actions resulted in an unjustifiable conviction, may be very difficult. Reasonable people—including attorneys—often can disagree over the appropriate course of action in a given situation. In fact, someone once said that if you lined ten attorneys up end-to-end they would all point in different directions.

BOX 5.7   The Issue of Attorney Competence: The Case of Florida

J. R. Phelps, director of The Florida Bar's Law Office Management Assistance Service, issued the following statement concerning attorney competence in 2002:

> Few attorneys would argue with the statement—Law schools do not graduate competent practicing lawyers. Instead, law schools graduate persons with "technical competency," i.e., graduates who have mastered substantive legal principles and know "how to think like a lawyer." These skills, however, are only half of the "competency equation," which is equal parts technical substantive skills ("technical competency") and the ability to bring those skills to bear for the benefit of and to the satisfaction of a client ("performance competency"). It is this performance competency, the ability to communicate adequately with a client and then timely perform services so that reasonable client expectations are met, which is missing from too many lawyers' erudition as demonstrated by Florida Bar disciplinary statistics.

He concluded:

> Equal emphasis should be placed on educating lawyers about both parts of the competency equation. Proven law firm management skills should be taught to everyone who would proclaim to be a competent lawyer so they can truly function professionally and competently with their clients' interests foremost in mind. The existing infrastructure of the Bar's continuing legal education (technical competence) efforts can be easily and economically combined with training in the equally-as-important area of practice management (performance competence) to serve as a sound corollary to the Bar's current professionalism efforts. In this way, the competency equation can be leveraged to its full potential.

Source: Phelps (2002).

Attorney incompetence may be very difficult to define. In fact, it may be comparable to Justice Potter Stewart's note about pornography in the case of *Jacobellis v. Ohio*, 378 U.S. 184 (1964). He said he could not always define hard-core pornography, but he "knew it when he saw it." In the abstract we may not be able to define ineffective assistance of counsel, but we *may* recognize it when we see it. Box 5.7 presents the view of one state on the issue of attorney competence.

In a previous section I discussed the various methods by which we provide attorneys to indigent defendants in both state and federal courts. These methods stand in contrast to privately retaining an attorney. It is important to remember, at this point, that courts will not appoint attorneys to defendants who can afford their own, and the assumption on the part of most people is that you get more and better quality representation when you pay for your own lawyer. However, is that true? Research by the Bureau of Justice Statistics can help us answer that question.

In examining state case outcomes from 1996 and federal case outcomes from 1998, the Bureau of Justice Statistics found that just over 75 percent of state defendants with public attorneys pleaded guilty or were found guilty, and 77 percent of state defendants with private attorneys pleaded guilty or were found guilty. Among federal criminal defendants in 1998, 92 percent with public attorneys and 91 percent of federal defendants with private attorneys were either found guilty or pleaded guilty to their charges (Harlow 2000:1).

One area of difference between the two types of attorneys was the likelihood of incarceration. More defendants with court-appointed attorneys were sentenced to some period of incarceration. However, the statistics compiled for the BJS report also indicate that except for state drug charges, state and federal inmates received very similar sentences whatever the type of attorney representing them. Additionally, the report found that individuals with publicly funded attorneys were more likely to be charged with more serious offenses— especially violence and drug offenses—than were those represented by privately financed attorneys (Harlow 2000:1,3).

The conclusion that we can reach in this matter is that there is relatively little difference in case outcomes for defendants represented by court-appointed attorneys and those that hire their own lawyers. Regardless of the perception that some defendants have, indigent defenders do a reasonable job of providing legal counsel for their clients.

ATTORNEYS IN CIVIL CASES

In the United States there are relatively few attorneys who specialize in criminal law. As I have mentioned elsewhere, the fee structure and the clientele make a criminal law practice especially undesirable for many attorneys. What we do find, however, are many attorneys in private practice who only handle civil cases, or who handle a mixed criminal and civil caseload, with most of the cases being on the civil side.

There are several explanations for why the practice of civil law is more appealing to attorneys. First, much of the coursework offered in law school focuses on particular elements civil law (torts, realty, contracts, civil procedure, etc.) versus one or two courses that might deal with the whole of criminal law. Second, many attorneys find the practice of civil law more interesting and challenging. Civil cases often can involve complex issues that require a great deal of research and the use of expert witnesses to testify to the liability of one party versus another. Finally, as I frequently have noted, and its significance cannot be stressed enough, civil cases are more financially rewarding for attorneys. Since cases may be taken on a fee-contingent basis, a plaintiff's attorney stands to win one-third or more of whatever the client receives. This could involve anywhere from several thousand dollars to millions of dollars.

The next section discusses the types of clients that are involved in civil cases. From this you will see further the nature of civil law and the appeal of focusing a legal practice on these cases.

CIVIL LITIGANTS

Civil litigants can be defined as a group that "includes individuals, organizations, and government officials who are trying to settle disagreements and to regulate their own behavior and the behavior of others" (Vago 2009: 94–95). There are several ways to view the litigants who get involved in civil disputes. In this section I consider the parties in civil cases along two dimensions: (1) the frequency with which the parties appear in court, and (2) the number of parties involved in the dispute or the extensiveness of the controversy.

In terms of the frequency with which litigants appear in court, Galanter (1974) provides us with two helpful categories: "**one-shotters**" and "**repeat players.**" As should be apparent, the one-shotters are litigants (either individuals or groups) that file suit only once or very infrequently. They have an issue to resolve, and once their case is over they go on with their lives. Examples of one-shot litigants would be parties involved in a divorce or a person injured in an automobile accident.

By contrast, repeat players frequently have business in court. They file law suits often, typically as a result of the types of commerce in which they engage. Examples of these litigants would be banks and other lending institutions that sue to recover for losses from loan defaults (such as mortgages). Insurance companies and commercial real estate firms that rent apartments also may appear as repeat players in litigation.

The second dimension along which we can classify litigants is the number of people involved in the dispute. In simplest terms, does this case involve an individual or does it involve an organization? Vago (2009: 298–307) has developed a typology of litigants that can be illustrated by the following two-by-two table.

As Table 5.3 illustrates, there are some cases that have individuals as both plaintiffs and defendants (Cell 1). As I mentioned before, the one-shot type of cases that involve parties to a divorce are also examples of situations where both the plaintiff

TABLE 5.3	A Typology of Civil Litigants	
	Individual	Organization
Individual	1	2
Organization	3	4

Source: Adapted from Vago (2009: 298–307).

and the defendant are individuals. The second situation deals with an organization as the plaintiff and an individual as a defendant (Cell 2). These cases result from banks or other lending institutions suing homeowners for defaults on their mortgages, or credit card companies that sue cardholders for not paying their bills on time. In the third circumstance, an individual is the plaintiff and an organization is the defendant (Cell 3). Typical cases here might involve a tenant who sues the company that owns an apartment complex for failing to properly maintain the apartments. An individual also could be the plaintiff in a personal injury suit against a business such as a grocery store where there has been a slip-and-fall case, or when there has been a traffic accident and an individual sues the insurance company of the other party. A suit by a person over employment discrimination also would typify an individual-versus-an-organization type of case. Finally, organizations can be plaintiffs and defendants in some cases (Cell 4). One example of an organization-versus-organization case would be when a parts supplier sues a manufacturing corporation for breach of contract. Also, the United States government (as an organization) also might be a plaintiff in a case against a corporation over a restraint-of-trade issue. This too would be a Cell 4 case.

To conclude this section, plaintiffs and defendants in civil cases can appear in a variety of configurations. Some litigants file suit only once in a lifetime or, at most, a few times over many years. Others regularly appear in court. Some plaintiffs and defendants are individuals and others are organizations. In the end, however, the most likely winners are the repeat players that have the greatest courtroom experience or financial resources (Galanter 1974).

SUMMARY

Courts are living, breathing institutions that consist of a variety of people who serve in them on behalf of society. Some of the individuals who serve in the courts are there for relatively long periods of time. Others just temporarily join what we have identified as the courtroom work group.

Prosecuting attorneys may be the most powerful individuals serving in the courts today. They are at the center of what has been characterized as an "exchange system" (Cole 2004) and have interactions with judges, defense attorneys, police officers, the news media, and the general public. It is an office of considerable influence in that they hold the ultimate authority over whether to prosecute a case or not.

Standing in opposition to the prosecuting attorney are defense attorneys. Many criminal defendants in the United States cannot afford their own attorneys, so they are at the mercy of the courts to appoint a competent attorney for them. Appointed attorneys may be public defenders, assigned counsel, contract attorneys, members of legal aid societies, or law students getting clinical experience. Evidence has demonstrated that appointed attorneys provide a reasonable level of legal representation, though they often find it difficult to shake their image as sub-par lawyers.

In civil cases, attorneys often take cases with no up-front guarantee of getting paid. The contingency-based fee of much civil litigation presents something of a big risk–big reward situation. When plaintiffs win their cases, their attorneys get a share of the award. This can make the practice of civil law especially appealing to many private attorneys.

The litigants in civil cases can best be understood by examining them along two dimensions: the frequency with which they go to court, and the size of the group they represent. As we have seen, filing suit is a reasonably infrequent occurrence for most people (some people never file suit), while for others it is a regular event. Also, some litigants are individuals and some are organizations. This means that civil cases can be complex and prolonged forms of litigation.

QUESTIONS FOR CRITICAL THINKING

1. What do we mean by the term "courtroom work group?" Who are the "regular" members of this work group, and what do they have in common?

2. The prosecuting attorney has been described as the most powerful person in the criminal court process. Do you agree or disagree with this assessment? Why?

3. You have recently graduated from law school, passed the bar exam, and you have taken your first criminal case. One of your non-lawyer friends asks the following question: "How can you defend guilty people in court?" How do you answer that question?

4. List and describe some of the pressures that promote the practice of plea bargaining by defense attorneys.

5. Some research has found that court-appointed attorneys fare about as well with their clients as privately retained lawyers. If that is the case, why do court-appointed attorneys often suffer from image problems concerning their competence?

6. Why would many lawyers prefer to practice civil law versus criminal law? Are there truly many criminal law specialists available? If you wanted to find one, how would you go about it?

7. What do we mean when we talk about litigants being "one-shotters" versus "repeat players?" Can you think of an example of each of these types?

RECOMMENDED READINGS

Abadinsky, Howard. *Law and Justice: An Introduction to the American Legal System, 6th ed.* (2007). Upper Saddle River, NJ: Prentice Hall. Abadinsky looks at a variety of aspects of the justice system in the United States, not just the courts. He examines both civil and criminal justice, as well as the judicial process as it impacts juveniles. The book looks at a number of theories or perspectives of law, and discusses the process of legal education in the United States, as well as the actors within the courts.

Heinz, John P., Robert L. Nelson, Rebecca L. Sandefur, and Edward G. Laumann (2005). *Urban Lawyers: The New Social Structure of the Bar.* Chicago: University of Chicago Press. These authors recognize that certain fundamental changes in the practice of law in the city of Chicago have taken place. They begin by looking at a survey that was taken of Chicago lawyers in 1975 and compare the results with another survey completed in 1995. In their study they look at who the lawyers are, what they do, the nature of different law firms in the city, the career paths pursued, incomes, the quality of the lawyers' personal lives, and the levels of satisfaction with the practice of law. Heinz et al. recognize that there is stratification of the urban bar based on income, gender, race, and even religious background.

Iglesias, David, with Davin Seay (2008). *In Justice: Inside the Scandal that Rocked the Bush Administration.* Hoboken, NJ: John Wiley & Sons. In this book, Iglesias (with the assistance of David Seay), one of the U.S. attorneys fired by Attorney General Alberto Gonzales during the George W. Bush Administration, tells the story of how political considerations can enter into the ostensibly apolitical world of the United States attorneys. Iglesias details the events leading up to his dismissal, along with seven other U.S. attorneys in 2006. The book provides an insight into the ways in which national politics can trickle down to the local level and intrude into the world of federal prosecutions.

Lewis, Anthony (1964). *Gideon's Trumpet.* New York: Random House. Lewis, a New York newspaper reporter, wrote this brief book to tell the story of Clarence Earl Gideon and his case that eventually reached the United States Supreme Court. Gideon was denied an attorney by a Florida judge, and after he was convicted he filed his own appeal to the Supreme Court. The attorney that argued his case before the Court (Abe Fortas) later himself became an Associate Supreme Court justice. The book provides the fascinating background story of one of the most significant cases ever to be decided by the Supreme Court.

KEY TERMS

assigned counsel system
barristers
case screening
contract defenders
indigent defendants
legal aid societies

legal clinics
one-shotters
panel attorneys
pro bono
prosecuting attorney
public defender

repeat players
right to counsel
solicitors
state attorney general
United States Attorneys
voucher system

REFERENCES

Abadinsky, Howard. *Law and Justice: An Introduction to the American Legal System,* 6th ed. (2007). Upper Saddle River, NJ: Prentice Hall.

American Bar Association (2010a). ABA-approved Law Schools. http://www.abanet.org/legaled/approvedlawschools/approved.html.

American Bar Association (2010b). Lawyer Demographics. http://new.abanet.org/marketresearch/PublicDocuments/Lawyer_Demographics.pdf.

Argersinger v. Hamlin, 407 U.S. 25 (1972).

Betts v. Brady, 316 U.S. 455 (1942).

Biskupic, Joan (2009). High Court Weighs Lawsuit against Prosecutors. *USA Today*, November 5, 2009, p. 2A.

Blumberg, Abraham S. (2004). The Practice of Law as a Confidence Game. In *The Criminal Justice System: Politics and Policies*, 9th ed., ed. George F. Cole, Marc G. Gertz, and Amy Bunger, 211–26. Belmont, CA: Wadsworth Publishing Co.

Bureau of Labor Statistics (2010). *Occupational Outlook Handbook, 2010–11*. Washington, DC: U.S. Department of Labor. http://www.bls.gov/oco/ocos053.htm.

Carp, Robert A., Ronald Stidham, and Kenneth L. Manning (2007). *Judicial Process in America*, 7th ed. Washington, DC: CQ Press.

Cole, George F. (2004). The Decision to Prosecute. In *The Criminal Justice System: Politics and Policies*, 9th ed., ed. George F. Cole, Marc G. Gertz, and Amy Bunger, 178–88. Belmont, CA: Wadsworth Publishing Co.

Cole, George F., Marc G. Gertz, and Amy Bunger, eds. (2004). *The Criminal Justice System: Politics and Policies*, 9th ed. Belmont, CA: Wadsworth Publishing Co.

Connelly, Michael (2005). *The Lincoln Lawyer*. New York: Little, Brown and Co.

DeFrances, Carol J. (2001). *State-funded Indigent Defense Services, 1999*. Washington, DC: U.S. Department of Justice.

DeFrances, Carol J., and Marika F. X. Litras (2000). *Indigent Defense Services in Large Counties, 1999*. Washington, DC: Bureau of Justice Statistics, U.S. Department of Justice.

Galanter, Marc (1974). Why the "Haves:" Come Out Ahead: Speculations on the Limits of Legal Change. *Law & Society Review* 9(1): 95–160.

Gideon v. Wainwright, 372 U.S. 335 (1963).

Hanson, Roger A., and Brian J. Ostrom (2004). Indigent Defenders Get the Job Done and Done Well. In *The Criminal Justice System: Politics and Policies*, 9th ed., ed. George F. Cole, Marc G. Gertz, and Amy Bunger, 227–50. Belmont, CA: Wadsworth Publishing Co.

Harlow, Caroline Wolf (2000). *Defense Counsel in Criminal Cases*. Washington, DC: Bureau of Justice Statistics, U.S. Department of Justice.

Heinz, John P., and Edward Laumann (1982). *Chicago Lawyers: The Social Structure of the Bar*, rev. ed. Evanston, IL: Northwestern University Press (in association with the American Bar Foundation).

Iglesias, David (2007). Why I Was Fired. *New York Times*, March 21. http://www.nytimes.com/2007/03/21/opinion/21iglesias.html.

Jacobellis v. Ohio, 378 U.S. 184 (1964).

Langton, Lynn, and Donald J. Farole, Jr. (2009). *Public Defender Offices, 2007—Statistical Tables*. Washington, DC: Bureau of Justice Statistics, U.S. Department of Justice.

Law School Admission Council (2010). http://www.lsac.org.

Lewis, Anthony (1964). *Gideon's Trumpet*. New York: Random House.

Longley, Robert (2007). About the United States Attorneys. http://usgovinfo.about.com/od/uscourtsystem/a/usattorneys.htm?p=1.

Melone, Albert P., and Allan Karnes (2008). *The American Legal System: Perspectives, Politics, Processes, and Policies*, 2nd ed. Lanham, MD: Rowman & Littlefield Publishers.

Miller v. Pate, 386 U.S. 1 (1967).

Orvis, Gregory P. (2002). Defense Counsel Systems. In *Encyclopedia of Crime and Punishment,* ed. David Levinson, 485–89. Thousand Oaks, CA: Sage Publications.

Perry, Steven W. (2006). *Prosecutors in State Courts, 2005*. Washington, DC: U.S. Department of Justice.

Phelps, J.R. (2002). What Does "Competent Representation" Really Mean? *The Florida Bar News*, March 1. http://www.floridabar.org/divcom/jn/jnnews01.nsf/8c9f13012b96763985256aa90062 4829/7aab34d8689c2423852574f900763606!OpenDocument.

Pottawattamie County, Iowa et al. v. McGhee et al. 129 S.Ct. 2002, 173 L.Ed. 2d 1083 (2009).

Powell v. Alabama, 287 U.S. 45 (1932).

Smith, Christopher E. (1991). *Courts and the Poor*. Chicago: Nelson-Hall Publishers.

Strickland v. Washington, 466 U.S. 668 (1984).

Subin, Harry I. (2002). The Criminal Lawyer's Different Mission: Reflections on the "Right" to Present a False Case. In *Crime & Justice in America,* 2nd ed., ed. Wilson Palacios, Paul F. Cromwell and Roger G. Dunham, 262–66. Upper Saddle River, NJ: Prentice Hall.

United States v. Cronic, 466 U.S. 648 (1984).

United States v. Wade, 388 U.S. 218 (1968).

U.S. Department of Justice (2008). *An Investigation into the Removal of Nine U.S. Attorneys in 2006.* Washington, DC: Offices of the Inspector General and Professional Responsibility.

U.S. Department of Justice (2009). United States Attorneys Mission Statement. http://www.justice. gov/usao/.

Uphoff, Rodney J. (2009). The Criminal Defense Lawyer: Zealous Advocate, Double Agent, or Beleaguered Dealer? In *Courts and Justice*, 4th ed., ed. G. Larry Mays and Peter R. Gregware, 332–65. Long Grove, IL: Waveland Press.

Vago, Steven (2009). *Law & Society*, 9th ed. Upper Saddle River, NJ: Pearson/Prentice Hall.

Walker, Samuel. (2006). *Sense and Nonsense About Crime and Drugs*, 6th ed. Belmont, CA: Wadsworth Publishing Co.

Worden, Alissa Pollitz (2009). Privatizing Due Process: Issues in the Comparison of Assigned Counsel, Public Defender, and Contracted Indigent Defense Systems. In *Courts and Justice*, 4th ed., ed. G. Larry Mays and Peter R. Gregware, 366–92. Long Grove, IL: Waveland Press.

ENDNOTES

[1] These states are Alaska, Arkansas, Colorado, Connecticut, Delaware, Hawaii, Iowa, Kentucky, Maryland, Massachusetts, Minnesota, Missouri, Montana, New Hampshire, New Jersey, New Mexico, North Dakota, Rhode Island, Vermont, Virginia, Wisconsin, and Wyoming.

[2] The states with county-operated public defender offices are Alabama, Arizona, California, Florida, Georgia, Idaho, Illinois, Indiana, Kansas, Louisiana, Michigan, Mississippi, Nebraska, Nevada, New York, North Carolina, Ohio, Oklahoma, Oregon, Pennsylvania, South Carolina, South Dakota, Tennessee, Texas, Utah, Washington, and West Virginia.

6

Jurors, Witnesses, and Others in the Judicial Process

Photo source: AP Images

INTRODUCTION

There are a number of ways that the general public can interact with the courts and the judicial process. They might be victims of crime, requiring their presence during the trial and at other hearings. They also might be the plaintiff or defendant in a civil case. However, it is most likely that members of the public will participate in the judicial process in one of two significant ways: either as members of a jury or as witnesses to some event that requires them to testify in court. This chapter explores the constitutional right to a jury trial, the nature of jury service in the United States, the various types of witnesses that might appear in court, and their differing functions, and those people who regularly appear in the courtroom but who remain somewhat outside of the core of the courtroom work group like security personnel, court clerks and administrators, court reporters, and interpreters or translators.

I begin the discussion of jurors with consideration of the constitutional right to a jury trial. Next I examine the individuals who serve as jurors in our courts. Each year many people get called to jury service in local, state, and federal courts, and this experience often can leave a lasting impression about the courts and the functions they serve in our society.

THE RIGHT TO A JURY TRIAL

In order to remember it easily, many think of the Sixth Amendment of the United States Constitution as the trial amendment. Among other protections provided by the Sixth

Amendment, it guarantees that "In all criminal prosecutions, the accused shall enjoy the right to a speedy and public trial, by an impartial jury of the State and district wherein the crime shall have been committed."

There are two very important points that should be noted about this provision in the Sixth Amendment. First, this right originally was applied to federal cases, but it was extended by the Supreme Court to state prosecutions by way of the Fourteenth Amendment (see, for example, *Duncan v. Louisiana*, 391 U.S. 145 [1968]). Second, the Sixth Amendment makes no provision for juries in civil cases. That right is spelled out in the Seventh Amendment, which says that "In suits at common law, where the value in controversy shall exceed twenty dollars, the right of trial by jury shall be preserved…." Again, this guarantee applies to federal courts and federal cases, and here the Supreme Court has never extended this right to the states. Nevertheless, most states have provisions in their constitutions or statutes that provide the right to a jury trial in most civil matters.

Having explained the constitutional basis for the right to a jury trial, it is essential to note that there are some exceptions to this guarantee (in addition to that of civil cases). For example, in the case of *McKeiver v. Pennsylvania*, 403 U.S. 528 (1971) the U.S. Supreme Court refused to extend the constitutional right to trial by jury to juvenile delinquency proceedings. In writing for a six-member majority, Associate Justice Harry Blackmun noted that the Supreme Court had never completely labeled juvenile court proceedings as criminal prosecutions. Additionally, "one cannot say that in our legal system the jury is a necessary component of accurate factfinding. There is much to be said for it, to be sure, but we have been content to pursue other ways for determining facts. Juries are not required, and have not been, for example, in equity cases, in workmen's compensation, in probate, or in deportation cases. Neither have they been generally used in military trials" (403 U.S. 544). He added that "There is a possibility, at least, that the jury trial, if required as a matter of constitutional precept, will remake the juvenile proceeding into a fully adversary process and will put an effective end to what has been the idealistic prospect of an intimate, informal protective proceeding" (403 U.S. 546). In summary, the Court held that "If the formalities of the criminal adjudicative process are to be superimposed upon the juvenile court system, there is little need for its separate existence. Perhaps that ultimate disillusionment will come one day, but for the moment we are disinclined to give impetus to it" (403 U.S. 529). The Supreme Court's decision in *McKeiver* allowed states to provide jury trials for juveniles, either constitutionally or by statute, but it did not require them to do so as a matter of guarantee under the United States Constitution. Today about a dozen states make provisions for jury trials in delinquency proceedings (Gardner 2009:238; Mays and Winfree 2006:23).

In addition to juvenile cases, juries are not mandated in petty offense cases (see *Duncan v. Louisiana*, 391 U.S. 145 [1968]). While there is no exact definition, generally the courts have decided that any crime that provides for incarceration of less than six months is a petty offense. What about situations where someone is charged with multiple petty offenses, each of which could result in a jail term of less than six months? The U.S. Supreme Court decided in *Lewis v. United States*, 518 U.S. 322 (1996) that defendants do not have a constitutional right to a jury trial in these situations. Therefore, while there is a broadly based constitutional right to a trial by jury, this right does not extend to all courts and all situations.

BOX 6.1

In Their Own Words: The Purpose of a Jury

In the United States Supreme Court case of *Taylor v. Louisiana*, 419 U.S. 522 (1975), Associate Justice Byron White, writing for an 8–1 majority, stated his perspective on the purpose of the jury. White said that "The purpose of a jury is to guard against the exercise of arbitrary power—to make available the commonsense judgment of the community as a hedge against the overzealous or mistaken prosecutor and in preference to the professional or perhaps over-conditioned or biased response of a judge" (419 U.S. 531). Thus, whatever the flaws and shortcomings associated with the jury system in the United States, in the end it is designed to protect every citizen who stands accused of a crime.

Source: *Taylor v. Louisiana*, 419 U.S. 522 (1975).

JURORS AND JURY SERVICE

As will be seen in Chapter 7, relatively few civil or criminal cases involve a jury trial. As Levine (2002:964) notes, "Either the case is settled before a jury is seated, or it is settled at some point during the trial, ending participation of the jury." Nevertheless, some cases make it to court, and some of these involve the utilization of **petit juries** or simply trial juries.

Most people hold one of two attitudes toward jury service. For some not only is it a civic obligation, but also it is an honor and privilege to serve on a jury. For others, being summoned to jury service is a hassle and a disruption of their daily lives and schedules. Some are glad to serve and others dread it and try their best to get out of jury service (see Kassin and Wrightsman 1988). In this section I examine the ways states go about calling people for jury service, and in the following subsection I discuss the actual jury selection process.

AGE QUALIFICATIONS

In some ways, jury service is looked upon as a universal obligation of citizenship in the United States. However, the history of courts in this country demonstrates that not everyone has been considered qualified for jury service, and some states have maintained exemptions for certain categories of individuals and occupations. For instance, traditionally states have excluded persons from jury service who have not reached the age of majority, and this continues to be the case. This meant that historically individuals under the age of twenty-one were not qualified to serve on juries. However, when the Congress passed the Twenty-sixth Amendment to the Constitution and the states ratified it on July 1, 1971, the voting age nationwide was reduced from twenty-one to eighteen. As a result of this change, most states also made eighteen the age of majority,

TABLE 6.1	Age Requirements and Limitations for Jury Service

Minimum Age

18—AK, AZ, AR, CA, CO, CT, DE, FL, GA, HI, ID, IL, IN, IA, KS, KY, LA, ME, MD, MA, MI, MN, MT, NV, NH, NJ, NM, NY, NC, ND, OH, OK, OR, PA, RI, SC, SD, TN, TX, UT, VT, VA, WA, WV, WI, WY (forty-six states plus the District of Columbia and Puerto Rico)

19—AL, NE

21—MS, MO

Maximum Age

65—IN, MS, NE, NC, SC, TN, WV

70—AK, CT, FL, GA, ID, LA, MD, MA, MI, MN, NV, NH, OR, TX, VA

72—WY

75—NJ

All other states have no maximum age stipulation.

Source: Rottman and Strickland (2006:218–21).

and this in turn qualified eighteen-, nineteen-, and twenty-year-olds to serve on juries. Table 6.1 shows the minimum and maximum ages for jury service in each state.

OTHER REQUIREMENTS FOR JURORS

States not only prescribe age restrictions, but other stipulations may be imposed as well. For instance, every state requires that potential jurors be citizens of the United States. Also, nearly every state requires that jurors must be able to read, speak, and understand English (Rottman and Strickland 2006:221). The exceptions to this requirement are Arkansas (where the judge may waive the requirement), Massachusetts (where potential jurors do not have to read English), New Mexico (where by state constitutional mandate jurors are not required to read, speak, or write either English or Spanish), and West Virginia (where American Sign Language is acceptable in place of spoken English).

FACTORS THAT DISQUALIFY POTENTIAL JURORS

Another condition placed on jury service is that individuals who have been convicted of a felony are disqualified from jury service. This stipulation arises out of court rulings such as the Virginia case of *Ruffin v. Commonwealth* 62 Va. 790 (1871), which held that convicted offenders become slaves of the state and, as such, they suffer a form of **civil death** (see Mays and Winfree 2009:302). In simplest terms, the notion of civil death means that convicted offenders (especially felons) lose a number of their rights of citizenship, including the right to vote, hold office, or be licensed for certain professions.

Today every state except Colorado disqualifies convicted felons from jury service. However, over one-third of the states allow convicted felons to vote if they have been pardoned, if their civil rights have been restored, or if some length of time has passed since conviction of the felony (seven or ten years, for example). Additionally, a few states include specific crimes that may or may not be felonies but still disqualify a person from jury service. Examples include people who have been convicted of crimes involving moral turpitude (Alabama), malfeasance in office (California and Montana), or "other infamous offenses" (Nevada and Tennessee). Perhaps the most unusual disqualifiers come from the State of Mississippi, where "bootleggers, habitual drunkards, and common gamblers" also are prevented from serving on juries (Rottman and Strickland 2006:219).

The final set of disqualifiers really should be classified as exemptions. These involve certain professions that have been excused from jury service by state legislatures. Twenty-six states offer no blanket exemptions from jury service based on a person's occupation. The other twenty-four states allow for exemptions for such diverse groups as judicial officers (including judges and court clerks), public officials, elected legislators, medical personnel (physicians, pharmacists, nurses, and dentists), attorneys, active duty military personnel, members of the clergy, firefighters, veterinarians, law enforcement personnel (including police officers, sheriff's officers, jailers, and probation/parole officers), sole proprietors of businesses, and certified public accountants. Some of these seem reasonable to exclude from jury service, but others seem somewhat unusual and puzzling.

BOX 6.2
Juries in Russia

Under the old Soviet system (prior to the fall of Communism in the 1980s), court cases in Russia were tried before a professional judge and two "people's assessors." In most instances the assessors agreed with the decision of the professional judge.

After the USSR dissolved and the loosely formed Commonwealth of Independent States emerged, there was a call for a more "democratic" legal system, one that employed twelve-person juries like those of many Western nations. Legal reforms within Russia resulted in juries being used in some jurisdictions, but the practice was not universally embraced. In fact, as a result of the acquittal of a group of Chechen rebels, the Russian parliament voted in 2008 to prohibit the use of juries in cases involving participation in "illegal armed units, violent seizure of power, armed rebellion and mass riots" (Amsterdam 2008). These cases are to be tried by judges.

Some observers have noted that the conviction rate in Russian courts using juries has gone from 100 percent to 80 to 90 percent, much in line with many other nations including the United States. This change is not completely welcomed, and while the use of juries in Russia is much more common now than in the past, it still does not have the wide acceptance that is witnessed in other countries.

Sources: Amsterdam (2008); Feofanov and Berry (1996:289–92).

BOX 6.3

In Their Own Words: Jury Trials

The case of *Duncan v. Louisiana* (1968) raised an interesting question for the U.S. Supreme Court: Does the right to trial by jury, stipulated in the Sixth Amendment to the Constitution, apply to state criminal proceedings and, if so, to which ones? Associate Justice Byron White, writing for a seven-member majority, said that

> The claim before us is that the right to trial by jury guaranteed by the Sixth Amendment meets these tests [of fundamental fairness]. The position of Louisiana, on the other hand, is that the Constitution imposes upon the States no duty to give a jury trial in any criminal case, regardless of the seriousness of the crime or the size of the punishment which may be imposed. Because we believe that trial by jury in criminal cases is fundamental to the American scheme of justice, we hold that the Fourteenth Amendment guarantees a right of jury trial in all criminal cases which—were they to be tried in a federal court—would come within the Sixth Amendment's guarantee. (391 U.S. 150).

In its opinion, the Court made it clear that the Sixth Amendment applied to state criminal prosecutions by way of the Due Process Clause of the Fourteenth Amendment. However, part of the dilemma in *Duncan* was whether this right applied to so-called "petty offenses." While the Supreme Court refused to draw a bright line between petty and serious offenses, it concluded in this case that "a crime punishable by two years in prison is, based on past and contemporary standards in this country, a serious crime and not a petty offense" (391 U.S. 163).

Source: *Duncan v. Louisiana*, 391 U.S. 145 (1968).

Additionally, before women earned the right to vote in the early 1900s, they too were routinely excluded from jury service (often because it was thought that their obligations in the home were more significant than their value to jury service). Currently no state automatically excludes women from jury service. However, it is important to note that in the process of selecting a jury, judges may exclude those individuals who assert that jury service would cause them "undue hardship [or] extreme inconvenience" or because of "public necessity or mental disability" (Rottman and Strickland 2006:213).

JURY SELECTION

States sometimes provide—by way of their constitutions or by statute—that the jury should be composed of a person's "**peers**." This word has a different meaning in a legal context versus how it might be used in a sociological setting. For instance, in sociology we might say that a person's peers are those individuals who are similar in age, social setting, group context, income, education, etc. By contrast, in a legal setting, peers are simply those who are qualified to serve as jurors. They may or may not (and in all likelihood probably do not) resemble the criminal defendant.

How, then, do we go about assembling a group of peers for jury service? The simplest answer to this question is through the use of **master lists** or **master wheels** (Levine 2002:965). These devices are employed to assemble the lists from which potential jurors will be drawn. In simplest terms, a master list is a compilation of all of those persons within a jurisdiction that are qualified for jury service (see Levine 2002:964–70). The master list will incorporate those individuals who are qualified to serve on juries, as well as exclude those who are not qualified or who are exempted from service for some reason. Each state has a slightly different process, but most fall into one of a handful of patterns, and many states use multiple sources of information to prepare the jury service master lists.

Forty states use voter registration roles as one source of information for compiling master lists for jury service. Additionally, forty-one states use the lists of registered drivers (with a minimum age of eighteen as a disqualifier), and fifteen states use tax rolls (typically property taxpayers) to supplement the lists of eligible persons for jury service. Other potential sources include city or country directories, motor vehicle registrations, telephone directories, and utility customers. Finally, three states (Maine, New Mexico, and Oklahoma) accept volunteers for jury service (Rottman and Strickland 2006:218–22).

The use of multiple data sources has become crucial for most states for at least two reasons. First, some states have been hard-pressed to assemble enough potential jurors for the number of trials scheduled. Second, some lists discriminate against certain categories of people. As an illustration, property tax rolls may not include those people who rent rather than own their own homes, and the lists of motor vehicle registrations and licensed drivers may exclude a significant portion of people who are disabled or who for some other reason do not drive. Therefore, the more lists that states can draw from, the more likely they are to include all qualified persons in the list of those summoned for jury service.

From the master lists, groups of potential jurors will be contacted and notified when and where they should report for jury service. These groups are know as the **venire**, and from this assemblage a jury plus alternates are chosen (Champion 2005:260; Levine 2002:965).

Before we leave the topic of juries, there are three other items that must be addressed. The first has to do with the office or individual responsible for summoning prospective jurors. The second deals with the frequency with which a person can be called for jury service, and the third is concerned with dismissal of individuals during the jury selection process.

COURT CLERKS AND/OR JURY COMMISSIONERS

In most jurisdictions in the United States, one of two groups is responsible for assembling the master lists and for summoning people for jury service. In some states these responsibilities fall on the county **court clerks** who come to their positions in different ways depending on state law (see Mays and Taggart 1986). In some states court clerks are elected, and this is a major county-wide office. The clerk may have court-related responsibilities such as maintaining court records, setting dockets, and summoning prospective jurors.

Other jurisdictions have moved toward the use of **jury commissioners** to deal with jury-related functions. These individuals may be appointed by the courts to oversee the responsibility of assembling the master lists and of coordinating with the judges (and possibly also the court clerks) to schedule enough potential jurors to meet the demands of the upcoming court trials. While they both may have jury-related responsibilities, one factor that typically distinguishes jury commissioners from court clerks is that jury commissioners have duties specifically focused on juries, and they do not have the additional responsibilities often associated with the office of court clerk, which often involves more interaction with the judges.

FREQUENCY OF JURY SERVICE

Since many people consider jury service to be a disruption of their normal routines, states try to minimize personal inconvenience in order to encourage more people to serve—or, alternately—to minimize the number of people who seek to be excused from jury service. Fourteen states provide that it must have been at least one year since the last time a person was called for jury service; fourteen states allow a two-year period between jury service; ten allow a three-year break; and two provide four years between summonses for service. The remaining states have various stipulations depending on whether a person actually was seated on a jury and the number of days (or trials) for which a person was summoned (Rottman and Strickland 2006:218–21).

EXCUSALS AT THE TIME OF TRIAL

In Chapter 7 you will see that one of the first functions that must be performed as a trial is set to begin is to pick the jury. No one knows for sure why, and the Supreme Court has labeled it an "historical accident," but juries in England and later in the United States traditionally have been composed of twelve members (Kalven and Zeisel 1966; *Williams v. Florida*, 1970). When we examine trial processes we see that some states use smaller juries, and some allow for non-unanimous verdicts. However, in most cases, depending on the nature of the trial, normally between thirty-six and forty-eight potential jurors will be assembled in order to get a jury of twelve with one or two alternates. In particularly sensational cases, even more people will be summoned for jury service.

The judge, the prosecuting attorney, and the defense attorney will begin the jury selection process of questioning potential jurors about their backgrounds and knowledge of the case at hand. This process is known as the *voir dire*, a term that means to speak the truth (Champion 2005:264). In most jurisdictions, when individuals are called for jury service they are required to complete and submit in advance a biographical document that details their place of residence, occupation, age, gender, education, and a number of other key pieces of information. These forms are made available to the attorneys before the jury selection process begins, and the lawyers for both sides have the opportunity to ask potential jurors about information contained in these biographical documents.

Before the questioning begins the attorneys understand that they have two possible ways to exclude people from the final jury. The first way is through **challenges for cause**. In reality, there is only one possible cause: prejudice or prejudging the case for either side, the facts of the case, the attorneys, or the defendant. There is no limit on the number of potential jurors that can be excused (or struck) for cause. However, when one of the attorneys asserts this as the justification for excusal, the judge still must be convinced that this person is unacceptable.

The second possible way jurors can be excused is through the use of **peremptory challenges**, which are available in limited numbers to each attorney. With peremptory challenges the attorneys do not have to provide a justification to the judge concerning why the person should be excused. It may be based on something the individual said in the process of being questioned, or it may be a nagging feeling that this person is just not suitable for jury service or not the right person for the present case. At times attorneys may go with a "gut hunch" that the person holds an unspoken bias, or that during questioning this individual was not attentive enough.

While the use of peremptory challenges would seem to give attorneys wide latitude in excluding people from jury service, this ability is not without its limits. For instance, in the case of *Batson v. Kentucky*, 476 U.S. 79 (1986) the U.S. Supreme Court said that attorneys (and particularly prosecutors) cannot use their peremptory challenges in a racially discriminatory way. In *Batson*, the defendant was African American, and the "prosecutor used his peremptory challenges to strike all four black persons on the venire, and a jury of only white persons was selected" (79). Box 6.4 contains an excerpt from the conclusion of the Supreme Court's majority opinion.

States vary in the number of peremptory challenges they allow, and the range may be different for civil cases versus criminal cases, and for courts of limited jurisdiction versus courts of general trial jurisdiction. As an example, in civil cases states may allow as few as one or two peremptory challenges per side, up to as many as six or eight (three, four, and six being the most common numbers). By contrast, for felony cases states allow anywhere from three or six up to twelve or even twenty (in California) peremptory challenges per side (see Rottman and Strickland 2006:228–31). In capital cases the numbers typically are even greater and range from eight or ten up to twenty or twenty-five because of pretrial publicity, the seriousness of the charges, and the potential consequences of a conviction.

To illustrate something of the number of people called for jury duty in a given year, Table 6.2 shows how many people were summoned for federal jury service from 2004 to 2008 and the numbers selected; challenged; and not selected, serving, or challenged.

As this table shows, the assembling of potential jurors for federal trials is a monumental task, and there are even more trials scheduled in state courts. Additionally, roughly six in ten of those called for jury duty are chosen, and about two in ten are challenged for various reasons.

BOX 6.4   In Their Own Words:
Peremptory Challenges and Race

Associate Justice Lewis Powell wrote the majority opinion for seven members of the Supreme Court in the *Batson v. Kentucky* case. In his conclusion he asserted that:

> While we recognize, of course, that the peremptory challenge occupies an important position in our trial procedures, we do not agree that our decision today will undermine the contribution the challenge generally makes to the administration of justice. The reality of practice, amply reflected in many state and federal court opinions, shows that the challenge may be, and unfortunately at times has been, used to discriminate against black jurors. By requiring trial courts to be sensitive to the racially discriminatory use of peremptory challenges, our decision enforces the mandate of equal protection and furthers the ends of justice. In view of the heterogeneous population of our Nation, public respect for our criminal justice system and the rule of law will be strengthened if we ensure that no citizen is disqualified from jury service because of his race.

Source: *Batson v. Kentucky*, 476 U.S. 79, 98–99 (1986).

The ultimate goal of each attorney is to pick the "best" jury possible, and this subjective definition implies the jury panel that is the most favorable to whichever side. The reality, however, is that after both the attorneys and the judges have had an opportunity to question potential jurors, the people who are obviously most likely favorable to the other side get eliminated. In this way a "neutral" jury gets seated by default.

JUROR DUTIES

In this final section on jurors I address the functions that jurors perform, along with technical considerations of jury size and the question of unanimity in decision making. I return to the issues of jury size and unanimity again in Chapter 7 when I examine the trial process.

JUROR FUNCTIONS

At the most fundamental level, juries are required to do one thing during a trial: They must carefully listen to all of the evidence presented and then decide what the truth is. Often, arriving at the truth involves choosing between two contradictory and mutually exclusive stories. In such cases jurors may describe their jobs as choosing the story that makes the most sense. In legal terms, the jury is responsible for deciding the facts in a case. This stands in contrast to the duty of the judge, who must decide the law.

TABLE 6.2	Jury Service in Federal District Courts, 2004–2008			
Years	Total jurors available	Percent selected	Percent challenged	Percent not selected, serving, or challenged
2004	607,673	60.1	20.5	19.4
2005	612,032	60.0	20.5	19.4
2006	579,706	59.4	20.5	20.2
2007	554,193	58.6	21.4	20.0
2008	544,565	58.0	21.7	20.3

Source: Pastore and Maguire (2009).

Once a jury is chosen, the members are sworn in by the judge with an oath to discharge their duties in a careful and lawful manner. Most jurisdictions do not allow jurors to take notes, and this requires jurors to pay particular attention to each witness and the testimony and physical evidence presented at the trial (McKeon 2005).[1] Box 6.5 includes one judge's observations on how his opinion had changed about allowing jurors to take notes.

One of the emerging problems facing courts today is the increasing use of social media such as Facebook and Twitter by jurors. In fact, cases have already started to appear where judges have asked for cell phone records from sitting jurors who may have discussed a case or the jury deliberations with outsiders on their Facebook pages, and the Florida Supreme Court is trying to limit social media use by jurors (Freeman 2010).

At the conclusion of all testimony and after both sides rest their cases and the attorneys have completed their closing arguments, the judge presents a charge to the jury. This involves a description of all of the legal considerations the jury must consider. Typically, the instructions to the jury include a description of guilt beyond a reasonable doubt (in criminal cases), as well as an explanation of any defenses (like entrapment, necessity, or alibi) that may have been introduced. Civil cases have similar instructions that judges also provide to jurors.

Once the jury receives its instructions, it retires to the jury room to begin deliberations. The first order of business in most instances is the election of the foreperson. In reality, this individual has no more authority than any other juror, but the position may imply something of the perceived status of this person. The foreperson presides over jury deliberations and, after a verdict is reached, delivers the verdict documents to the court clerk and judge.

After selecting a foreperson, many juries immediately take a preliminary vote (sometimes called a straw poll) to see where they are in the deliberation process. If all of the members agree on the defendant's guilt or innocence, they may continue to discuss the case for a little while just so it does not appear that their decision was in haste.

BOX 6.5
In the News: Allowing Jurors to Take Notes

Historically, judges have not allowed jurors to take notes during a trial. Some of them felt that it was distracting to see jurors scribbling notes when something was said in court, and others thought that it kept jurors from focusing on both what witnesses were saying and how they looked when they testified. One such judge was Michael McKeon, a trial court judge in New York State. As the following quote shows, he has since changed his mind:

> As one of 50 judges from New York selected by Judge Judith Kaye, chief judge of the Court of Appeals, to study innovative jury practices, I agreed to experiment with several innovations, including note taking by jurors. As a result of my experience, I am convinced that it is a much better practice to allow jurors to take notes than not.

> Much to my surprise, my opinion changed not because the data from the 91 jury trials which allowed note taking seemed to prove that jurors can take notes and pay attention at the same time, but rather because of a comment made to me by one juror.

> After one criminal trial, while handing out juror questionnaires designed to record the thoughts and comments on innovations used during the trial, one juror thanked me for allowing her to take notes. She went on to say that in order for her to process, understand and retain information, it was necessary for her to take notes.

> She further related that had she not been able to take notes, her effectiveness as a juror would have been seriously compromised in that she would have been put in a position to make a decision on guilt or innocence based on an incomplete recollection of the facts and the law to be applied to the case.

Source: McKeon (2005).

Then they notify the bailiff, who notifies the judge that a verdict has been reached. In some states the jury foreperson signs the verdict documents and may be the only jury member whose name is associated with any court records. A few states still allow the foreperson the option of reading the verdict in court, compared with other states where the judge performs this function. Finally, in the State of Oklahoma, in cases in which the death penalty is imposed, the jury foreperson's name actually appears on the death warrant.

The two following sections examine the issues of jury size and unanimity, since both of these factors may have an influence on the decision making process. I discuss these two factors further in Chapter 7.

JURY SIZE

The traditional size for trial juries in both civil and criminal cases has been twelve members. No one knows for certain how this number was arrived at, but somewhere back in the distant past this was the number that emerged in England, and the United States (and many other common law countries) have chosen to use this number as well. Having said that, it is important to note that today thirty-three states make specific constitutional or statutory provisions for the use of less than twelve-person juries in some instances. For example, Florida was one of the first states to use six-person juries in felony cases that did not involve the death penalty (*Williams v. Florida*, 1970). Other states have followed suit in criminal cases, and several states and the federal government now routinely use six-person juries in civil cases (see Waters 2004). Furthermore, six-person juries may be employed for serious misdemeanor cases (such as drunk driving cases), as well as for juvenile cases in states such as New Mexico that permit jury trials for juveniles in delinquency matters (*New Mexico Statutes Annotated* 32A-2-16, 2010).

The United States Supreme Court has sanctioned the use of juries with fewer than twelve members. However, while the Supreme Court has never definitively ruled on the issue, in cases that involve capital punishment the Court has suggested that since all states require twelve-person juries in death penalty cases, these more than likely should continue to be utilized (see Justice White's majority opinion in *Williams v. Florida* [1970]).

To date the research on jury size has established one very important fact: Smaller juries save jurisdictions time and money in the jury selection process. More juries can be seated from the same venires when there are six-person juries compared with twelve-person juries. This also might make jurors serve on fewer cases or for fewer jury days, and this could make jury service more palatable to more people called for jury duty. However, there are lingering issues about smaller juries. For example, research has demonstrated that smaller juries are less likely to be truly representative of the communities they serve. This may mean smaller groups of minorities seated as jurors. Additionally, there is concern over juror dynamics in the decision making process with smaller juries. Smaller groups might be able to put more pressure on holdout jurors. Nevertheless, today roughly two-thirds of the states (plus the federal government) make some provision for the use of smaller than twelve-person juries (Waters 2004).

JURY UNANIMITY

Just as the use of twelve-person juries has been traditional, the requirement that verdicts must be unanimous also is traditional. Some observers believe that a unanimous verdict is one way to quantify guilt beyond a reasonable doubt. This means that the prosecuting attorney must convince all members of the jury of the defendant's guilt, while the defense attorney must simply convince one who will hold out for acquittal. However, if there is a **hung jury** (that is, they cannot come to a unanimous verdict), the judge has the option of dismissing the charges or of scheduling the case for retrial.

While the requirement of unanimous verdicts is still found in most jurisdictions in the United States, there are some states that allow for non-unanimous verdicts (see, for example, *Apodaca v. Oregon*, 406 U.S. 404 [1972] and *Johnson v. Louisiana*, 406 U.S. 356 [1972]). The U.S. Supreme Court has spoken on this issue, and it has sanctioned the use of divided verdicts of 10-2 and 9-3.

However, there are limits on when and where non-unanimous verdicts can be accepted. The first major limitation is that all states require unanimous verdicts in death penalty cases. Also, the Supreme Court has said in the case of *Burch v. Louisiana*, 441 U.S. 130 (1979) that when states use smaller juries—such as six-person juries—unanimous verdicts should be required. Writing for a unanimous Court, then-Associate Justice William Rehnquist said that the *Burch* case "lies at the intersection of our decisions concerning jury size and unanimity. As in *Bellew* [*v. Georgia*, 435 U.S. 223 (1978)], we do not pretend the ability to discern *a priori* a bright line below which the number of jurors participating in the trial or in the verdict would not permit the jury to function in the manner required by our prior cases" (441 U.S. 138). However, Rehnquist added that "much the same reasons that led us in *Bellew* to decide that use of a five-member jury threatened the fairness of the proceeding and the proper role of the jury led us to conclude now that conviction for a nonpetty offense by only five members of a six-person jury presents a similar threat to preservation of the substance of the jury trial guarantee, and justifies our requiring verdicts rendered by six-person juries to be unanimous" (441 U.S. 139).

In summary, we can say that courts can use smaller than twelve-person juries and that they may permit non-unanimous verdicts. However, as Table 6.3 shows, most jurisdictions have remained with the traditions of twelve-person juries requiring unanimous verdicts.

WITNESSES

When a trial begins there are two types of witnesses that may be called to testify. The most common witnesses in both civil and criminal cases are **lay witnesses** (also called **eyewitnesses**). Lay witnesses are individuals who saw some event or who have some type of personal knowledge of what occurred. For example, if a driver was stopped for a red light and saw two cars collide in the middle of an intersection, this driver would be considered a lay witness, and he or she could testify as to what transpired before, during, and after the accident. The drivers of the two vehicles involved in the accident might testify at a trial, but their testimonies might be discounted by a jury because they were participants and their testimonies are influenced by their own subjective perspectives.

Eyewitnesses can testify to anything they have perceived by their physical senses (smell, taste, sight, hearing, or touch). They may be able to testify as to their opinions if they are asked to do so by one of the attorneys and the judge allows the testimony. Normally, however, they can only testify to those facts that they know based on their personal experiences or observations. Lay witnesses testify based on civic duty and the requirement of the court.

In contrast to the testimony of eyewitnesses, **expert witnesses** are called to testify to their professional (expert) opinions on particular issues. Expertise by these witnesses

| TABLE 6.3 | Jury Size and Unanimity Requirements in State Felony Cases | | |
State	Jury size	Unanimous verdicts required
Alabama	12	Yes
Alaska	12	Yes
Arizona*	12 or 8	Yes
Arkansas	12	Yes
California	12	Yes
Colorado	12	Yes
Connecticut*	6	Yes
Delaware	12	Yes
Florida*	6	Yes
Georgia	12	Yes
Hawaii	12	Yes
Idaho	12	Yes
Illinois	12	Yes
Indiana*	12 or 6	Yes
Iowa	12	Yes
Kansas	12	Yes
Kentucky	12	Yes
Louisiana*	12	Yes*
Maine	12	Yes
Maryland	12	Yes
Massachusetts	12	Yes
Michigan	12	Yes
Minnesota	12	Yes
Mississippi	12	Yes
Missouri	12	Yes
Montana	12	Yes
Nebraska	12	Yes
Nevada	12	Yes
New Hampshire	12	Yes
New Jersey*	12	Yes
New Mexico	12	Yes
New York	12	Yes
North Carolina	12	Yes
North Dakota	12	Yes
Ohio	12	Yes
Oklahoma	12	Yes
Oregon	12	No*

TABLE 6.3	*Continued*	
State	**Jury size**	**Unanimous verdicts required**
Pennsylvania*	12	Yes
Rhode Island	12	Yes
South Carolina	12	Yes
South Dakota	12	Yes
Tennessee	12	Yes
Texas	12	Yes
Utah*	12 or 8	Yes
Vermont	12	Yes
Virginia	12	Yes
Washington*	12	Yes
West Virginia	12	Yes
Wisconsin	12	Yes
Wyoming	12	Yes

Notes: Arizona, Connecticut, Florida, Louisiana, and Utah require twelve-person juries in death penalty cases, but smaller juries may be utilized otherwise. Indiana requires twelve-person juries for the most serious felony cases. Louisiana allows non-unanimous (10–2) verdicts in all but death penalty cases and those mandating confinement at hard labor. New Jersey allows defendants in death penalty cases to request smaller than twelve-person juries. Oregon allows for 11–1 verdicts in all but death penalty cases. Pennsylvania and Washington allow defendants to opt for less than twelve-person juries in non-capital cases.

Source: Rottman and Strickland (2006:233–37).

is established by their professional work experience, their educational backgrounds, and the degree to which they may have been consultants or conducted research in a particular field of knowledge. Expert witnesses may testify based on civic duty, but normally are paid for their time and expertise as well.

For both civil cases and criminal cases, before either side can call an expert witness, attorneys for the other side must be informed of the potential use of the witness and be allowed to depose the witness. A **deposition** is a formal interview with a witness outside of the courtroom, but during which the witness is under oath and the questions and answers are recorded and transcribed. Giving a deposition allows counsel for the opposing side to know in advance the nature of the witness's expertise and the substance of the potential testimony.

Before an individual can be called as an expert witness, the court will conduct a hearing during which the attorneys can assert or challenge the person's expertise. This process is called "qualifying the witness," and ultimately the judge will decide whether the witness has sufficient credentials to be recognized as an expert witness. At times, all parties recognize the level of expertise demonstrated by the proposed witness and they simply stipulate (agree with one another, and before the court) that the person is acceptable as an expert witness.

Expert witnesses typically are paid by the party that intends to call them (although the courts may make provisions for the pay of expert witnesses as well). Occasionally, this is raised as an issue when the witness is being qualified, or questioned about his or her expertise. For instance, if the prosecutor intends to call a ballistics expert the defense attorney may ask the expert, in the presence of the jury, "Mr. Jones, isn't it true that you are being paid for your testimony here today?" Sometimes that causes concern on the part of jurors, but most recognize this as a tactical ploy by the attorney.

If an individual is accepted as an expert, the attorney for the side calling the witness will get to question the person first (direct examination), and then the other side will get to cross-examine. In the final analysis, the best expert witnesses are those who appear neutral, and who serve as resources for the judge and jury and not just cheerleaders for one particular side (Anderson and Winfree 1987).

BAILIFFS AND OTHER SECURITY PERSONNEL

Virtually as long as we have had courts, some provisions have been necessary for security in and around the courtrooms. Within the past few decades, and particularly in light of the 9/11 events, courthouse security nationwide has been substantially increased. In this section I examine some of the types of incidents that have been confronted by the courts, and the personnel that are responsible for providing security for judges, attorneys, witnesses, and the other participants in the judicial process.

Defense attorneys may receive threats from their clients who are unhappy with the results of their cases. Not all of these incidents are reported, and currently there does not seem to be an effective recordkeeping system for those that are reported. However, on the prosecution side we know that in 2005 40 percent of the 2,344 state prosecutors' offices nationwide received a work-related threat. For large offices (serving populations of 1 million or more) 84 percent received some type of threat (Perry 2006).

Judges also seem particularly vulnerable to threats and actual incidents of violence. Box 6.5 details one such event, but there have been others as well, including the case of federal district Judge Joan H. Lefkow, of the Northern District of Illinois, whose husband and mother were both killed in their home. The police later stopped a suspect identified as Bart Ross, who had been a plaintiff in a medical malpractice suit dismissed by Judge Lefkow. When the police approached Ross he shot himself to death, and later the police found a suicide note with details into the shooting of Judge Lefkow's husband and mother.

Such cases make it challenging to provide security both in the courthouse setting as well as for judicial officers as they come and go from work. In the following sections I look at some of the actors in the judicial process that are responsible for courthouse security.

Bailiffs are courtroom actors who are responsible for security and order in the courtroom. If the bailiffs do their jobs correctly they can very easily blend into the background in the courtroom. Among the jobs performed by bailiffs are providing security at the entrances of courthouses and individual courtrooms. They often require courthouse visitors to sign in, and they may screen visitors with metal detectors or portable screeners (wands) much like security points in airports. Primarily they are trying to ensure that no unauthorized person brings a weapon into the courts.

Bailiffs also are responsible for announcing the entry of judges into the courtroom, which may be the most visible function they perform. They call the courtroom to order and warn all spectators that they should behave respectfully.

As part of their broader security duties, bailiffs are assigned the responsibility of escorting members of the jury to and from the courtroom. They stand guard outside the jury room while jurors decide on a verdict, and they may have overnight security responsibilities at restaurants and hotels or motels where jurors may be sequestered during their deliberations. **Sequestered juries** present a particular problem, since

BOX 6.6

In the News: Courthouse Security

On March 11, 2005, an accused rapist went on a shooting spree at the Fulton County Courthouse in Atlanta, Georgia. When the shooting stopped, three people had been killed, including Judge Rowland Barnes. While some people might believe that this is an isolated incident, it is not. Almost every state has recently witnessed threats or actual assaults against courtroom personnel, and the U.S. Marshals Service reported that in 2005 there were almost seven hundred serious threats against federal judges.

The threats come from a variety of sources, including detained jail inmates who are appearing in court, families of criminal defendants, and disgruntled litigants, especially in divorce cases. The news reports of the shooting in Atlanta summarized some of the problems associated with courtroom security:

A committee assigned to investigate the Atlanta courthouse shootings revealed that Nichols [the shooter] exploited what some say were security weaknesses in one of the nation's busiest courthouses. The grandmotherly deputy assigned to take him from his holding cell should not have been armed, but she was. The two deputies assigned to watch the TV screens of his cell were not at their posts.

Since last year, eight deputies have been fired at the Atlanta courthouse, and new cameras have been hooked up in most areas. But more precautions need to be taken, some say.

"There's a great lack of education with these deputies and it's not their fault," says Dennis Scheib, an Atlanta attorney who anticipated a problem in the city's courthouse and described what could happen in a letter to a local paper two years before the Nichols incident. "It doesn't seem like [county officials] have learned a lot by what has happened."

Source: Jonsson (2006).

the judge does not want jurors to have contact with members of the public (including their own families). Jurors are also prohibited from seeing or hearing news reports that might refer to the trial, and they are not allowed to discuss the case outside of the jury room. All of this presents a significant challenge to members of the courthouse security staff, as it involves unusual working hours and unique security concerns.

Bailiffs may exercise a number of miscellaneous duties related to their positions. For example, they may be required to monitor public areas of the courthouse to make sure that hallways and waiting rooms are neat and clean. They also may have to periodically search areas open to the public to make sure that no explosive devices or weapons have been hidden in places where they can be retrieved for an attack on courthouse personnel. In many courts the bailiffs also are responsible for calling witnesses to the stand and in assisting witnesses being sworn in before they testify. Bailiffs also may hand-carry files between the court clerk's office or judges' offices and the courtrooms to make sure that they are not compromised. They also may be trained in emergency first aid procedures in case there are accidents or medical emergencies such as heart attacks (Criminal Justice USA 2010). Ultimately, the bailiff is required to prevent any disruptions and to maintain order in the courtroom.

In federal courts the duties involving courtroom security are performed by both the United States Marshals Service and security personnel provided by the Department of Homeland Security's Office of Federal Protective Service (Federal Protective Service 2009). Active duty deputy U.S. Marshals are responsible for transporting federal prisoners, and either active duty or retired deputy marshals provide courthouse and courtroom security and maintain decorum.

COURT CLERKS AND ADMINISTRATORS

Although I already have discussed the role of court clerks in regards to the jury process, it is important to note some of their additional functions relative to the smooth operation of the courts. For example, in many jurisdictions court clerks have scheduling responsibilities for courtrooms and trials. They set the dates that judges and courtrooms are available and place the cases on what is called the court's **docket**. In multi-judge districts, there may be a master docket or calendar of cases with judges being assigned new cases in rotation. This approach keeps cases from backing up as the result of one judge being assigned a long-lasting or complex trial. Other jurisdictions assign cases to judges on individual dockets (see Mays and Taggart 1986). In this way it is possible for lawyers, judges, and others to see which judges are keeping current on their dockets. At times this is an unofficial measure of judicial efficiency, although not one without problems.

Court clerks also may be responsible for scheduling the **court reporters** needed for trials. While I discuss this function in the next section, it is important to recognize that the clerks may be responsible for actually producing the transcripts that are created by the court reporters and for distributing copies to the judges and attorneys.

Court clerks also become the managers of the records repositories in most courthouses. This means that any type of record that is produced in any judicial proceeding must be recorded and stored for some specified period of time. In that regard, court clerks have become the chief housekeepers for most courts.

Finally, court clerks also may have the administrative responsibility for collecting fees and fines. In some states the court clerks have a range of non-court-related functions such as issuing automobile license plates, business licenses, and marriage licenses.

Given the range of duties that court clerks have assigned—by statute, constitution, or tradition—many courts have created the position of **court administrator** to shift some of the administrative burden off of the court clerks. The notion of judicial administration can be traced back to a 1906 speech given by Roscoe Pound to the American Bar Association (Pound 1906). Although Pound cannot be given full credit for the movement to professionalize judicial administration, his 1906 speech and the writings that followed for several years proposed four principles that would serve as the basis for court reform efforts for decades to come. The four principles were:

- Court unification—states should move in the direction of eliminating specialized courts (opting instead for specialized judges) and reducing the amount of courts with concurrent jurisdiction.

- Judicial superintendents—every state should have someone who ultimately was responsible for overseeing the structure and operations of the state courts. In most instances this would be a chief judge or the chief justice of the state supreme court.

- Administrative personnel—courts at all levels should employ individuals who could exercise administrative control over the daily operations of the courts.

- Policy research—courts should engage in ongoing research to monitor the workloads and other duties and responsibilities that they must discharge. Ultimately the question is "What are the outcomes of court processes?" (Wheeler 2006–2007:954–56).

The second of Pound's principles—dealing with administrative personnel—became the basis for the court administration movement in the United States. The first court administrator positions were created in the early 1900s as a result of the work of Roscoe Pound; Arthur Vanderbilt, president of the American Bar Association and Chief Justice of the New Jersey Supreme Court; Supreme Court Chief Justice William Howard Taft, Herbert Harley of the American Judicature Society, and others (Wheeler 2006–2007).

However, court administration did not really begin to emerge as a profession until the early 1970s, largely as a result of the expansion of the field of public administration and the influence of a book on court management written by Friesen, Gallas, and Gallas (1971). Additionally, a report was issued by the National Advisory Commission on Criminal Justice Standards and Goals (1973) calling for professionalization in the field of court administration. These two influential documents advocated the creation of a cadre of professionally trained administrators who would be responsible for several essential administrative functions faced by the courts. The primary responsibilities handled by many court administrators are: budgeting, personnel administration, jury management, and case scheduling or case-flow management (see Mays and Taggart 1985; Taggart and Mays 1984).

In the United States, court administrators are found at all levels from trial courts through appellate courts. Most states now have an **Administrative Office of Courts,** and there also is an AOC for the federal courts as well. Box 6.7 summarizes the responsibilities of the Administrative Office of U.S. Courts.

Court administrators, unlike court clerks, typically are appointed by the chief judge of the particular district, or by a panel of judges, and they serve at the pleasure of the judge(s). Some of them have law degrees and act almost as judicial adjuncts or extensions of the judges. Others have degrees in business administration, public administration, criminal justice, or a variety of different fields (see Taggart and Mays 1984).

BOX 6.7
The Administrative Office of U.S. Courts

Created in 1939, the Administrative Office of the United States Courts serves the Federal Judiciary in carrying out its constitutional mission to provide equal justice under law. The AO, as it is called, is the central support agency for the Judicial Branch. It provides a wide range of administrative, legal, financial, management, program, and information technology services to the federal courts. The AO provides support and staff counsel to the Judicial Conference of the United States and its committees, and implements and executes Judicial Conference policies, as well as applicable federal statutes and regulations. The AO facilitates communications within the Judiciary and with Congress, the Executive Branch, and the public on behalf of the Judiciary.

The agency is a unique entity in government. Neither the Executive Branch nor the Legislative Branch has any one comparable organization that provides the broad range of services and functions that the Administrative Office does for the Judicial Branch. The agency's lawyers, public administrators, accountants, systems engineers, analysts, architects, statisticians, and other staff provide a long list of professional services to meet the needs of judges and the more than 32,000 Judiciary employees working in more than 800 locations nationwide. The Director of the Administrative Office is the chief administrative officer for the federal courts and secretary to the Judicial Conference of the United States.

Source: The Federal Judiciary (2009).

For a number of years there were two national organizations that represented court managers: the National Association for Court Administration (largely representing elected managers) and the National Association of Trial Court Administrators (primarily representing appointed managers). In 1985 these two organizations merged to form the National Association for Court Management, an organization of more than two thousand members that is committed to improving the administration of justice, providing education and training, and improving public access to the courts (National Association for Court Management 2009).

Research in the 1980s found that although court administrators have taken over many of the management functions of the courts, some of these duties continue to be shared by judges and court clerks. The result can be that there is conflict among these three offices over who is responsible for which functions (see Mays and Taggart 1986).

OTHER COURTROOM PERSONNEL

In the section on court clerks, I mentioned the job of court reporter. Court reporters have a very specific responsibility. They must maintain a verbatim transcript of all in-court proceedings. This transcript becomes critical if an appeal is filed in a case, because appellate courts review proceedings based on transcripts and written and oral arguments of attorneys. They do not simply retry the case. Court reporting has become something of a science, and technological devices such as computers and videotaping have greatly impacted the work of court reporters (see Hartmus and Levine 2000).

Many state trial courts today have recognized the need to employ interpreters. These include individuals who speak and can interpret "common" foreign languages such as Spanish, as well as "exotic" Eastern European and Asian languages. Additionally, there often is a need for American Sign Language interpreters in courts for defendants (or even jurors) who are deaf. Currently, all states report that they provide foreign language and sign language interpreters, paid for by the county, the state, or out of court fees (Rottman and Strickland 2006:83–97).

SUMMARY

One of the most important ways the public can participate in the judicial process is through jury service. While we often describe jury service as a "civic duty," many people try diligently to get out of serving on juries. Some people view this obligation of citizenship as a major disruption of their lives. Nevertheless, a great deal of time and effort goes in to assembling proper pools of potential jurors for the occasional trials that do occur.

A variety of methods have been employed to ensure that representative juries are chosen from the community. Some states have relied on property tax rolls to summon prospective jurors. Obviously, this overlooks the substantial number of people who are renters rather than property owners. Other states have chosen to use voter registration lists as the source for summoning people for jury duty. Again, this method only captures the names of those people who are registered to vote, and in some jurisdictions that may exclude significant segments of the population (such as young adults and minorities). This approach also has the tendency to overselect middle age and senior adults, who tend to register to vote in comparatively high numbers. As a result of the inherent deficiencies of each of these methods, several states now include lists of licensed drivers (with an exclusion of those under the age of eighteen) in an effort to provide a more representative group of potential jurors. Most states now use multiple sources of information to summon people for jury duty.

Once the pool of potential jurors (the venire) is assembled, the judge and the attorneys engage in a period of questioning concerning possible biases that people may hold. Typical questions include whether the person has served in law enforcement (or has a family member who has); whether prospective jurors know the defendant, the attorneys, or any of the witnesses in the case; and whether they have read or heard anything about the case that would cause them to form an opinion about guilt or innocence before hearing the evidence. If potential jurors have already prejudged the case—that is, they express some degree of prejudice—they can be dismissed for cause. However, both the prosecution and the defense are given a certain number of dismissals where they do not have to state a particular reason. The latter group is called peremptory challenges, and attorneys must be careful in exercising these exclusions so as not to discriminate against racial minorities or other "protected" groups (e.g., such as women).

In most criminal trials, a great deal of the evidence is introduced through the testimony of witnesses. Generally speaking, we can say that there are two groups of witnesses that could appear in any case. The first group can be characterized as lay witnesses or eyewitnesses. These are individuals who experienced something with their physical senses (they saw, heard, smelled, tasted, or felt something) to which they can testify in court. The second group is comprised of expert witnesses who can be employed by both sides, and in most instances these individuals are compensated for their courtroom appearance and the time (and sometimes analysis) involved in their appearing. Unlike eyewitnesses, expert witnesses can testify to their opinions based on their education, training, and experience. Some cases, such as those that depend on forensic analysis and those involving the insanity defense, are especially dependent upon the testimony of expert witnesses to help both the judge and jury understand what has taken place.

Security, both inside of the courtroom and outside of the courthouse, has become extremely important. There have been assaults on judges and attorneys, as well as victims and witnesses in cases. As a result, most courthouses in the United States are starting to employ heightened security measures to protect the people who work in courthouses along with all of the people involved in trials. Much of the responsibility for security falls on the bailiffs and other security personnel employed by the courts. In state and local courts security typically is provided by active duty or retired police officers or sheriff's deputies. Active duty or retired deputy U.S. Marshals provide security for the federal courts.

The day-to-day administrative duties of courts in the United States often are handled by elected court clerks. In fact, in some states these individuals hold positions that are provided for by the state constitution. Court clerks may be responsible for a variety of trial-related duties such as scheduling cases (or docketing), summoning potential jurors, and providing courtroom ancillaries such as court reporters.

However, in a great many jurisdictions court clerks have functions outside the realm of the judicial process. For example, they may be responsible for issuing business licenses, marriage licenses, and even automobile registrations. As a result of the many duties that fall the lot of court clerks, some jurisdictions have started to employ trained administrators to deal with budgeting and personnel issues, and even docketing and jury management in some instances. Furthermore, courts may also employ jury commissioners to deal with the complex task of assembling the pools of potential jurors that are necessary to ensure the smooth processing of the hundreds of thousands of both civil and criminal cases processed by the courts in the United States each year.

Finally, trial courts of general jurisdiction have employed court reporters to maintain transcripts of all proceedings. In the past, much of this work was done with the use of stenotype machines that typed shorthand that could be converted into the verbatim transcripts. Today a great deal of the transcription is computer-assisted or done through the use of videotaping. In addition, courts have had to expand the types of other employees they must use to process cases. Today it is not unusual to see interpreters (both foreign language and American Sign Language) appearing in courts. In fact, these professionals have become an indispensible part of many court proceedings today.

QUESTIONS FOR CRITICAL THINKING

1. In some states youngsters accused of delinquent offenses are guaranteed the right to a jury trial by state statute. Since persons younger than eighteen are not qualified for jury service, does this mean that juveniles are denied a right to a trial by a jury of their peers? Explain.

2. Should people who have been convicted of a felony be disqualified from jury service? Why should this stipulation be imposed (or should it be imposed)?

3. What is the justification for excluding people such as police officers, attorneys, doctors, and the clergy from jury service? Does this seem like a reasonable course of action? Why or why not?

4. You have been summoned for jury duty in one of your local courts. As a full-time college student, serving on a jury would disrupt your class and perhaps part-time work schedule. Would you seek to be excused from jury duty? Should you be excused? Would/should the same considerations apply for your professor?

5. Have you ever witnessed a traffic accident or a crime? Have you been called to court to testify as an eyewitness? How would you characterize your experience to others who have not had the chance to appear on the witness stand?

6. Students sometimes hear about the fees that are charged by expert witnesses, and one of their first questions is "How do I get a job like that?" What would you say the general qualifications should be for someone to serve as an expert witness?

7. The use of expert witnesses in a trial can be characterized as a "swearing match," with the experts for one side squaring off with the experts for the other side. How should juries deal with situations where there is conflicting expert testimony?

8. Courthouses have become the scene of a number of high-profile incidents of workplace violence. Why are the courts potentially dangerous places to work?

9. Who within the courtroom work group are the most likely targets of violence and why? What can be done to keep the courts accessible to the public, yet safe places to work?

10. Who should manage the courts? Is this a responsibility that judges should not delegate? Should elected court clerks (many of whom hold constitutional positions) be the court managers, or should "professional" managers be appointed to handle the daily administrative tasks of the courts?

RECOMMENDED READINGS

Dwyer, William L. (2002). *In the Hands of the People: The Trial Jury's Origins, Triumphs, Troubles, and Future in American Democracy*. New York: St. Martin's Press. Dwyer believes that jury service is one of the pillars of democracy in the United States. He is concerned with the fact that many people believe that juries could be eliminated from our court system with little effect on the quality of justice. His assertion is that if one day we wake up and the historical jury we have known is gone, something will have changed in the fundamental way we operate our justice system in this country.

Kassin, Saul M., and Lawrence S. Wrightsman (1988). *The American Jury on Trial: Psychological Perspectives*. Bristol, PA: Taylor & Francis. The authors of this book are psychologists who examine how juries operate, how they process the information presented to them, and how to go about conducting research on jury deliberations. One of the chapters focuses on the use of so-called scientific selection of jurors, a topic that has been much debated in some of the recent high-profile trials in the United States.

Levine, James P. (2001). *Juries and Politics*. Belmont, CA: Wadsworth Publishing Co. Levine's book sets out to answer the question: "What makes juries tick?" The author's perspective is that juries are part of the political system of the United States and that, as such, they act in political ways. Levine provides a very thorough review of the literature on juries. He discusses the constitutional basis for juries and how attorneys and witnesses attempt to influence jurors and jury deliberations.

Saari, David J. (1982). *American Court Management: Theories and Practices*. Westport, CT: Quorum Books. Saari examines courts as legal, political, and social institutions. The book was one of the first modern texts to apply contemporary administrative approaches to the administration of courts in the United States.

KEY TERMS

Administrative Office of Courts
bailiffs
challenges for cause
civil death
court administrator
court clerks
court reporters

deposition
docket
expert witnesses
eyewitnesses
hung jury
jury commissioners
lay witnesses
master lists

master wheels
peers
peremptory challenges
petit juries
sequestered juries
venire

REFERENCES

Amsterdam, Robert (2008). No More Juries in Russia. http://www.robertamsterdam.com/2008/12/no_more_juries_in_russia.htm.

Anderson, Patrick, and L. Thomas Winfree, Jr. (1987). *Expert Witnesses: Criminologists in the Courtroom*. Albany, NY: State University of New York Press.

Apodaca v. Oregon, 406 U.S. 404 (1972).

Batson v. Kentucky, 476 U.S. 79 (1986).

Bellew v. Georgia, 435 U.S. 223 (1978).

Burch v. Louisiana, 441 U.S. 130 (1979).

Champion, Dean J. (2005). *The American Dictionary of Criminal Justice*, 3rd ed. Los Angeles, CA: Roxbury Publishing Co.

Criminal Justice USA (2010). http://www.criminaljusticeusa.com/bailiff.html.

Duncan v. Louisiana, 391 U.S. 145 (1968).

The Federal Judiciary (2009). http://www.uscourts.gov/adminoff.html.

Federal Protective Service (2009). http://www.dhs.gov/xabout/structure/gc_1253889058003.shtm.

Feofanov, Yuri, and Donald D. Berry (1996). *Politics and Justice in Russia: Major Trials of the Post-Stalin Era*. Armonk, NY: M. E. Sharpe.

Freeman, Adam (2010). Will Stricter Guidelines on Jurors Using Facebook, Twitter Work? http://www.wtsp.com/news/local/story.aspx?storyid=152396.

Friesen, Ernest C., Edward C. Gallas, and Nesta M. Gallas (1971). *Managing the Courts*. Indianapolis: Bobbs-Merrill Co.

Gardner, Martin R. (2009). *Understanding Juvenile Law*, 3rd ed. Newark, NJ: Matthew Bender/LexisNexis.

Hartmus, Diane M., and James P. Levine (2000). Videotaped Trial Transcripts for Juror Deliberations. In *Courts and Justice*, 2nd ed., ed. G. Larry Mays and Peter R. Gregware, 175–82. Prospect Heights, IL: Waveland Press.

Johnson v. Louisiana, 406 U.S. 356 (1972).

Jonsson, Patrik (2006). A Year After Atlanta Shootings, Courthouse Security is "Spotty." *The Christian Science Monitor*, March 13. http://www.csmonitor.com/2006/0313/p04s01-usju.html.

Kalven, Harry, and Hans Zeisel (1966). *The American Jury*. Boston: Little, Brown and Co.

Kassin, Saul M., and Lawrence S. Wrightsman (1988). *The American Jury on Trial: Psychological Perspectives*. Bristol, PA: Taylor & Francis.

Levine, James (2002). Jury System. In *Encyclopedia of Crime and Punishment*, ed. David Levinson, 964–70. Thousand Oaks, CA: Sage Publications.

Lewis v. United States, 518 U.S. 322 (1996).

Mays, G. Larry, and L. Thomas Winfree, Jr. (2009). *Essentials of Corrections*, 4th ed. Belmont, CA: Wadsworth/Cengage.

Mays, G. Larry, and L. Thomas Winfree, Jr. (2006). *Juvenile Justice*, 2nd ed. Long Grove, IL: Waveland Press.

Mays, G. Larry, and William A. Taggart (1985). Local Court Administration: Findings From a Survey of Appointed Managers. *Judicature* 69(1):29–35.

Mays, G. Larry, and William A. Taggart (1986). Court Clerks, Court Administrators, and Judges: Conflict in Managing the Courts. *Journal of Criminal Justice* 14(1): 1–7.

McKeiver v. Pennsylvania, 403 U.S. 528 (1971).

McKeon, Judge Michael F. (2005). How Experience Changed My Practice on Juror Note Taking. *The Daily Record*, April 29. http://www.nyjuryinnovations.org/materials/Hon._Michael%20McKeon,_How_Experience_Changed_My_Practice_on_Juror_Note-Taking.pdf.

National Advisory Commission on Criminal Justice Standards and Goals (1973). *Task Force Report on the Courts*. Washington, DC: U.S. Government Printing Office.

National Association for Court Management (2009). http://www.nacmnet.org.

New Mexico Statutes Annotated (2010). http://law.justia.com/codes/new-mexico/2006/nmrc/jd_32a-2–16-d405.html.

Pastore, Ann L., and Kathleen Maguire, eds. (2009). *Sourcebook of Criminal Justice Statistics* [Table 1.95.2008]. http://www.albany.edu/sourcebook/pdf/t1952008.pdf.

Perry, Steven W. (2006). *Prosecutors in State Courts, 2005*. Washington, DC: Bureau of Justice Statistics, U.S. Department of Justice.

Pound, Roscoe (1906). The Causes of Popular Dissatisfaction with the Administration of Justice. *American Law Review* 40:729–49.

Rottman, David B., and Shauna M. Strickland (2006). *State Court Organization 2004*. Washington, DC: Bureau of Justice Statistics, U.S. Department of Justice.

Ruffin v. Commonwealth 62 Va. 790 (1871).

Saari, David J. (1982). *Court Management: Theories and Practices*. Westport, CT: Quorum Books.

Taggart, William A., and G. Larry Mays (1984). Preparing to Manage the Courts: The Educational Backgrounds of Court Administrators. *Judicature* 67(6): 284–91.

Taylor v. Louisiana, 419 U.S. 522 (1975).

Waters, Nicole L. (2004). *Does Jury Size Matter?* Williamsburg, VA: National Center for State Courts.

Wheeler, Russell R. (2006–2007). Roscoe Pound and the Evolution of Judicial Administration. *South Texas Law Review* 48:943–67.

Williams v. Florida, 399 U.S. 78 (1970).

ENDNOTE

[1]As one example, Pennsylvania amended its rules of criminal procedure in August 2008 to allow jurors to take notes in criminal trials.

PART THREE

TRIALS AND RELATED FUNCTIONS

7

Trials and Trial Procedures

Photo source: Exactostock/SuperStock

INTRODUCTION

Nothing attracts public attention like the drama associated with a high-profile criminal trial, and the more spectacular the crime, the more notorious the parties involved in the case, or the more sympathetic the victim, the more attention a case will get. For most members of the general public, a criminal trial represents the essence of the criminal justice process in the United States. However, relatively few cases—either civil or criminal—make it to trial in this country; most are resolved in a less formal, more routine manner through guilty pleas (with or without explicit plea bargaining) and other types of negotiated settlements.

This chapter considers those events that take place before a trial actually begins, and then the various stages that occur when there is a trial. Separate from the trial I examine the processes of jury deliberation and sentencing, including the range of sentencing options that may be available to judges and juries. Finally, I address the grounds upon which appeals can be based, and the different appellate mechanisms that are available to convicted criminal defendants.

PRETRIAL PROCEDURES

Before cases ever go to trial several steps must be completed. In order to understand pretrial procedures completely, we should begin with an **arrest**. Garner (2000:40) says that arrest is a "seizure or forcible restraint. The taking or keeping of a person in custody by legal authority, especially in response to a criminal charge."

ARREST

The police can make an arrest with or without a warrant (Kamisar, LaFave, Israel, King, and Kerr 2008); however, consideration must be given to whether the offense is a felony or a misdemeanor. For felonies and misdemeanors, law enforcement officials can make arrests any time they have arrest warrants. Additionally, for felonies they can make arrests without a warrant (if the offense is committed in their presence) or upon probable cause (for example, a citizen complainant tells an officer that an armed robbery has occurred and points out the suspected robber).

By contrast, in misdemeanor cases, while officers can make arrests if the offense is committed in their presence, there are limited circumstances when they can do otherwise. For example, a few states (New Mexico being one of them) allow officers to make warrantless arrests for specified misdemeanor offenses, such as shoplifting or domestic violence, that they did not personally observe.

After officers have made an arrest, the next stage typically is to place the suspect into a police lockup or similar short-term detention facility for processing, or to book the suspect directly into the local jail. The courts allow suspects to be detained without release options for short time periods in order to allow officers to continue their investigations. It is often at this point that custodial interrogations take place in police department or jail interrogation rooms.

BAIL

Once the booking and investigation processes have been completed, suspects generally are allowed to make bail. **Bail** is the process of securing a person's release prior to the next scheduled court appearance. It is designed to ensure that a suspect will appear for the next court hearing (see Champion 2005:21). The surety posted in order to make bail is called the **bond**, and frequently the two words appear together on signs or in telephone directories as "bail bonds."

In some jurisdictions, accused offenders must physically appear before a judge or magistrate to have bail set initially. Other locations throughout the country employ what are called "bail schedules." These forms are posted in the booking offices of local jails, and they list the normal amounts of bail that would be required by judges. These figures become the presumptive bail amounts that are required, and the use of these schedules allows jail inmates to post bail (assuming they are otherwise eligible) without having to appear before a judge.

One of the clauses that appears in the Eighth Amendment to the U.S. Constitution provides that "Excessive bail shall not be required." There are at least two issues that arise out of this provision. First, does this mean that there is a constitutional right to bail? Most observers believe that this is not the case, and that bail is a privilege extended by the courts and not a right. Nevertheless, some courts systems begin with the presumption that every case is eligible for bail unless the government can demonstrate otherwise. Second, what does the word "excessive" really mean? Here, again, is a place where the Constitution's wording is vague. A few judges have taken the view that any amount of bail that defendants cannot make is excessive. Most judges, however, try to examine the characteristics of the offense and the offender to determine the amount of bail that reasonably supports public safety and ensures that the accused will appear at the next scheduled court date.

A few cases at both the state and federal levels qualify for what is called **preventive detention**. Preventive detention is based on the notion that a few situations require that the accused remain incarcerated, and bail should not be set (Wice 2002). The primary justifications for this approach are: (1) the accused presents a significant risk for flight, and (2) the accused presents a significant public safety threat if released. Concern over the commission of additional crimes on pretrial release status also has been associated with preventive detention. Historically, judges could achieve the same results by setting incredibly high amounts of money bail. However, with passage of the federal Bail Reform Act of 1984 (and a number of similar state statutes) incarceration without bail was allowed. Today, while it is used relatively infrequently, judges still have the option to refuse to set bail if the case seems to warrant it (see *United States v. Salerno* 1987).

There are a number of lingering issues associated with the practice of preventive detention. Although the Supreme Court has settled the question of legality by sanctioning the use of this option for judges, what do we know about the effects of preventive detention on the individuals who are detained? First, we know that predicting future human behavior such as dangerousness may be nearly impossible for judges (see Fagan and Guggenheim 1996). Second, accused offenders find it much more difficult to consult with their attorneys when they are detained. This makes preparation of their cases complicated. The end result may be a greater willingness to plea bargain rather than going to trial. In effect, it may give the government even greater leverage over criminal defendants (Corrado 1996).

Suspected offenders can post bail in several different ways, depending on state laws and local legal practices. The least restrictive way of posting bail is to post an unsecured bond, or to be released on the individual's own recognizance. This may be called an OR bond or ROR (for **release on recognizance**). In these situations, people accused of crimes may be released from custody by offering their word that they will appear for their next scheduled court hearing. In some ways, when a motorist is issued a traffic ticket for a moving violation and asked to sign the form by the officer, this is a release on recognizance.

Another way of posting bail is through a cash deposit. In many jurisdictions judges provide jails with what are sometimes called a "bail schedule" that allow suspects charged with routine offenses to know what the amount of bail will be before they make a court appearance. If a cash deposit is required, the suspect, or the suspect's family, may be able to post the entire amount of the bail and thereby secure release. In these situations, if the accused makes all of the scheduled court appearances on time, the bail amount may be entirely refunded, minus any administrative costs that the courts may impose.

A third way of posting bail is through the use of property bonds. Many states will allow property owners to sign a lien against their property if it is worth as much as the amount of bail. If the suspect fails to appear for a hearing the court can order the bail forfeited and the property can be seized as a payment for the bail.

The most common way for many people to post bail is through the services of a **bail bondsman**. Bail bondsmen are private businesspersons who act on behalf of the courts. If a money bail is set at $2,000 by a judge, the bail bondsman will sign a promissory note for that amount with the court in exchange for a fee from the jailed individual. The customary fee for the bondsman is 10 percent of the bail amount, but it really could be any amount up to the face value of the promissory note. Especially if there is a concern about the accused person being a flight risk, the fee may be increased from the normal amount. Whatever the outcome of the case, the bonding fee stays with the bail bondsman as cost of using this service.

If a suspect fails to appear in court, the judge can order the bail bond forfeited, and most bonding companies will employ the services of bond agents, sometimes called "bounty hunters" or "skip-tracers," to track down the now-fugitive. The television show based on the life of Dwayne "Dog" Chapman chronicles the adventures of bond agents who track down some of the people who have become fugitives, or who simply failed to show up for court.

Finally, a few states have modified the bail bonding process to allow percentage deposits to be posted with the courts. Instead of employing the services of a private bail bondsman, the courts allow individuals waiting in jail to post a percentage of the bail in exchange for release. For example, if the bail amount is $2,000 the court may charge 10 percent ($200) in order to release a suspect. If the person shows up for all of the scheduled hearings, once the case is concluded the court may deduct a certain percentage (perhaps 10 percent or $20) of the deposit for administrative fees and return the rest to the accused. In effect, this process puts the courts into competition with other bail bonding agents.

INITIAL APPEARANCE

The next stage of processing for serious misdemeanor and felony suspects is to schedule an **initial appearance** before a judge or magistrate. This hearing considers whether there was probable cause to make an arrest without a warrant and to review the charges, address the issue of representation by an attorney, and discuss whether a reduction in bail or a release on recognizance with or without conditions is appropriate. These initial appearances can occur almost immediately after the arrest, but frequently happen within the first twenty-four to forty-eight hours. In the United States Supreme Court case of *County of Riverside v. McLaughlin*, 500 U.S. 44 (1991), Justice Sandra D. O'Connor wrote for a five-member majority. She said that the policy of excluding Saturdays, Sundays, and holidays from the forty-eight-hour rule for probable cause determinations did not "comport fully with the principles" that had been outlined by the Court in previous cases, and "the County's regular practice [of excluding these days] exceeds the 48-hour period" the Court viewed as permitted by the Constitution.

BOX 7.1 Legal Representation for Defendants: Denmark

Often it helps to understand the legal system in the United States by examining the systems employed by other nations. The following excerpt from the *World Factbook of Criminal Justice Systems* produced by the Bureau of Justice Statistics illustrates the use of legal counsel in Denmark:

Everyone accused has the right to legal assistance by counsel of his own choice. Defense counsel is mandatory in all criminal cases of a more serious nature, regardless of the financial situation of the accused. The defense counselor is appointed either at the request of the accused or, more often, chosen by the court from a body of qualified lawyers previously selected by the Ministry of Justice. The police must inform the accused of his right to a publicly assigned defense counsel. If the convicted is unable to pay his defense counsel the [national] Treasury will in most cases provide the lawyer's fee and cover other costs. In case of acquittal the State will nearly always cover all costs. It is the right of the accused to have his defense counsel present during police interrogation and court hearings, and he is entitled to consult with counsel in private at all times. The counselor is informed of the evidence gathered by the police but in some cases he may not notify the accused of the contents.

Source: Ravn (2009).

PRELIMINARY HEARING

After the initial appearance, both misdemeanor and felony cases may be scheduled for a **preliminary hearing**. Many defendants, especially those who are indigent, may waive the right to a preliminary hearing, and the case proceeds to the next stage. In most states, preliminary hearings occur in the courts of limited jurisdiction (see Chapter 8 for a description of these courts).

At the preliminary hearing the judge once again informs the defendants of the charges against them. There also is a discussion of the right to counsel if the defendant is not already represented by an attorney. If a defense attorney is present, there may be another discussion about reducing the amount of bail for defendants who still are incarcerated. Once these items are disposed of, and assuming the defendant does not waive the right to a preliminary hearing, the state begins presenting some of its evidence. This normally is a fairly brief process, with a police officer and some of the prosecution witnesses taking the stand in an effort to convince the judge that there is sufficient probable cause in the case in order to move it forward toward trial.

GRAND JURY

If the prosecutor can demonstrate probable cause to the satisfaction of the judge—and this happens in virtually every instance—in some states the case is then bound over to the **grand jury**. All federal felony cases are heard by grand juries under the Fifth Amendment provision of the U.S. Constitution that specifies that "No person shall be held to answer for a capital, or otherwise infamous crime, unless on a presentment or indictment of a Grand Jury." However, only seventeen states continue to require grand juries as screening devices for some or all felonies (Rottman and Strickland 2006:215–17).[1] The states that do not require grand jury indictments for felonies typically employ a more thorough preliminary hearing process or the use of a criminal information filed by the prosecuting attorney in order to establish probable cause (Rottman and Strickland 2006:213; Walsh and Hemmens 2008:65).

In some ways, the grand jury is one of the most private and least known aspects of the entire criminal justice system (Melone and Karnes 2008:248–51). This is the case for two reasons. First, grand jury hearings are held behind closed doors and the defendant, the news media, and the general public do not have access to the hearings. Second, unlike the members of petit or trial juries, grand jury members are forever sworn to secrecy concerning the testimony presented and the voting that occurs in the grand jury room.

The size of grand juries varies among jurisdictions, and they can be composed of as few as six or seven members (Indiana and Iowa, respectively), up to as many as twenty-three members in California, Colorado, Georgia, Maine, Massachusetts, Minnesota, New Hampshire, New Jersey, New York, Pennsylvania, Rhode Island, and Vermont (Rottman and Strickland 2006:215–17). Citizens are summoned for grand jury service in much the same way as they would be for trial juries. Once selected, they are "empanelled" for some length of time, and they may meet daily or only periodically to hear cases. Most jurisdictions have one of the assistant prosecuting attorneys serve as the legal advisor to the grand jury, and this individual is present during the testimony by the witnesses. However, when it comes time for the grand jury to vote, the prosecutor is dismissed from the grand jury room. Unlike trial juries, grand jury decisions do not have to be unanimous. In fact, many states only require an affirmative vote by two-thirds or three-fourths of the grand jury members in order to return a **true bill** or an **indictment.** This document is a formal accusation of the crime against the defendant. If the grand jury fails to find probable cause in the case, it returns a no true bill or not true bill (Bureau of Justice Statistics 2009). However, given that grand juries only hear the prosecution's side of the case, and the requirement that their decision does not have to be unanimous, grand juries return indictments in the vast majority of the cases they hear.

As previously mentioned, some states bypass the preliminary hearing and grand jury stages through the use of **criminal information**. This is a document prepared by the prosecuting attorney setting forth the facts of the case and the substance of the government's accusations. In some jurisdictions the criminal information document is only used with misdemeanor cases, but other jurisdictions use them exclusively for felonies as well (Bureau of Justice Statistics 2009; Champion 2005; see also Melone and Karnes 2008:248).

ARRAIGNMENT

After the grand jury hands down an indictment or the information has been served by the prosecutor, a court of general trial jurisdiction schedules the case for an **arraignment**. At the arraignment the judge may once again need to deal with the issues of counsel and bail. However, in most cases the defendants —who need not be present, in which case the defense attorney—are informed of the charges against them. This is done once again since the charges may have been adjusted up or down at the time of the grand jury hearing and indictment. Furthermore, the defendants are advised of the range of due process rights available to them. Some of these include the right to a speedy and public trial, the right to confront the accusing witnesses in the case, and the right to be tried by a jury. At this point the judge asks the defendant if he or she is prepared to enter a plea. The options available—depending on the jurisdiction—are not guilty, guilty, and *nolo contendere* or no contest, guilty but mentally ill, not guilty by reason of insanity, and what is called an "Alford plea." The Alford plea gets its name from the Supreme Court case of *North Carolina v. Alford* (1970). This approach allows the defendant to enter a guilty plea as a result of plea bargaining without admitting to guilt.

If the defendant refuses to enter a plea or stands mute, the court will enter a plea of not guilty on his or her behalf. This is done in order to support the initial presumption of innocent until proven guilty. It also demonstrates the perspective by the courts that they should protect people accused of crimes even when they refuse to cooperate or defend themselves.

Depending on the type of counsel the defendant has—privately retained or court-appointed—lawyers may have very specific plea recommendations for their clients. These recommendations are based on many factors, from the client's financial status or ability to pay to the lawyer's experience with similar types of cases.

If a not-guilty plea is entered, the judge coordinates with the court clerk as well as the prosecuting attorney's office and the defense attorney to try to set a trial date. Often these initial dates are changed if scheduling conflicts arise later, or if one of the attorneys needs additional time to prepare for the case. If a guilty plea is entered, the judge will carefully question the accused to make sure he or she is fully aware of the rights he/she is surrendering (including the protection against self-incrimination, the right to a jury trial, the right to confront accusers, and the right to appeal).

Once the judge is satisfied with the voluntariness of the plea a sentencing date is established in order to allow the probation department to prepare a **presentence investigation report** (or PSR). The PSR examines the work and education history of the convicted person, along with the family situation and prior criminal history. Afterward, the probation officer who prepares the PSR makes a recommendation to the judge concerning whether the offender should be incarcerated or placed on probation. If the court orders probation, then the probation officer draws up a probation contract with a list of conditions that must be met in order to avoid incarceration.

In cases where the defendant chooses to plead *nolo contendere*, meaning that the accused person does not contest the charges against him or her, the judge can treat this like a guilty plea and set a sentencing date. *Nolo contendere* pleas may be entered in cases where the defendant does not want to go through a criminal trial but where

BOX 7.2

In Their Own Words: Plea Bargaining

In the United States Supreme Court case of *Brady v. United States* (1970) Associate Justice Byron White, writing for a unanimous Court, noted:

> That a guilty plea is a grave and solemn act to be accepted only with care and discernment has long been recognized. Central to the plea and the foundation for entering judgment against the defendant is the defendant's admission in open court that he committed the acts charged in the indictment. He thus stands as a witness against himself and he is shielded by the Fifth Amendment from being compelled to do so—hence the minimum requirement that his plea be the voluntary expression of his own choice. But the plea is more than an admission of past conduct: it is the defendant's consent that judgment of conviction may be entered without a trial—a waiver of his right to trial before a jury or a judge. Waivers of constitutional rights not only must be voluntary but must be knowing, intelligent acts done with sufficient awareness of the relevant circumstances and likely consequences.

Seven years later, in the Supreme Court case of *Blackledge v. Allison* (1977), Associate Justice Potter Stewart, writing again for a unanimous Court, reemphasized the key role of plea bargaining in the justice system:

> Whatever might be the situation in an ideal world, the fact is that the guilty plea and the often concomitant plea bargain are important components of this country's criminal justice system. Properly administered, they can benefit all concerned. The defendant avoids extended pretrial incarceration and the anxieties and uncertainties of a trial; he gains a speedy disposition of his case, the chance to acknowledge his guilt, and a prompt start in realizing whatever potential there may be for rehabilitation. Judges and prosecutors conserve vital and scarce resources. The public is protected from the risks posed by those charged with criminal offenses who are at large on bail while awaiting completion of criminal proceedings. These advantages can be secured, however, only if dispositions by guilty plea are accorded a great measure of finality.

Sources: Blackledge v. Allison, 431 U.S. 63 (1977); *Brady v. United States*, 397 U.S. 742 (1970).

civil charges may be pending. In cases of no-contest pleas, since the defendant has not pleaded guilty and has not been found guilty, the plaintiff cannot use this against the defendant in subsequent civil proceedings. Thus, no-contest pleas often are a tactical maneuver by the defendant facing other potential legal proceedings.

At this point it is critical to point out that most of the criminal defendants charged in the United States do not go to trial (Sanborn 2009). Their cases are resolved with something other than a trial, and often this means a guilty plea, with or without a

plea bargain. Some defendants faced with overwhelming evidence simply plead guilty to the charges against them. Others, through the agency of their attorneys, actively engage in plea bargaining with the prosecuting attorney's office. While there are mixed feelings within the criminal justice community about the use of plea bargaining, it has been at least implicitly sanctioned by the United States Supreme Court (see, among other cases, *Bordenkircher v. Hayes* [1978]; *North Carolina v. Alford* [1970]; *Santobello v. New York* [1971]). Box 7.2 contains the perspectives of two U.S. Supreme Court justices on the issue of plea bargaining.

The advantage to the defendant of entering a guilty plea is that the fear of the unknown trial result is alleviated. When a trial looms, defendants are aware of the maximum possible sentence for the crime of which they stand accused, and the result of a guilty plea often falls significantly far short of that sentence. Also, the time and stress of a trial is completely removed when a guilty plea is filed.

A great deal of research has been done on plea bargaining and the forces at work during the plea bargaining process. Several facts seem clear. First, the prosecuting attorney clearly is in the position of power in the plea bargaining process (Cole 2004; Heumann 2004). The ultimate threat is that if the defendant does not accept the plea deal, the prosecuting attorney will take the case to trial and will make every effort to get a conviction and go for the maximum sentence (see, for example, *Bordenkircher v. Hayes* 1978; Gershman 2009). Faced with the prospect of a long sentence or additional charges, many defendants will plead guilty.

Second, the members of the courtroom work group typically have a good understanding of the "going rate," or what a case is really worth in terms of time, effort, and potential punishment (Walker 2006). Therefore, when a plea deal is offered the defense attorney can say to the client with some degree of certainty whether this is a "good deal" or not. Knowing the going rate helps all of the parties involved expedite case processing.

Third, given the presence and widespread knowledge of the "going rate" by the courtroom work group, the deal offered by the prosecutor may not be substantially different than the outcome that would have resulted if the case had gone to trial. Of course, no one can know that for certain.

Fourth, the defendant is almost totally at the mercy of the prosecutor and the defense attorney. While defense attorneys are sworn to protect the rights of their clients and to provide a vigorous defense, often they find themselves in the role of an "agent-mediator" trying to persuade the defendant (and perhaps the defendant's family) that a guilty plea is the best thing for everyone involved. When defense attorneys act in this capacity, one observer has said that the practice of law becomes a "confidence game" (Blumberg 2004; see also Uphoff 2009).

Fifth, the plea bargaining process does not really involve bargaining over a plea. In fact, three different elements—the potential sentence, the charges that have been filed, and the number of counts against the defendant—all become part of the bargaining process. In the end, the defendant is seeking some sort of leniency, and an adjustment in any of the three elements might provide that leniency.

Sixth, the judge may play little or no role in the initial plea bargaining process. Some states employ canons of judicial ethics that prohibit judges from being engaged in the negotiations, and other states allow or even encourage judges to be involved (Frontline 2009). It is important to remember, though, that judges have to approve any bargain that has been reached by the opposing attorneys. However, since all of the members of the courtroom work group know and understand the "going rate," attorneys seldom strike a bargain that they know will be unacceptable to a judge.

Finally, the overwhelming assumption is that plea bargaining exists because of the sheer volume of the cases. However, research has demonstrated that large courts and small courts, urban courts and rural courts all have about the same level of cases disposed of by plea bargaining (somewhere between 80 and 90 percent). Therefore, it must be something other than caseload that drives the plea bargaining process (Sanborn 2009; Rosett and Cressy 1976). In simplest terms, plea bargaining allows everyone to win something. Prosecuting attorneys get a win, and this helps their "batting average." Defense attorneys, especially public defenders, get another case moved off of their frequently very large caseloads. Judges keep their dockets moving. And defendants presumably receive some degree of leniency. What everyone in the process gets is *certainty*. Going to trial can be a risky and time-consuming proposition for both sides. Plea bargaining lets prosecutors and defense attorneys have some control over the outcome of their cases, rather than entrusting them into the uncertain hands of jurors (Eisenstein and Jacob 1977; Findlaw.com 2009).

BOX 7.3

Does Everyone Plea Bargain?

Given the pervasiveness of plea bargaining in the United States, it is easy to assume that every nation employs this mechanism for disposing of cases. The truth is that some nations do not use plea bargaining at all, and others (like Mexico from the following quote) may have greatly restricted opportunities for plea bargaining.

> Mexico does not have a system of plea negotiations (such as in the United States of America and other places) where a defendant can agree to plead guilty in exchange for some considerations from the state, such as a reduced charge or a more lenient sentence. That is, defendants cannot convict themselves by pleading guilty. They all must go through a trial to be convicted. Nevertheless, negotiation between defendants and the state regarding the final outcome of the case happens in certain cases.

Source: Lopez Portillo (2009).

PRETRIAL MOTIONS

After an individual has been through a preliminary hearing, has been indicted by a grand jury, and has gone through an arraignment, he or she officially is transformed from a suspect into a defendant. However, before the defendant goes to trial there still are a few stages in the process that must be completed. For example, in most locations the courts of general trial jurisdiction schedule hearings for pretrial motions. Attorneys do not file pretrial motions in every case, but common motions include: motions for dismissal of some or all of the charges, motions for a change of venue, motions to sever charges (if there are multiple charges or counts to try the defendant on one charge at a time), motions to suppress physical evidence or confessions, and motions for discovery (see, for example, Kamisar et al. 2008). Sometimes privately retained attorneys file motion to demonstrate to their clients that something is being done in the case (Blumberg 2004). Court-appointed attorneys also may file pretrial motions. However, many of the motions filed by all attorneys are summarily dismissed by the judge. One group of legal observers has said that pretrial motions result in dismissals of fewer than 5 percent of felony cases (Kamisar et al. 2008). However, this does not mean that the motions filed by either privately retained or court-appointed attorneys are frivolous.

In this section we will examine some of the most common pretrial motions. The possible list of motions is so extensive that it would require an entire book to list and give examples of all of the motions; therefore, I will focus on the most common pretrial motions encountered in criminal trials (see Federal Rules of Criminal Procedure 2009; ProDoc 2009).

Discovery

Probably the most common pretrial motion is one for **discovery**. Discovery is the "compulsory disclosure, at a party's request of information that relates to litigation" (Garner 2000:203). It is a part of the judicial process system as a result of the value we place on liberty, and in order to minimize the situations in which persons can be wrongfully convicted.

Discovery motions routinely are filed by defense attorneys (some jurisdictions also allow prosecutors to file motions for discovery as well). The substance of a discovery motion is that the defense attorney is asking the court to provide for a review and examination of the prosecutor's case by the defense. This could include the list of potential witnesses, their roles in the case, the amount and nature of physical evidence, and the results of any laboratory analyses. The justification for discovery motions is that they level the playing field for the defense in response to the overwhelming resources possessed by the state. While it might seem like the prosecution would want to keep from disclosing the nature of its case against the defendant, discovery actually may convince the defense attorney (and, in turn, the defendant) that entering a guilty plea would be a wise course of action.

Motions in Civil Cases

In civil cases, attorneys also may enter what are called *in limine* **motions**. These motions request that the court limit the issues or evidence that may be presented at trial. In criminal cases defense attorneys can file suppression motions that challenge the introduction of certain evidence by the prosecutor. An example of a suppression motion would be a request that the judge not allow some of the evidence gathered by the police and/or a confession by the defendant. The justification could be that the evidence was obtained through an unlawful search, or that the confession obtained from the defendant was coerced.

Dismissal of Charges

There also can be pretrial motions to dismiss some or all of the charges against the defendant. As should be obvious from our discussion of plea bargaining, it is often the case that multiple charges are filed against criminal defendants. In reality, only the most serious charge is of concern to the prosecuting attorney. Therefore, the defense attorney may request that the judge dismiss all of the lesser charges in order to allow the defense to focus its efforts in preparing for trial.

Defense attorneys also may file motions to sever some of the charges. In this way it makes the defendant look less culpable (if only tried on one crime at a time), than if the jury is faced with deciding guilt or innocence on six or eight charges, for instance. The same strategy might be employed if there are several defendants in a case. Defense attorneys almost always file motions to sever the trials of codefendants, especially if there is some question about the degree to which each one may have contributed to the crime.

Change of Venue

When there has been a substantial amount of pretrial publicity, and either the prosecution or the defense is concerned about the effect that publicity has on a fair trial, there may be a motion for a **change of venue**. With celebrated murder cases and situations of child abuse resulting in death, the attorneys may be concerned about the ability to pick an impartial jury. This especially can be the case when the crime has been committed in a relatively small or rural jurisdiction. To ensure the greater likelihood that a fair trial will result (and minimize the necessity for appeals), the case may be moved to a distant city. If the case involves state charges, then the trial could occur anywhere in the state. With federal cases, the trial could be moved to any federal district court in the United States and its territories.

Continuance

A common pretrial motion is one that calls for a **continuance**. Practically every attorney—prosecution or defense, civil or criminal—has filed a motion for a continuance at some time or another. There are a variety of reasons for such motions. The most obvious reason for a continuance is that either the prosecution or the defense has not had adequate time to prepare its case. Additionally, there can be scheduling conflicts for attorneys who are handling multiple cases in multiple courts. Inevitably, two cases will end up being scheduled in different courts at the same time and the attorneys with conflicting schedules have to engage in delicate negotiations with judges, all of whom think their courts and dockets are the most important.

Prosecutors have to be especially mindful of speedy trial concerns when they file continuance motions. All state and federal courts have limits on the amount of time the government has to bring a case to trial. In most instances, if prosecutors ask for continuances the speedy trial clock keeps ticking. By contrast, when defendants ask for continuances they waive their right to a speedy trial and the deadline for bringing the case to court is moved forward.

Once the attorneys have filed their pretrial motions and the judge has ruled on each one, the case is ready for trial. There can still be other motions filed once the trial has commenced, but many of the issues that are raised can be dealt with by objections from the attorneys during the proceedings.

THE TRIAL

The few cases not resolved through the dismissal of charges or guilty pleas end up being set on trial court dockets. Although they remain relatively rare, most people associate the criminal trial with the very essence of the criminal justice system. In this section I will examine those processes that occur after a grand jury indictment has been handed down or a criminal information has been filed, through the completion of the trial itself.

BENCH TRIAL OR JURY TRIAL?

Once the pretrial motions are disposed of, the judge will set a date for the trial. Before that date arrives, the defendant can waive his/her right to a trial by jury and instead request a **bench trial** (Bureau of Justice Statistics 2009). When a bench trial occurs the judge is placed in the dual roles as both the trier of facts and trier of law. In effect, one person becomes the judge and jury. Relatively few major felony cases utilize bench trials, and they are generally requested in a case that may be particularly grisly or one that would induce sympathy for the victim in the eyes of the jury. In such situations the defense attorney may believe that if a judge decides the case, he or she may be less moved by sympathy or emotion. Instead, most rely on the provision of the Sixth Amendment of the United States Constitution that guarantees that "In all criminal prosecutions, the accused shall enjoy the right to a speedy and public trial, by an impartial jury of the State and district wherein the crime shall have been committed." However, it is important to note that this provision, like others in the Bill of Rights, was originally applied in federal courts to federal cases. In *Duncan v. Louisiana*, 391 U.S. 145 (1968) the Supreme Court emphasized that this protection applied to state court proceedings as well.

ASSEMBLING THE JURY POOL

Before it comes time to select a jury, several events have transpired behind the scenes. As discussed in Chapter 6, in many jurisdictions the court clerk or a jury commissioner has been assembling a master list of people who are eligible to serve on juries. For most states the minimum requirements are that the person must be at least eighteen years of age, a legal resident of the jurisdiction, and not a convicted felon. Many states assemble the lists of potential jurors from the property tax or voter registration rolls. In order to expand the numbers of potential jurors, since not everyone owns property or is registered to vote, some states have started to supplement their lists with driver's license registrations with a stipulation of a minimum age of eighteen.

When people are needed for jury duty, the appropriate official will send summonses to a sufficient number of individuals to constitute juries for some time period.[2] From the **master list** of persons eligible to serve, smaller pools of potential jurors are assembled. These groups that go through the jury selection process are called **venires**. A venire consists of between thirty and forty-five members, depending on the nature of the case, and from this pool the final group of jurors is selected. Most states still use the traditional number of twelve jurors for felony cases, while some use six jurors for serious misdemeanors and some civil cases. No one is quite sure where the number twelve came from, but in the case of *Williams v. Florida*, 399 U.S. 78 (1970) the U.S. Supreme Court labeled it an historical artifact and held that six-person juries are permissible in all but capital cases.

JURY SELECTION

The actual jury selection process is known as the ***voir dire***, which means to speak the truth. The assumption is that attorneys are trying to pick a completely neutral jury. The reality is that each side would like to have a jury favorable to its cause. In the process of give-and-take in selecting a jury, the most biased jurors should be eliminated. Some judges allow the prosecuting and defense attorneys to ask their own questions of the pool, but in some courts the attorneys submit lists of potential questions and the judge actually interrogates members of the jury pool. Common questions include:

> "Have you ever worked in law enforcement, or has anyone in your family been employed in law enforcement?"
>
> "Do you know any of the parties (the attorneys, witnesses, the defendant, or victim) involved in this case?"
>
> "Have you seen, read, or heard anything about this case?"
>
> "Have you been a victim of a crime (the same or similar to the one in this case)?"

If the answer is yes to any of the inquiries, then there is often a follow-up question: "Would any of these factors influence your ability to make an impartial decision in this case?"

After the *voir dire* is complete, the judge and the attorneys may retire to the judge's chambers to discuss who is acceptable or not acceptable to each side as a juror. Both the prosecution and defense have an unlimited number of "strikes" for cause (the primary cause being prejudice), although the judge may have to be convinced that the potential juror should be removed. However, each side also has a limited number of **peremptory challenges**. These "strikes" may be based on nothing more than intuition or a certain feeling of uneasiness by the attorney. Depending on the nature of the case, attorneys may have from six to twelve peremptory challenges that allow them to remove potential jurors for no stated cause (see the discussion in Chapter 6 on peremptory challenges). The only restriction governing peremptory challenges is that they cannot be exercised in a racially discriminatory manner (see *Batson v. Kentucky*, 476 U.S. 79, 1986), or to exclude any other identifiable group such as all women, all men, or members of certain religious groups (see, for example, *J.E.B. v. Alabama ex rel. T.B.*, 511 U.S. 127 [1994]).

Attorneys may differ in their orientations toward the jury selection process. Some consider it an art, and others think of it as a science (Seitzer 2010; Tindale and Nagao 1986). In fact, around the nation companies have been started that can help in the "scientific" approach to jury selection in high-profile cases like the O.J. Simpson trial. However, whatever the orientation held by an attorney, a very strong belief exists among lawyers that cases may be won or lost during jury selection.

OPENING ARGUMENTS

After the jury has been selected and the courtroom proceedings begin, each side is permitted to present its opening arguments. The prosecuting attorney gets to go first in opening arguments, and this is the time when each side gives an overview of its case. Oftentimes attorneys describe this process as explaining their "theory" of the case or, essentially, how they perceive the crime was committed. After the prosecutor is finished the defense presents opening arguments, and when the defense concludes, it is time to begin questioning witnesses.

WITNESS EXAMINATION

As with the opening arguments, the prosecution gets to go first in questioning its witnesses. The initial questioning is done by the side calling the witness, and this is known as **direct examination**. After the prosecutor finishes with each witness, the defense has the opportunity (if it so desires) to conduct a **cross-examination** of the witness. The prosecutor can then ask questions on re-direct and the attorneys can go back and forth until both sides are satisfied that they have had their questions adequately answered.

When the prosecutor announces that he or she has no more witnesses to call, the defense has the opportunity to ask the judge for a directed verdict of acquittal based on the fact that the state has failed to prove its case beyond a reasonable doubt. This tactic practically never works, but occasionally the judge will agree with the defense motion and dismiss some or all of the charges.

If the charges are not dismissed, the judge invites the defense to call its first witness. At this point, it is essential to note that the defense is under no obligation to present a case. The burden of proof rests with the state, and the defense can inform the court that it does not intend to call any witnesses and that it will rest its case (this does not happen very often, either).

The defense attorney questions his or her witnesses, and the prosecutor has the opportunity to cross-examine these witnesses. Again, as with the prosecutor's witnesses, both sides may go back and forth until they have exhausted their questions.

When this process has been completed and both sides have rested their cases, the attorneys for each side have one more opportunity to address the jury: closing arguments. (These are discussed after the following subsection.)

SCIENTIFIC EVIDENCE IN COURT

Most of the witnesses that testify in a trial are lay witnesses or eyewitnesses. However, another group of individuals also may be called to testify in a case when there is scientific analysis that may be admitted into evidence. These witnesses are called **expert witnesses** and, unlike eyewitnesses, they are permitted to testify to their opinions. However, these opinions are based on scientific analysis and the research experience of the experts.

The use of scientific evidence in court is one of the most hotly debated subjects in legal circles today. We often take for granted the use of physical evidence such as fingerprints, shoe prints, tire and tool marks, and serological evidence (body fluids). However, each of these has had a long history of development before it was accepted as legally sufficient evidence. As with many other legal procedures, appellate courts (and especially the U.S. Supreme Court) had to articulate standards for when physical evidence can be admitted, and the types of evidence and scientific analysis that are acceptable.

One of the earliest legal tests for the admissibility of scientific evidence for federal courts was articulated in *Frye v. United States*, 293 F. 1013 (D.C. Cir., 1923). Under the *Frye* test the party trying to introduce the evidence had to convince the court that "the tests or procedures...have gained general acceptance in their particular field" (Garner 2000:285). However, this test has been overruled by the U.S. Supreme Court case of *Daubert v. Merrell Dow Pharmaceuticals*, 509 U.S. 579 (1993).

Now under the *Daubert* test, federal courts "must decide whether the proposed expert testimony meets the requirements of relevance and reliability," and the party attempting to introduce the evidence "must show that the expert's underlying reasoning or methodology, and its application to the facts, are scientifically valid" (Garner 2000:181). In order to establish scientific validity, the court must consider factors such as "(1) whether the theory can be or has been tested, (2) whether the theory has been subjected to peer review or publication, the theory's known or potential rate of error and whether there are standards that control its operation, and (4) the degree to which the relevant scientific community has accepted the theory" (Garner 2000:181). In addition to being utilized by the federal courts, the *Daubert* test and similar standards are applied in state courts as well. As result of such stringent requirements, attorneys have been prevented from introducing the results of polygraph examinations in most states, but they have been allowed to introduce the results of DNA testing (see Mays, Purcell, and Winfree 1992; Purcell, Winfree, and Mays 1994).

The area of scientific crime analysis is a rapidly developing and ongoing field. In the future we will see further technological advances that will present challenges to the courts in terms of the admissibility of scientific testing relative to the legal search for the truth.

CLOSING ARGUMENTS AND JURY INSTRUCTIONS

Unlike every other stage of the case, in the closing argument phase typically the defense goes first. The defense attorney tries to highlight for the jury any problems with the prosecutor's evidence and any inconsistencies in testimony among the state's witnesses. By the same token, the prosecutor once again emphasizes the strength of the evidence presented and the jury's obligation to find the defendant guilty.

When both sides have concluded their closing arguments, the judge reads the instructions to the jury. This sometimes is called the **charge to the jury**. The judge has a number of standard charges; these include explanations of the state's obligation to prove all points of the offense and to have established guilt beyond a reasonable doubt. The judge also may admonish the jury to consider what each witness said, and what stake they might have in testifying the way they did. Judges often ask the attorneys to submit lists of potential special instructions that should be provided to the jury. This is especially the situation where there are affirmative defenses like duress, entrapment, and insanity. Once the jury has received its charge, the judge dismisses the members to select a foreperson and to begin the deliberation process.

JURY DELIBERATIONS AND VERDICTS

One of the first considerations for the courts is whether to sequester the jury or not, and this is not an automatic decision. A **sequestered jury** is one in which the jury members are locked behind closed doors during deliberations, and they are not allowed to go home, watch television news shows, or read the newspaper until they have reached a verdict and the trial has been concluded (Levine 2009). Most courts have arrangements with local hotels to provide housing for sequestered juries, and jurors are housed together and they eat together under the watchful eyes of court bailiffs.

Judges may sequester juries in high-profile and notorious cases in order to prevent "tampering and exposure to publicity" that may influence the verdict (Garner 2000:621). However, whether the jury is sequestered or not, the judge will warn jury members that they are not to discuss the case with each other until all the evidence has been presented. The judge will also emphasize to jurors that they are not to read anything, or listen to or watch news reports about the case. If there is any question about the potential for prejudicial publicity, the judge will normally err on the side of caution and order the jury to be sequestered.

Once the jury has retired from the courtroom, in some ways it is very difficult to know what goes on inside the jury room. Jurors in some high-profile cases may speak openly once the case is concluded, and some have even written books about their experiences.[3] Nevertheless, based on what has been reported publicly and the results from jury experiments, we do know some of what transpires during jury deliberations (see Kassin 2009).

For example, after electing a jury foreperson the first thing many juries do is take a vote. In fact, they may vote before they have even discussed the evidence in the case. Former jurors have explained this by saying that if everyone is in agreement there is no need to spend a lot of time rehashing certain of the issues. If there is not agreement, then the deliberation process begins.

We know from anecdotal accounts and from jury experiments that gender makes a difference in jury processes. Non-minority males with high-status jobs often are selected as the jury foreperson. While this position is largely symbolic, the foreperson may be able to direct the discussions and may have some power of persuasion over indecisive jurors. Males also tend to dominate the jury discussions and deliberations, and some may try to intimidate reluctant jurors, especially if they are females (see, for example, *Online Encyclopedia of Criminal Justice* 2009).

If the jury unanimously votes to convict, then the case moves forward to sentencing. If they vote to acquit, the defendant is set free. Sometimes in the deliberation process jurors deadlock over a particular issue or they deadlock over the entire verdict. When this happens the court declares that there is a **hung jury**. Several things can happen when this is the situation (Kassin 2009). Frequently the jury will send a message to the judge that they cannot reach a decision, and they may indicate the tally of the last vote taken. The judge might be able to send in further instructions or provide clarification that will help break the deadlock. For example, the judge might remind the jury that if they cannot reach a verdict on the original charge, there are lesser included offenses to most crimes that might provide the jury with another option.

With hung juries the judge also might bring the case to a halt by declaring a mistrial and resetting it for a future trial date. This is not considered double jeopardy, since the jury was unable to reach a verdict. In some cases, if the judge is convinced by the vote of the jury (for example, an overwhelming majority voting in favor of acquittal), the charges simply may be dismissed and the defendant released.

As we have previously mentioned, most states still use twelve-member juries for felony cases, and most still require unanimous verdicts. However, in a series of different cases the U.S. Supreme Court has upheld the use of smaller juries and has ruled that jury verdicts in non-capital cases need not be unanimous (see, for example, *Apodaca v. Oregon*, 406 U.S. 404, 1972; *Johnson v. Louisiana*, 406 U.S. 356, 1972; *Burch v. Louisiana*, 441 U.S. 130, 1979; *Williams v. Florida*, 399 U.S. 78, 1970).

When the jury has reached a verdict, the foreperson sends a note to the judge and all of the parties involved in the case reassemble in the courtroom. At this point the verdict is passed to the judge in written form, and the judge announces the verdict aloud. If there is some doubt about what the jurors have decided, the defense attorney might ask to have the jurors polled individually in court to make sure that this was the verdict they rendered. If there is no change in the verdict, the judge sets a date for sentencing and orders the probation department to prepare a presentence investigation report (PSR).

SENTENCING

I deal with sentencing at much greater length in the next chapter. However, within the context of the trial process I must at least briefly mention some of the considerations that enter into the picture.

First, there are at least five major theories or philosophies behind sentencing. One of the oldest of these notions is **retribution**. Retribution looks to the past and assumes that the offender is worthy of punishment for the sake of punishment as a result of breaking the law. Next, many laws are based on the philosophy of **deterrence**, which looks to the future. Deterrence presumes that when offenders are punished sufficiently, this will prevent future law violations by that person (specific deterrence) as well as others in society (general deterrence). Another theory behind sentencing is **incapacitation**. In simplest terms, incapacitation means that when we incarcerate people we limit their ability to commit crimes against society. The last of the major justifications associated with sentencing is **rehabilitation**. Somewhat like deterrence, rehabilitation looks to the future. It is based on the concept that if we provide treatment (such as substance abuse counseling, educational programming, and job skills training) to offenders to remedy their personal and social deficiencies, we can reduce the amount of crime that they might commit in the future. Finally, since the 1980s, some courts increasingly have focused on restoration as a goal of sentencing (Bazemore 1992; Armstrong, Maloney, and Romig 1990). Restoration, or **restorative justice**, is not a new philosophy. In fact, it is a very old one. The concept can be traced back to Native American groups and other tribal societies where maintaining group cohesion is important. At its most basic, restorative justice seeks to correct the imbalance that was created between individuals and groups within a society when a violation of the law occurred.

Second, in most instances sentencing is a function performed by the judge. After the verdict has been returned, the judge sets a future date for sentencing that allows the probation department to prepare the presentence investigation report (PSR). In most instances, the presentence investigation report contains information on details of the current offense, the person's criminal history, level of educational achievement, work history, military record (if applicable), family situation, and issues such as drug and alcohol usage. The report concludes with recommendations to the judge for either probation or incarceration (Mays and Winfree 2009:94–95).

Once this report is completed, the judge in consultation with the probation department will decide whether community-based sanctions or some period of incarceration are most appropriate, and then order those sanctions imposed. The major exception to this is in capital cases. The United States Supreme Court has ruled in a cluster of cases that capital sentencing must be carried out by juries, and that it is constitutionally insufficient to allow the judge alone to impose these sentences (see Bernat 2009; *Ring v. Arizona*, 536 U.S. 584 [2002]).

Third, in imposing sentences where there are multiple charges, the judge must decide whether the sentences will be **concurrent sentences** (that is, all at the same time) or **consecutive sentences** (one after the other). This choice can have a substantial influence on the amount of time that actually must be served.

Finally, judges may have the authority to suspend some or all of certain sentences. In effect, this can allow defendants to be released without having to be on probation or without serving a jail or prison sentence. In the end, these decisions are prescribed by the sentencing laws enacted by legislative bodies.

APPEALS

In Chapter 11 I examine the courts of appellate jurisdiction at both the state and federal levels in much greater depth. However, in this section let us consider appeals as they relate to the outcomes of the trial process.

Appellate procedures can vary based on whether the case involves a misdemeanor or a felony. Since misdemeanor convictions normally occur in the courts of limited jurisdiction, and most often these are courts of non-record (that is, they do not keep verbatim transcripts), appeals of misdemeanors typically go to the courts of general trial jurisdiction. This is done through the process of conducting an entirely new trial, or what is known as a **trial *de novo***. By contrast, in most states criminal appeals resulting from felony convictions go to the courts of intermediate appeals, where they exist, or to the courts of last resort (see Kamisar et al. 2008).[4]

In terms of the bases for appeals, it is very important to note that "the right to appeal is limited to the right to have an appellate court examine the record of the trial proceedings for error. If error is found, the appellate court either may take definitive action—such as ordering that the prosecution be dismissed—or it may set aside the conviction and remand the case for a new trial" (Allen and Kuhns 1985:19). It is also essential to consider that relatively few cases are appealed. For instance, between 1985 and 1993 the percentage of federal criminal cases appealed ranged from 13 percent to 23 percent (Scalia 2001), and although we do not have comparable numbers for state criminal cases there is every reason to believe that the percentages are similar. Additionally, in forty-six large counties in the United States, between 2001 and 2005, about 15 percent of the civil cases were appealed (Cohen 2006). This means that roughly one in every five or six cases will result in an appeal.

There are several reasons for the relatively small numbers of appeals, but the primary one is that an appeal must be based on an error of law, not an error of fact. The person most likely to be responsible for an appeal being filed is the judge overseeing a trial. This is the case because, as we have noted, the judge is the "trier of law," while the jury is the "trier of fact."

Some of the common errors of law include ineffective assistance of counsel; false or lost evidence, or problems with the laboratory analysis of evidence; admission of illegally obtained evidence (either physical evidence or admissions and confessions); improper instructions to the jury (see Steele and Thornburg 2009; sentencing errors; improper prosecutorial arguments; or plea negotiation errors (see King, Cheesman, and Ostrom 2007). Judges are responsible for ensuring that the state obtains a conviction by a fair process and, as Supreme Court Justice Sutherland noted, the prosecutor may "prosecute with earnestness and vigor—indeed he should do so. But, while he may strike hard blows, he is not at liberty to strike foul ones" (*Berger v. United States*, 295 U.S. 78, 88, 1935). Therefore, the during the trial process the judge should ensure that all of the procedures employed by the state against the defendant are fundamentally fair.

SUMMARY

As this chapter has demonstrated, the process that goes from arresting someone for a crime and bringing that person to court and getting a conviction is a long and winding road. Multiple stages of case processing are involved as well as multiple actors in the criminal justice system. For example, even before a trial can begin there are a variety of decisions and actions that must be taken. When the police arrest a suspect and book that individual into jail, the issue of bail immediately arises. Judges may set bail in person or they may have the jails post a bail schedule for the most commonly occurring offenses. If the suspect cannot make bail, he or she will have to stay in jail until the court can schedule a bail hearing or an initial appearance. At the time of the initial appearance the judge will inform the individual of the charges against him or her and review the issues relating to representation by counsel and bail.

In many states, after the initial appearance is completed a date is set for a preliminary hearing. The purpose of the preliminary hearing is to determine if there is sufficient probable cause to send the case along to the next stage. Typically, the state presents just enough of its evidence to convince the judge that there is sufficient reason for the case to go forward. Often this means that only the arresting or investigating officer testifies. A few states bypass the preliminary hearing process altogether and use criminal presentments or information prior to an actual trial.

Slightly over half the states still use grand juries for some or all of their felony cases. The grand jury is a group of citizens that meets to consider whether probable cause exists to take the case to trial. It is important to remember that grand juries meet in secret, typically only the prosecution presents its case (the defendant and the defense attorney are not present), and an indictment or true bill can be handed down on some fractional vote of the grand jury members (often two-thirds or three-fourths). Indictments become the formal accusations upon which trials proceed, and they result in the trial courts setting a date to hold an arraignment on the indictment.

Arraignments are one step in the pretrial procedures that must be conducted before a trial can commence. The arraignment deals with issues such as bail and the right to counsel and, perhaps for the first time, the defendant is asked to enter a plea. Once the arraignment has been held and pretrial motions filed and dispensed with, the judge sets a date for the trial.

It is essential to emphasize that relatively few cases (probably less than 10 percent) in the United States ever make it all the way to a trial. In a few instances the charges are dismissed, but in most situations a plea agreement is reached between the prosecutor and the defense attorney concerning the defendant's willingness to plead guilty in exchange for some form of leniency. For many people, however, the degree of plea bargaining present in the courts of the United States brings into serious question the amount and quality of justice dispensed. Many of the actors in the system—often with a sorrowful look—will announce that they do not really like plea bargaining, but that it remains something of a "necessary evil." In reality, virtually everyone in the process, from the defendant and the defense attorney to the prosecutor and the judge, gets something out of plea bargaining. In some sense, the "going rate" (Walker 2006) allows the courtroom work group to process cases in a routine and accelerated way. In many of the cases, very few facts are in dispute, and this allows the members of the court-room work group to dispose of those cases expeditiously and to move on to the cases where questions and unresolved issues remain.

The trial itself—while somewhat rare in most jurisdictions—still remains the hall-mark of the justice system in the United States. The initial stages of the trial focus on jury selection and the opening arguments from the prosecutor and defense attorney. Jury selection garners a great deal of attention from lawyers, and a whole consulting industry has developed in the United States focusing on "scientific" jury selection.

Once the trial begins the state presents its case. After the prosecutor finishes, the defense may ask the judge for a directed motion of acquittal or proceed with its case. Interestingly, the defense does not have to present a case at all since the burden of proof or persuasion rests with the prosecutor.

When both sides have completed their presentations and summations, the judge issues instructions to the jury concerning the process of deliberation. The jury may be free to go home during the period of its deliberations, or they may be sequestered. When they reach their verdict, they return to the courtroom and the verdict is announced.

Once the verdict has been rendered, the judge requests a presentence investigation report from the probation department, and the probation officer recommends condi-tional community supervision or incarceration. Judges and probation officers agree in a large percentage of the sentencing decisions. In most criminal cases the judge has the responsibility of imposing the appropriate sentence, but in some jurisdictions (and particularly in capital cases) a mandatory sentence may be required, or the jury may recommend the sentence.

The final stage in the trial process is the filing of appeals. If the defense attorney believes that there have been errors of law, and that these are substantial errors (that is, they have negatively influenced the outcome of the case), there is an opportunity to file an appeal. Most criminal convictions are not appealed, and of those that are few proceed beyond the first appellate review. Some convictions are overturned, and new trials are ordered in a few cases, but in most instances the convictions stand.

QUESTIONS FOR CRITICAL THINKING

1. In both this chapter and earlier in the book I discussed police procedures rela-tive to arrests. Compare and contrast the circumstances in which the police can make an arrest with or without a warrant.

2. What is bail? What purposes does bail serve? What are some of the different options for posting a bond?

3. Should a private businessperson (a bail bondsman) be performing services for the courts? Is this different in any way from private police (security) personnel or private corrections? Explain.

4. In some ways there is an incredible amount of ignorance about the function of grand juries in the United States. What is a grand jury, and what roles do grand juries perform? Is your state one that requires grand jury indictments, or is some other procedure (or procedures) employed?

5. Take a position—pro or con—on the following proposition: Plea bargaining undermines fundamental justice processes in the United States.

6. Observers suggest that the prosecuting attorney is the most powerful person in the criminal justice process. Do you agree or disagree? Why?

7. Describe the process of selecting people for jury duty and choosing a jury for a trial. Are the parties involved in the process really trying to choose a neutral jury? What does this say about who ultimately gets chosen for jury duty?

8. One of the most controversial procedures in the jury selection process is the use of peremptory challenges. Should attorneys be allowed to "strike" potential jurors for no reason whatsoever? Should the use of peremptory challenges be discontinued in the United States? Why or why not?

9. Attorneys occasionally complain about what they call "witness management problems." What do you think they mean by this term? Explain.

10. While the U.S. Supreme Court has sanctioned the use of less-than-unanimous jury verdicts, most states still require unanimous verdicts. Why is this still such a common requirement? Do you support the use of less-than-unanimous verdicts? Why or why not?

11. Some states limit the amount of discretion a judge may exercise by the imposition of sentencing guidelines. Should legislatures and sentencing commissions exercise this authority, or is this a violation of judicial independence by removing judges' discretion?

12. Relatively few criminal convictions are ever appealed, and even fewer defendants are successful in their appeals. However, the public has the perception that courts are turning criminal defendants loose in droves. Why is this perception so pervasive? What fuels these kinds of attitudes toward the courts?

RECOMMENDED READINGS

Israel, Jerold H., Yale Kamisar, Wayne R. LaFave, and Nancy J. King (2009). *Criminal Procedure and the Constitution: Leading Supreme Court Cases and Introductory Text*. Eagan, MN: West/Thomson Reuters. This is a casebook used in law schools all over the United States. However, much of the introductory material that has been provided by the authors is very helpful for understanding how cases progress from arrest to trial. The chapters on guilty pleas, trial by jury, fair trial/free press, and the role of counsel are especially useful.

Rosett, Arthur I., and Donald R. Cressy (1976). *Justice by Consent: Plea Bargains in the American Courthouse*. Philadelphia: J. B. Lippincott. Although this book is now over three decades old (and probably a little hard to find outside of university libraries), it is one of the definitive works on the process of plea bargaining. The authors offer a very thorough treatment of the subject of plea bargaining, particularly the factors that promote the high levels of plea bargaining in courts of all sizes.

Thompson, R. Alan, Lisa S. Nored, John Worrall, and Craig Hemmens (2008). *An Introduction to Criminal Evidence: Cases and Concepts*. New York: Oxford University Press. This book is somewhat brief, but it provides a good overview of key trial concepts such as burden of proof, proof beyond a reasonable doubt, and affirmative defenses. Particularly useful are the chapters on witness competency, the examination of witnesses, and expert witnesses and scientific evidence.

KEY TERMS

arraignment
arrest
bail
bail bondsman
bench trial
bond
change of venue
charge to the jury
concurrent sentences
consecutive sentences
continuance
criminal information
cross-examination
deterrence

direct examination
discovery
expert witnesses
eyewitnesses
grand jury
hung jury
incapacitation
indictment
initial appearance
in limine motions
master list
nolo contendere
peremptory challenges
plea bargain

preliminary hearing
presentence investigation
   report
preventive detention
rehabilitation
release on recognizance
restorative justice
retribution
sequestered jury
trial *de novo*
true bill
venires
voir dire

REFERENCES

Allen, Ronald J., and Richard Kuhns (1985). *Constitutional Criminal Procedure*. Boston: Little, Brown and Co.

Apodaca v. Oregon, 406 U.S. 404 (1972).

Armstrong, Troy L., D. Maloney, and R. Romig (1990). The Balanced Approach in Juvenile Probation: Principles, Issues, and Application. *Perspectives* 14(1): 8–38.

Batson v. Kentucky, 476 U.S. 79 (1986).

Bazemore, Gordon (1992). On Mission Statements and Reform in Juvenile Justice: The Case of the Balanced Approach. *Federal Probation* 56(3):64–70.

Berger v. United States, 295 U.S. 78 (1935).

Bernat, Frances P. (2009). *Ring*ing in Arizona: Did the U.S. Supreme Court's Decision in *Ring v. Arizona* Adversely Impact the State High Court's Workload? In *Courts and Justice*, 4th ed., ed. G. Larry Mays and Peter R. Gregware, 250–62. Prospect Heights, IL: Waveland Press.

Blackledge v. Allison, 431 U.S. 63 (1977).

Blumberg, Abraham S. (2004). The Practice of Law as a Confidence Game. In *The Criminal Justice System: Politics and Policies*, 9th ed., ed. George F. Cole, Marc G. Gertz, and Amy Bunger, 211–26. Belmont, CA: Wadsworth Publishing Co.

Bordenkircher v. Hayes, 434 U.S. 357 (1978).

Brady v. United States, 397 U.S. 742 (1970).

Burch v. Louisiana, 441 U.S. 130 (1979).

Bureau of Justice Statistics (2009). http://bjs.ojp.usdoj.gov

Champion, Dean J. (2005). *The American Dictionary of Criminal Justice*, 3rd ed. Los Angeles: Roxbury Publishing Co.

Cohen, Thomas H. (2006). *Appeals from General Civil Trials in 46 Large Counties, 2001–2005*. Washington, DC: Bureau of Justice Statistics, U.S. Department of Justice.

Cole, George F. (2004). The Decision to Prosecute. In *The Criminal Justice System: Politics and Policies*, 9th ed., ed. George F. Cole, Marc G. Gertz, and Amy Bunger, 178–88. Belmont, CA: Wadsworth Publishing Co.

Corrado, Michael L. (1996). Punishment and the Wild Beast of Prey: The Problem of Preventive Detention. *Journal of Criminal Law and Criminology* 86(3): 778–814.

County of Riverside v. McLaughlin, 500 U.S. 44 (1991).

Daubert v. Merrell Dow Pharmaceuticals, 509 U.S. 579 (1993).

del Carmen, Rolando (1991). *Criminal Procedure: Law and Practice*. Pacific Grove, CA: Brooks/Cole Publishing Co.

Duncan v. Louisiana, 391 U.S. 145 (1968).

Eisenstein, James, and Herbert Jacob (1977). *Felony Justice: An Organizational Analysis of Criminal Courts*. Boston: Little, Brown and Co.

Fagan, Jeffrey, and Martin Guggenheim (1996). Preventive Detention and the Judicial Prediction of Dangerousness for Juveniles: A Natural Experiment. *Journal of Criminal Law and Criminology* 86(2): 415–48.

Federal Rules of Criminal Procedure (2009). Rule 12. http://www.law.cornell.edu.

Findlaw.com (2009). Plea Bargains and Judicial Economy. http://criminal.findlaw.com/crimes/criminal_stages-plea-bargains/plea-bargains-judges-incentives.html.

Frontline (2009). The Plea. http://www.pbs.org/wgbh/pages/frontline/shows/plea/faqs.

Frye v. United States, 293 F. 1013 (D.C. Cir., 1923).

Garner, Bryan A., ed. (2000). *A Handbook of Criminal Law Terms*. St. Paul, MN: West Group.

Gershman, Bennett L. (2009). Why Prosecutors Misbehave. In *Courts and Justice*, 4th ed., ed. G. Larry Mays and Peter R. Gregware, 321–31. Prospect Heights, IL: Waveland Press.

Heumann, Milton (2004). Adapting to Plea Bargaining: Prosecutors. In *The Criminal Justice System: Politics and Policies*, 9th ed., ed. George F. Cole, Marc G. Gertz, and Amy Bunger, 189–210. Belmont, CA: Wadsworth Publishing Co.

J.E.B. v. Alabama ex rel. T.B., 511 U.S. 127 (1994).

Johnson v. Louisiana, 406 U.S. 356 (1972).

Kamisar, Yale, Wayne R. LaFave, Jerold H. Israel, Nancy J. King, and Orin S. Kerr (2008). *Basic Criminal Procedure*, 12th ed. Eagan, MN: West/Thomson Reuter.

Kassin, Saul M. (2009). The American Jury: Handicapped in the Pursuit of Justice. In *Courts and Justice*, 4th ed., ed. G. Larry Mays and Peter R. Gregware, 154–83. Prospect Heights, IL: Waveland Press.

King, Nancy J., Fred L. Cheesman II, and Brian J. Ostrom (2007). *Habeas Litigation in U.S. District Courts: An Empirical Study of Habeas Corpus Cases Filed by State Prisoners Under the Antiterrorism and Effective Death Penalty Act of 1996 (Executive summary)*. Washington, DC: U.S. Department of Justice.

Levine, James P. (2009). The Impact of Sequestration on Juries. In *Courts and Justice*, 4th ed., ed. G. Larry Mays and Peter R. Gregware, 184–97. Prospect Heights, IL: Waveland Press.

London Daily Mail Online (2005). With Books Planned, Jurors Say Jacko's Guilty. http://www.daily-mail.co.uk/tvshowbiz/article-358204/With-books-planned-jurors-say-Jackos-guilty.html.

Lopez Portillo, Ernesto (2009). Mexico. *World Factbook of Criminal Justice Systems*. http://bjs.ojp.usdoj.gov/index.cfm?ty=pbdetail&iid=1435.

Mays, G. Larry, Noreen Purcell, and L. Thomas Winfree, Jr. (1992). DNA (Deoxyribonucleic Acid) Evidence, Criminal Law, and Felony Prosecutions: Issues and Prospects. *Justice System Journal* 16(1): 111–22.

Mays, G. Larry, and L. Thomas Winfree, Jr. (2009) *Essentials of Corrections*, 4th ed. Belmont, CA: Wadsworth Publishing Co.

Melone, Albert P. and Allan Karnes (2008). *The American Legal System*, 2nd ed. Lanham, MD: Rowman & Littlefield Publishers.

North Carolina v. Alford, 400 U.S. 25 (1970).

The Free Dictionary. Jury Deliberation. http://legal-dictionary.thefreedictionary.com/Jury+deliberation

ProDoc (2009). Texas Criminal Prosecution. http://www.prodoc.com/texas/forms_list/tx_crim_pros.pdf.

Purcell, Noreen, L. Thomas Winfree, Jr., and G. Larry Mays (1994). DNA (Deoxyribonucleic Acid) Evidence and Criminal Trials: An Exploratory Survey of Factors Associated with the Use of "Genetic Fingerprinting" in Felony Prosecutions. *Journal of Criminal Justice* 22(2): 145–57.

Ravn, Lene (2009). Denmark. *World Factbook of Criminal Justice Systems*. http://bjs.ojp.usdoj.gov/index.cfm?ty=pbdetail&iid=1435

Ring v. Arizona, 536 U.S. 584 (2002).

Rosett, Arthur I., and Donald R. Cressy (1976). *Justice by Consent: Plea Bargains in the American Courthouse*. Philadelphia: J. B. Lippincott.

Rottman, David B., and Shauna M. Strickland (2006). *State Court Organization 2004*. Washington, DC: Bureau of Justice Statistics, U.S. Department of Justice.

Sanborn, Joseph B., Jr. (2009). Pleading Guilty and Plea Bargaining: The Dynamics of Avoiding Trial in American Criminal Courts. In *Courts and Justice*, 4th ed., ed. G. Larry Mays and Peter R. Gregware, 109–27. Prospect Heights, IL: Waveland Press.

Santobello v. New York, 404 U.S. 257 (1971).

Scalia, John (2001). *Federal Criminal Appeals, 1999 with Trends, 1985–99*. Washington, DC: Bureau of Justice Statistics, U.S. Department of Justice.

Seitzer, Richard (2010). Scientific Jury Selection: Does It Work? *Journal of Applied Social Psychology* 36(10): 2417–35.

Steele, Walter W., and Elizabeth G. Thornburg (2009). Jury Instructions: A Persistent Failure to Communicate. In *Courts and Justice*, 4th ed., ed. G. Larry Mays and Peter R. Gregware, 141–53. Prospect Heights, IL: Waveland Press.

Tindale, R. Scott, and Dennis H. Nagao (1986). An Assessment of the Potential Utility of "Scientific Jury Selection": A "Thought Experiment" Approach. *Organizational Behavior & Human Decision* 37:409–25.

United States v. Salerno, 481 U.S. 739 (1987).

Uphoff, Rodney J. (2009). The Criminal Defense Lawyer: Zealous Advocate, Double Agent, or Beleaguered Dealer? In *Courts and Justice*, 4th ed., ed. G. Larry Mays and Peter R. Gregware, 332–65. Prospect Heights, IL: Waveland Press.

Walker, Samuel (2006). *Sense and Nonsense about Crime and Drugs*, 6th ed. Belmont, CA: Wadsworth Publishing Co.

Walsh, Anthony, and Craig Hemmens (2008). *Law, Justice, and Society*. New York: Oxford University Press.

Wice, Paul B. (2002). Preventive Detention. In *Encyclopedia of Crime and Punishment*, ed. David Levinson, 1217–20. Thousand Oaks, CA: Sage Publications.

Williams v. Florida, 399 U.S. 78 (1970).

ENDNOTES

[1]The states are Alabama, Alaska, Delaware, Florida, Maine, Mississippi, New Hampshire, New Jersey, New York, North Carolina, Ohio, Rhode Island, South Carolina, Tennessee, Texas, Virginia, and West Virginia.

[2]In some jurisdictions potential jurors may serve for up to three months. Other jurisdictions have experimented with shorted periods of service to encourage more people to serve on juries. These states or counties may call people for jury duty for no more than one month (and some even shorter time periods).

[3]For instance, at least three jurors in the Michael Jackson child molestation trial initially voted to convict the singer then changed their votes to not guilty. After the trial each of these jurors indicated a desire to write a tell-all book indicating that they believed the singer truly to be guilty of child molestation (see London Daily Mail Online 2005).

[4]As I have mentioned previously in the text, often the courts of last resort are called supreme courts, but this title can be used for trial courts as well (in states like New York). Also, Oklahoma and Texas have divided courts of last resort, and their Courts of Criminal Appeals are the final appellate courts in those states (see Rottman and Strickland 2006).

8

Sentencing

Photo source: AP Images

INTRODUCTION

The focus in this chapter is on the sanctions legislatively prescribed for criminal cases. Since civil cases result in monetary awards and equitable relief, those types of cases are not part of this discussion (as they have been in many other places in the text). Instead we will only look at the dispositions that occur once an individual has been convicted of a crime.

Several factors enter into the picture at the time courts impose sentences. First, it is important to remember that state legislatures (for state crimes) and the U.S. Congress (for federal crimes) determine the specific sanction or range of sanctions for each criminal offense. Second, depending on the state or the particular crime involved, the judge may be responsible for selecting the appropriate sentence or this may be the responsibility of the jury. In death penalty cases, the United States Supreme Court decided in *Ring v. Arizona*, 536 U.S. 584 (2002) that the jury must serve as the sentencing body (Bernat 2009; Bureau of Justice Statistics 2009).

Third, criminal cases may involve a broad range of potential sentences. For example, at the most lenient end of the guilty verdict continuum are **probation**, **fines**, and **community service**. In fact, judges often use these three sanctions in combination with each other. At the next level of severity are sentences that require some period of incarceration. These periods of confinement can be from a few days up to one year in jail for misdemeanors, and from one year to life in prison for felonies. The ultimate punishment, of course, is the death penalty, which now can be imposed in 34 states (Death Penalty Information Center 2011).[1] In this chapter we will examine the range of issues associated with sentencing those individuals who have been convicted of crimes. We will look at who has the responsibility for selecting the appropriate sentence, the types of sentences that can be imposed, the factors that enter into the sentencing decision making process, and the various sentencing strategies that are available. We will also consider the impact that race, ethnicity, and gender have on sentencing, as well as some of the current trends in sentencing. As you will see, all of these factors have some influence on the very complex concept of criminal sentencing.

RESPONSIBILITY FOR SENTENCING DECISIONS

In some ways, the responsibility for sentencing rests with all members of the court-room work group. Prosecuting attorneys and defense attorneys each get to contribute something to the sentencing decision making process, along with probation officers who prepare the **presentence investigation report** (PSR) for the judge. The prosecutor's control over sentencing begins with the initial charges filed against the defendant. This decision defines the parameters within which the sentencing options will fall.

The influence over sentencing by both the prosecutor and the defense attorneys additionally can be seen in the process of plea bargaining. In those cases the lawyers hammer out a bargain that the judge is likely to sanction and, in effect, the bargain that is agreed to presents the judge with a suggested sentence (Sanborn 2009). As I indicated in Chapter 3 on the courtroom work group, and again in Chapter 7 on trial processes, the core members of the courtroom work group understand the "going rate," or what a reasonable sentence would be given the circumstances in the case (Walker 2006). Therefore, there is a reasonable amount of consensus concerning the appropriate sentence in most cases, whatever the law may prescribe.

Ultimately, however, the sentencing decision rests with the judge. Even when there has been a plea bargain, the judge must agree to the sentence that is offered and must be assured that the defendant has freely accepted the plea. In virtually every case, the law authorizes the judge to prescribe a sentence that is consistent with the sanctions established by the legislature. As noted at the beginning of the chapter, the major exception to this involves capital cases. In those situations the jury is responsible for deciding whether the death penalty should be imposed or not.

In civil cases the issues of liability and compensation typically rest with the jury. If the defendant is found to be liable for damages, the jury can award the plaintiff compensatory damages (covering the actual losses suffered) as well punitive damages (providing a degree of civil punishment for the wrong inflicted by the defendant). The judge may play some role in accepting the jury's verdict or in modifying the award.

SENTENCING OPTIONS AVAILABLE

The options for sentences are largely defined by whether the offense was a misdemeanor or a felony. In this section I present the different types of sanctions that judges or juries may assign based on the severity of the crime.

MISDEMEANOR SENTENCES

As I have noted elsewhere in the text, not all misdemeanors are created equally. At the least serious end of the continuum we have what can be called **petty misdemeanors** or **infractions**; these include violations of city ordinances and virtually all traffic offenses. At the other end of the spectrum are the serious misdemeanors. The following penalties might be utilized by courts for either type of case.

Probation

In situations that involve both petty and serious misdemeanors, judges typically have at least four sentencing options. One of the first options is that after a guilty plea or a conviction the judge could assign a guilty misdemeanant to probation. **Probation** has been defined as the commitment of criminal offenders "to a period of correctional supervision in the community generally in lieu of incarceration" (Glaze and Bonczar 2007:1). There are four elements associated with probation that should be noted. First, probation is a sentence. Receiving probation following a conviction does not mean that the offender simply "got off." Second, probation is a judicial function. In simplest terms this means that a judge is responsible for imposing probation on convicted offenders. Third, probation is conditional. Every probationer will have conditions imposed by the court and enforced by the appropriate probation agency. Fourth, while there is such a sanction as unsupervised probation, in most instances probationers are supervised in the community by probation officers (Mays and Winfree 2009:62).

Some local court systems around the United States have city or county probation departments in addition to statewide probation agencies. For example, the Kootenai County Adult Misdemeanor Probation Department in Coeur d'Alene, Idaho, has as its mission the proactive supervision of probationers to "promote public safety, court order compliance, and accountability." This department also strives to "help reduce incarceration rates and mitigate the risks for re-offense by directing and assisting probationers in personal and community adjustment" (Kootenai County 2010). Ventura County, California, also has a county probation department, and this agency employs 350 probation officers and has an annual budget of $64 million. This organization supervises both convicted misdemeanants and felons (County of Ventura 2010).

If the judge decides that an **active probation** sentence is appropriate, the newly convicted offender has to report to a probation officer and is required to abide by any conditions imposed by the court and enforced by the probation department. However, it is possible that the judge could impose probation without supervision. This **informal probation** (sometimes called **summary probation**) arrangement often is based on the presumption that a particular offender does not need active supervision, and the primary stipulation is that no further violations occur. In effect, some of the people convicted of petty misdemeanors are self-monitored.

Community Service

Second, either as stand-alone penalties or in addition to probation, the judge might require a convicted misdemeanant to do a certain number of **community service** hours. Community service projects can consist of cleaning up city property such as parks; the removal of graffiti; washing police cars, ambulances, or fire trucks; or working at an animal rescue shelter. The justification for this type of sentence is to minimize the negative effects of the sanction while giving something back to the community.

Fines

Third, one of the most common penalties (particularly for petty misdemeanors) is a fine. **Fines** are overwhelmingly used in traffic violation cases. The problem with most systems that employ fines is that not everyone appearing before the court has the same ability to pay. In other words, fines fall disproportionately harder on those in the lowest economic brackets of society. As a result, some jurisdictions have experimented with the system of **day fines** that has been utilized in some European countries (see Winterfield and Hillsman 2004). Under a day fine program, each offense has a certain number of "penalty days" attached to it. If, for example, the charge is reckless driving, the number of penalty days assigned might be three. In this system, the ultimate fine is determined by multiplying the number of penalty days by the amount of money the individual earns per day. The result is that a fine might be $60 for one person and $260 for another. While some people might be offended at the seeming injustice of day fines, it is important to remember that proportionately day fines provide a more equitable economic penalty system.

Incarceration

The final disposition for misdemeanors is jail time. If the case is a petty misdemeanor the law may provide for fines only and no jail time, or it may permit the imposition of sentences up to six months in the local jail. For serious misdemeanors, sentences normally will run from six months up to one year. It is possible, though, that judges can impose consecutive misdemeanor sentences and extend the amount of time served beyond one year (see, for example, *Lewis v. United States*, 518 U.S. 322 [1996]). However, it is also important to note that in every case the judge has the option of suspending some or all of the jail time.

FELONY SENTENCES

Felony sentences in the United States typically fall into one of five categories: **community-based sanctions**, probation, **economic sanctions**, incarceration, and **capital punishment**. Any sentencing option other than probation or prison fits into the wide range of sanctions that typically are called **intermediate sanctions**. I will discuss each of these in turn.

Community-Based Sanctions

Community-based sanctions primarily involve placement into live-in facilities such as **half-way houses** and **residential treatment centers** (RTCs). These kinds of facilities provide the opportunity for treatment, and they allow for more structure—while maintaining some degree of freedom—than would be the case if convicted felons were incarcerated in a jail or prison (see Mays and Winfree 2009:110–11).

Probation

Researchers have found that the offenders most likely to receive probation were those convicted of property offenses or drug offenses (30 percent each). Those convicted of "other" offenses and weapons offenses received probation 29 percent and 27 percent of the time, respectively. By contrast, individuals convicted of violent offenses (including murder/non-negligent manslaughter, rape/sexual assault, robbery, and aggravated assault) only received probation 20 percent of the time (Durose and Langan 2007).

The growth in the number of convicted felons sentenced to probation has slowed somewhat in recent years. Compared with 1994, convicted felons in 2004 were less likely to receive probation and more likely to be incarcerated (Glaze and Bonczar 2007). Nevertheless, in 2008 nearly 5.1 million people were on probation. This compares with 828,169 who were on parole and 1.5 million who were in prison. Table 8.1 shows the growth in correctional populations in the United States from 2000 to 2008. As this table shows, in 2008 probationers represented 58 percent of the nation's total correctional population. This compares with about 21 percent of the correctional population housed in prisons. The essential point to note here is that probation plays a significant role in the sanctioning and supervision of convicted offenders in the United States.

BOX 8.1
Parole in Canada

Canada is much like the United States in that it employs parole as a means of providing early release from incarceration for certain inmates. Parole is "a discretionary executive process, a function of an administrative board. The National Parole Board, under the authority of the solicitor general of Canada, reviews parole applications made by inmates of federal penitentiaries. The board also has jurisdiction over prisoners in provinces where no provincial parole board exists" (Lemire and Duckett 2010). The National Parole Board defines parole as a "carefully constructed bridge between incarceration and return to the community. It is a conditional release, which allows some offenders to continue to serve the balance of their sentences outside of the institution" (National Parole Board of Canada 2010).

Canadian law requires that most offenders must serve the final one-third of their sentences under what is called statutory release. While the National Parole Board of Canada does not decide on statutory release, the Board can impose conditions related to release. In Canada, after inmates have served one-third of their prison term they are eligible to apply to the National Parole board for "full parole." Unlike the United States, which has parole boards in a number of individual states, Canada maintains a national parole board.

Sources: Lemire and Duckett (2010); National Parole Board of Canada (2010).

TABLE 8.1	Correctional Populations in the United States, 2000–2008			
Year	Total correctional population	Probation	Parole	Prison
2000	6,445,100	3,826,209	723,898	1,316,333
2001	6,581,700	3,931,731	732,333	1,330,007
2002	6,758,800	4,024,067	750,934	1,367,547
2003	6,924,500	4,120,012	769,925	1,390,279
2004	6,995,000	4,143,792	771,852	1,421,345
2005	7,051,900	4,166,757	780,616	1,448,344
2006	7,182,100	4,215,361	799,875	1,492,973
2007	7,247,300	4,234,471	821,177	1,517,867
2008	7,308,200	4,270,917	828,169	1,518,559

Source: Glaze and Bonczar (2009:3).

BOX 8.2

In the News: Current Applicaton of the Rico Act

The federal government's fight against traditional organized crime in the United States (exemplified by the Mafia) was aided by passage of the 1970 Racketeer Influenced and Corrupt Organizations Act. However, in the 1980s attorneys began to recognize the potential of Section 1964(c) of the Act which allowed for civil claims by anyone injured in their person or property as a result of an organized criminal act. This section of the Act provided that a person successful in a RICO suit would receive a judgment three times their actual damages and additionally would receive costs plus attorneys' fees. The predictable result was that lawyers all over the United States tried to establish any type of federal civil claim as a RICO case. As a result of the proliferation of such suits, the federal courts now have established a number of obstacles limiting such litigation. One lawyer who specializes in this field has noted that

> As a result of this effort, civil litigants must jump many hurdles and avoid many pitfalls before they can expect the financial windfall available under RICO, and RICO has become one of the most complicated and unpredictable areas of the law. Today, RICO is almost never applied to the Mafia. Instead, it is applied to individuals, businesses, political protest groups, and terrorist organizations. In short, a RICO claim can arise in almost any context. (Grell 2010)

In fact, the range of federal RICO cases has included groups and individuals as diverse as Major League Baseball, financier Michael Milken, the Hell's Angels, the Latin Kings street gang, and anti-abortion protest groups.

Sources: Grell (2010); Legal Information Institute (2010).

Economic Sanctions

As I mentioned in a previous section, economic sanctions such as fines typically are thought of in misdemeanor cases, but over the past two to three decades the courts increasingly have turned to economic sanctions in felony cases. In most instances, economic sanctions are used with crimes that have a profit motive, such as drug trafficking and organized criminal activity. In fact, when the U.S. Congress passed the **Racketeer Influenced and Corrupt Organizations (RICO) Act** (18 U.S.C. Sections 1961–1968) in 1970 it was largely viewed as the chief means of prosecuting La Cosa Nostra or the so-called Mafia in the United States. For much of the Act's early history that was precisely the way it was utilized by federal law enforcement agencies and federal prosecutors around the country.

A key element of the RICO Act has been the ability of the federal courts to impose economic sanctions against those parties convicted of organized criminal activities in order to make such acts less profitable. These sanctions include hefty fines and the possibility of **forfeiture of property** that can be tied to the profits gained from organized criminal activity. At times these sanctions are imposed as stand-alone penalties, though they can also be added to other punishments including imprisonment. As Box 8.2 shows, the RICO Act now is often used against organizations and individuals other than the traditional organized crime groups that prompted passage of the statute to begin with.

Incarceration

Finally, felony sentences also might involve short periods of incarceration—for example, of less than one year—followed by an extended period of probation. These sentences frequently are considered a form of **shock incarceration**. Some of these short-term sentences are served in jails and other types of local detention facilities. Convicted offenders also may be housed in regular prisons to give them a brief taste of prison life. Shock incarceration is designed to be a specific deterrence (see the discussion of theories of punishment in Chapter 7), and one of the goals of shock incarceration programs is to help minor felons or first-time offenders develop an appreciation for what a long prison term might entail. The result should be the prevention of future violations that might bring about a period of long-term confinement.

Furthermore, some convicted felons may receive sentences involving periods of incarceration in local jails that would not be considered shock incarceration. In 2004, 30 percent of the felons convicted in state courts received local jail sentences. When looking at these dispositions by the type of crime, they ranged from a low of 24 percent for violent offenders to a high of 35 percent for "other offenses" and 31 percent for property crimes (Durose and Langan 2007:3).

Conviction of a felony also may result in prison sentences ranging from one year to life, and at the extreme might result in the execution of the offender when a capital crime has been committed. In 2004, of the 194,570 felons convicted of violent offenses, 54 percent were sentenced to serve time in state prisons. The second largest group was the 44 percent who were convicted of weapons offenses.[2] Table 8.2 shows the complete breakdown of dispositions of convicted state felons in 2004.

The average prison sentence imposed for all felons in state courts in 2004 was fifty-seven months. However, as Table 8.3 shows, this ranged from a high of ninety-two months for violent offenders to a low of forty-one months for "other offenses" and forty-five months for property offenses. This table also shows the length of jail and probation terms in 2004.

As can be seen from Tables 8.2 and 8.3, violent offenders were the most likely to receive prison sentences (54 percent), and they were sentenced to the longest prison terms (between seven and eight years on average). Convicted felony drug offenders in state courts averaged prison terms of four and one-half years, and this compared with federal drug sentences of seven years (Durose and Langan 2007:3).

At the topmost extreme of felony sentencing are life sentences and the death penalty. As the Bureau of Justice Statistics notes, of the 8,400 people convicted of murder or non-negligent manslaughter in 2004, about one-fifth received life sentences. Additionally, during the same year state courts imposed capital sentences on 115 people from twenty-nine states (Durose and Langan 2007:3).

TABLE 8.2	Percent of Dispositions for State Felons Convicted in 2004			
Most serious offense	Prison	Jail	Probation	Other
All offenses	40	30	28	2
Violent offenses	54	24	20	2
Weapons offenses	44	28	27	1
Drug offenses	37	30	30	3
Property offenses	37	31	30	2
Other offenses	34	35	29	2

Source: Durose and Langan (2007:3).

TABLE 8.3	Average Sentence Lengths in Months for State Felons in 2004			
Most serious offense	Total	Prison	Jail	Probation
All offenses	37	57	6	38
Violent offenses	68	92	7	44
Weapons offenses	32	47	7	34
Drug offenses	31	51	6	38
Property offenses	29	45	6	38
Other offenses	24	41	6	38

Source: Durose and Langan (2004:3).

Capital Punishment

The death penalty has been in the news a great deal over the past decade, principally as a result of a number of high-profile cases that have highlighted the problem of wrongful convictions. I address the issue of wrongful convictions in Chapter 12, but in this section I discuss the scope of capital sentencing in the United States.

To begin with, capital punishment has been part of the sentencing scheme in the United States since the founding of the nation. The framers of the Constitution noted in the Fifth Amendment that "No person shall be...deprived of *life*, liberty, or property, without due process of law" [emphasis added]. The assumption was that since capital punishment had been used in England and in the colonies, it would also be available in the new nation. Since prisons as we know them did not emerge until the early 1800s, corporal punishment (for less serious crimes) and capital punishment (for more serious crimes) were widely practiced.

By the time the twentieth century arrived, states had decided whether capital punishment would be available for certain offenses. The majority of states (about thirty-eight for most of the twentieth century) allowed the death penalty to be imposed for a handful of offenses, but most used it only in cases of murder. Roughly one-fourth of the states opted not to have the death penalty and instead imposed long prison terms. From the 1960s until the 1970s, executions continued to decline, and in the early 1970s the United States Supreme Court heard the case of *Furman v. Georgia*, 408 U.S. 238 (1972) that sought to end capital punishment, which it asserted were arbitrary and capricious. Indeed, the majority opinion in *Furman* found that the death penalty as it was being imposed in most states gave entirely too much discretion to sentencing juries. The Court did not say then, and it has not said yet, that the death penalty was, in and of itself, unconstitutional.

As a result of the *Furman* decision, Georgia and most other states went back and rewrote their death penalty laws. Several factors resulted from this effort. For example, states now separate the jury's responsibility in determining guilt from its responsibility in deciding the appropriate punishment. This process is known as a **bifurcated hearing** procedure.

Additionally, juries must consider both **aggravating circumstances** and **mitigating circumstances** in arriving at a sentencing decision. Aggravating circumstances are those factors that appear to make the offense more serious or worthy of additional punishment, while mitigating circumstances make the offense appear less serious. Aggravating circumstances might include elements such as the crime was especially heinous or there was extreme cruelty, there was a combination of crimes (rape or robbery and murder), the offense was committed by a group of individuals, the crime was committed with the use of a weapon (especially a firearm), the offender had an extensive criminal history, or the victim was especially vulnerable (very young or very old). By contrast, examples of mitigating circumstances might be youthfulness, diminished mental capacity, or killings prompted by domestic violence (although in situations that might not be considered self-defense).

Furthermore, states require sentencing juries to arrive at unanimous verdicts in regard to imposition of the death penalty. Finally, all states but one (South Carolina) now provide for an automatic appeal of a capital sentence to the state court of last resort.

With these changes in place, Georgia's revised death penalty law was challenged in the case of *Gregg v. Georgia*, 428 U.S. 153 (1976), and in 1977 executions began again with the State of Utah putting Gary Gilmore to death by firing squad (see Mailer 1980).

Currently, 34 states plus the federal government provide for capital punishment, and since Gary Gilmore's execution, through the end of 2009, there have been 1,188 people executed in the United States, or about thirty-seven people per year on average. Of this number, the State of Texas leads by far with 447 executions, followed by Virginia with 105, Oklahoma with 91, Florida with 68, and Missouri with 67. Six states with the death penalty had only one execution each, and another nine reported no executions for the period 1977 to 2009 (Snell 2010:18).

At the end of 2009 there were 3,173 people on death row in the United States, and this was 37 fewer than at the end of 2008. The states with the largest death row populations in 2009 were California (with 668), Florida (with 391), Texas (with 356), and Pennsylvania (with 223). These four states house just over half of the nation's death row inmates.

Out of the 3,173 inmates under a capital sentence in 2009, only 58 were women. Additionally, 1,795 of the total (57 percent) were white and 1,343 (42 percent) were black (Snell 2010:8). It is important to note, though, that since 1977, 672 whites (57 percent) have been executed compared with 411 (35 percent) blacks (Snell 2010:16). Even though blacks are executed in smaller numbers than their percentages on death row (35 percent versus 42 percent), these numbers represent—but do not fully explain—the racial disproportionality of the death penalty in the United States.

THE SENTENCING DECISION MAKING PROCESS

I have mentioned in a number of places throughout this text that several actors in the judicial process have an impact on sentencing as well as other decisions. At this point I will focus on the roles that prosecutors and judges in particular play in sentencing decisions.

The prosecuting attorneys have a number of tactics at their disposal that can impact the sentencing process. In Chapter 7 we examined the plea bargaining process, but here I need to highlight some of the tactics that enhance the prosecuting attorney's strategic role both in plea bargaining and in the sentencing of convicted offenders.

One of the prosecutor's major powers lies in the decision whether to prosecute or not (see Cole 2004). Simply put, the prosecutor can decide not to file criminal charges in spite of the facts uncovered in a police investigation.

Next, the prosecutor exercises a great deal of influence over the particular crimes (and how many crimes) with which the defendant actually gets charged. This authority allows prosecutors to engage in overcharging for tactical advantages, and there are two ways the prosecutor can overcharge. First, the prosecutor can employ **horizontal overcharging**, or charging the defendant with as many different offenses, or as many counts of a single offense, as possible (Holten and Lamar 1991). Attorneys sometimes call this approach "bed sheeting," implying that the prosecutor is trying to cover the defendant with every possible offense.

Prosecutors also can engage in **vertical overcharging**. This strategy can be seen in cases where the defendant is charged with a more serious crime than the evidence might be able to support at trial. For example, defendants routinely may be charged with first degree murder, even in situations where the facts uncovered in the police investigation would indicate a second degree murder or even manslaughter charge. Both of these overcharging strategies give the prosecutor a tactical advantage in plea bargaining as well as at trial. While some people might raise questions about the ethics of overcharging, some prosecutors routinely do it, and there is nothing legally impermissible about the practice (see Gershman 2009).

Judges can also exercise discretion in sentencing, and one of the primary ways is through their choice among the variety of sentences that have been defined by the legislature. As we have seen, they can impose probation, fines and other economic sanctions, community service, jail terms, and prison terms. Even in situations where the law very narrowly prescribes the appropriate sentence, judges still can exercise discretion. For example, in appropriate circumstances the law may allow judges to suspend all or part of the sentence.

Additionally, a significant factor that can enter into the sentencing equation is the option of **concurrent sentences** versus **consecutive sentences**. With concurrent sentences, the judge allows the sentences for several charges to be served at the same time. This could mean that the actual time served might be determined by the most severe crime for which the defendant was charged and convicted. By contrast, consecutive sentences allow judges to "stack" multiple terms of imprisonment one on top of the other. The net effect is to make the offender serve all or a large part of one sentence before beginning the next sentence. This procedure allows judges to increase the total time served, sometimes substantially. The imposition of consecutive sentences allows judges to extend the time served for especially heinous crimes, in situations where a repeat offender is being sentenced, or where the offender seems unrepentant concerning the offense.

In addition to the option of concurrent versus consecutive sentences, states also provide for different approaches in determining the appropriate sentence length. In the next section we will examine the sentencing schemes that define whether a prison term is of a fixed amount or whether it falls within a permissible range.

SENTENCING STRATEGIES EMPLOYED

INDETERMINATE SENTENCING

A number of other factors must be considered in the process of imposing sentences. Beginning in the nineteenth century, **indeterminate sentences** started to emerge as one way of dealing with offenders that would stress individualization and rehabilitation. From the 1930s until the 1970s, every state and the federal government utilized indeterminate sentences. Some states still employ these sentencing systems where there is sometimes a minimum sentence specified, but the criminal statutes establish a maximum period of potential confinement (Tonry 1999). For instance, with the least serious felonies the law may provide for a sentence of not less than one year and not more than five years in a state prison. However, once the judge imposes the sentence, the actual time served will be determined by the state parole-granting authority, usually the parole board (Bonczar 2008; Glaze and Bonczar 2009).

Today, approximately two-thirds of the states still retain some form of indeterminate sentencing, and Michael Tonry offers three reasons why indeterminate sentencing still dominates the sentencing schemes of most states:

(1) Inertia—as is true of most governmental policies and practices, once they are in place they are difficult to change.

(2) Efficiency—indeterminate sentencing gives judges, prisons, and parole authorities increased flexibility to adjust correctional populations to suit resource availability.

(3) General satisfaction—actors and agencies within the criminal justice system may simply feel that indeterminate sentencing helps them achieve a number of legitimate correctional goals. (Tonry 1999: 3).

BOX 8.3

In Their Own Words: Indeterminate Sentencing

Michael Tonry is one of the nation's leading scholars on criminal justice policy, especially as it relates to the courts and sentencing. He observes that there are two primary goals of indeterminate sentencing—rehabilitation and public safety—that keep it as a viable method of imposing criminal sanctions. In relation to rehabilitation Tonry says:

> Indeterminate sentencing views human beings as malleable and redeemable and, accordingly, allows maximum scope for efforts to provide services to offenders and to expose them to opportunities for self-improvement and advancement (1999:5).

In terms of public safety, Tonry adds:

> Indeterminate sentencing allows judges and corrections officials routinely to take public safety considerations into account when making decisions about individual offenders. Decisions about parole release can take account of offenders' risk profiles, and decisions about probation conditions, supervision, and revocations can be fine-tuned to the particular risks individual offenders present and the temptations they face (1999:5).

While these are not the only goals associated with indeterminate sentencing, they are among the most frequently mentioned.

Source: Michael Tonry is Professor of Law and Public Policy at the University of Minnesota School of Law.

DETERMINATE SENTENCING

In contrast to indeterminate sentences, since the mid-1970s a number of states have moved in the direction of **determinate sentences** (Steen 2002). This movement was the result of criticisms from both ends of the political spectrum. Liberals believed that indeterminate sentencing coupled with traditional parole decision-making gave judges broad-based discretion that could be employed in a discriminatory way. By contrast, conservatives saw indeterminate sentencing as being untruthful in that the sentence imposed by the court frequently was not the sentence actually served. In some ways, they saw indeterminate sentencing as providing merely a "slap on the wrist" to convicted offenders rather than imposing on them the punishment they deserved.

A 1996 national survey of state sentencing practices found that thirteen states—Arizona, California, Delaware, Florida, Illinois, Maine, Minnesota, Mississippi, New Mexico, North Carolina, Oregon, Virginia, and Washington—had what could be classified as determinate sentencing systems (Bureau of Justice Assistance 1996). Determinate sentences provide for a specific amount of time to be served by a convicted offender—such as two years—and most of the states that employ determinate sentences have abolished discretionary parole as an early-release mechanism. In place of parole most determinate sentencing states now establish the release date based on the sentence imposed by the courts minus any **good time credits** accumulated.

BOX 8.4   In the News: Determinate Sentencing and Prison Populations

One of the consistent themes in criminal justice literature is that when states shift from indeterminate sentencing to determinate sentencing this has an impact on state prison populations: namely, the number of inmates increases, sometimes substantially. However, what does the evidence really show? A research project conducted by the Vera Institute examined state sentencing policies and prison populations from 1975 to 2006 and found the following:

(1) Surprisingly, states that had determinate sentencing combined with presumptive sentencing guidelines "had lower incarceration rates and smaller growth in incarceration rates than other states."

(2) States that utilized determinate sentencing along with voluntary sentencing guidelines "had larger growth in incarceration rates than other states."

(3) Non-policy factors such as higher property crime rates, larger minority populations, higher per capita incomes, higher numbers of arrests for drug offenses, and more religiously conservative general populations all were as likely to influence incarceration rates as sentencing policies.

Source: Stemen, Rengifo, and Wilson (2006).

One of the concerns associated with determinate sentencing is the impact this sentencing system has on prison populations. Box 8.4 provides information on recent findings about how different sentencing schemes might influence the size of inmate populations in various states.

STRUCTURED SENTENCING

In addition to indeterminate sentencing and determinate sentencing, guided or **structured sentences** now play a major role in the sentencing process. Beginning in 1983 in the State of Minnesota, **sentencing guidelines** and other forms of guided sentences (such as presumptive sentences) define for judges the appropriate sentences for each crime (Blumstein 1984; Knapp 1982, 1984; Tonry 1999).

Most sentencing guidelines systems utilize a two-dimensional sentencing grid that considers the present offense with which the defendant is charged, and the defendant's criminal history. Figure 8.1 provides an example of a sentencing guidelines grid. Factors such as age, race, socio-economic status, drug use, and employment history—which could all be associated with prejudice—are not considered relevant in most guided sentencing schemes. In fact, one of the major justifications in utilizing sentencing guidelines is to reduce judicial discretion and thus to reduce sentencing disparities.

Structured sentences in their various forms are designed to accomplish a number of goals. There seem to be four primary objectives that have emerged from the states that pioneered structured sentencing. First, structured sentencing allows policymakers to have control over sentencing policies. Traditionally, this has been a function of legislatures, and most legislative approaches have proven to be inflexible. Second, structured sentences can be linked to available prison space. This means that, if necessary, sentences can be restructured to prevent prison crowding and the costly litigation that often results from such a situation. Third, structured sentencing can promote the development and expansion of community corrections alternatives. As most states have realized, because of the tremendous costs involved, they cannot rely on institutional options as the primary way of supervising their correctional populations. Finally, the primary goal of most structured sentencing systems is to eliminate "unwarranted racial, ethnic, gender, and geographical disparities in sentencing" (Tonry 1999:8). Some debate exists over the degree to which structured sentencing has been able to accomplish these goals (or whether it can accomplish them), but structured sentences demonstrate another way that states have tried to deal with the dissatisfaction often expressed over traditional sentencing methods.

MANDATORY SENTENCING

Currently the federal government and all states have some form of **mandatory minimum sentences** (Parent, Dunworth, McDonald, and Rhodes 1997). This approach is designed to assure that certain convicted offenders will receive a specified prison term for their crimes. These sentences may range from required prison terms or sentence enhancements for certain drug or weapons crimes, to **habitual offender laws** that

FIGURE 8.1 SENTENCING GUIDELINES GRID

SEVERITY LEVEL OF CONVICTION OFFENSE (Common offenses listed in italics)		CRIMINAL HISTORY SCORE						
		0	1	2	3	4	5	6 or more
Murder, 2nd Degree (intentional murder; drive-by-shootings)	XI	306 261–367	326 278–391	346 295–415	366 312–439	386 329–463	406 346–480[2]	426 363–480[2]
Murder, 3rd Degree Murder, 2nd Degree (unintentional murder)	X	150 128–180	165 141–198	180 153–216	195 166–234	210 179–252	225 192–270	240 204–288
Assault, 1st Degree Controlled Substance Crime, 1st Degree	IX	86 74–103	98 84–117	110 94–132	122 104–146	134 114–160	146 125–175	158 135–189
Aggravated Robbery, 1st Degree Controlled Substance Crime, 2nd Degree	VIII	48 41–57	58 50–69	68 58–81	78 67–93	88 75–105	98 84–117	108 92–129
Felony DWI	VII	36	42	48	54 46–64	60 51–72	66 57–79	72 62–86
Assault, 2nd Degree Felon in Possession of a Firearm	VI	21	27	33	39 34–46	45 39–54	51 44–61	57 49–68
Residential Burglary Simple Robbery	V	18	23	28	33 29–39	38 33–45	43 37–51	48 41–57
Nonresidential Burglary	IV	12[1]	15	18	21	24 21–28	27 23–32	30 26–36
Theft Crimes (Over $2,500)	III	12[1]	13	15	17	19 17–22	21 18–25	23 20–27
Theft Crimes ($2,500 or less) Check Forgery ($200–$2,500)	II	12[1]	12[1]	13	15	17	19	21 18–25
Sale of Simulated Controlled Substance	I	12[1]	12[1]	12[1]	13	15	17	19 17–22

☐ Presumptive commitment to state imprisonment. First Degree Murder is excluded from the guidelines by law and continues to have a mandatory life sentence. See section II.E. Mandatory Sentences for policy regarding those sentences controlled by law.

▨ Presumptive stayed sentence; at the discretion of the judge, up to a year in jail and/or other non-jail sanctions can be imposed as conditions of probation. However, certain offenses in this section of the grid always carry a presumptive commitment to state prison. See sections II.C. Presumptive Sentence and II.E. Mandatory Sentences.

[1] One year and one day

[2] M.S. § 244.09 requires the Sentencing Guidelines to provide a range of 15% downward and 20% upward from the presumptive sentence. However, because the statutory maximum sentence for these offenses is no more than 40 years, the range is capped at that number.

Effective August 1, 2006

Source: Minnesota Sentencing Guidelines Commission (2007).

stipulate long prison terms, sometimes without parole, for those convicted or three or more felonies. The most famous of the habitual offender laws are those designated by the phrase "three strikes and you're out" used by California and several other states. In California, offenders convicted of a third strike are sentenced to prison terms of twenty-five years to life (Dodge, Harris, and Burke 2009).

There have been a number of legal challenges to these laws, arguing that they constitute "cruel and unusual punishment" in violation of the Eighth Amendment to the

Constitution. However, in a series of cases the U.S. Supreme Court has found virtually all of these laws to be constitutional (see, for example, *Rummel v. Estelle*, 445 U.S. 263 [1980]), and like the other challenges to habitual offender laws, the Supreme Court has upheld the constitutionality of three-strikes laws (see *Ewing v. California*, 538 U.S. 11 [2003]; *Lockyer v. Andrade*, 538 U.S. 63, [2003]).[3]

RACE, ETHNICITY, AND GENDER IN SENTENCING

I deal with concerns over race, ethnicity, and gender in the judicial process more fully in Chapter 12; however, in this section I briefly examine the impact that sentencing has on different racial or ethnic groups, and the disparities that may exist among males and females as they are processed by the courts.

MINORITIES AND SENTENCING

To begin with, there is a long-standing debate over the degree to which sentencing disproportionately affects racial and ethnic minorities in this country. A large number of factors can enter into the sentencing equation, and while this is a complex issue a report from the Bureau of Justice Statistics sheds some light on the question. The Census Bureau estimates that in 2008 12.8 percent of the U.S. population was black. By contrast, of all felons sentenced in state courts in 2004 38 percent were black, and the numbers vary by offense category. For example, the smallest numbers of blacks with felony sentences (27 percent) were in the "other" offense category. This contrasts with 46 percent who were sentenced for drug crimes and 55 percent who were sentenced for weapons offenses (Durose and Langan 2007: 2).

In comparison, the percentages of whites sentenced for felonies in 2004 ranged from a low of 43 percent for weapons charges to a high of 64 percent for property crimes and 69 percent for the "other" category of offenses. Therefore, while whites constituted the majority of felons sentenced in every category except weapons offenses, blacks were significantly overrepresented in felony convictions compared with their numbers in the general population.

GENDER AND SENTENCING

The picture of sentencing and gender is substantially different than that of sentencing and race/ethnicity. The Census Bureau estimates that in 2008 50.7 percent of the population in the United States was female. However, in terms of the 2004 felony sentencing statistics, females only constituted 18 percent of the total number of people sentenced for having committed a felony. The three largest categories for which women were sentenced for felonies were: property crimes (26 percent), drug offenses (18 percent), and "other" felonies (13 percent). These numbers demonstrate that women are tremendously underrepresented in the offender statistics in this country.

Three different explanations have been offered for this phenomenon: (1) women are better at the crimes they commit and they escape apprehension; (2) culturally, biologically, or for some other reason, women are less likely to commit crimes than men; and

(3) in most instances the criminal justice system is much less likely to sanction women than men. The last explanation has been called the **chivalry hypothesis**, and there is a great body of literature related to this idea (see Mays and Winfree 2006:71).

The second and third explanations offered for the underrepresentation of women in crime have been subjected to the greatest research. In terms of biological differences, "Some criminologists believe that the human traits that produce violence and aggression have been advanced by the long process of human evolution" (Siegel 2011:118). From this perspective, aggressive males have a greater likelihood of finding suitable mates and passing along their genetic traits (including behavioral patterns) to their offspring. Thus, males are overrepresented in crimes of violence. Additionally, biological researchers have found that higher levels of the male hormone testosterone are associated with aggressive behavior (see, for example, Bernhardt 1997). Finally, some research from the mid-1980s found that different actors within the criminal justice system were likely to respond to most female offenders in a much less severe way than were male offenders (see, Smith, Visher, and Davidson 1984; Visher 1983).

TRENDS IN SENTENCING

I have touched on a number of topics that could be included as trends in sentencing already. However, as I bring this chapter to a conclusion I want to highlight more clearly four changes—determinate sentencing, sentencing guidelines, mandatory minimum sentences, and truth in sentencing—that have been occurring in the sentencing environment of courts in the United States (see, for example, Ditton and Wilson 1999).

CHANGES IN SENTENCING POLICY

Beginning in the mid-1970s, two major changes occurred in sentencing policies nationwide. First, a number of states moved away from their traditional reliance on indeterminate sentencing. Popular dissatisfaction concerning the "coddling of criminals" from conservatives, and the discretion associated with both sentencing and early release by parole boards from liberals spurred the change. The movement toward determinacy was supposed to provide more certain and realistic sentencing for felony offenders. In some states the changes in sentencing policies brought about significant increases in prison populations. In other states the changes were smaller or they did not occur at all (see Stemen et al. 2006; Tonry 1999).

Second, to help reduce unwarranted sentencing disparities, several states implemented structured sentences, typified by sentencing guidelines (Tonry 1999). One of the primary goals of structured sentences was to limit the amount of discretion that judges had in choosing the appropriate sentence for the crime. These sentences were designed to restrict judges' sentencing options to legally relevant factors. In most instances, structured sentences were based on (1) the instant offense with which the individual was charged and convicted, and (2) the offender's criminal history. No longer could education, work history, family structure, drug use, or other extra-legal factors be taken into consideration.

In order to help correctional authorities control the impact of sentencing changes on prison populations, most states instituted two policies. First, states (including those that had retained indeterminate sentencing systems) granted good time credits for inmates who exhibited good behavior and those who participated in programming efforts. The result was discount rates—sometimes substantial—that reduced the amount of time inmates served. These rates ranged from 54 days per year (a 15 percent reduction) up to one day of good time credit for each day served (a 50 percent reduction). In most states the allocation of good time credits resulted in mandatory releases instead of the discretionary procedures that had been in place with parole. Second, states like Minnesota that had implemented sentencing guidelines often tied the structure of the guidelines to state prison capacities. In effect, these states decided in advance how many prison inmates they could afford to house.

While good time credits and other early release mechanisms gave correctional officials some control over prison populations, the fact that inmates did not serve the sentences actually imposed again brought about criticisms. As you will see in the next section, states responded with additional changes in sentencing laws that resulted in even greater punitiveness.

INCREASED PUNITIVENESS

Three trends in sentencing policies exemplified an increasingly punitive attitude toward offenders. First, a number of states passed or expanded their habitual offender laws. These statutes were aimed at providing substantially longer sentences for offenders that had been convicted of three or more felonies in the past. As I have mentioned previously in this chapter, California's "three-strikes and you're out" law was one of the most visible of these laws.

The second change toward more punitive sentences has been the introduction of mandatory minimum sentences. All states and the federal government mandate specific minimum prison sentences for certain offenses. Occasionally, these mandatory minimum sentences are for drug offenses, but most frequently they are tied to violent crimes, particularly those committed with a firearm.

The third indication of increasing punitiveness is the "**truth in sentencing**" movement. Conservatives have pushed for the implementation of truth in sentencing, especially in states that had established determinate sentencing schemes. In 1994 the United States Congress passed the Violent Crime Control and Law Enforcement Act. This federal legislation provided incentive grants to states that adopted a truth-in-sentencing orientation.

The idea behind this policy has been that inmates should have to serve all or at least most of the sentences that the courts imposed on them, and there are substantial restrictions on discretionary parole and good time credits. Truth in sentencing was modeled on the sentencing system employed by the federal government that allowed federal prison inmates to accumulate fifty-four days of good time credit per year. This meant that inmates now would have to serve at least 85 percent of the sentence they had been given in these states (Ditton and Wilson 1999). Table 8.4 shows the states that met the federal truth-in-sentencing funding requirement in 1999.

The net effect of these two trends has been to increase prison populations in the states that utilized them. States that made sentencing policies more punitive generally have had incarceration rates that were greater than those that had not established such policies (Ditton and Wilson 1999; Stemen et al. 2006).

CAPITAL PUNISHMENT

An additional area where there has been some change in the past two decades is in the imposition and execution of capital punishment. Generally speaking, since 1998 there has been a downward trend in the number of people sentenced to die in the United States. Likewise, the number of actual executions has dropped from a modern-day high of ninety-eight in 1999 to thirty-seven in 2008 (Snell 2009).

While it may be difficult to account for all of the reasons these numbers have declined, a significant factor may be the issue of wrongful convictions that has been witnessed in a number of states. We will return to this issue in Chapter 12, but it is significant to note that in 2008 there were 111 people who received death sentences in the United States, and there were eighty-two people removed from death row for reasons other than executions. Some of these people died before they could be executed, a few had their sentences commuted to life in prison, but some were found to have been wrongfully convicted and they were unconditionally released from prison. Therefore, while we continue to impose capital punishment in thirty-four states, the average offender is still spending nearly thirteen years on death row (Snell 2010). This would

TABLE 8.4 States Meeting the Truth-in-Sentencing Requirement, 1999	
Arizona	Missouri
California	New Jersey
Connecticut	New York
Delaware	North Carolina
Florida	North Dakota
Georgia	Ohio
Illinois	Oklahoma
Iowa	Oregon
Kansas	Pennsylvania
Louisiana	South Carolina
Maine	Tennessee
Michigan	Utah
Minnesota	Virginia
Mississippi	Washington

Note: These states require some or all of their prison inmates to serve 85 percent of the sentence imposed by the courts. This list is accurate as of January 1999. Other states may have been added or deleted more recently.

Source: Ditton and Wilson (1999:2).

seem to indicate that most of the states show relatively little interest in moving quickly to execute the offenders they have on death row.

SUMMARY

Sentencing is one of the most complex tasks undertaken by the courts in the United States. Given the fact that relatively few cases go to trial, a considerable amount of time spent by the courtroom work group surrounds this issue of sentencing.

As we have seen in this chapter, much of the sentencing responsibility falls on the judge. Once a guilty verdict has been returned by a jury, the judge—typically with input from the probation department—must decide on the appropriate sentence. However, it is important to note that the prosecuting attorney and the defense attorney also may influence sentencing decisions. Furthermore, in cases that are resolved through plea bargaining the prosecutor and the defense attorney will negotiate an agreeable sentence and then present this to the judge. The judge, in turn, must be assured that the defendant is entering the plea voluntarily, and that he or she understands the consequences of a guilty plea—such as forgoing the option of appeal. In most instances the judge will accept the plea agreement that was reached.

After guilt has been established, either by a guilty plea or a verdict of guilt, the judge must select the appropriate sentence from among the available options. The choices will be influenced by whether the offense was a misdemeanor or a felony. The most common sentences for misdemeanors are fines, probation (potentially with restitution or community service), and local jail time. For felonies, the potential sanctions include economic sanctions (fines and forfeitures), probation, incarceration for a certain number of years (one year or more), life imprisonment (possibly without the opportunity for parole), and the death penalty. State and federal statutes establish the options that face the judge in each case, but judges still retain a great deal of discretion in the sentencing process.

In many criminal cases the prosecutor will file a variety of charges. Some of this is a tactical decision that allows the prosecutor greater negotiating room in the plea bargaining process. However, when these cases go to trial it is possible that a defendant will be convicted of multiple charges or counts. In those situations the judge must decide on the appropriateness of concurrent sentences versus consecutive sentences. Most of the time judges allow defendants to serve multiple sentencing concurrently (at the same time), which is the typical approach to sentencing. In some instances, however, the judge may choose to impose consecutive sentences (one after the other). Defendants who have committed particularly heinous crimes, those who seem unrepentant, and those who appear to be career criminals may receive consecutive sentences as a demonstration of society's disdain over the criminal acts.

Nationwide, today criminal sentencing involves a complex array of possible options. In fact, it is nearly impossible to easily summarize how states now have structured their sentencing systems. For much of the twentieth century the dominant sentencing scheme in the United States was indeterminate sentencing. With indeterminate sentences the judge would impose a range of punishment that was prescribed by law.

The final decision about the release of the offender came through the process of discretionary parole. As a result of discontent from a numbers of quarters, a number of states now have moved to determinate sentencing where convicted offenders receive a definite prison sentence, less any good time credits they may accumulate.

In addition to the consideration of indeterminate versus determinate sentencing, some states now have structured sentences typified by sentencing guidelines. The picture of structured sentences is complicated by the fact that some states have mandatory guidelines, whereas in other states the guidelines are voluntary or advisory. A few states take guided sentences one step further and impose what are called presumptive sentences. These sentences are the norm that must be selected by the judge, except in cases that justify a substantial departure—either up or down. Finally, the imposition of mandatory minimum sentences has become more common in many states. These sentences may be imposed in certain drug offenses, for crimes committed with a firearm, or in situations where the offender may be labeled a career criminal or a habitual offender. In general, when mandatory minimum sentences are employed frequently by a state they have the result of increasing prison populations.

There are several trends in sentencing that have been witnessed by the courts. As we have mentioned, some states have moved in the direction of determinate sentencing with the elimination of discretionary parole. Following the lead of Minnesota, a handful of states have developed sentencing guidelines in an effort to curb some of the discretion (and sentencing disparity) traditionally associated with judges and sentencing. In order to further restrict the use of early release mechanisms, a few states have embraced the so-called "truth in sentencing" movement. These states now require some or all prison inmates to serve at least 85 percent of the sentences imposed. Naturally, with restricted release procedures like these, prison populations tend to grow.

In the end, sentencing policy in the United States continues to be a major topic of discussion among policy makers and academics. The public may or may not be fully informed about the various options available to the courts, but they are concerned if they feel that offenders are not receiving the amount and types of punishments they deserve.

QUESTIONS FOR CRITICAL THINKING

1. You are a new probation officer and you are preparing your first presentence investigation report. What kinds of factors (information) should go into such a report? Is there anything that should not be included?

2. It has been said that probation officers and judges agree on the appropriate sentence in a case over 90 percent of the time. Is this a function of the "going rate?" Are probation officers likely to make a recommendation that the judge would reject outright? Why? What could the consequences be?

3. Why is probation recommended for so many misdemeanor and felony cases? Is probation really a sanction? Justify your answer.

4. If judges order restitution and/or community service, who has the responsibility to make sure that the requirements are fulfilled? Does this create a problem?

5. In organized crime cases (however we define them), what purposes do fines and property forfeitures serve?

6. An interesting exercise is to poll the members of your class on their attitudes toward the death penalty. Give them the following three options: (a) "I am opposed to the death penalty in all situations," (b) "under the appropriate circumstances (for example, first degree murder) I am in favor of the death penalty," and (c) "I really can't decide how I feel about the death penalty."

7. What are some of the primary reasons people are in favor of or opposed to capital punishment? What problems have arisen recently concerning the death penalty?

8. Why would prosecuting attorneys engage in overcharging criminal defendants? Although this practice is not illegal, does it seem ethical to you? Why or why not?

9. One of the justifications for indeterminate sentencing is rehabilitation. Is rehabilitation a viable concept in today's correctional climate? How do you think the public feels about rehabilitation?

10. Sentencing guidelines were developed to address a number of perceived problems in sentencing. One of these problems was sentence disparities. Do judges have too much discretion in sentencing? Does discretion lead to discrimination? Explain.

11. What do we mean by "truth in sentencing?" What has led to the movement in a number of states?

RECOMMENDED READINGS

Champion, Dean J. (1989). *The U.S. Sentencing Guidelines: Implications for Criminal Justice.* New York: Praeger Publishers. The United States Sentencing Guidelines were implemented in 1987. In the two years following this event Champion edited this volume that has thirteen contributions from a group of legal and social science scholars who comment on different aspects of guided sentences and the likely consequences of the federal courts utilizing sentencing guidelines. It is interesting to look back over the past two decades to see how the various scholars speculated that the federal sentencing guidelines would turn out, and now to observe the actual consequences of these guidelines.

Griset, Pamala L. (1991). *Determinate Sentencing: The Promise and the Reality of Retributive Justice.* Albany, NY: State University of New York Press. Griset traces the political factors that led to the implementation of determinate sentencing in several states during the 1970s and 1980s. Her basic premise is that "the determinate ideal is a myth founded on false notions of power and purpose" (1991:1). She specifically examines the movement to determinate sentencing in New York State, and suggests that retributive justice abandons the notion of rehabilitation in order to pursue punishment for the sake of punishment.

Spohn, Cassia (2009). *How Do Judges Decide?* 2nd ed. Thousand Oaks, CA: Sage Publications. Spohn covers topics such as the goals of sentencing and the sentencing process. She particularly focuses on the ways that judges decide and the impact that sentencing decisions have on gender, race, and ethnicity.

KEY TERMS

active probation
aggravating
circumstances
bifurcated hearing
capital punishment
chivalry hypothesis
community-based
sanctions
community service
concurrent sentences
consecutive sentences
day fines
determinate sentences
economic sanctions

fines
forfeiture of property
good time credits
habitual offender laws
half-way houses
horizontal overcharging
indeterminate sentences
informal probation
infractions
intermediate sanctions
mandatory minimum
sentences
mitigating circumstances
petty misdemeanors

presentence investigation
report
probation
Racketeer Influenced and
Corrupt Organizations
Act
residential treatment
centers
sentencing guidelines
shock incarceration
structured sentences
summary probation
truth in sentencing
vertical overcharging

REFERENCES

Bernat, Frances P. (2009). *Ring*ing in Arizona: Did the U.S. Supreme Court's Decision in *Ring v. Arizona* Adversely Impact the State High Court's Workload? In *Courts and Justice*, 4th ed., ed. G. Larry Mays and Peter R. Gregware, 250–62. Long Grove, IL: Waveland Press.

Bernhardt, Paul (1997). Influences of Serotonin and Testosterone in Aggression and Dominance: Convergence with Social Psychology. *Current Directions in Psychological Science* 6:44–48.

Blumstein, Alfred (1984). Sentencing Reforms: Impact and Implications. *Judicature* 68:129–39.

Bonczar, Thomas P. (2008). *Characteristics of State Parole Supervising Agencies, 2006*. Washington, DC: Bureau of Justice Statistics, U.S. Department of Justice.

Bureau of Justice Assistance (1996). *National Survey of State Sentencing Structures*. Washington, DC: U.S. Department of Justice.

Cole, George F. (2004). The Decision to Prosecute. In *The Criminal Justice System: Politics and Policies*, 9th ed., ed. George F. Cole, Marc G. Gertz, and Amy Bunger, 178–88. Belmont, CA: Wadsworth Publishing Co.

County of Ventura (2010). Probation Agency. http://portal.countyofventura.org/portal/page/portal/Probation.

Ditton, Paula M., and Doris James Wilson (1999). *Truth in Sentencing in State Prisons*. Washington, DC: Bureau of Justice Statistics, U.S. Department of Justice.

Dodge, Mary, John C. Harris, and Alison Burke (2009). Calling a Strike a Ball: Jury Nullification and "Three Strikes" Cases. In *Courts and Justice*, 4th ed., ed. G. Larry Mays and Peter R. Gregware, 393–403. Long Grove, IL: Waveland Press.

Durose, Matthew R., and Patrick A. Langan (2007). *Felony Sentences in State Courts, 2004*. Washington, DC: Bureau of Justice Statistics, U.S. Department of Justice.

Ewing v. California, 538 U.S. 11 (2003).

Furman v. Georgia, 408 U.S. 238 (1972).

Gershman, Bennett L. (2009). Why Prosecutors Misbehave. In *Courts and Justice*, 4th ed., ed. G. Larry Mays and Peter R. Gregware, 321–31. Long Grove, IL: Waveland Press.

Glaze, Lauren E., and Thomas P. Bonczar (2007). *Probation and Parole in the United States, 2006*. Washington, DC: Bureau of Justice Statistics, U.S. Department of Justice.

Glaze, Lauren E., and Thomas P. Bonczar (2009). *Probation and Parole in the United States, 2008*. Washington, DC: Bureau of Justice Statistics, U.S. Department of Justice.

Gregg v. Georgia, 428 U.S. 153 (1976).

Grell, Jeff (2010). "The RICO Act." http://www.ricoact.com/.

Griset, Pamala L. (1991). *Determinate Sentencing: The Promise and the Reality of Retributive Justice*. Albany, NY: State University of New York Press.

Holten, N. Gary, and Lawson L. Lamar (1991). *The Criminal Courts: Structures, Personnel, and Processes*. New York: McGraw-Hill.

Knapp, Kay A. (1982). Impact of the Minnesota Sentencing Guidelines on Sentencing Practices. *Hamline Law Review* 5:237–56.

Knapp, Kay A. (1984). *The Impact of the Minnesota Sentencing Guidelines*. St. Paul, MN: Minnesota Sentencing Commission.

Kootenai County (2010). Adult Misdemeanor Probation. http://www.kcgov.us/departments/justiceservices/adultmis/

Legal Information Institute (2010). Chapter 96-Racketeer Influenced and Corrupt Organizations. http://www.law.cornell.edu/uscode/18/pIch96.html.

Lemire, Guy and Mona T. Duckett (2010). Probation and Parole. *The Canadian Encyclopedia*. http://www.thecanadianencyclopedia.com.

Lewis v. United States, 518 U.S. 322 (1996).

Lockyer v. Andrade, 538 U.S. 63 (2003).

Mackenzie, Geraldine, Nigel Stobbs, and Jodie O'Leary (2009). *Principles of Sentencing*. Devon, UK: Willan Publishing.

Mailer, Norman (1980). *The Executioner's Song*. New York: Random House.

Mays, G. Larry, and L. Thomas Winfree, Jr. (2009). *Essentials of Corrections*, 4th ed. Belmont, CA: Wadsworth Publishing Co.

Mays, G. Larry, and L. Thomas Winfree, Jr. (2006). *Juvenile Justice*, 2nd ed. Long Grove, IL: Waveland Press.

Minnesota Sentencing Guidelines Commission (2007). *Update Report on Drug Offender Sentencing Issues*. St. Paul, MN: State of Minnesota.

National Parole Board of Canada (2010). "Parole." http://www.pbc-clcc.gc.ca/parle/parle-eng.shtml

Parent, Dale, Terence Dunworth, Douglas McDonald, and William Rhodes (1997). Key Legislative Issues in Criminal Justice: Mandatory Sentences. *NIJ Research in Action*. Washington, DC: U.S. Department of Justice.

Ring v. Arizona, 536 U.S. 584 (2002).

Rummel v. Estelle, 445 U.S. 263 (1980).

Sanborn, Joseph B., Jr. (2009). Pleading Guilty and Plea Bargaining: The Dynamics of Avoiding Trial in American Criminal Courts. In *Courts and Justice*, 4th ed., ed. G. Larry Mays and Peter R. Gregware, 109–28. Long Grove, IL: Waveland Press.

Siegel, Larry J. (2011). *Criminology: The Core*, 4th ed. Belmont, CA: Wadsworth/Cengage.

Smith, David, Christy A. Visher, and L. A. Davidson (1984). Equity and Discretionary Justice: The Influence of Race on Police Arrest Decisions. *Journal of Criminal Law and Criminology* 75:36–66.

Snell, Tracy L. (2007). *Capital Punishment, 2005*. Washington, DC: Bureau of Justice Statistics, U.S. Department of Justice.

Snell, Tracy L. (2010). *Capital Punishment, 2009—Statistical Tables*. Washington, DC: Bureau of Justice Statistics, U.S. Department of Justice.

Steen, Sara (2002). Determinate Sentences. In *Encyclopedia of Crime and Punishment*, ed. David Levinson, 509–12. Thousand Oaks, CA: Sage Publications.

Stemen, Don, Andres Rengifo, and James Wilson (2006). *Of Fragmentation and Fermentation: The Impact of State Sentencing Policies on Incarceration Rates, 1975–2002.* Washington, DC: U.S. Department of Justice.

Tonry, Michael (1999). *Reconsidering Indeterminate and Structured Sentencing.* Washington, DC: National Institute of Justice, U.S. Department of Justice.

Visher, Christy A. (1983). Gender, Police Arrest Decisions, and Notions of Chivalry. *Criminology* 21:5–28.

Walker, Samuel (2006). *Sense and Nonsense About Crime and Drugs*, 6th ed. Belmont, CA: Wadsworth Publishing Co.

Winterfield, Laura A., and Sally T. Hillsman (2004). The Staten Island Day-Fine Project. In *Courts and Justice*, 3rd ed., ed. G. Larry Mays and Peter R. Gregware, 443–55. Long Grove, IL: Waveland Press.

ENDNOTES

[1]Since the last Bureau of Justice Statistics report was prepared, the State of New Mexico has abolished the death penalty and several other states are considering similar measures.

[2]Some of the sentences for weapons charges may involve the illegal possession of a weapon, or the possession of a prohibited weapon, rather than the use of a firearm in the commission of another crime such as robbery.

[3]Under California's three-strikes law, not only do felony convictions count in determining eligibility for a habitual offender sentence, but also certain misdemeanors—termed "wobblers"—might be taken into account as well. Furthermore, while many people believed that the law originally was aimed at violent, personal offenders, most of the people convicted under California's law have been persistent property offenders (Dodge, Harris, and Burke 2009).

PART FOUR

COURT STRUCTURE

9

Courts of Limited Jurisdiction and Specialized Courts

INTRODUCTION

In the state courts systems of the United States, the real workhorses in terms of the numbers of cases processed are the lower-level trial courts. Often these tribunals are called **courts of limited jurisdiction**, courts of inferior jurisdiction, or sometimes special courts. I first introduced these courts in Chapter 1 in a discussion of hierarchical jurisdiction. You might refer back to that section as a brief refresher.

My focus here is on the limited jurisdiction courts, especially since these are the types of courts that most people are likely to encounter as victims, offenders, plaintiffs, and defendants. Quite often the lower levels courts are characterized as "the people's courts," and the reality is that they process a great deal of the people's legal business on a daily basis (Mansfield 1999). Therefore, these frequently overlooked seats of justice are worthy of our attention if for no other reason than the sheer volume of cases they are called upon to process annually.

In this chapter we will consider both state and federal courts of limited jurisdiction. However, before we go any further I need to explain my primary focus on state courts, with much less treatment of federal courts. The principal reason for this orientation is that the state courts of limited jurisdiction are the most pervasive courts of any type in the United States. In fact, forty-six of the fifty states have at least one type of limited jurisdiction court, and some have a variety of different types (see Table 9.1). By contrast, the federal judicial system has four limited jurisdiction courts, plus the United States magistrate judges. Therefore, in the following sections I examine both the state and federal courts of limited jurisdiction and illustrate the differences between the two.

TABLE 9.1	State Courts of Limited Jurisdiction, 2004*
State	**Types of Courts**
Alabama	District Court
	Municipal Court
	Probate Court
Alaska	District Court
Arizona	Justice of the Peace Court
	Municipal Court
Arkansas	City Court
	District Court
Colorado	County Court
	Municipal Court
Connecticut	Probate Court
Delaware	Alderman's Court
	Court of Chancery
	Court of Common Pleas
	Family Court
	Justice of the Peace Court
Florida	County Court
Georgia	City Court
	Civil Court (2 counties)
	County Recorder's Court
	Juvenile Court
	Magistrate Court
	Municipal Court
	Probate Court
	State Court
Hawaii	District Court
Idaho	Magistrates Division
Indiana	City Court
	County Court
	Small Claims Court (1 county)
	Town Court
Kansas	Municipal Court
Kentucky	District Court
Louisiana	City and Parish Courts
	Justice of the Peace Court
	Mayor's Court
Maine	Probate Court
Maryland	District Court
	Orphan's Court

Continued

TABLE 9.1	*Continued*
State	**Types of Courts**
Massachusetts	Boston Municipal Court
	District Court
	Housing Court
	Juvenile Court
	Land Court
	Probate & Family Court
Michigan	District Court
	Municipal Court
	Probate Court
Mississippi	Chancery Court
	County Court
	Justice Court
	Municipal Court
Missouri	Municipal Court
Montana	City Court
	Justice of the Peace Court
	Municipal Court
Nebraska	County Court
	Juvenile Court (3 counties)
	Workers' Compensation Court
Nevada	Justice Court
	Municipal Court
New Hampshire	District Court
	Probate Court
New Jersey	Municipal Court
	Tax Court
New Mexico	Magistrate Court
	Metropolitan Court (1 county)
	Municipal Court
	Probate Court
New York	City Court
	Civil Court (NYC)
	Court of Claims
	Criminal Court (NYC)
	District Court
	Family Court
	Surrogates' Court
	Town and Village Justice Court

Continued

TABLE 9.1	*Continued*
State	**Types of Courts**
North Carolina	District Court
North Dakota	Municipal Court
Ohio	County Court
	Court of Claims
	Mayors Court
	Municipal Court
Oklahoma	Court of Tax Review
	Municipal Court Not of Record
	Municipal Court of Record
Oregon	County Court
	Juvenile Court
	Municipal Court
Pennsylvania	District Justice Court
	Philadelphia Municipal Court
	Philadelphia Traffic Court
	Pittsburgh City Magistrates
Rhode Island	District Court
	Family Court
	Municipal Court
	Probate Court
	Traffic Tribunal
	Workers' Compensation Court
South Carolina	Family Court
	Magistrate Court
	Municipal Court
	Probate Court
South Dakota	Magistrate Court
Tennessee	General Sessions Court
	Juvenile Court
	Municipal Court
Texas	Constitutional County Court
	County Court at Law
	Justice of the Peace Court
	Municipal Court
	Probate Court
Utah	Justice Court
	Juvenile Court

Continued

TABLE 9.1	Continued
State	**Types of Courts**
Vermont	Environmental Court Probate Court Vermont Judicial Bureau
Virginia	District Court
Washington	District Court Municipal Court
West Virginia	Family Court Magistrate Court Municipal Court
Wisconsin	Municipal Court
Wyoming	Circuit Court Municipal Court

Note: States not listed do not have limited jurisdiction courts.
Source: Rottman and Strickland (2006:268–319).

THE STRUCTURE OF LIMITED JURISDICTION COURTS

In this country both civil and criminal cases begin in what are called the courts of **original jurisdiction**, or simply trial courts. These are the courts that are called upon to hold several types of initial hearings and trials. The next section examines the federal courts that fit into this classification, and the following section discusses the various state courts of limited jurisdiction.

FEDERAL COURTS

The federal courts of limited jurisdiction can be classified under two broad categories. First, there are the Article III courts. These are established by the judicial article of the U.S. Constitution. Next, there are the Article I courts. These courts are created under the authority given to Congress by the Constitution to establish certain types of courts. The two limited jurisdiction Article III courts are the U.S. Court of Claims and the U.S. Court of International Trade.

The U.S. Court of Claims meets in Washington, DC, and it has as its sole jurisdiction to hear suits filed against the federal government. The U.S. Court of International Trade meets in New York City, and it deals with cases arising from disputes over **tariffs** (taxes on goods that are imported into the United States) and international trade disputes that involve companies based in the United States (U.S. Courts 2009).

In addition to the two Article III limited jurisdiction federal courts, there are two Article I courts (the U.S. Tax Court and the Bankruptcy courts), plus the United States magistrate judges and two specialized appellate courts. Let us consider the U.S. magistrate judges first.

Technically speaking, the U.S. magistrate judges do not comprise a separate court. Instead, as I have noted in Chapter 4, they serve limited terms of office, and they act as judicial adjuncts to the federal district judges who appoint them (Smith 2009). The U.S. magistrate judges frequently are responsible for the issuance of arrest and search warrants, they conduct initial appearances and some types of hearings (bond, evidentiary, etc.), and they can try civil cases when both sides agree to let them do so. They also may sit in judgment in federal misdemeanor cases.

The United States Tax Court is responsible for cases that involve tax payments and other types of tax issues, especially disputes over the amount taxes paid and the amount owed. Federal bankruptcy courts have exclusive jurisdiction over issues relating to personal and business bankruptcy, and these cases may involve financial restructuring or complete liquidation.

Finally, although I cover appellate courts in Chapter 11, at this point I should note that there are two specialized appellate courts in the federal system: the U.S. Court of Military Appeals and the U.S. Court of Veterans' Appeals. As their names indicate, Congress has given them very narrow jurisdictions.

STATE COURTS

In some state systems there is only one type of court of original jurisdiction, and these are the courts of general trial jurisdiction. Those states do not have separate inferior courts. This is the situation in California, Illinois, Iowa, and Minnesota (Rottman and Strickland 2006). The remaining states have one or more types of limited jurisdiction courts. Table 9.1 provides a list of the different types of limited jurisdiction courts in each state.

As Table 9.1 shows, Arizona, Delaware, Louisiana, Montana, Nevada, and Texas are the sole remaining states that still utilize the old English common law office of **justice of the peace** (Mansfield 1999; Rottman and Strickland 2006). In 2001 Arkansas combined its justice of the peace courts with the municipal courts, and in 2003 Wyoming combined its justice of the peace courts with the circuit courts. Many of the other states that did have justices of the peace eliminated this judicial office during the 1960s and 1970s.

Justices of the peace normally are elected judicial officials, and some serve full-time whereas others serve only part-time. Historically, there were two major criticisms or deficiencies associated with this office. First, there was a notable lack of legal training for the justices of the peace. In fact, no formal legal training was required. Second, in a number of states there was the tradition of paying justices of the peace on a **fee system.** In other words, to cover their salaries and office expenses they were provided with a certain percentage of the fees and fines they collected. This led to a strong suspicion that there was an added incentive to find defendants guilty. As a result of these criticisms, and as many states reformed their court systems in the twentieth century, all states but six eliminated this office or merged it with other courts of limited jurisdiction (Rottman and Strickland 2006; see also, Carp, Stidham, and Manning 2007).

As some states reorganized their court systems in the 1960s and 1970s they abolished the office of justice of the peace and replaced it with a different limited jurisdiction court, such as the **magistrates' courts**. Magistrate judges still are elected, but they have regular offices and courtrooms, and they are paid a salary instead of relying on the fee system for funding. Additionally, many states also allow cities and towns to create their own **municipal courts**. These, too, are courts of limited jurisdiction, but they differ from justice of the peace or magistrate courts in that their jurisdiction is confined to traffic cases and violations of municipal ordinances.

In Chapter 10 I discuss the courts of general trial jurisdiction. There I mention chancery courts, or courts of equity. These courts are something of vestiges from our English common law tradition, and in the three states (Delaware, Mississippi, and Tennessee) where these courts exist they may have overlapping responsibilities with civil jurisdiction courts. However, in some ways chancery courts should be recognized as courts of limited jurisdiction.

As Table 9.1 shows, some states have other types of limited jurisdiction courts. Some of the most common are juvenile courts, district courts, and county courts. A few have very specialized courts, and I discuss some of these later in the chapter.

OPERATIONS OF LIMITED JURISDICTION COURTS

As is the case with all courts, limited jurisdiction courts have their authority prescribed by the state constitution, the state legislature, or both. Where they exist, the limited jurisdiction courts normally hear minor civil disputes, in which case they become the state's **small claims courts**. In such instances, landlords can sue for breaches of rental contracts, and creditors can file suits with the courts (often without the need for a lawyer) in an attempt to recover money owed for a consumer credit loan, for example. The jurisdiction of these civil cases typically will be set at a specific dollar amount, such as $2,000 or $5,000, but in some states the amounts are as much as $25,000 or higher (see Mansfield 1999). Creditors who win such cases obtain a "judgment" which, in most instances, is no more than an official court document that says they won. It does not necessarily mean that they will be able to collect the outstanding debt.

On the criminal side of the docket, courts of limited jurisdiction have authority to hear and dispose of misdemeanor cases. These could include petty offenses such as traffic cases, violations of city ordinances, or serious misdemeanors such as simple assault or drunk driving. In most states these cases can result in a fine and/or jail time up to one year in a city or county jail, or some other type of local detention facility.

Limited jurisdiction courts also can have "front-end" responsibilities for high-profile felony cases. By that we mean these courts may have authority for issuing search or arrest warrants, holding **initial appearances** (often within 48 hours of arrest), and conducting **preliminary hearings**, sometimes called probable cause hearings. During the initial appearances the judge must advise the defendants of the charges, deal with the issue of bail, and appoint an attorney if the defendants are indigent. In a preliminary hearing, if the judge finds that there is sufficient probable cause for further action the case can be bound over to the grand jury or set on the docket of a court of general trial jurisdiction. All in all, these responsibilities mean that the lower-level courts handle heavy caseloads, and the courtrooms that house these tribunals typically are always busy. In fact, in many urban areas these courts operate from the early morning through late-night hours.

Before going further we need to consider the features that cause the courts of limited jurisdiction to be labeled "inferior courts." Some have suggested that these courts are inferior courts because of the quality of justice they dispense. In fact, the lower criminal courts have even been accused of imposing a form of "rough justice" (Robertson 1974). Related to this point, Malcolm Feeley (1992:3) says of these courts that

> Lower level courts are a world apart. They bear little resemblance either to the popular image of trial courts or to actual practices of higher trial courts which handle far fewer cases. In the lower courts trials are rare events, and even protracted plea bargaining is an exception…. These courts are chaotic and confusing; officials communicate in verbal shorthand wholly unintelligible to accused and accuser alike, and they seem to make arbitrary decisions, sending one person to jail and freeing the next. But for the most part they are lenient; they sentence few people to jail and impose few large fines. Their facilities are terrible. Courtrooms are crowded, chambers are dingy, and libraries are virtually nonexistent. Even the new courtrooms age quickly, worn down by hard use and constant abuse.

In the end, Feeley says, "the process is the punishment" for the criminal defendants who are dealt with by these courts. However, a number of features of these courts must be considered carefully before we jump to the conclusion that the level of justice they allocate is inherently poor.

First, the courts of limited jurisdiction are responsible for adjudicating the vast majority of civil and criminal cases in the United States. To illustrate this we simply need to look at the number of misdemeanor cases disposed of by state courts. A confounding factor here is that there is no single, complete source for this information. Nevertheless, Table 9.2 shows the growth in misdemeanor cases for the years 1985 to 1998 for twenty-six states plus the District of Columbia and Puerto Rico. Clearly the caseload is large, and while there are some year-to-year fluctuations, overall the numbers grew by 37 percent for the years covered. Extrapolating from these jurisdictions to the population of the entire United States gives us an estimated misdemeanor caseload of 11,604,745 for all states in 1998 (Cohen 2000).[1] As one additional measure of workload, Table 9.3 shows the number of small claims (civil) cases that were filed in thirty-six states in 2005. These numbers range from a low of 3,237 cases in Vermont to a high of 297,152 in Indiana. Given these numbers, it is easy to see that the lower-level courts operate under exceed-

TABLE 9.2	Misdemeanor Cases in 28 U.S. Jurisdictions, 1985–1998*
Year	Number of Misdemeanor Cases
1985	5,324,051
1986	5,510,401
1987	5,745,251
1988	6,040,281
1989	6,102,018
1990	6,412,383
1991	6,216,517
1992	6,301,257
1993	6,251,759
1994	6,544,873
1995	6,789,173
1996	6,822,396
1997	6,975,050
1998	7,278,473

*Note: The jurisdictions included in this table are Alaska, Arizona, California, the District of Columbia, Florida, Hawaii, Idaho, Illinois, Indiana, Iowa, Kansas, Kentucky, Maine, Maryland, Massachusetts, Michigan, Missouri, New Hampshire, North Carolina, North Dakota, Ohio, Oklahoma, Puerto Rico, Texas, Vermont, Virginia, Washington, and West Virginia.
Source: Cohen (2000).

ingly large civil and criminal caseloads and that fact has an impact on the amount of time judges and lawyers can spend with each of these cases.

Second, it can generally be said that courts of limited jurisdiction are not courts of record. This means that almost none of the trials conducted in these courts have verbatim transcripts prepared by a court reporter. In most cases this is not a serious deficiency. However, when cases are appealed from limited jurisdiction courts they must go forward to general trial courts under a process known as **trial *de novo***, which functions as a completely new trial since no transcript is available (Walsh and Hemmens 2008:92).

Third, for a substantial number of civil cases and criminal cases neither side is represented by an attorney in limited jurisdiction courts. Assistant prosecutors are present for the most serious misdemeanor cases, such as those involving assaults or drunk driving, but for routine traffic charges and other **petty offenses** police officers or the victims themselves may serve as their own prosecutors. In civil proceedings, plaintiffs may hire attorneys, but frequently they present their own cases, especially

TABLE 9.3	Number of Small Claims Cases Filed in 35 States for 2005	
State	Limit of Claim	Total Cases
Alabama	$3,000	98,900
Alaska	$10,000	10,339
Arizona	$2,500	27,117
Arkansas	$5,000	20,069
California	$5,000	255,630
Colorado	$7,500	13,588
Connecticut	$5,000	72,249
Florida	$5,000	235,602
Hawaii	$3,500	3,237
Idaho	$4,000	20,028
Illinois	$5,000	123,590
Indiana	$6,000	297,152
Iowa	$5,000	94,035
Kansas	$4,000	10,171
Kentucky	$1,500	17,633
Maine	$4,500	9,458
Massachusetts	$2,000	123,476
Michigan	$3,000	91,108
Minnesota	$7,500	52,934
Missouri	$3,000	16,057
Nebraska	$2,700	7,339
New Hampshire	$5,000	17,342
New Jersey	$3,000	57,066
New Mexico	$10,000	35,813
North Carolina	$5,000	274,449
North Dakota	$5,000	5,468
Ohio	$3,000	85,700
Oregon	$5,000	73,030
Rhode Island	$2,500	16,642
South Carolina	$7,500	118,540
Utah	$7,500	34,953
Vermont	$3,500	7,361
Washington	$4,000	28,020
West Virginia	$5,000	44,936
Wisconsin	$5.000	166,504

Source: LaFountain et al. (2006)

if the disputes fit into the category of small claims. Civil and criminal defendants also may attempt to represent themselves in what are known as **pro se proceedings**. The U.S. Supreme Court has held that in most circumstances defendants have the right to represent themselves (see *Faretta* v. *California*, 422 U.S. 806 [1975]).

Without the presence of attorneys, judges carry a much greater burden in assuring that proper legal procedures are followed. This situation also creates the potential for judicial misconduct, since in some limited jurisdiction courts the judge may not be a licensed attorney, and potentially no one trained in the law is present to hold the judge accountable (Mansfield 1999).

Fourth, many states do not routinely provide for jury trials in inferior courts. This means that **bench trials** are the rule instead of the exception. There are departures from this rule, however. If the case is a non-petty offense—that is, a crime that could result in incarceration for six months or more—the Supreme Court has held that constitutionally the option of a jury trial must be provided (*Duncan v. Louisiana*, 391 U.S. 145, [1968]). To accommodate the occasional jury trial, some states provide for six-person instead of twelve-person juries in inferior courts.

Finally, is it important to emphasize that some inferior courts (such as municipal, district, or county courts) may require judges to be licensed attorneys, and this is increasingly the trend. However, some states still allow for **lay judges** (that is, non-lawyer judges) in certain courts of limited jurisdiction. For example, in 1968 the State of New Mexico eliminated the office of justice of the peace and replaced this position with magistrate judges who serve in limited jurisdiction courts in twelve of the state's thirteen judicial districts. These judges, like the justices of the peace before them, still are not required to be licensed attorneys. They only must meet three general qualifications for elected offices in the state: (1) they must be a qualified voter, (2) they must reside in the district from which they are elected, and (3) they must possess a high school diploma or GED (*New Mexico Statutes Annotated* 2009, Sec. 35–2-1).

In courts presided over by lay judges, the various participants may be at the mercy of the judge's common sense, past experience, or any training that he or she may have received after election. To assist these judges, organizations like the various state administrative offices of courts (AOCs) or the National Judicial College at the University of Nevada, Reno, offer training programs for non-lawyer judges, and many states encourage their lay judges to attend these training programs.

All of these factors taken together give us a picture of the environment within which the limited jurisdiction courts operate. They handle high volumes of cases, often with relatively little in the way of support staffs or other resources. Most cases are processed rapidly, and the outcomes seldom are dramatic. Nevertheless, these courts frequently are criticized for the ways in which they operate, even though in most situations they have relatively little say in the resources they receive and they often are overwhelmed by the number of cases they must process.

TYPES OF CASES HEARD BY LOWER LEVEL COURTS

I already have briefly mentioned some of the types of cases heard by the courts of limited jurisdiction. However, in this section I deal more specifically with the most typical cases encountered.

TORT CLAIMS

First, among the civil cases processed, some states give these courts jurisdiction over **tort claims** below a certain dollar value. In simplest terms, a tort is a civil wrong. Champion (2005:252) says that a tort is "A private or civil wrong or injury, other than a breach of contract, for which the court will provide a remedy in the form of an action for damages." The Bureau of Justice Statistics, in its definition of torts, says that these are "Claims arising from personal injury or property damage caused by negligent or intentional acts of another person or business" (Langton and Cohen 2008:11).

For example, assume you have gone to the supermarket to do your weekly shopping. While in the store you stop at the produce section where the store employees have just sprayed all of the produce to make it look fresher and more attractive. In the process of having sprayed the produce some water has gotten on the floor and you slip and fall fracturing your knee. Your course of action against the store typically would be a tort claim. Or if you live in an area with significant snowfall in the winter, stores may be required to keep their sidewalks clear to keep people from falling. This type of slip-and-fall accident also could result in a tort claim. In successful tort claims by a plaintiff, the result would be an award of monetary damages. It is important to note, at this point, that in some states only negligent torts (arising from traffic cases) are heard in limited jurisdiction courts, and the remainder are heard in trial courts of general jurisdiction.

BREACHES OF CONTRACT

In addition to tort claims, the lower levels courts also may have jurisdiction over **breaches of contract**. Again, these will be claims involving damages below a certain dollar amount. These types of cases frequently arise out of consumer credit loans and landlord–tenant disputes. For example, you purchase a car and finance it through a lending agency (a bank or credit union, for instance). At some point you fall behind in your payments, and after some specified grace period and attempts to collect the missed payments, the lending institution initiates proceedings to repossess the vehicle. In many states this type of case could be heard in one of the courts of limited jurisdiction. A similar kind of situation could arise when people who rent apartments or houses fall behind in their monthly payments or, on the other side, when the landlord fails to live up to obligations to keep the property adequately maintained. As with torts, contract cases may be heard by courts of general trial jurisdiction in some states.

PROBATE CASES

Finally, some lower-level courts have jurisdiction over **probate** matters. I talk about specialized probate courts in the next section, but at this point I need to provide a summary definition of what probate entails. In most states, probate law is concerned with the disposition of wills and questions of inheritance, especially if a person dies *intestate*—that is, without a will. In legal terms, "the probate process involves collecting the decedent's assets, liquidating liabilities, paying necessary taxes, and distributing property to heirs" (*Black's Law Dictionary* 1991:835). Probate matters can be extremely complex, especially when there is no will, and eighteen states have at least one court dealing specifically with probate matters, with some having one per county (see Rottman and Strickland 2006:268–319).

SPECIALIZED COURTS

In this section we will take a brief look at some of the specialized courts within state judicial systems. Some of these courts are long-standing tribunals, and some have more recently been created to deal with specific social or administrative problems. Again, the exact labels and subject matter jurisdictions of these courts may vary from state to state, but we will deal with the categories of specialized courts that appear most commonly.

JUVENILE COURTS

One of the most frequently found specialized courts is the **juvenile court**. The first juvenile court was created in Cook County, Illinois, in 1899 (Feld 2003; Mays and Winfree 2006). Juvenile courts were established with the idea that children who violate the law should not be treated the same as adults. The first juvenile courts were founded on the English common law legal doctrine of ***parens patriae***. This concept came into being when English children were orphaned and they had no one to enact legal proceedings for them, since they were not persons before the law and could not act on their own behalf. In such situations the king would appoint one of his advisors (a chancellor) to represent the child's best interests. From this came the idea that the king was the "father of the country" (*parens patriae*) who ultimately was responsible for protecting the legal interests of children.

Age Jurisdiction

English common law, later incorporated into the laws of several states, viewed age as a limiting factor in the process of forming criminal intent. For instance, children under the age of seven were deemed incapable of forming criminal intent by the courts. These children might be in need of guidance, protection, or some type of treatment, but they were not to be treated as criminals. Youngsters between the ages of seven and fourteen were deemed incapable of forming criminal intent. The presumption was that the typical child in this category did not have a fully developed sense of right and wrong and had little appreciation for the consequences of his or her actions. However, this was a presumption that the state could attempt to overcome at the time of a trial. Finally, persons over the age of fourteen were presumed capable of forming criminal intent, and they were to be held legally accountable for their actions. In these cases the defense could assert that the child should not be held culpable, and in those situations the burden of proof would shift to the defendant (Gardner 2009; Mays and Winfree 2006).

Age jurisdiction is the primary defining characteristic of juvenile courts, and three ages are of particular significance. First, there is the minimum age at which juvenile courts take jurisdiction over youngsters. Some states follow the common law tradition and begin jurisdiction at the age of seven. Other states have increased that number and do not accept cases involving law violations until youngsters reach the age of ten. A final group of states do not specify a particular age at all and allow the juvenile court judges to decide when to accept cases (see Sickmund 2003).

The second age of importance in juvenile courts is the maximum age of jurisdiction. Currently, thirty-seven states and the District of Columbia use the age of seventeen as the maximum age for their juvenile courts. Three states (Connecticut, New York, and North Carolina) use fifteen as the maximum age for juvenile courts. Another ten states (Georgia, Illinois, Louisiana, Massachusetts, Michigan, Missouri, New Hampshire, South Carolina, Texas, and Wisconsin) have sixteen as the maximum age for juvenile courts (Sickmund 2003:3).

The final age of importance in juvenile courts is the age at which juveniles can be transferred to criminal courts to be tried as adults. States have a variety of ages at which youngsters can be tried as adults, with the youngest age being twelve. The most common age for transfers is sixteen, and some states (New Mexico being one of them) have adopted what are called **blended sentencing** systems that allow the judges to decide after the case has been tried whether juvenile penalties or adult penalties are most appropriate (Mays and Gregware 1996).

Since the beginning of juvenile courts, states have employed some mechanism for deciding whether to try juveniles as adults. In most states the primary, if not exclusive, method for making this decision is what is known as the judicial waiver. The juvenile court judge must conduct a transfer hearing—consistent with the U.S. Supreme Court guidelines articulated in *Kent v. U.S.,* 383 U.S. 541 (1966)—determine whether the youngster is a threat to public safety or lacks amenability to treatment. At the present time forty-six states have statutory provisions for judicial waivers of delinquent youngsters to adult courts. However, in addition to judicial waivers, fifteen states allow prosecuting attorneys to direct-file cases with adult criminal courts, bypassing the juvenile courts altogether. Twenty-nine states also provide for statutory exclusions whereby the legislature can remove some offenses (typically the most serious ones) and have them automatically tried in adult courts (see Mays and Winfree 2006:139–40). Whatever the method employed, every year between 1 percent and 2 percent of the delinquency cases filed nationwide end up being transferred to adult courts (currently this is about seven thousand cases each year).

Subject Matter Jurisdiction

The primary areas of subject matter jurisdiction for juvenile courts are cases involving **delinquency**, **dependency**, and **neglect** (see McCarthy, Patton, and Carr 2003;

Smithburn 2002). Delinquency offenses are violations of the law that would be a crime for an adult. By contrast, dependency is not an act of the child, but rather is a state of want or need in which the child is found that results from no fault of the parents or guardians. Neglect is a state of want or need in which the child is found that results from deliberate acts, or failures to act, on the part of the parents or guardians.

The first juvenile courts also had jurisdiction over what were termed **status offenses**. Unlike delinquency, these were acts that were illegal for juveniles, but which would not be crimes for adults. Examples of status offenses include curfew violations, running away, and truancy. Originally status offenses were treated as a form of delinquency, and status offenders could be incarcerated in secure juvenile correctional institutions. Today most states treat status offenses as a form of dependency, and some states label status offenders as children in need of supervision or services (CHINS; see Mays 2003).

In some states, juvenile cases dealing with delinquency, dependency, and neglect are handled by the courts of general trial jurisdiction. By contrast, in states like Georgia and Texas many counties have separate courts to address matters concerning individuals under the age of majority (seventeen years of age and under in the vast majority of states). Some states (Colorado being one example) also have particular counties with their own separate juvenile courts.

FAMILY COURTS

Another category of specialized courts is **family courts** or **domestic relations courts**.[2] It is important to note that some states—like Delaware, Hawaii, New York, Rhode Island, South Carolina, and Vermont—have separate courts handling marriage annulments, divorces, paternity suits, custody disputes, and awards of child support. At times these issues are handled by separate judges under the broad umbrella of a family court. Box 9.1 shows the perspectives of a retired family court judge.

PROBATE COURTS

A third common category of specialized courts includes probate courts. In the previous section I discussed this area of law as it is handled by the courts of limited jurisdiction. To repeat briefly, these courts handle matters related to wills and inheritances. Some also oversee the legal affairs of orphans, adoptions, mental health issues, and transfers of property. The states of Alabama, Arkansas, Colorado (Denver), Connecticut, Georgia, Indiana, Maine, Maryland (Orphan's Court), Massachusetts, Michigan, New Hampshire, New Mexico, New York (Surrogates' Courts), Rhode Island, South Carolina, Tennessee, Texas, and Vermont have courts that in whole or in part are responsible for probate matters.

OTHER SPECIALIZED COURTS

Additionally, a few states have very specialized specialized courts (see Rottman and Strickland 2006). The following list gives examples:

- tax court (Arizona, Indiana, New Jersey, Oklahoma, Oregon)
- police court (Arkansas)
- water court (Colorado, Montana)
- mayor's court (Louisiana)
- administrative court (Maine)
- housing court (Massachusetts)

BOX 9.1

In Their Own Words: Judge Angela Jewell

There is a perception that the Family Court Bench is a stepping stone to other more serious courts (i.e., civil and criminal). It is my perception, having been both a Family Court and Criminal Court Judge, that Family Court and Children's Court are the courts that resolve serious issues before they become issues to be addressed in Criminal Court and other Courts. There is a proverb of Ghana that embodies my belief: "The ruin of a nation begins in the homes of its people."

A truly effective Family Court provides what I like to call "long-term justice." Family Court should not be the forum for scorched earth tactics, where long after the dust settles—the attorneys and experts have been paid for their services and the Court has exhausted its resources—the parties finally realize that they, like Dorothy from the *Wizard of Oz*, had the power all along. Early intervention is the key to the concept of long-term justice. Parties should be empowered as quickly as possible to resolve conflict over their issues using the tools of mediation and/or settlement facilitation. This limits litigation to the remedy of last resort, and absolutely necessary.

The true victims of Family Court litigation are the children. I have heard, from so many court clinicians, who testify after they have conducted interviews of the children, that what they really want is for their parents to stop fighting. Children do not make the same judgments about their parents that the parents make about each other. They want each parent's permission to love and spend time with the other parent, and they want them to be able to co-parent with respect and reasonable communication.

The true power of Family Court judges is empowering the litigants appearing before them. I tell litigants, when I refer them to co-parenting education classes and other community resources, that by attending these classes, they are empowering themselves to work with each other as co-parents, long after the Court makes its decisions.

Source: Angela Jewell is a retired Family Court Judge from the Second Judicial District, Albuquerque, New Mexico.

- land court (Massachusetts)

- workers' compensation court (Montana, Rhode Island)

- court of claims (New York, Ohio)

- environmental court (Vermont)

While most state court structures remain relatively stable, over time two trends have emerged. First, with the court modernization and unification movements, the trend throughout much of the twentieth century was to eliminate most, if not all, specialized state courts. However, a significant number of states still retain some of their specialized courts. Second, at the end of the twentieth century—largely as a result of the emergence of the concept of therapeutic jurisprudence—even some states with unified court systems reversed that trend by creating a limited number of specialized, problem-solving courts.

In the next section we will examine therapeutic jurisprudence and how it has contributed to the development of specialized courts that deal with specific social problems. For the most part, these courts have emerged since the 1980s, and they have continued to proliferate nationwide. As you will see, problem-solving courts tend to focus on specialized social issues that traditionally would not have been the concern of the courts.

THERAPEUTIC JURISPRUDENCE

The concept of **therapeutic jurisprudence** extends the notion of specialized courts into the realm of dealing with a range of social problems or trends. The principles behind therapeutic jurisprudence have been a part of some ancient cultures and American Indian societies for centuries (see Braswell, Fuller, and Lozoff 2001; Nielson and Zion 2005). However, the idea began to emerge in the United States around 1989 when the first **drug court** was created in Miami, Florida. By the end of 2005 there were about 1,500 drug courts nationwide and today there are almost 2,000 of these courts (National Association of Criminal Defense Lawyers 2009; Schmitt 2006). The drug court model stands in contrast to the traditional legal model of adjudicating drug-involved offenders. The National Institute of Justice, in reviewing the operations of drug courts after the first decade of their existence, noted that:

> Traditionally, the courts use legal sanctions, including incarceration, both to punish drug-involved offenders and to deter them from further criminal activity. On the other hand, the treatment community emphasizes therapeutic relationships to help motivate addicts to reduce their dependence on drugs, change their behavior, and take control of their lives.... Drug courts offer an alternative to incarceration, which, by itself, has not been effective in breaking the cycle of drugs and crime (Schmitt 2006:1).

In the traditional approach to dealing with criminal offenses the court is focused on deciding guilt and determining the appropriate sentence. Both the prosecution and the defense stand in an adversarial posture, and there is relatively little concern with finding a solution to any underlying problems exhibited by the defendant. By contrast, the drug court model involves ten essential elements that help demonstrate the difference between the traditional legal approach to processing cases and the therapeutic jurisprudence or problem-solving approach. The ten elements are:

1. Substance abuse treatment is to be integrated into the system of traditional case processing.

2. Prosecutors and defense attorneys are to operate in a nonadversarial mode that protects both public safety and the rights of defendants.

3. Potential participants should be identified and placed into the program early in the legal process.

4. There should be an array of treatment and rehabilitation services available to program participants.

5. Program clients should be subjected to frequent testing for drug and alcohol use.

6. To promote compliance by program participants, there should be coordination among the judges, prosecutors, defense attorneys, and treatment personnel.

7. Judges should maintain ongoing contacts with the individuals participating in the program.

8. Each drug court program should have a system in place to monitor and evaluate outcome effectiveness.

9. There should be interdisciplinary educational efforts to making program planning, implementation, and operations more effective.

10. Drug courts should work with public agencies and community organizations to promote local support for drug courts. (Schmitt 2006:3)

While drug courts generally have met with a great deal of acceptance, they are not without their critics. In fact, in 2007 the National Association of Criminal Defense Lawyers (NACDL) began a nationwide study of drug courts to assess the effectiveness of these programs along with the costs that might accrue to criminal defendants. The final report was issued on the twentieth anniversary (2009) of the first drug court beginning operations in Miami.

One of their conclusions was that drug addiction should be treated as a medical or public health problem, and not a matter for the criminal justice system. They recognized that there would be cases in which drug-involved clients would be defendants and that the leniency offered by drug courts was preferable to the punishment offered through traditional adjudication processes. However, in response to the uncritical acceptance of drug courts, the NACDL issued the following list of five recommendations:

1. Defendants should not be required to plead guilty in order to receive drug court treatment—in some drug courts in the United States defendants must

first plead guilty before they are accepted into treatment programs; this approach may require them to waive many of the constitutional rights and protections that might become important if they do not successfully complete the program and later they face traditional criminal prosecution.

2. Prosecutors should surrender their role as gatekeepers into the drug courts, and admission criteria should be objective and fair—if prosecuting attorneys have control over who is admitted to the drug court, there may be a tendency to exclude high-risk offenders (such as those charged with drug-related violence), and some of these offenders might benefit the most from the drug court program.

3. Drug courts must incorporate strong ethical frameworks—criminal defense lawyers must not be required to surrender their obligation to vigorously defend their clients for the sake of the teamwork approach mandated by drug courts.

4. Drug courts should be used for high-risk clients, and low-risk defendants should be referred to other, less-stringent treatment programs—like many adult and juvenile treatment programs, drug courts have been accused of skimming off the cases most likely to succeed and referring the high-risk cases to the normal channels for adjudication; the result is that the low-risk cases produce artificially high rates of success.

5. There should be rigorous research efforts that establish that drug courts are open to all appropriate clients irrespective of race, economic status, or national origin—some drug courts have been guilty of unfairly excluding minorities and the economically disadvantaged, while focusing on community members of relative status or influence (National Association of Criminal Defense Lawyers 2009:11–13).

Nevertheless, the appeal and early reports of success of drug courts for adult offenders have resulted in expansion of the concept to include the creation of juvenile drug courts (Butts and Roman 2004), as well as drug courts for accused DWI offenders (Mays, Ryan, and Bejarano 1997). Nationwide, this shift in focus for courts has gained reasonably wide acceptance among judges and attorneys as a way to treat offenders with substance abuse problems, rather than incarcerating them for some period of time.

The drug court concept has spawned the development of similar courts dealing with other social problems as well. In addition to drug courts, we now have teen or youth courts (Heward 2004), mental health courts (Slate 2004), and domestic violence courts (Harrell, Castro, Newmark, and Visher 2008). A number of states also have created firearms-related crime courts or so-called gun courts. Box 9.2 summarizes the operations of the nation's first gun court in Providence, Rhode Island. While some people have characterized these specialized tribunals as "boutique courts," the notion of therapeutic jurisprudence and the types of specialized courts associated with it now are firmly established in our judicial process.

BOX 9.2   In the News: The Providence, Rhode Island, Gun Court

The first gun court in the United States was established in 1994 in Providence, Rhode Island. A surprising element of this court was that it had the joint support of the National Rifle Association as well as gun-control groups. The court was created in response to a very harsh gun law passed in Rhode Island in 1989. That law provided that offenders convicted of crimes of violence committed with a firearm would receive minimum sentences of a shocking 310 years for the first offense, 1,020 years for the second offense, and 15 years to life for a third offense. However, some of these cases did not reach court in a timely manner, and not all of them had these harsh sentences imposed. As a result, the rate of firearms-related crimes continued to increase. Therefore, the newly established court took the approach that gun-related crimes should be set on the docket quickly (they were to be set for trial within sixty days). The result was that the speed of dispositions increased and the imposition of the prescribed tough sentences went from 67 percent to 82 percent of the cases. The view taken by Rhode Island officials was that "if you use a gun in Providence, you are going to jail." While this is not necessarily a therapeutic jurisprudence perspective, it does show the nature of the court specialization movement relative to specific social problems.

Source: National Criminal Justice Reference Service (2009).

BOX 9.3

Specialized Courts in Australia

As a common law system nation like the United States, Australia has a judicial system that includes many specialized courts dealing with a variety of social problems. For example, each state and territory has a juvenile court or children's court and, much like the early U.S. juvenile courts, the proceedings are closed to the public.

In addition to specialized juvenile courts, Australia also has coroner's courts to investigate suspicious deaths. There are also family courts, industrial courts, small claims courts, licensing courts, mining courts, and environmental courts. These tribunals have relatively narrowly defined jurisdictions, and few are charged with litigating criminal matters.

Source: Biles (2010).

SUMMARY

As I close this chapter there are several points that I need to touch on by way of summary. In this chapter we have examined the courts of limited jurisdiction within the federal and state court systems. While these courts are sometimes also called courts of inferior jurisdiction, they are not inferior relative to the size of the caseload they carry. In fact, these lower level tribunals are the workhorses of most state court systems, since they process the vast majority of civil and criminal cases filed.

In the federal system there is a relatively small range of limited jurisdiction courts. The U.S. magistrate judges perform many of the duties that would be associated with limited jurisdiction courts. However, they do not operate in separate federal courts; instead, they serve as adjuncts to the federal district judges. The specialized courts within the federal system include the U.S. Court of Claims and the U.S. Court of International Trade. There also are the U.S. Tax Court and the Bankruptcy courts.

In terms of state courts of limited jurisdiction, there are a number of factors that need to be reemphasized. First, all but a few states have one or more lower-level trial courts. These vary in name and may be called municipal courts, magistrate courts, justice of the peace courts, county courts, or even district courts (in a few states).

Second, typically these courts are responsible for processing petty misdemeanor cases (such as traffic offenses) and serious misdemeanors (such as simple assault and drunk driving), and for conducting some initial appearances and preliminary hearings for felony cases. Furthermore, the courts of limited jurisdiction normally serve as the small claims courts, adjudicating minor civil cases in which the amount in dispute is below a certain specified level (this differs from state to state).

A third unique element of the lower-level courts is that in some states they may not require judges to be licensed attorneys. Also, they often are courts of non-record (that is, they normally do not have a court reporter present for most cases to produce a verbatim transcript of proceedings). This means that when cases are appealed, they will go to the general trials courts on a process known as trial *de novo*. Additionally, some states do not provide for jury trials in the lower-level courts, so all cases are tried before a judge with no option of a jury. Other states can provide jury trials if requested and in serious misdemeanor cases, and they may use six-person rather than twelve-person juries.

In addition to the courts of limited trial jurisdiction, a number of states also operate what could be characterized as specialized courts. The most common ones among this group are juvenile courts, family or domestic relations courts, and probate courts. To carry this principle of court specialization even further, many states now have applied the concept of therapeutic jurisprudence to solving social problems such as drunk driving, mental health issues, weapons offenses, and domestic violence.

Today there is a wide variety of these problem-solving courts operating within the structure of the court systems of many states. The basic premise underlying each of these courts is that the traditional retributive or punitive response of the law (fines, probation, and jail or prison time) does not solve the fundamental social problems at work in so many of these situations. The success of these courts depends to a large extent on funding for treatment available, and the degree to which judges and lawyers buy into the notion of therapeutic jurisprudence as a way to solve problems rather than just to process cases.

QUESTIONS FOR CRITICAL THINKING

1. Go online to your state court system's website and look for the organizational structure of the courts in your state. Is there a court of limited jurisdiction? If so, what is it called? Is there more than one type of lower-level court in your state?

2. Should all judges be required to have a law degree and to have had experience practicing law? Does it really matter that much in the case of judges in the limited jurisdiction courts? Why or why not?

3. The courts of limited jurisdiction often are called "the people's courts." What do we mean by this characterization? What kinds of cases would be most closely associated with "the people's court?"

4. Build a case for or against the following proposition: All misdemeanor cases should have the availability of a jury trial.

5. Based on our discussion of juries in Chapter 6, what are some of the advantages and disadvantages of six-person versus twelve-person juries?

6. Have you ever gone to court for a traffic ticket? Did you serve as your own attorney? How did it turn out?

7. What is a tort, and how is a tort claim different from a crime? Are the two completely different, or are there some similarities? Explain.

8. Does your state have separate juvenile and adult courts, or are the juvenile courts part of the courts of general trial jurisdiction? If juvenile courts are separate limited jurisdiction courts, what does this say about their status or stature within the state court system?

9. What is a status offense, and how do status offenses differ from delinquent offenses? Should the juvenile courts be concerned with children who commit status offenses, or is this a social services issue?

10. What do we mean by therapeutic jurisprudence? Does it require a different orientation by judges and lawyers? Is this an entirely different way of looking at how courts operate? Is this a new idea or a very old one? Maybe an Internet search will help inform your answer.

RECOMMENDED READINGS

Feeley, Malcolm (1992). *The Process Is the Punishment: Handling Cases in a Lower Criminal Court.* New York: Russell Sage Foundation. Feeley takes a look at the way minor criminal cases are processed in an urban court setting. The conclusion that one can draw from his research for this book could be that while these courts do not do much good, neither do they do a lot of harm to the accused that come before them. The actual punishment doled out by these courts is simply having to go through the process of being accused of a crime and having to appear in the least appealing of the courts within our court system.

Nielson, Marianne O., and James W. Zion, eds. (2005). *Navajo Nation Peacemaking: Living Traditional Justice*. Tucson, AZ: University of Arizona Press. If you want to know where the concepts of restorative justice and therapeutic jurisprudence have their roots, this book is a good place to start. The readings included in this volume help Western-oriented legal scholars obtain a view of courts and case processing that is effective, but largely different from the European-based model with which most of us are familiar.

Packer, Herbert (1968). *The Limits of the Criminal Sanction*. Palo Alto, CA: Stanford University Press. I cite this book several times throughout this text, and I recommend it for further reading in other chapters. However, Packer's book is without equal, especially in terms of understanding the concept of "assembly line justice" and the typical operations of the lower-level courts. For those of you interested in working in the courts (as an attorney or in some other capacity), this is a must-read work.

Robertson, John, ed. (1974). *Rough Justice: Perspectives on Lower Criminal Courts*. Boston: Little, Brown and Co. This book is somewhat dated and long out-of-print, but it clearly is a classic in the field of judicial process. The readings included look at the structure and operations of the lower level criminal courts from a number of perspectives. Perhaps you can find a copy in your university library or in a used book store; the search will be worth it.

KEY TERMS

bench trials

blended sentencing

breaches of contract

delinquency

dependency

domestic relations courts

drug court

family courts

fee system

courts of limited
  jurisdiction

initial appearances

justice of the peace

juvenile court

lay judges

magistrates' courts

municipal courts

neglect

original jurisdiction

parens patriae

petty offenses

preliminary hearings

probate

pro se proceedings

small claims courts

status offenses

tariffs

therapeutic jurisprudence

tort claims

trial *de novo*

REFERENCES

Biles, David (2010). Australia. *World Factbook of Criminal Justice Systems*. Washington, DC: Bureau of Justice Statistics, U.S. Department of Justice. http://bjs.ojp.usdoj.gov/content/pub/ascii/WFBCJAUS.TXT.

Black's Law Dictionary, 6th ed. (1991). St. Paul, MN: West Publishing Co.

Braswell, Michael, John Fuller, and Bo Lozoff (2001). *Corrections, Peacemaking and Restorative Justice: Transforming Individuals and Institutions*. Cincinnati, OH: Anderson Publishing Co./LexisNexis.

Butts, Jeffrey A., and John Roman, eds. (2004). *Juvenile Drug Courts and Teen Substance Abuse*. Washington, DC: Urban Institute Press.

Carp, Robert A., Ronald Stidham, and Kenneth L. Manning (2007). *Judicial Process in America*, 7th ed. Washington, DC: CQ Press.

Champion, Dean J. (2005). *The American Dictionary of Criminal Justice*, 3rd ed. Los Angeles, CA: Roxbury Publishing Co.

Cohen, Thomas H. (2000). Court research associate, National Center for State Courts, personal correspondence.

Feeley, Malcolm (1992). *The Process is the Punishment: Handling Cases in a Lower Criminal Court*. New York: Russell Sage Foundation.

Feld, Barry C. (2003). *Juvenile Justice Administration*. St. Paul, MN: West Group.

Gardner, Martin R. (2009). *Understanding Juvenile Law*, 3rd ed. San Francisco: Matthew Bender/ LexisNexis.

Harrell, Adele, Jennifer Castro, Lisa Newmark, and Christy Visher (2008). *Final Report on the Evaluation of the Judicial Oversight Demonstration*. http://www.ncjrs.gov/pdffiles1/nij/grants/219384.pdf.

Heward, Michelle E. (2004). The Organization and Operation of Teen Courts in the United States: A Comparative Analysis of Legislation. In *Courts and Justice*, 3rd ed., ed. G. Larry Mays and Peter R. Gregware, 400–22. Long Grove, IL: Waveland Press.

Kent v. U.S., 383 U.S. 541 (1966).

LaFountain, Robert C., Richard Y. Schauffer, Shauna M. Strickland, William E. Raftery, and Chantal G. Bromage, eds. (2006). *Examining the Work of State Courts*. Williamsburg, VA: National Center for State Courts.

Langton, Lynn, and Thomas H. Cohen (2008). *Civil Bench and Jury Trials in State Courts, 2005*. Washington, DC: Bureau of Justice Statistics, U.S Department of Justice.

Mansfield, Cathy Lesser (1999). Disorder in the People's Court: Rethinking the Role of Non-lawyer Judges in Limited Jurisdiction Court Civil Cases. *New Mexico Law Review* 29(Winter): 119–200.

Mays, G. Larry (2003). Status Offenders. In *Encyclopedia of Juvenile Justice*, ed. Marilyn D. McShane and Frank P. Williams III, 354–58. Thousand Oaks, CA; Sage Publications.

Mays, G. Larry, and Peter R. Gregware (1996). The Children's Code Reform Movement in New Mexico: A Qualitative Analysis. *Law and Policy* 18(1, 2): 179–93.

Mays, G. Larry, Stephen G. Ryan, and Cindy Bejarano (1997). New Mexico Creates a DWI Drug Court. *Judicature* 81(3): 122–25.

Mays, G. Larry, and L. Thomas Winfree, Jr. (2006). *Juvenile Justice*, 2nd ed. Long Grove, IL: Waveland Press.

McCarthy, Francis Barry, William Wesley Patton, and James G. Carr (2003). *Juvenile Law and Its Processes: Cases and Materials*, 3rd edition. San Francisco: Matthew Bender/LexisNexis.

National Association of Criminal Defense Lawyers (2009). *America's Problem-Solving Courts: The Criminal Costs of Treatment and the Case for Reform*. Washington, DC.

National Criminal Justice Reference Service (2009). "Gun Court—Providence, RI: Profile No. 37." http://www.ojjdp.ncjrs.org/pubs/gun_violence/profile37.html.

New Mexico Statutes Annotated (2009). Charlottesville, VA: Matthew Bender/LexisNexis.

Nielson, Marianne O., and James W. Zion, eds. (2005). *Navajo Nation Peacemaking: Living Traditional Justice*. Tucson, AZ: University of Arizona Press.

Robertson, John A. (1974). *Rough Justice: Perspectives on Lower Criminal Courts*. Boston: Little, Brown and Co.

Rottman, David B., and Shauna M. Strickland (2006). *State Court Organization 2004*. Washington, DC: Bureau of Justice Statistics, U.S. Department of Justice.

Schmitt, Glenn R. (2006). *Drug Courts: The Second Decade*. Washington, DC: National Institute of Justice, U.S. Department of Justice.

Sickmund, Melissa (2003). *Juveniles in Court*. Washington, DC: Office of Juvenile Justice and Delinquency Prevention, U.S. Department of Justice.

Slate, Risdon N. (2004). Mental Health Courts: Striving for Accountability While Looking to the Future and Holding Civil Liberties and Public Safety in the Balance. In *Courts and Justice*, 3rd ed., ed. G. Larry Mays and Peter R. Gregware, 423–39. Long Grove, IL: Waveland Press.

Smith, Christopher E. (2009). From U.S. Magistrates to U.S. Magistrate Judges: Developments Affecting the Federal District Courts' Lower Tier of Judicial Officers. In *Courts and Justice*, 4th ed., ed. G. Larry Mays and Peter R. Gregware, 95–108. Long Grove, IL: Waveland Press.

Smithburn, J. Eric (2002). *Cases and Materials in Juvenile Law.* Cincinnati, OH: Anderson Publishing Co.

U.S. Courts (2009). Understanding Federal and State Courts. http://www.uscourts.gov/outreach/resources/fedstate_lessonplan.htm.

Walsh, Anthony, and Craig Hemmens (2008). *Law, Justice, and Society.* New York: Oxford University Press.

ENDNOTES

[1] The National Center for State Courts reported that in 2005 limited jurisdiction courts in the United States had a criminal caseload of 14.2 million cases (LaFountain et al. 2006:45).

[2] In a few states the probate courts also have some domestic relations responsibilities.

10

Courts of General Trial Jurisdiction

CHAPTER OUTLINE

INTRODUCTION

In the United States the bulk of trial work—both civil and criminal—is handled by the state courts of original jurisdiction. These courts may be judicial forums of limited jurisdiction, such as the ones discussed in Chapter 9, or the general trial jurisdiction courts that we will consider in this chapter. They may be unified courts with both civil and criminal caseloads, or they may be specialized courts handling only one or a limited number of types of cases. State courts may handle cases at law, equity cases, or both.

Cases at law are based on a "rigid and formalized legal system" (Altschuler and Sgroi 1996:424) arising from the "strictly formulated rules of common law" (*Black's Law Dictionary* 1991:374). By contrast, "[e]quity is a body of jurisprudence, or field of jurisdiction, differing in its origin, theory, and methods from the common law" (*Black's Law Dictionary* 1991:374). Equity cases are designed to provide fairness when the legal remedies might produce "inadequate or unacceptable results" (Altschuler and Sgroi 1996:424). As I indicated in Chapter 1, most states today have merged equity and law courts into one legal system. However, the states of Delaware, Mississippi, and Tennessee still maintain separate equity courts that are known as **chancery courts** (Rottman and Strickland 2006).[1] As indicated in Chapter 9, where they exist chancery courts are courts of relatively limited jurisdiction.

Another feature to consider relative to state courts is the funding mechanisms under which they operate. For instance, state courts may be completely state funded, locally funded, or a blend of both. These courts also may have very simple or extremely complex structures. The judges of these courts in most situations are required to be licensed attorneys, but in a few instances, involving the limited jurisdiction courts, they are required neither to be trained in the law nor even to possess a college degree (Langton and Cohen 2007).

In a way, these factors are what make it very difficult to simply or briefly explain what state courts in the United States really look like. Therefore, I will make an attempt to describe these courts in the most general terms possible. To provide some clarity, in some instances I will use specific state court systems to illustrate the particular points I am making.

CREATION OF STATE COURTS

As I have noted elsewhere in this book, the reality is that the United States is a country of fifty-two court systems—with each state having its own system, in addition to a court system for the federal government and one for the District of Columbia. The federal government has trial and appellate courts that are addressed later in this chapter and in the chapter that follows, and each state has its own relatively unique court system.

The differences in structures can be explained partially by the time period during which different states entered the Union. Some of the distinctions can be accounted for by the distinct political and legal cultures and traditions of the various states. For example, Louisiana differs from the other forty-nine states (and the federal government, for that matter) in that its legal system is based on the French Napoleonic or civil code tradition discussed in Chapter 2 (see Abadinsky 2007; Melone and Karnes 2008). Patterns of immigration from other countries also influenced what can be called the **"local legal culture"** of each state, and even different regions or jurisdictions within a state. The notion of the local legal culture was discussed earlier in the text, but to review, this is a shorthand reference to the titles and authorities of the actors, as well as the interactions, customs, and legal norms demonstrated by each unique legal jurisdiction in the United States. This means that the local legal culture is likely to vary from one county to the next, and even between cities within the same county. Certainly the local legal culture varies between state and federal courts, and from one federal court district to the next.

JURISDICTION OF STATE COURTS

State court jurisdictions ultimately are defined by state constitutions. In most states, the constitution delegates to the state legislature the authority to define and alter court jurisdictions and structures. This parallels the authority of the United States Congress in reference to the federal courts. In the end, the simplest statement that we can make is that while there are similar patterns in state court structures, each state actually has something of its own unique organizational pattern. Some of these have changed radically over the years. Others remain much the same today as they were a century ago.

Different states have different numbers of tiers or levels of courts. For example, Figure 10.1 shows the simplest form of state courts: a two-tiered court system in South Dakota. By contrast, Figure 10.2 illustrates the three-tiered court system of Minnesota, and Figure 10.3 shows Kentucky's four-tiered system. In some states, like Tennessee, the lower tiers may contain several different types of courts. Therefore, the easiest way to classify them is to divide all state courts into two categories: (1) trial courts or courts of original jurisdiction, and (2) courts of appellate jurisdiction. The types of appellate courts are dealt with more fully in Chapter 11.

Courts of original jurisdiction are often simply called trial courts. In the most fundamental sense this means that these are the courts where civil and criminal cases

FIGURE 10.1   SOUTH DAKOTA COURT STRUCTURE, 2004

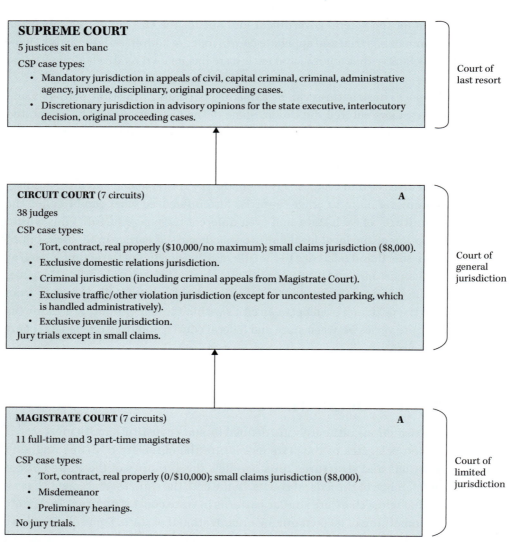

SUPREME COURT

5 justices sit en banc

CSP case types:

- Mandatory jurisdiction in appeals of civil, capital criminal, criminal, administrative agency, juvenile, disciplinary, original proceeding cases.
- Discretionary jurisdiction in advisory opinions for the state executive, interlocutory decision, original proceeding cases.

Court of last resort

CIRCUIT COURT (7 circuits)   **A**

38 judges

CSP case types:

- Tort, contract, real properly ($10,000/no maximum); small claims jurisdiction ($8,000).
- Exclusive domestic relations jurisdiction.
- Criminal jurisdiction (including criminal appeals from Magistrate Court).
- Exclusive traffic/other violation jurisdiction (except for uncontested parking, which is handled administratively).
- Exclusive juvenile jurisdiction.

Jury trials except in small claims.

Court of general jurisdiction

MAGISTRATE COURT (7 circuits)   **A**

11 full-time and 3 part-time magistrates

CSP case types:

- Tort, contract, real properly (0/$10,000); small claims jurisdiction ($8,000).
- Misdemeanor
- Preliminary hearings.

No jury trials.

Court of limited jurisdiction

Source: Rottman and Strickland 2006:310.

FIGURE 10.2 MINNESOTA COURT STRUCTURE, 2004

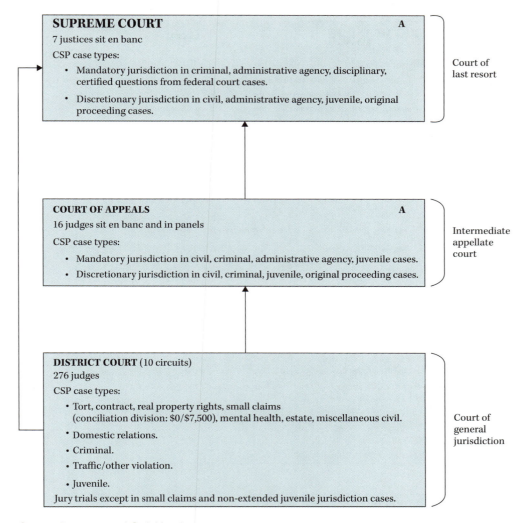

SUPREME COURT   A

7 justices sit en banc

CSP case types:

- Mandatory jurisdiction in criminal, administrative agency, disciplinary, certified questions from federal court cases.

- Discretionary jurisdiction in civil, administrative agency, juvenile, original proceeding cases.

Court of last resort

COURT OF APPEALS   A

16 judges sit en banc and in panels

CSP case types:

- Mandatory jurisdiction in civil, criminal, administrative agency, juvenile cases.
- Discretionary jurisdiction in civil, criminal, juvenile, original proceeding cases.

Intermediate appellate court

DISTRICT COURT (10 circuits)

276 judges

CSP case types:

- Tort, contract, real property rights, small claims (conciliation division: $0/$7,500), mental health, estate, miscellaneous civil.
- Domestic relations.
- Criminal.
- Traffic/other violation.
- Juvenile.

Jury trials except in small claims and non-extended juvenile jurisdiction cases.

Court of general jurisdiction

Source: Rottman and Strickland 2006:291.

are originally heard and recorded. In fact, these are the tribunals most people think of when we talk about a case "going to court." Trial courts hear evidence and decide winners and losers in civil cases and decide guilt and innocence in criminal cases. For civil cases, once liability has been determined, these courts decide the appropriate remedies, including monetary awards and equitable relief. When a conviction results from a criminal case, the trial courts are responsible for imposing the appropriate sentence or other sanction on the criminal defendant.

For some states, the courts of original jurisdiction constitute only one level of the state's court structure (see Figure 10.1). As you will see later in this chapter, this is

FIGURE 10.3 KENTUCKY COURT STRUCTURE, 2004

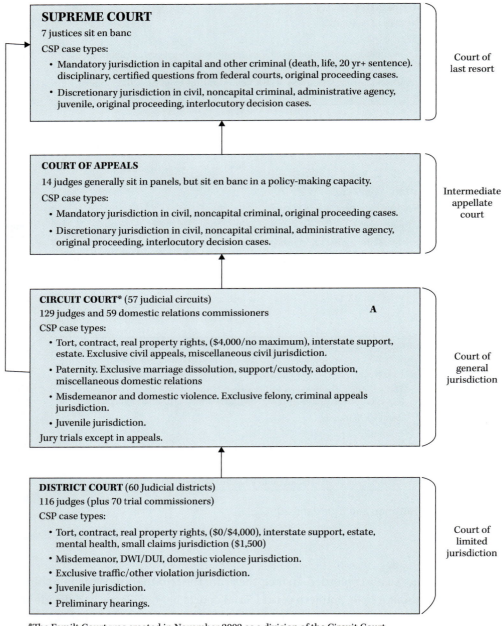

SUPREME COURT

7 justices sit en banc

CSP case types:

- Mandatory jurisdiction in capital and other criminal (death, life, 20 yr+ sentence). disciplinary, certified questions from federal courts, original proceeding cases.
- Discretionary jurisdiction in civil, noncapital criminal, administrative agency, juvenile, original proceeding, interlocutory decision cases.

Court of last resort

COURT OF APPEALS

14 judges generally sit in panels, but sit en banc in a policy-making capacity.

CSP case types:

- Mandatory jurisdiction in civil, noncapital criminal, original proceeding cases.
- Discretionary jurisdiction in civil, noncapital criminal, administrative agency, original proceeding, interlocutory decision cases.

Intermediate appellate court

CIRCUIT COURT* (57 judicial circuits)   A

129 judges and 59 domestic relations commissioners

CSP case types:

- Tort, contract, real property rights, ($4,000/no maximum), interstate support, estate. Exclusive civil appeals, miscellaneous civil jurisdiction.
- Paternity. Exclusive marriage dissolution, support/custody, adoption, miscellaneous domestic relations
- Misdemeanor and domestic violence. Exclusive felony, criminal appeals jurisdiction.
- Juvenile jurisdiction.

Jury trials except in appeals.

Court of general jurisdiction

DISTRICT COURT (60 Judicial districts)

116 judges (plus 70 trial commissioners)

CSP case types:

- Tort, contract, real property rights, ($0/$4,000), interstate support, estate, mental health, small claims jurisdiction ($1,500)
- Misdemeanor, DWI/DUI, domestic violence jurisdiction.
- Exclusive traffic/other violation jurisdiction.
- Juvenile jurisdiction.
- Preliminary hearings.

Court of limited jurisdiction

*The Familt Court was created in November 2002 as a division of the Circuit Court. The Family Court has 33 judges and is located in 42 counties.

Source: Rottman and Strickland 2006:285.

similar to the district courts that serve as the courts of trial jurisdiction for the federal system. As I discussed in the previous chapter, though, some states have more than one level of trial courts. Therefore, we can divide the courts of original jurisdiction into two further categories: (1) courts of limited or inferior jurisdiction, and (2) courts of general trial jurisdiction. The courts of limited jurisdiction were addressed in Chapter 9.

To help us understand the operation of various levels of courts, Walker (2006:34–44) has developed what he terms the "**wedding cake model**." The following list describes the types of cases processed by each layer of the wedding cake:

Level I—these are what we can call "celebrated cases." Celebrated cases are notorious because of the nature of the crime (Theodore Kaczynski of the Unabomber case or serial murderers like Ted Bundy, John Wayne Gacy, or Jeffrey Dahmer), the celebrity status of the person charged with committing the crime (such as Martha Stewart or Michael Jackson), or the celebrity status of the person against whom the crime is committed (the murder of former Beatle John Lennon). Some cases contain all of these elements and they become the "super-celebrity" cases. Celebrated cases typically go through the entire judicial process and constantly are in the public eye as a result of the media attention given them.

Level II cases—here we find the most serious felonies. Many of these cases involve crimes of personal violence, and in every way they may be as heinous as the celebrated cases, if not more so. However, for some reason they do not gain the notoriety and they do not attract the level of media attention that surrounds the celebrated cases. A high percentage of the serious felony cases go to trial because the defendants face long prison sentences and they have nothing to lose and everything to gain by insisting on a trial. Plea bargaining occurs in a much smaller percentage of the serious felony cases compared with other felonies.

Level III—these are less serious felonies. Here we find the common property crimes such as auto thefts, burglaries, and grand larcenies. We also might find some routine drug and other vice-related offenses here. Because the percentage of cases plea bargained increases as we go down through the various levels of the wedding cake, offenders at this level try to have charges reclassified as serious misdemeanors, or try to get sentences reduced to probation and no prison time.

Level IV—this is the misdemeanor level; these cases can include county or municipal ordinance violations. If the wedding cake is drawn to scale, we find more cases here than in the other three levels combined. This is the level of criminal cases processed by the courts of limited jurisdiction, and these are the courts to which citizens are most often exposed.

As I have previously mentioned, misdemeanor cases are most often processed in the courts of limited jurisdiction. By contrast, felony cases (Levels I, II, and III of the wedding cake) are tried in the general jurisdiction courts. Those three levels of criminal cases, along with major civil cases, are the focus of the remainder of this chapter.

COURTS OF GENERAL JURISDICTION

The **general trial jurisdiction courts** are authorized to try any state crimes. As a practical matter there may be a division of labor, with minor civil disputes and misdemeanors being heard in limited jurisdiction courts and major civil cases and felony trials being processed in the general trial courts. However, appeals from inferior courts make the general trial courts ultimately responsible for all state cases.

A variety of factors distinguish general trial courts from the limited jurisdiction courts. One of the first is that while trial courts have significant caseloads, they handle substantially fewer cases than the limited jurisdiction courts. For example, in 1994 there were 872,220 people convicted of felonies in state courts. By comparison, in 2004 there were 1,079,000 felony cases disposed of by state courts of general jurisdiction (Durose and Langan 2007:1). In addition to the criminal caseload, in 2005 state courts of general jurisdiction had 7.4 million civil cases filed in them, and they disposed of nearly 27,000 of these cases through either bench or jury trials (Langton and Cohen 2008). While these numbers demonstrate a substantial volume of cases, it is only a small fraction compared with the misdemeanor caseloads of the inferior courts discussed in Chapter 9.

Additionally, unlike the limited jurisdiction courts (which may have only limited recording capabilities), general trial courts are courts of full record. This means that a court reporter is present for all trials and most other hearings to record the proceedings and to produce a verbatim transcript. Transcripts are important when cases are appealed, because they become the record on which appeals are based.

A further distinguishing factor is the presence of attorneys. It would be an unusual case indeed in which no attorneys appeared in general trial courts. Most prosecutors' offices regularly assign one or more assistant prosecutors to trial courts, depending on the size of the jurisdiction. Likewise, defense attorneys—either privately retained or court-appointed—represent virtually all criminal defendants charged with felonies. The only exceptions to this would be the few situations in which defendants waive their right to an attorney and attempt to represent themselves.

General trial courts also are characterized by the regular presence of juries. The Sixth Amendment to the United States Constitution guarantees the right to a trial by jury. As I have mentioned elsewhere, the United States Supreme Court has said that this right applies to all but petty cases (*Duncan v. Louisiana*, 391 U.S. 145 [1968]), and the presumption is that felony cases will be tried by a jury. There is the option, however, to waive the right to a jury trial and proceed with a **bench trial**, before a judge with no jury. Bench trials may be chosen in particularly complex civil cases (where understanding especially intricate points of law is crucial), in criminal cases that may involve a great deal of negative pretrial publicity toward the defendant, or in cases where a crime is particularly heinous and a jury will likely be extremely effected by the evidence (such as child sexual abuse or very brutal violence). A defense attorney may recommend a bench trial in any of these cases, believing it will lead to a more favorable outcome for the defendant. The choice over a jury trial versus a bench trial, however, always remains with the defendant.

Courts of general trial jurisdiction may also have very different physical appearances than the courts of limited jurisdiction. At times, both types of courts may share common courtrooms in the city or county courthouse. At other times, the limited jurisdiction courts operate in small rooms in police stations or county justice centers, or even in storefront space such as strip malls. By contrast, the general trial courts tend to be the most dignified looking of the courts, with wood paneling, carpeting, prominently displayed state seals, and other official-looking decorations.

The final distinguishing factor for the general trial courts is the requirement of law-trained judges. Virtually all states require judges of general trial jurisdiction courts to possess a law degree (Langton and Cohen 2007; Rottman and Strickland 2006). Furthermore, states ranging from Alaska and California to New York and Ohio require candidates for judge to have been licensed, practicing attorneys for anywhere from five to 10 years before their term as judge (Rottman and Strickland 2006).

Now that I have discussed some of the features that distinguish general trial courts from courts of limited jurisdiction, it is time to turn our attention to workloads of the general jurisdiction courts. While the limited jurisdiction courts process substantially more cases, the general trial courts tend to deal with cases of greater significance.

BOX 10.1
Trial Courts in Germany

The general trend for courts in Germany (with roughly 83 million inhabitants) has been the movement away from the traditional continental European inquisitorial system of justice, and toward a more Anglo-American adversarial system of justice, especially since the advent of the European Union. The most recent significant event so far was, in September 2009, the introduction of a couple of explicit bargaining options for the prosecution and the courts (including plea and sentence bargaining) into the law text of national German Penal Procedure Code. Therefore, there are some new-found similarities between the German court system and that of the United States, but there are still some significant differences as well.

For example, state and federal courts alike are ultimately defined by one and the same national constitution called "Basic Law" of the Federal Republic of Germany, as further specified by the national Court Organization Act. Like the system of courts in the United States, German courts are organized at several levels. There were, as of January 2010, 661 local courts of first instance (*Amtsgerichte*) at the lowest level of courts. They are much like the courts of limited jurisdiction in the United States, and they hear small claims civil cases as well as criminal cases. In criminal matters there are single sitting Criminal Judges dealing with only misdemeanor offenses, and the maximum sentence they can impose is two years of imprisonment. The local bench courts

Continued

BOX 10.1

Continued

(*Schoeffengerichte*), however, can handle any type of criminal case, including felonious crimes, as long as the maximum sentence will not exceed four years of imprisonment. These local bench courts are normally composed of one professional judge and two lay judges. At the next level are the 116 regional courts (*Landgerichte*) that are responsible as courts of first instance for major civil and criminal cases; however, they act also (and in the majority of actual affairs) as courts of appeal (in fact and law) against decisions made by the local courts. When hearing first-instance criminal cases in trial, they sit in so-called "criminal chambers" with three professional judges and two lay judges. The criminal chambers have unlimited sentencing power within the general penalty frame as drawn by the Penal Code (that is, from one month up to fifteen years or life imprisonment).

There also are, on the state level, higher regional courts (*Oberlandesgerichte*), twenty-four in total, respectively one to three in each state, depending upon the size of the state respective to its population. Those courts may act, in criminal matters, as bench courts of first instance in the most serious cases of terrorism or high treason and similar political crimes, if the office of the federal prosecutor general has decided to charge defendants before those courts instead of before standard regional courts. (Note: This prosecutor general is quite different from its linguistic American counterpart. The latter one would in Germany not be called prosecutor general, but minister of justice.) Their main jurisdiction in practice, however, is to serve as appellate courts that hear further appeals from the lower courts, but only in matters of interpreting the law. When acting in trial, they sit in so-called "criminal senates" consisting of three professional judges or exceptionally, in very difficult and voluminous cases, five professional judges.

Finally, there are five federal courts that have appellate jurisdiction only in civil and criminal law matters (*Bundesgerichtshof*), labor law matters (*Bundesarbeitsgericht*), social welfare and social security law matters (*Bundessozialgericht*), and in tax and customs law matters (*Bundesfinanzhof*). Federal courts of appeal sit in trial with five professional judges. The federal constitutional court (*Bundesverfassungsgericht*) forms, along with the German basic law, one of the four central federal authorities and has therefore as such not to answer to any other federal institution.

As far as its jurisdiction as a proper court is concerned, one may see it structurally positioned "apart from" rather than "above" all other courts of law in Germany. It sits in trial with two senates of eight justices each. The German constitutional court deals with questions of constitutional significance in

Continued

BOX 10.1
Continued

many fields, but only as far as they may violate the basic law, especially regarding (a) legally valid court decisions of any type, (b) valid (but only federal) laws of all sorts, (c) international contracts and general rules of international law, and (d) valid acts or instruments of the European Union. Any person having his or her constitutional complaint rejected or declared substantially invalid by a decision of the German constitutional court is legally entitled to file a petition to the European Court of Human Rights in Strasbourg (France) with the claim of suffering from infringement with his or her human rights as defined by the so-called European Convention of Human Rights, more precisely the "European Convention for the Protection of Human Rights and Fundamental Freedoms" (drafted in 1950 and in force since 1953).

Unlike the courts in the United States, the German courts operate on a continental European model in terms of legal codes and the ways in which judges are prepared for office. Unlike common law countries, Germany has a very thorough system of more or less comprehensive legal codes, and additionally special codes or acts of law that govern the decisions made by judges. If there is not a codified prohibition against some action, then the behavior does not constitute a crime.

Likewise, professional judges are prepared for their careers beginning with their law school training. After they have completed their legal educations, law students must pass the so-called first state examinations that allow them to begin a two-year apprenticeship that prepares them for the practice of law. At the end of the apprenticeship period they must pass the so-called second state examinations that allow them then to become a lawyer by their own motion or to formally apply for getting a higher (law-related) position in one of the many state institutions. If they choose to apply for the position of a judge, they need first to be elected or approved, at the federal level and in the majority of the states, by a judges' council. In the second instance they may be appointed by the respective state prime minister or the president of the republic, who may delegate their constitutional power to a special ministry, like the ministry of justice. The first appointment is, in any case, a probationary one, lasting for a period from a minimum of two and maximum of five years' duration. Later regular appointments are valid for lifetime, similar to the position of tenured state or federal civil servants.

Source: Hans-Juergen Kerner, Professor and Director, Institute of Criminology, University of Tuebingen, Germany.

STATE COURT WORKLOADS

I already have made passing reference to the numbers of cases processed by the state courts, but in this section I will deal with this issue more fully. The inescapable conclusion is that state courts process the vast majority of civil and criminal case workloads in the United States. In fact, in 2004 the overwhelming number of felony convictions came in state courts versus federal courts (94 percent compared with 6 percent, respectively). The following sections outline the types and volume of cases processed by the state general trial courts.

CIVIL CASES

The largest percentages of cases processed by state courts are civil. While issues of justice and punishment (in the form of monetary awards) are present in civil cases, the financial stakes in these cases were one of the primary motivations behind the 24 percent increase in civil case filings in the decade from 1984 to 1994 (National Center for State Courts 2000). However, the recent trend is for some decline in the number of civil cases, and in the nation's seventy-five most populous counties the number of civil trials declined by 51.8 percent from 1992 to 2005 (Langton and Cohen 2008:9). Nevertheless, in 2005 there were 7.5 million civil cases compared with 6.6 million criminal cases filed in general trial jurisdiction courts. This includes states that had **unified court systems**, or those with only one level of trial courts (LaFountain, Schauffer, Strickland, Raftery, and Bromage 2006).

The civil cases processed by state courts include issues such as breaches of contract, tort claims, personal injury suits, and a whole range of domestic relations issues. While this list does not cover the full range of civil disputes (for example, there may

BOX 10.2   In the News: Large Civil Judgment Against a Major Retailer

In December of 2005, a civil jury in Alameda County, California, returned a verdict that awarded $172 million to 116,000 employees and former employees of the retail giant Wal-Mart. The suit had been brought on behalf of the employees who alleged that Wal-Mart had violated a California employment law that required companies to give thirty-minute lunch and dinner breaks to individuals who worked more than six hours. A number of legal observers noted that the California law is unique in the nation and, therefore, the verdict would have no bearing in other states. Attorneys for Wal-Mart announced their intention to appeal the award which consisted of $57 million in compensatory damages and $115 million in punitive damages.

Sources: CNN (2005); Lee (2005:A-1).

be some probate cases included in the count), these categories are typical of the most common controversies addressed in civil litigation. I consider each of these issue areas briefly in the following paragraphs.

Breaches of Contract

Individuals and businesses in the United States rely on the courts to enforce their legal rights in relation to **breaches of contract**. For commercial enterprises, periodically a customer or another business will breach a contract into which they have entered with a company. When this happens the company—or individual, for that matter—against whom the breach has occurred can go to court to have the contract nullified or the specific provisions enforced by court order (Altschuler and Sgroi 1996). This type of protection allows businesses in the United States to know that the courts can be relied on to provide legal protection for their economic interests (Abadinsky 2007; Altschuler and Sgroi 1996). In 2005, out of the 26,948 civil trials conducted in state courts, roughly one-third (or 8,917 cases) involved contract disputes. The most common category (2,883 cases) included disputes where a seller was the plaintiff. The second most common group (2,591 cases) involved situations where buyers were the plaintiffs. The remainder involved fraud, rental/lease disputes, employment discrimination, partnership disputes, and a number of other types of cases (Langton and Cohen 2008:2).

Tort Claims

The second type of commonly occurring civil litigation involves **torts**. A tort is a "private or civil wrong or injury, other than breach of contract, for which the court will provide a remedy in the form of an action for damages" (Champion 2005:252). A tort is said to occur when an individual or company is legally obligated to act or not to act and the entity does the opposite of what the law expects or requires. A tort can also occur when there is "injury, loss, or damage from the negligent or intentional acts of the defendant(s)" (Langton and Cohen 2008:2). In 2005, tort cases were the most common type of civil trial conducted by state courts in the United States. In fact, six of every ten trials involved a tort claim of some sort.

In 2005, the types of tort cases most frequently handled by state courts included, in descending order: automobile accidents (57.5 percent), medical malpractice (14.9 percent), **premises liability** (11.3 percent), **intentional tort** (4.4 percent), other/unknown tort (4 percent), **conversion** (2.3 percent), product/asbestos liability (2.2 percent), **slander** or **libel** (1.1 percent), professional malpractice other than medical (0.9 percent), animal attack (0.8 percent), and **false arrest** or **false imprisonment** (0.3 percent) (Cohen 2009:1–2).

Some of the types of tort cases are self-explanatory (for example, automobile accidents and medical malpractice). The others may require some explanation. For example, premises liability cases arise from situations where there has been bodily damage or death as a result of dangerous conditions that exist in either residential or commercial properties. Intentional torts are those harms to either persons or property that result from the deliberate acts of another person. Conversion occurs when someone engages in the unauthorized use of another person's property and there is resulting personal injury or property damage. Slander and libel are related in that they result from damage to the reputation of a person as a result of false statements made by another person. The difference between the two is that slander results from spoken comments, whereas libel occurs when the statements appear in writing. Finally, while false arrest and false imprisonment suits can arise as a result of the actions of private citizens, in most circumstances these suits are directed at law enforcement or correctional personnel.

A number of tort suits arise from circumstances in which there have been personal injuries. Personal injury suits, as examples of tort claims, can result from several different types of situations. However, the most common source of these cases involves motor vehicle accidents. Typically, when a person is injured in an accident the insurance company for the other party will try to make a quick settlement to pay for medical expenses and for the repair or replacement of the damaged automobile. If a settlement cannot be reached, a personal injury suit can be filed and the sometimes protracted process begins. The most common types of state civil trials in 2005 were traffic accident cases. Motor vehicle accident cases constituted 57.5 percent of the tort trials and 34.9 percent of all state civil trials in 2005 (Langton and Cohen 2008:2).

Occasionally, tort claims are filed against state and local governments as well. For instance, if an inmate slips and falls in the shower at the county jail, the injured person might contact an attorney and have the lawyer serve notice on the county that a tort claim is anticipated. The assumption is that the county could have known (or should have known) that the wet floor posed a hazard and that steps should have been taken to keep inmates from slipping when they take showers. Tort claims also may be filed when police officers or corrections officers act in ways that exceed their authority. An example of this would be a case where there was alleged to be excessive use of force that caused bodily harm to an individual. Additionally, in 2005 there were fifty-eight state trials for tort actions based on false arrest or imprisonment (Langton and Cohen 2008:2). Some of these tort claims seek damages of a few thousand dollars, and some run into the millions.

Domestic Relations

Domestic relations law has become a specialty for some attorneys. **Domestic relations** issues concern a broad range of matters that center on marriages and families. These cases can involve divorces and annulments of marriages, the disposition of wills and inheritances (sometimes handled by separate probate courts), paternity suits, and child custody settlements. To simplify domestic relations issues, many states instituted more liberal uncontested or "no fault" divorces in the late 1960s and early 1970s; by the 1980s virtually all states had adopted some version of this model. These cases often can be handled by the parties themselves or they may be referred to a mediator, and such cases may not require the services of attorneys at all.

It is at this point that I should mention two very crucial factors relating to civil suits. First, unlike the situation with criminal cases, there is no constitutional right to counsel in civil litigation (see Farole 2009). Second, also unlike criminal cases, there is no speedy trial provision for civil cases. Briefly, I will expand on both of these points and the implications they have for the processing of civil cases, since these two factors can have a profound impact on civil litigation in the United States.

BOX 10.3
Civil Jurisdiction in Hong Kong

Civil court jurisdiction in other nations often is very similar to that experienced in the United States. For example, the following list includes the types of civil cases normally heard by the District Court of Hong Kong.

The most common types of civil action that the District Court deals with are:

- Contract
- Quasi-contract
- Tort (including personal-injuries claims)
- Recovery of land or premises
- Claims in equity such as administration of estate of a deceased person, trust, mortgage, specific performance, maintenance of infant, dissolution of partnership, relief against fraud or mistake
- Distress
- Employees' compensation cases (there is no limit on the amount claimed)
- Sex discrimination, disability, and family status discrimination cases
- Matrimonial cases including divorce, maintenance, custody and adoption of children (the Court which handles these types of cases is also known as the Family Court)

These types of cases would regularly appear on the dockets of most civil courts in the United States as well.

Source: Court Services & Facilities (2009).

To begin with, since there is no right to counsel for civil litigation, in many personal injury suits lawyers accept cases on a **contingency fee** basis. Quite often attorneys will advertise on billboards, television, in the telephone book, or in the newspaper with slogans like "no up-front fees," or "if you don't win, we don't get paid." This means that attorneys are speculating on a win and will take a certain percentage of the damages recovered for cases settled out of court (typically one-third) and a larger percentage (sometimes up to one-half) for cases that go to trial.

Since there is not a speedy trial guarantee for civil cases, these suits may take a number of years to resolve. At times the parties with the deepest pockets (for instance, insurance companies and other large corporations) may employ a strategy of trying to wait out the other side in hopes of a more favorable settlement. While it may not be possible to prove delay by one party to the suit, there has been increasing concern over the delay in civil cases in many states (Grossman, Kritzer, Bumiller, and McDougal 1992; Litan 1992), and some reformers have been lobbying for swifter resolution of civil cases.

Before I begin the discussion of criminal cases, it is important once again to emphasize that there are substantially more civil suits compared with criminal cases in state courts. Some of these civil cases concern very complex issues—such as violations of patent and copyright laws or breaches of multi-billion dollar contracts—and any number of them touch on some of the deepest human emotions. This means that in some sense, while criminal cases may be more sensational, civil cases may be more difficult to resolve in a routine manner.

CRIMINAL CASES

In terms of the caseloads of criminal courts in the United States, 872,220 felony cases were processed by state courts in 1994. By 2004 that number had grown to over 1 million cases, or an increase of about 24 percent (Durose and Langan 2007). Aside from the growth in the number of cases, three other trends are particularly noteworthy. First, from 1994 to 2004 the percentage of property offenses dropped from 32 percent to 29 percent; this was a total of 310,680 cases in 2004. While the percentage change does not seem that dramatic, it is important to remember that property offenses typically represent the bulk of the criminal case workload at the state level. Thus, the change in volume of cases is substantial.

Second, the percentage of felony drug convictions increased from 31 percent in 1994 to 34 percent. This meant that in 2004 there were 362,850 felony drug convictions. Finally, the combined categories of violent offenses and weapons offenses decreased from 23 percent in 1994 to 21 percent. This meant that state courts accounted for 227,580 felony convictions in these categories in 2004 (Durose and Langan 2007:2).

As I mentioned in Chapter 9, the misdemeanor cases processed by limited jurisdiction courts typically are adjudicated in a very routine manner and in many situations without attorneys for either side. By contrast, felony cases take more time, and virtually all involve both a prosecuting attorney and a defense attorney. However, the one place where felony case processing departs from the public image is in the level of plea bargaining involved. Plea bargaining was discussed at length in Chapter 7. However, a few points concerning this method of disposing of cases are worth repeating.

For instance, a variety of numbers historically have been quoted on this topic, but the most frequently cited figures are that somewhere between 80 percent and 90 percent of all felony cases in this country result in guilty pleas—with or without the presence of explicit plea bargaining. The most recent numbers are even more astounding, because in 2004 the Bureau of Justice Statistics reported that 95 percent of the state felony sentences resulted from a guilty plea, while the remainder were convicted after a trial (Durose and Langan 2007:1).

Therefore, the television and movie image of criminal cases being hard-fought in the courtroom actually applies to a relatively small number of high-stakes, hotly disputed cases. In the overwhelming majority of criminal cases the facts are not in dispute, and the courtroom work group has a fairly clear understanding of the "going rate," or the amount of punishment appropriate for this case (Eisenstein and Jacob

1977; Walker 2006). The vast majority of criminal cases are decided on paper, then, and not in the courtroom.

Now that we have briefly examined the state courts of general trial jurisdiction, let us turn our attention to their federal counterparts. One of the points I have made throughout this text is that we have a variety of courts at different levels of government in the United States. In fact, if we count the separate court systems in each state, the federal courts, and the courts in the District of Columbia, we are a nation of fifty-two similar, yet distinct, court systems (Langton and Cohen 2007; Pastore and Maguire 2009). For the average person, contact with the courts means courts at the state or local level. However, it is important to remember that the federal courts of original jurisdiction handle a large number of both civil and criminal cases as well. Sometimes the jurisdictions of state and federal courts are very distinct. At other times the jurisdictions are very similar and even overlap. This is called **concurrent jurisdiction**. In the remainder of this chapter I will examine the basis for the authority, subject matter jurisdiction, and structure associated with the federal courts of original jurisdiction.

ESTABLISHMENT OF THE FEDERAL DISTRICT COURTS

Understanding the federal courts is important not only because of the number of cases they adjudicate, but also because the kinds of cases they handle can impact all of the civil and criminal justice systems in the United States. Of particular importance in recent years have been those cases dealing with organized criminal enterprises (the federal **Racketeer Influenced and Corrupt Organization Act**—or RICO), and civil rights violations directed at individuals and agencies in the criminal justice system.

Most of the federal courts owe their existence, structure, and jurisdiction fundamentally to Article III of the United States Constitution. Article III, Section 1 provides that "The judicial power of the United States, shall be vested in one supreme court, and in such inferior courts as the Congress may from time to time ordain and establish." This simply means that the Constitution specifically establishes the Supreme Court of the United States and broadly defines the types of cases it may hear. However, the Constitution leaves the number, types, jurisdiction, and staffing of other federal courts to the discretion of Congress, and implies that the federal court system will change as Congress sees fit as well.

The result of this arrangement is that we have what can be called **constitutional courts**, or Article III courts as they often are known, and **legislative courts**, created under Article I's powers granted to Congress (Carp and Stidham 2001). While the focus of the following sections largely is on Article III courts (the federal district courts), brief mention also will be made of some of the legislative courts. One of the chief differences between constitutional and legislative courts is that constitutional courts only have judicial powers, while legislative courts may exercise judicial, legislative, and administrative powers (Abraham 1998).

The nature of the federal court system was a topic of much debate during the Constitutional Convention of 1787. Wheeler (1992:5) says that "The very idea of a federal court system in addition to the existing state courts...was a source of vigorous opposition to the Constitution's ratification." The two political parties of the day—the **Anti-Federalists** and the **Federalists**—held divergent views on many aspects of the proposed national government, including what role, if any, there should be for a system of federal courts.

The Anti-Federalists, who opposed a strong central government, were very concerned that national courts "could become instruments of tyranny" (Wheeler and Harrison 2005: 2). Therefore, the Anti-Federalists lobbied strongly for a limited and weak federal judiciary. In fact, the Anti-Federalists proposed that virtually all legal matters should be handled by the state courts (see, for example, Wheeler and Harrison 2005). By contrast, the Federalists (the political party of George Washington) favored not only the establishment of a national Supreme Court, but also of a system of lower-level federal trial courts.

In the end the Federalist position won out, and in 1789 President George Washington signed one of the first pieces of legislation to be passed by Congress: "An Act to Establish the Federal Courts of the United States." Quite often this legislation is simply referred to as the **Judiciary Act of 1789**. The Judiciary Act of 1789 contained a number of provisions that impacted the administration of justice early in our nation's history, and many of these stipulations continue to have an effect today. Among the most important elements of the Act were:

- Creation of federal courts below the level of the Supreme Court
- Creation of a series of circuit courts with limited appellate jurisdiction
- Establishment of the size of the membership of the Supreme Court originally with a Chief Justice and five Associate Justices
- Appointment of United States marshals, United States attorneys, and an attorney general, all to be chosen by the President

Three particular provisions of the Judiciary Act were compromises offered to the Anti-Federalists. First, district courts and circuit courts were given limited jurisdictions so as not to intrude into state legal matters. Second, no district or circuit court boundary could cut across a state line. Third, judges were chosen from the district or circuit within which they resided (Wheeler 1992:5). This arrangement, which still exists today, tied the organization and operations of the lower-level federal courts to the states.

As the nation grew and expanded, Congress continued to modify the federal court structure. The following sections provide information on the specific legislative changes that defined the jurisdiction of the federal courts and the organizational structure of those courts.

JURISDICTION OF THE FEDERAL DISTRICT COURTS

In the debate between the Federalists and the Anti-Federalists a great deal of controversy existed over the subject matter jurisdiction of federal courts, particularly the lower courts. Initially, the Judiciary Act of 1789 granted federal trial courts jurisdiction in cases relating to admiralty, diversity of citizenship, the United States as a plaintiff, and federal crimes (see especially Wheeler and Harrison 2005:6–7).

MARITIME CASES

Admiralty cases involve what is also known as maritime law. Specifically, this concerns "the system of law which particularly relates to marine commerce and navigation, to business transacted at sea or relating to navigation, to ships and shipping, to seamen, to the transportation of persons and property by sea, and to marine affairs generally" (*Black's Law Dictionary* 1991:668). With a new nation bounded by oceans and crossed by substantial inland waterways, this area of jurisdiction seemed especially important to the new national government. Very little controversy existed over federal courts exercising admiralty jurisdiction, and these cases were the main business of the district courts when they first were created (Wasby 1993).

DIVERSITY OF CITIZENSHIP

By contrast, **diversity of citizenship** jurisdiction seemed to be an especially thorny issue for both the Constitutional Convention and the First United States Congress. Article III, Section 2 of the Constitution provides that federal courts shall have jurisdiction in cases involving "controversies between two or more states;…between a state and citizens of another state;…between citizens of different states;…between citizens of the same state claiming lands under grants of different states, and between a state, or the citizens thereof, and foreign states, citizens or subjects." Diversity of citizenship "extends to cases between citizens of different states, designating the condition existing when the party on one side of a lawsuit is a citizen of one state, and the party on the other side is a citizen of another state, or between a citizen of a state and an alien [non-citizen]" (*Black's Law Dictionary* 1991: 331).

The Federalists seemed especially concerned about diversity of citizenship jurisdiction for two reasons. First, in the original states the legislatures appointed most of the judges, and there was the abiding concern that state judges would be influenced by the legislatures that appointed them. Second, there was at least the implicit concern of a "home field advantage," or bias in favor of in-state litigants over out-of-state litigants. Whether these were likely outcomes or not, they seemed to be real concerns in the minds of many national leaders, especially the Federalists.

U.S. GOVERNMENT AS A PARTY

As I mentioned previously, Article III, Section 2 of the Constitution also provided federal court jurisdiction over "controversies to which the United States shall be a party." This seemed to cover both civil and criminal jurisdiction, and initially it appeared to have little potential impact. It is important to remember, however, that when the Judiciary Act of 1789 was passed, and for some time to follow, "federal statutory law was quite limited in the early years" (Wheeler and Harrison 2005:6). Therefore, state courts were responsible for many of the types of cases that later would also become concerns for the federal courts.

At the most fundamental level, the United States Constitution prescribes the types of cases federal courts may hear. Beyond the broad parameters provided for in the Constitution, Congress can further expand or contract federal court jurisdiction. For instance, in diversity jurisdiction cases Congress has determined that the amount in dispute must exceed $75,000 (not including costs and interest) for federal courts to have jurisdiction; this amount was increased from $50,000 in 1996. Otherwise, these cases are to be handled by state courts.

CASE AND CONTROVERSY RULE

Two final factors need to be emphasized in regard to federal court jurisdiction. First, the Constitution limits the federal courts to deciding "cases and controversies." This means that the courts must be presented with actual disputes involving opposing parties who have a real stake in winning or losing. Thus, federal courts are constrained from answering hypothetical questions or from issuing advisory opinions (see Abraham 1998; Melone and Karnes 2008).

FLEXIBILITY OF JURISDICTION

Second, federal court jurisdiction can be a very fluid concept. While some jurisdictional elements are relatively fixed, others are flexible and have been changed over time by court interpretations (case law and rules of procedure) and Congressional enactments (statutory law) to meet the needs of an ever-changing society. Box 10.4 contains a short summary of the types of cases heard by the federal district courts.

BOX 10.4

Responsibilities of the Federal District Courts

The United States district courts are the trial courts of the federal court system. Within limits set by Congress and the Constitution, the district courts have jurisdiction to hear nearly all categories of federal cases, including both civil and criminal matters. There are ninety-four federal judicial districts, including at least one district in each state, the District of Columbia, and Puerto Rico. Each district includes a United States bankruptcy court as a unit of the district court. Three territories of the United States—the Virgin Islands, Guam, and the Northern Mariana Islands—have district courts that hear federal cases, including bankruptcy cases.

There are two special trial courts that have nationwide jurisdiction over certain types of cases. The Court of International Trade addresses cases involving international trade and customs issues. The United States Court of Federal Claims has jurisdiction over most claims for money damages against the United States, disputes over federal contracts, unlawful "takings" of private property by the federal government, and a variety of other claims against the United States.

Source: Understanding the Federal Courts (2009).

STRUCTURE OF THE FEDERAL DISTRICT COURTS

As Figure 10.4 illustrates, the current structure of federal courts in the United States can be illustrated as a three-tiered pyramid (see *Understanding the Federal Courts* 2009). At the top of the pyramid is the U.S. Supreme Court. At the next level are the U.S. Court of Appeals for the Armed Forces and the thirteen U.S. Courts of Appeals. These two levels of federal appellate courts are discussed further in Chapter 11.

Below the Courts of Appeals are the ninety-four district courts and a group of specialized courts including the Tax Court, U.S. Claims Court, Court of Veterans Appeals, and the Court of International Trade. Many of these courts originally were created as types of legislative courts that were previously mentioned in this chapter. However, Congress has changed the status of all of these to constitutional courts except the U.S. Tax Court, the U.S. Court of Military Appeals, and the Territorial Courts (Abraham 1998; *Understanding the Federal Courts* 2009).

Since they are the federal courts of first instance, the district courts are the primary focus of this chapter. One of the reasons these courts are so important is that most federal cases never progress beyond this stage (Wasby 1993). The district courts have both criminal and civil jurisdiction, and they serve as the courts of general trial jurisdiction for the federal system. In reality, however, the "primary trial court" designation for the district courts really did not occur until passage of the Circuit Court of Appeals Act of 1891 (Wheeler and Harrison 2005:18).

The federal court system that exists today has evolved slowly since the founding of the nation. In fact, with passage of the Judiciary Act on September 24, 1789, the structure of the federal court system initially was outlined. The first eleven states to ratify the Constitution, in alphabetical order, were Connecticut, Delaware, Georgia, Maryland, Massachusetts, New Hampshire, New Jersey, New York, Pennsylvania, South Carolina, and Virginia. These states, plus the districts of Kentucky and Maine, comprised the first thirteen federal districts, and each of these districts had one judge. Additionally, eleven of the districts were grouped into three circuits—Eastern, Middle,

FIGURE 10.4   FEDERAL COURT STRUCTURE

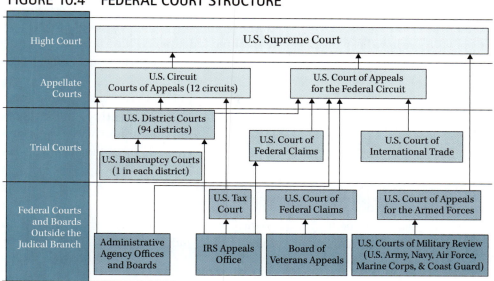

and Southern—within which a district court judge and two Supreme Court justices comprised the circuit court bench. The districts of Kentucky and Maine were not included in one of the three circuits, and the district courts there initially had both trial and appellate jurisdiction (see Wheeler and Harrison 2005:5–8).

The original **circuit riding** dimension of the federal appellate courts was something of a hold-over from the way state courts had previously operated. This approach to structuring and assigning the federal judiciary accomplished two things: (1) it kept the federal appellate courts close to their state court roots, and (2) it kept Congress from having to provide a separate corps of judges to staff the circuit courts.

As the United States expanded, the district court structure that had been established provided flexibility for expansion. In 1802 there were twenty district courts, and by 1837 the number had increased to thirty-four. The real difficulty in federal court organization came about as a result of the forced circuit court and Supreme Court link. For instance, in 1802 there were six federal circuits and six Supreme Court justices. By 1837 the number of circuits had increased to nine, and the number of Supreme Court justices was increased to nine also, in order to provide oversight for the new Eighth and Ninth Circuits (Wheeler and Harrison 2005).

Eventually, the policy of adding justices in relation to the number of federal circuits increased the size of the Supreme Court to ten members in 1863, and some people (President Abraham Lincoln being one of them) criticized the ineffectiveness of this approach to structuring the appellate level of the federal judiciary (Wheeler and Harrison 2005:12). There were fluctuations in the Supreme Court's size from 1863 until 1870 when Congress finally set the Court's size at nine, the number of justices that continues until the present day. I discuss more of the structure and functions of the federal courts of appeals (the circuit courts) and the U.S. Supreme Court at greater length in the next chapter.

WORKLOAD OF THE FEDERAL DISTRICT COURTS

Most of the cases appearing in federal district courts are heard by one judge, typically in a jury trial rather than a bench trial. However, throughout the history of the federal courts there have been instances where three-judge panels have been utilized (see especially Wasby 1993). These panels are comprised of two district court judges and a court of appeals judge.

The first three-judge courts were used beginning in 1903 to respond to requests for injunctions against the Interstate Commerce Commission. In 1910 three-judge courts were used for injunctions against state laws and in 1913 this authority was expanded to cover the administrative actions of states. Finally, use of three-judge courts was extended to injunctions against federal statutes in 1937.

The problem with the three-judge courts was that appeals of their decisions bypassed the courts of appeals and went directly to the U.S. Supreme Court. These mandatory appeals overloaded the Supreme Court's discretionary (certiorari) docket. Therefore, in 1976 Congress ended the use of three-judge courts in all cases except those involving legislative reapportionment, the Civil Rights Act of 1964, and the Voting Rights Act (Wasby 1993).

In 1998 the number of civil cases filed in federal district courts declined for the first time since 1991 (*The Third Branch* 1998:1). Two types of cases—those involving personal injuries and prisoner petitions—largely contributed to this decline. The number of personal injury cases related to breast implant litigation increased substantially beginning in 1992, and by 1998 most of these cases had been settled. Additionally, prisoner petitions decreased 7 percent as a result of Congressional passage of the Prison Litigation Reform Act of 1996. This legislation made it more difficult for prison inmates to file suit in federal court, among other ways by requiring filing fees. Additionally, as previously mentioned in this chapter, in 1996 Congress increased the amount in dispute required for federal diversity jurisdiction cases from $50,000 to $75,000 (*The Third Branch* 1998:2). This resulted in a decline of 11 percent in diversity cases.

Recent figures demonstrate something of the magnitude of what could be labeled the "normal" workloads of federal district courts. Table 10.1 shows the number of civil and criminal cases filed in the district courts from 2004 to 2008. Three features of this table are particularly noteworthy. First, there are some slight year-to-year variations, but the general trend for both types of cases is upward. The number of criminal cases filed in 2008 was virtually the same as in 2004. However, there had been a decline of about 4,000 cases per year from 2004 to 2006, but in 2007 the numbers started back up. Thus, the 2008 criminal case filings represented a 3.6 percent increase over 2007.

Second, in terms of civil filings in federal district courts, the numbers grew by nearly 49,000 cases annually from 2004 to 2008; this was an 18.3 percent increase in just five years. The exception to growth was from 2006 to 2007.

Third, as is readily apparent, there are nearly four times as many civil cases as there are criminal cases filed in federal district courts. These two types of cases (along with a brief mention of bankruptcy cases) are dealt with in the following sections.

TABLE 10.1 Criminal and Civil Cases Filed in U.S. District Courts, 2004–2008		
Year	Criminal Cases Filed	Civil Cases Filed*
2004	70,397	218,338
2005	68,996	253,273
2006	66,365	259,541
2007	67,910	257,507
2008	70,429	267,257

Note: These numbers represent the total case filings including original filings in the district courts, cases that were removed from state courts, remands from the courts of appeals, cases that were reopened, and transfers.
Source: Duff (2008).

CIVIL RIGHTS CASES

Civil rights cases can be pursued under state laws in some situations, however, in most instances the federal district courts are the preferred forum for litigating civil rights actions. Most of the cases that come to the federal courts deal with employment discrimination of some type, issues surrounding housing and other types of accommodations, welfare rights and benefits, and voting rights. The Bureau of Justice Statistics notes that "A civil rights claim [may] arise when an individual or group asserts they have been discriminated against on the basis of their race, sex, religion, age, physical limitation, or previous condition of servitude" (Kyckelhahn and Cohen 2008:1).

The federal government expanded civil rights laws at the beginning of the 1990s and, as a result, the total number of civil rights cases that were filed in the federal district courts increased from 18,922 in 1990 to a high of 43,278 in 1997. Since that time there has been a steady decline in cases, including a decrease of about 20 percent from 2003 to 2006 (Kyckelhahn and Cohen 2008). Table 10.2 shows the number of private civil rights suits (those not involving the government as a party) from 1990 to 2006, indicating the types of issues involved.

In 2006, about 13 percent of all of the federal civil cases filed involved civil rights claims. As Table 10.2 shows, roughly half of the civil rights cases filed in any year concern employment discrimination issues. The other large category involves "other civil rights complaints" and these either cannot be identified from court records, or they include issues other than those specifically identified in the table.

One final item of interest concerning federal civil rights lawsuits is the number of these cases that actually make it to trial. In 2006, 72 percent of the civil rights actions filed in federal court were dismissed. Of this number, 37 percent were settled out of court, and another 11.4 percent were voluntarily dismissed. The remaining cases were disposed of by the courts for lack of jurisdiction, want of prosecution, or other reasons.

TABLE 10.2	Private Civil Rights Suits Filed in Federal District Courts, 1990–2006*					
Year	Total Number	Employment	Voting	Housing	Welfare	Other
1990	16,310	6,936	114	284	107	8,869
1995	33,574	17,374	188	582	103	15,327
2000	37,888	19,245	141	1,202	73	17,227
2001	37,878	19,371	173	1,151	53	17,130
2002	37,391	19,225	209	1,231	61	16,665
2003	37,602	18,768	139	1,261	63	17,371
2004	37,374	18,040	152	1,169	54	17,959
2005	33,390	15,344	143	821	48	17,034
2006	30,405	13,042	122	593	49	16,599

Note: These include the suits filed by private individuals and do not include the cases filed by the federal government as plaintiff.
Source: Kyckelhahn and Cohen (2008: 4).

From the 28 percent of cases that remained active, only 3 percent actually went to trial (Kyckelhahn and Cohen 2008:5).

In summary, although federal civil rights cases composed a relatively small part of the overall federal trial court docket, these cases are important because of the kinds of issues they encompass. Especially significant are the cases dealing with discrimination in employment, housing and accommodations, and voting rights.

CRIMINAL CASES

One measure of the crimes processed by the federal courts can be gathered from the numbers of cases disposed of by the United States Attorneys. For example, in 1995 the U.S. Attorneys concluded 102,309 criminal cases. By 2005, that number had grown to 143,640 (about a 4 percent per year increase). During this period, property crimes decreased substantially from 33,888 to 25,570. This was a decrease from 5.3 percent of all criminal cases concluded to 3.8 percent of the federal criminal cases. All of the other categories of cases increased, some slightly and some significantly: violent offenses from 5,399 to 5,485, drug offenses from 31,261 to 40,038, public order offenses from 18,469 to 21,583, weapons offenses from 5,732 to 13,689, and immigration offenses from 6,660 to 36,559 (Motivans 2008:3).

The annual report prepared by the Director of the Administrative Office of the U.S. Courts provides even more recent and complete numbers. As was shown in Table 10.1, the total number of federal criminal cases filed declined from 2004 to 2006 and started to increase again in 2007 and 2008. While they are not shown in Table 10.1, the following numbers illustrate some of the changes in federal criminal cases within certain categories comparing 2004 with 2008 (Duff 2008:224–27):

- Violent offenses decreased from 2,701 in 2004 to 2,232 in 2008.
- Property offenses (including burglary, larceny, embezzlement, fraud, forgery/counterfeiting, and auto theft) increased from 11,890 to 12,048.
- Interestingly (given the attention often given to federal drug laws), drug offenses decreased from 18,414 to 15,784 (the all-time high for drug crime cases was 2002 when there were 19,184).
- Firearms and explosives offenses declined from 9,609 to 8,045.
- Sex offenses (particularly possession and production of sexually explicit materials) increased from 1,632 to 2,634.
- Immigration offenses, primarily illegal entry into the country, increased from 17,033 to 21,313.

Although these numbers do not include all of the classes of federal crimes, they do demonstrate the trends in a number of key categories.

Before we leave this discussion of the processing of federal criminal cases, it is important to note the influence of speedy trial legislation.[2] The Sixth Amendment to the Constitution provides, in part, that "the accused shall enjoy the right to a speedy and public trial." For much of our nation's history, and especially in relation to state cases, what constituted a "speedy" trial largely was left to the discretion of trial judges (see, for example, *Klopfer v. North Carolina*, 386 U.S. 213 [1967] and *Barker v. Wingo*, 407 U.S. 514 [1972]). However, when Congress passed the **Speedy Trial Act of 1974**, the notion of a speedy trial took on a very specific meaning (see 18 U.S.C. Sections 3161–3174).

Under the Speedy Trial Act, federal authorities have thirty days from the time of arrest to file a criminal information or to bring forth a grand jury indictment. From information or indictment there is an additional seventy-day period within which the case must be tried or the charges may be dismissed (Carp, Stidham, and Manning 2007). There are allowances within the law for extensions based on filing pretrial motions and requests for continuances and other situations in which judges determine that delays are necessary and desirable. All states now have followed the lead of the federal government, and have speedy trial provisions that range from 90 to 180 days in which to bring criminal cases to trial.

BANKRUPTCY CASES

From 1993 to 1997 the number of federal bankruptcy cases filed increased 43 percent. Two factors associated with this trend need to be mentioned. First, in 1996 the number of bankruptcy cases surpassed the 1 million mark for the first time in our nation's history (*The Third Branch* 1998:3). Second, 96 percent of the bankruptcies filed in 1997 were personal (that is, non-business) bankruptcies. A report issued by the federal courts maintained that "The rise in bankruptcy filings is most likely connected to the great availability of consumer credit—which has produced record levels of debt as a percentage of personal income" (*The Third Branch* 1998:4).

The crash of the housing market in the United States and the economic downturn that started in 2008 also had a major impact on bankruptcy filings. For instance, the most recent figures available show that the number of bankruptcy filings (both personal and business) increased from 801,269 in 2007 to 1,042,993 in 2008. These cases ranged from simple personal bankruptcies to situations involving multi-billion dollar international businesses such as Chrysler Corporation and General Motors. Obviously, the more extensive and complex the case, the more time the federal bankruptcy courts must spend on it.

BOX 10.5

In the News: Changes in Bankruptcy Laws

In 2005, the Bankruptcy Code was amended to require that most individual debtors complete a special briefing from an approved credit counseling agency before filing a bankruptcy case. In most states, the United States trustee is responsible for approving the providers that offer this special pre-bankruptcy briefing and in the six districts located in Alabama and North Carolina, the bankruptcy administrator assigned to those districts approves them. The United States trustee and the bankruptcy administrators maintain a list of approved providers.

Source: Administrative Office of the U.S. Courts (2009).

SUMMARY

It is a major challenge to provide a detailed description of state courts in the United States, and a small volume could be written on each state and its court system. In fact, check one of your local libraries to see if some group such as the state bar association or the administrative office of courts in your state has prepared such a book. The difficulty comes from the fact that while the basic court structural features may be similar, each state has its own distinctive legal history and unique court system. Most of the state court systems began to evolve in the 1700s and 1800s, while many of the states still were colonies or territories. In the twentieth century several states modernized their court systems one or more times, but a number of states still have historical vestiges of their original court systems, such as the offices of the justice of the peace or chancery courts.

State courts have their jurisdictions defined by their constitutions or respective legislatures. State legislatures also are responsible for deciding the number of judges needed and the budgets necessary to support the court systems. This creates a dynamic tension. On the one hand, the judiciary is a separate and theoretically coequal branch of government. On the other hand, courts and their employees are dependent on the legislative branch to fund and define the scope of their operations. They also must depend on the executive branch to enforce the laws and any orders handed down by the courts.

The workloads of state courts are somewhat related to the state populations and the amount of commerce present in the state. However, almost irrespective of the jurisdiction size, many judges will characterize their dockets as full and their workloads as heavy. I discussed the courts of inferior jurisdiction—those responsible for processing small claims and misdemeanors—in Chapter 8, and these courts continue to deal with a tremendous number of cases compared to the general trial courts. Nevertheless, in most states the trial courts have large caseloads when compared to their federal counterparts. Therefore, we can conclude that most of the court "business" in the United States is handled by the state courts. These are the courts with which most people are familiar, if they have had contact with courts at all.

Having said that, it is important to emphasize that federal courts also have a broad range of responsibilities and demanding workloads. The federal district courts are responsible for a number of criminal and civil matters that are unique parts of their jurisdictions. For example, immigration violations; admiralty cases; and patent, copyright, and trademark suits fall into the exclusive purview of the federal courts. Additionally, certain types of cases such as bank robberies, kidnapping, drug offenses, and stolen vehicles that are taken across state lines may be handled by the federal courts, but some of these cases also might be prosecuted in state courts instead.

While the federal district courts process about 70,000 criminal cases filed each year, their real workload involves civil cases and bankruptcies. For instance, in 2008 there were 70,429 criminal cases filed in federal district courts compared with 267,257 civil cases and over 1 million bankruptcies. By any definition, this is a heavy workload for the nation's 678 federal district judges and the 352 bankruptcy judges assigned to their districts.

As you have seen, both the state and federal courts of general trial jurisdiction are responsible for issues that affect a broad range of society. Not all of us will be victims of crime, but some may be involved in automobile accidents that will result in a lawsuit. Furthermore, several people each year are victims of discrimination relative to their employment, the purchase of a home or the rental of an apartment, and to a lesser extent other forms of discrimination. Some of these situations may be handled informally, but some will result in litigation that will find its way into the trial courts of general jurisdiction.

QUESTIONS FOR CRITICAL THINKING

1. Choose one of the following positions and develop a list of reasons to defend it:

   (a) there should be one set of laws and one court system in the United States and not separate state and federal courts; or

   (b) because each state is unique each needs its own laws and court system.

2. How many levels of courts exist in your state? Are there specialized courts to handle certain types of cases? What justifications can you think of for having specialized courts?

3. Talk to a judge or attorney (preferably both) in your area. Suggest that your state's court system would be better if it was like a neighboring state. What kind of reaction did you get? Why?

4. What do we mean by the "local legal culture?" What kinds of factors influence this culture?

5. What is Walker really trying to show us by his "wedding cake"? Does this characterization help you understand the processing of different kinds of cases, or is it overly simplistic? Explain.

6. List and discuss some of the features that seem to distinguish courts of limited jurisdiction from the courts of general trial jurisdiction.

7. Why would anyone choose a bench trial over a jury trial? Why might a lawyer recommend one or the other?

8. What is meant by a "unified court system?" If you do an Internet search (or look through books on courts), do you find a consistent definition?

9. In general, do courts process more criminal cases or civil cases? Why is there such a disparity in the caseloads of the two types of cases?

10. Within the federal court structure, what is the difference between constitutional courts and legislative courts? Give an example of each type.

11. To what extent do civil rights lawsuits affect the way actors in the criminal justice system perform their duties? Can you think of actions that may be undertaken by law enforcement officers or corrections personnel that could result in a civil rights suit?

12. Are you a member of any "protected class" that might have a reason to file a civil rights suit?

RECOMMENDED READINGS

LaFountain, Robert C., Richard Y. Schauffer, Shauna M. Strickland, William E. Raftery, and Chantal G. Bromage, eds. (2008). *Examining the Work of State Courts, 2007.* Williamsburg, VA: National Center for State Courts. This is one in a series of reports prepared by the National Center for State Courts that outlines what state courts do at the trial and appellate levels. It examines the number of cases filed and disposed of by these courts in terms of the categories of cases processed. This document may be available in your college or public library, but it also can be found online at http://www.ncsconline.org/d_research/csp/2007b_files/EWSC-2007-v21-online.pdf.

Stolzenberg, Lisa, and Stewart J. D'Alessio, eds. *Criminal Courts for the 21st Century.* Upper Saddle River, NJ: Prentice Hall, 1999. This book contains twenty readings on various facets of the criminal court process. A number of the selections deal with the structures and processes of state courts. The readings also deal with the social and political dynamics of courts and the criminal justice system.

Walker, Samuel (2006). *Sense and Nonsense about Crime and Drugs*, 6th ed. Belmont, CA: Wadsworth Publishing Co. While Walker's book is not specifically about courts and the judicial process, he does examine the ways in which the criminal justice system deals with certain types of offenders and offenses. Of particular interest in his book is the characterization of court processing as a "wedding cake," and his treatment of the "going rate" and plea bargaining dynamics.

KEY TERMS

admiralty
Anti-Federalists
bench trial
breaches of contract
chancery courts
circuit riding
concurrent jurisdiction
constitutional courts
contingency fee
conversion
diversity of citizenship

domestic relations
false arrest
false imprisonment
Federalists
general trial jurisdiction
   courts
intentional tort
Judiciary Act of 1789
legislative courts
libel
local legal culture

premises liability
Racketeer Influenced and
   Corrupt Organization
   Act
slander
Speedy Trial Act of 1974
torts
unified court systems
wedding cake model

REFERENCES

Abadinsky, Howard, and L. Thomas Winfree, Jr. (1992). *Crime & Justice*, 2nd ed. Chicago: Nelson-Hall Publishers.

Abraham, Henry J. (1998). *The Judicial Process*, 7th ed. New York: Oxford University Press.

Administrative Office of the U.S. Courts (2009). *Federal Courts: Bankruptcy*. http://www.uscourts.gov/bankruptcycourts.html.

Altschuler, Bruce E., and Celia A. Sgroi (1996). *Understanding Law in a Changing Society*, 2nd ed. Upper Saddle River, NJ: Prentice Hall.

Barker v. Wingo, 407 U.S. 514 (1972).

Black's Law Dictionary, 6th ed. (1991). St. Paul, MN: West Publishing Co.

Carp, Robert A., and Ronald Stidham (2001). *The Federal Courts*, 4th ed. Washington, DC: CQ Press.

Carp, Robert A., Ronald Stidham, and Kenneth L. Manning (2007). *Judicial Process in America*, 7th ed. Washington, DC: CQ Press.

Champion, Dean J. (2005). *The American Dictionary of Criminal Justice*. 3rd edition. Los Angeles: Roxbury Publishing Co.

CNN (2005). Jury Slaps Wal-Mart with $172 million Ruling. http://www.mindfully.org/Industry/2005/Wal-Mart-$172M-Lunch22dec05.htm.

Cohen, Thomas H. (2009). *Tort Bench and Jury Trials in State Courts, 2005*. Washington, DC: Bureau of Justice Statistics, U.S. Department of Justice.

Court Services & Facilities (2009). http://www.judiciary.gov.hk/en/crt_services/pphlt/html/dc.htm.

Duff, James C. (2008). *Annual Report of the Director*. Washington, DC: Administrative Office of the U.S. Courts.

Duncan v. Louisiana, 391 U.S. 145, (1968).

Durose, Matthew R., and Patrick A. Langan (2007). *Felony Sentences in State Courts, 2004*. Washington, DC: Bureau of Justice Statistics, U.S. Department of Justice.

Eisenstein, James, and Herbert Jacob (1977). *Felony Justice: An Organizational Analysis of Criminal Courts*. Boston: Little, Brown and Co.

Farole, Donald J. (2009). *Contract Bench and Jury Trials in State Courts, 2005*. Washington, DC: Bureau of Justice Statistics, U.S. Department of Justice.

Grossman, Joel B., Herbert M. Kritzer, Kristin Bumiller, and Stephen McDougal (1992). Measuring the Pace of Civil Litigation in Federal and State Trial Courts. In *Judicial Politics,* ed. Elliot E. Slotnick, 337–44. Chicago: American Judicature Society.

Klopfer v. North Carolina, 386 U.S. 213 (1967).

Kyckelhahn, Tracey, and Thomas H. Cohen (2008). *Civil Rights Complaints in U.S. District Courts, 1990–2006*. Washington, DC: Bureau of Justice Statistics, U.S. Department of Justice.

LaFountain, Robert C., Richard Y. Schauffer, Shauna M. Strickland, William E. Raftery, and Chantal G. Bromage, ed. (2006). *Examining the Work of State Courts*. Williamsburg, VA: National Center for State Courts.

Langton, Lynn, and Thomas H. Cohen (2007). *State Court Organization, 1987–2004*. Washington, DC: Bureau of Justice Statistics, U.S. Department of Justice.

Langton, Lynn, and Thomas H. Cohen (2008). *Civil Bench and Jury Trials in State Courts, 2005*. Washington, DC: Bureau of Justice Statistics, U.S. Department of Justice.

Lee, Henry K. (2005). Gigantic Verdict Against Wal-Mart: Oakland Jury Orders $172 million Paid for Lack of Lunch Breaks. *San Francisco Chronicle*, December 23: A-1.

Litan, Robert E. (1992). Speeding Up Civil Justice. In *Judicial Politics*. ed. Elliot E. Slotnick, 329–36. Chicago: American Judicature Society.

Melone, Albert P., and Allan Karnes (2008). *The American Legal System*, 2nd ed. Lanham, MD: Rowman & Littlefield Publishers.

Motivans, Mark (2008). *Federal Justice Statistics, 2005*. Washington, DC: Bureau of Justice Statistics, U.S. Department of Justice.

National Center for State Courts (2000). http://www.ncsc.dni.us/RESEARCH/CSP/csphigh.htm.

Pastore, Ann L., and Kathleen Maguire, eds. (2009). *Sourcebook of Criminal Justice Statistics* [Online]. http://www.albany.edu/sourcebook/toc_5.html.

Rottman, David B., and Shauna M. Strickland (2006). *State Court Organization, 2004*. Washington, DC: Bureau of Justice Statistics, U.S. Department of Justice.

The Third Branch (1998). Washington, DC: Administrative Office of the U.S. Courts. December.

Understanding the Federal Courts (2009). http://www.uscourts.gov/understand03/content_3_0.html.

Walker, Samuel (2006). *Sense and Nonsense About Crime and Drugs*, 6th ed. Belmont, CA: Wadsworth Publishing Co.

Wasby, Stephen L. (1993). *The Supreme Court in the Federal Judicial System*, 4th ed. Belmont, CA: Wadsworth/Cengage.

Wheeler, Russell R. (1992). *Origins of the Elements of Federal Court Governance*. Washington, DC: Federal Judicial Center.

Wheeler, Russell R., and Cynthia Harrison (2005). *Creating the Federal Judicial System*, 3rd ed. Washington, DC: Federal Judicial Center.

ENDNOTES

[1] In 2001 the State of Arkansas merged their chancery and probate courts into the existing Circuit Courts, thus eliminating some of the state's limited jurisdiction tribunals.

[2] It is important to recognize that these provisions apply to criminal cases only. There are not similar requirements for civil cases.

11

Courts of Appellate Jurisdiction

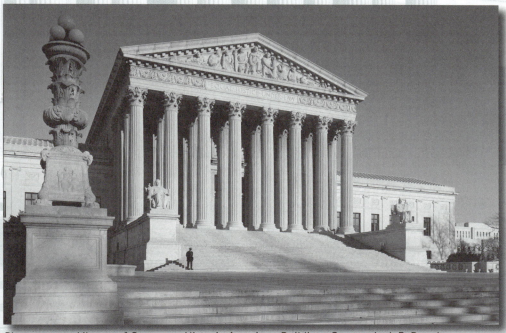

Photo source: Library of Congress: Historic American Buildings Survey, Jack E. Boucher, February 1975

INTRODUCTION

In an ideal legal system appellate courts would not be necessary because no errors would need to be corrected as a result of civil and criminal trial processes. However, since the people working in the courts are recruited from the human race, errors inevitably occur. This means that appellate courts always have a ready supply of cases for review and possible correction. In this chapter we will look at the functions of appellate courts—what they do, what they do not do, and how they go about performing their functions—as well as the similarities and differences between state appellate courts and federal appellate courts. We also will examine the judges who sit on the appellate benches in the various courts and the size and nature of appellate court caseloads. Before I go further, however, it is important to lay a brief foundation for what appellate courts do.

Unlike trial courts, whose job it is to determine matters of fact and law, appellate courts are responsible for reviewing "issues of law in connection with decisions made in specific cases previously adjudicated by other [trial] courts and decisions made by administrative agencies" (Bureau of Justice Statistics, 1981:54). These courts have four general characteristics: (1) they normally do not have original jurisdiction, (2) they hear appeals from trial courts or administrative boards and agencies, (3) they are collegial courts (their hearings are conducted by groups of judges), and (4) they are courts of record. In relation to the last point, appellate courts produce written records of their decisions that constitute what I called case law in Chapter 2.

Although it is not clear from the definition provided by the Bureau of Justice Statistics, appellate courts actually perform two distinct but related functions (see Marvell 1989:285). First, appellate courts are called on to correct errors of law that may have occurred in trial courts or, in some instances, in hearings conducted by administrative courts or agencies. Correcting errors of law might include the improper introduction of some types of evidence at trial, inadequate representation by counsel, or impermissible jury instructions. Second, they are responsible for developing law. Law creation occurs in situations where legislative bodies have failed to act on a certain issue, or where the legislation that has been passed is vague. One of the clearest cases relating to the "creation of law" occurred in the U.S. Supreme Court case of *Griswold v. Connecticut*, 381 U.S. 479 (1965) where the 7–2 Court majority recognized a right to privacy or a zone of privacy within marriages that covered the distribution of birth control devices and information by Planned Parenthood. No such right explicitly exists in the Constitution, and prior to the *Griswold* case the Court had not recognized such a right. Most of the error correction takes place in the **intermediate appellate courts**. By contrast, law development—what some might call law creation—happens much less frequently, but it typically takes place in the **courts of last resort**.

In the federal system and in thirty-nine state systems there are intermediate appellate courts that hear first-level appeals from trial courts and administrative agencies (Bureau of Justice Statistics 1981; Rottman and Strickland 2006). In almost every state, these intermediate appellate courts are called the courts of appeals, and they are "intermediate" because their decisions are reviewable by the state court of last resort, most commonly called the supreme court (although as you will see the exact name may vary from state to state). The state courts of last resort normally have the final say in appellate matters. However, it is important to recognize that in rare instances cases may be appealed from state courts of last resort into the federal system.

From this brief introduction I move now into an examination of state appellate courts and follow that with a discussion of federal appellate courts. As will become readily apparent, there are some similarities and there are some differences between state and federal courts of appeals. However, the same can be said when comparing appellate courts in one state with those in other states. As has been my practice throughout the book I present a general discussion and provide specific examples as illustrations.

STRUCTURE OF STATE APPELLATE COURTS

As is true of the courts of original jurisdiction, states vary in terms of the numbers of courts of appellate jurisdiction they have. As mentioned previously, thirty-nine states have intermediate-level appellate courts in addition to their courts of last resort. The remaining eleven states—Delaware, Maine, Montana, Nevada, New Hampshire, North Dakota, Rhode Island, South Dakota, Vermont, West Virginia, and Wyoming—have only a single level of appellate courts (courts of last resort).

INTERMEDIATE COURTS OF APPEALS

First level (or intermediate) courts of appeal are relatively recent additions to the court structures of most states. Rottman and Strickland (2006:131) note that in 1957 only thirteen states had intermediate appellate courts, but over the past fifty years twenty-six additional states have added these courts. Intermediate appellate courts most frequently meet in a centralized location such as the state capital. Though this is the arrangement in most states, in others, because of the state size or court workload the judges may "ride circuit" and meet at different locations, or the court may be structured in regional divisions (see Barclay 1998). Multiple meeting locations can ease travel burdens for attorneys and others involved in the appeals process. This is the model California (nine locations), Idaho (nine locations), Ohio (twelve locations), New York (four locations, and Texas (fifteen locations) follow, for example (see Marvell 1989; Rottman and Strickland 2006:9–10).

As a result of different approaches to how intermediate appellate courts are structured and where they meet, the number of judges on these courts varies widely from state to state. For instance, the states of Alaska and Idaho have three judges on their courts of appeals, and Hawaii and Nebraska have six. By contrast, California has eighty-eight courts of appeals judges, Texas has eighty, Ohio has sixty-eight, Florida has sixty-two, New York has fifty-seven, and Illinois and Louisiana have fifty-three each. The average nationwide for states with only one intermediate appellate court is about twenty-seven judges.[1]

The intermediate appellate courts dispose of the vast majority of state appeals. Some cases, particularly civil cases with large monetary judgments and high-profile criminal cases eventually may be appealed to the state court of last resort.

COURTS OF LAST RESORT

It is difficult to generalize about the names by which the courts of last resort are known, as is true with many features of state court systems. For example, in quite a few states the state supreme court is the court of last resort for both civil and criminal cases. However, in both Texas and Oklahoma the state supreme courts have jurisdiction over civil matters exclusively (Rottman and Strickland 2006). In those two states, the court of last resort for criminal cases is the court of criminal appeals. Furthermore, in New York State the "supreme court" actually is the court of general trial jurisdiction (New York State Unified Court System 2009; Rottman and Strickland 2006). Therefore, it is difficult to use one label that adequately describes all of the courts of last resort. Nevertheless, since the most common label (the one that is used in forty-eight states) is "supreme court," that is the designation I use here.

State supreme courts vary in size. Six states have nine supreme court justices, twenty-six have seven justices, and eighteen have five justices. As I discuss at length in the following section, the judges (or justices, as they often are called) are chosen in a number of different ways. Some states—Alabama, Illinois, Louisiana, Ohio, Pennsylvania, Texas, and West Virginia—elect state supreme court justices in partisan elections. Others employ a system of appointments, and still others use some form of the Missouri Plan (or merit selection of judges).

Unlike their federal counterparts, state supreme court justices normally serve fixed terms—ranging from six to twelve years—but there are some exceptions to this generalization. For example, in Indiana justices serve an initial two-year term and then stand for retention election every ten years. In Massachusetts and New Hampshire, justices are appointed by the governor and may serve until the age of seventy. Finally, the major exception is Rhode Island, where state supreme court justices have life tenure like federal judges (Rottman and Strickland 2006).

States also employ a variety of mechanisms for disciplining or removing judges who prove unfit for service. Currently, every state has some board or commission that is responsible for addressing issues related to judicial conduct or discipline. Some states have boards that are comprised entirely of judges, but in most there are judges, lawyers, and lay persons who serve as members. In several states the judicial conduct commission has the responsibility for imposing discipline upon judges who have engaged in unethical or illegal conduct, and in other situations substantiated charges are referred to the state supreme court or similar judicial body for final disposition. The outcomes of these hearings can range from a simple written reprimand for a judge up to and including dismissal from office (Rottman and Strickland 2006:56–59).

As I have indicated previously, in every state except Oklahoma and Texas a single court of last resort has both criminal and civil jurisdiction. The bulk of the appellate workload by these courts involves civil appeals, and the same is true of the federal appellate courts. As an illustration, in 2008 there were 45,121 cases appealed from federal district courts to the U.S. Courts of Appeals. Of this number, 31,454 involved civil cases and 13,667 were criminal appeals. Thus, in the federal system civil appeals filed outnumbered criminal appeals filed by just over two-to-one (see Maguire 2010). Similar percentages of cases are referred to the U.S. Supreme Court.

One type of case heard by state supreme courts is particularly important, not because of the number of appeals but because of the visibility of these cases. When states redesigned and reimplemented their death penalty statutes in the wake of the U.S. Supreme Court's ruling in *Furman* v. *Georgia*, 408 U.S. 238 (1972), most included a provision that allows for automatic appeals from the trial court to the state court of last resort (see *Gregg* v. *Georgia*, 428 U.S. 153, 1976). These appeals do not have to be initiated by the person convicted of the crime, and they bypass the intermediate appellate courts in states that have them.

While death penalty rulings by state supreme courts obviously are not the final word in many of the cases, such appeals are important because they give appellate courts the responsibility for ensuring that the trials and the resulting death penalty verdicts are as free of mistakes as humanly possible.

Unfortunately, as has been revealed in several well-publicized cases from a number of states, errors still occur, and in some instances innocent people have been convicted of crimes they did not commit and have been sentenced to death (see, for example, Grisham 2006). As a result of some of these cases, in January 2000 then-Governor George Ryan suspended executions in the State of Illinois after several wrongful convictions were revealed. Ryan issued the following public statement:

> I now favor a moratorium [on executions], because I have grave concerns about our state's shameful record of convicting innocent people and putting them on Death Row. I can't support a system which in its administration has proven to be so fraught with error and has come so close to the ultimate nightmare: the state's taking of innocent life (CBSnews.com 2000).

Similar calls for moratoriums in states like Texas have not produced the same kinds of results to date.

Most of the time, state supreme court justices labor in relative obscurity. Oftentimes the average citizen would have a hard time naming any of the justices serving on their state supreme court. However, as a result of automatic death penalty appeals—and the errors that have occurred in states like Illinois—state courts of last resort have come under increasing scrutiny any time they are asked to review a death penalty case. It is possible that such reviews can bring unfavorable publicity to state supreme court justices. In fact, in Tennessee a successful statewide effort was mounted by a citizens' group to defeat Associate Justice Penny White in her retention election to the state supreme court over what were perceived as lenient decisions in death penalty cases (see Box 4.2 in Chapter 4; Reid 1999; see also Brown 1998).

A more recent example was seen in the 2010 election when Iowa supreme court justices David Baker, Michael Streit, and Marsha Ternus were not retained by the state's voters as a result of their ruling in favor of gay marriages ("Vote 2010"). Such efforts may not occur often, and when they do they may not be successful. However, these cases, as well as that of state supreme court justice Rose Bird in California, illustrate that some groups may give state appellate court judges more publicity than they are accustomed to receiving.

STRUCTURE OF FEDERAL APPELLATE COURTS

Like many of their state counterparts, the federal courts employ a two-tiered appellate system. In fact, given the early development of federal court structure in our nation's history, it is probably accurate to say that the federal courts provided the pattern that was adopted by many states.

As discussed in Chapter 1, the United States Supreme Court was established under the authority of Article III of the Constitution. This court truly is the court of last resort in the United States, although as you will see in one of the following sections the decisions by the Supreme Court may not be as final as most people would assume. It is possible that a Supreme Court decision may be only one point in a circular process that can also involve the President and Congress.

Beyond the U.S. Supreme Court, the U.S. Courts of Appeals were created very early in our nation's history, but their current structure and the practices they follow have developed over a long period of time. The next section examines the structure and functions of these federal intermediate appellate courts.

UNITED STATES COURTS OF APPEALS

The official title for the intermediate federal appellate courts is the Courts of Appeals. However, many scholars who write about the federal courts continue to call them the

Circuit Courts. This comes from the early **circuit riding** practices of district court judges and justices of the Supreme Court who served on the benches of the initial courts of appeals. The circuit court designation also continues to be used as a result of these courts being numbered and labeled the Court of Appeals for the First (or whatever number) Circuit.

The circuit courts were created by the Judiciary Act of 1789. Originally these courts were given limited appellate jurisdiction. In fact, not until over one hundred years later, with passage of the Circuit Court of Appeals Act of 1891, did the courts of appeals take on the functions with which we now associate them. With this legislation Congress "shifted the appellate caseload burden from the Supreme Court to new courts of appeals, and, in so doing, made the federal district courts the system's primary trial courts" (Wheeler and Harrison 1994:18).

In Chapter 4 I provided you with a map that has the outline of federal district courts and courts of appeals jurisdictions. You may want to refer to Figure 4.1 to refresh your memory. The present structure for the federal court system provides for eleven numbered courts of appeals plus an intermediate appellate court for the District of Columbia and one for the federal circuit (both of these located in Washington, DC). These intermediate appellate courts handle the vast majority of the cases appealed in the federal system. The caseload includes issues originally litigated in state courts but appealed to the federal district courts (like state prisoner habeas corpus petitions), as well as cases that originated in the federal district courts. A relatively small percentage of cases are ever appealed, and for those that are, most never go beyond the intermediate appellate courts. To illustrate this point, Tables 11.1 and 11.2 list the numbers of cases filed, terminated, and pending (or remaining on the docket) for the U.S. Courts of Appeals and the Supreme Court from 1991 to 2007 or 2008.

Each year a relatively small number of the felony convictions and even fewer misdemeanor convictions handed down by state and federal trial courts in the United States are appealed. For instance, in 2004 there were 12,506 criminal appeals from United States District Courts to the U.S. Courts of Appeals out of 74,782 federal felony cases processed; by 2008 this number had increased to 13,667 out of 70,896 federal felony cases processed (Pastore and Maguire 2010). These appeals represent around 17 percent of the criminal cases tried. In addition to the criminal caseload, there were 31,454 federal civil appeals filed with the U.S. Courts of Appeals in 2008. It is important to emphasize once again that the bulk of the nation's trial and appellate court caseload is at the state court level; in 2004 there were 1,078,920 state felony cases terminated and 240,531 criminal appeals filed in state appellate courts. This was slightly more than one in five of the case total number (Schauffler et al. 2005).

These two tables show that although there are year-to-year fluctuations, the general trend for both the Courts of Appeals and the Supreme Court is increasing numbers of cases filed and terminated for the years 1991 to 2007 and 2008. For instance, in 1991 the Supreme Court had 6,770 cases filed, and by 2007 this had increased by nearly 30 percent to 9,602. The numbers of cases disposed of by the Court also increased from 5,894 to 8,420 (again, a 30 percent increase). By comparison, the cases processed by the Courts of Appeals expanded from 43,027 in 1991 to 61,104 in 2008, and the number of cases disposed of went from 41,640 to 59,096. Both of these values represented a 30 percent increase.

TABLE 11.1 Number of Cases Appealed, Terminated, and Pending for the U.S. Courts of Appeals, 1991–2008

Year	Appeals filed	Cases terminated	Pending cases
1991	43,027	41,640	33,428
1992	47,013	44,373	35,799
1993	50,224	47,790	38,156
1994	48,322	49,184	37,269
1995	50,072	49,805	37,310
1996	51,991	50,413	38,774
1997	52,319	51,194	39,846
1998	53,805	52,002	41,666
1999	54,693	54,088	42,225
2000	54,697	56,512	40,261
2001	57,464	57,422	39,996
2002	57,555	56,586	40,149
2003	60,847	56,396	44,690
2004	62,762	56,381	51,226
2005	68,473	61,975	57,450
2006	66,618	67,582	56,178
2007	58,410	62,846	51,063
2008	61,104	59,096	53,071

Source: Pastore and Maguire (2010).

It appears, then, that the caseloads of both the Courts of Appeals and the Supreme Court are increasing at the same rate. The major difference is in the numbers of cases processed at each level.

THE COURT OF LAST RESORT

Unlike its state counterparts, the federal court of last resort—the U.S. Supreme Court—is much easier to characterize. However, because of the vast amount written about the Supreme Court and the justices that have served over the Court's history, it is difficult to summarize.

The general authority for the Supreme Court is provided for in Article III of the U.S. Constitution. Article III broadly provides that there will be a supreme court and other courts that Congress may decide to establish. It also provides that federal court jurisdiction includes

all Cases, in Law and Equity, arising under this Constitution, the Laws of the United States, and Treaties made, or which shall be made, under their Authority;…to all Cases affecting Ambassadors, other public Ministers and Consuls;…to all

TABLE 11.2	Numbers of Cases Appealed, Terminated, and Remaining on the Docket for the U.S. Supreme Court, 1991–2007		
Year	Cases appealed	Cases terminated	Remaining on docket
1991	6,770	5,894	876
1992	7,245	6,402	843
1993	7,786	6,721	1,065
1994	8,100	7,170	930
1995	7,565	6,649	916
1996	7,602	6,739	863
1997	7,692	6,759	933
1998	8,083	7,045	1,038
1999	8,445	7,369	1,076
2000	8,965	7,762	1,203
2001	9,176	8,072	1,104
2002	9,406	8,388	1,018
2003	8,882	7,836	1,046
2004	8,588	7,542	1,046
2005	9,608	8,240	1,368
2006	10,256	8,923	1,333
2007	9,602	8,420	1,182

Source: Pastore and Maguire (2010).

Cases of admiralty and maritime Jurisdiction;…to Controversies to which the United States shall be a party;…to Controversies between two or more States; between a State and Citizens of another State;…between Citizens of different States;…between Citizens of the same State claiming Lands under Grants of different States, and between a State, or the Citizens thereof, and foreign States, Citizens or Subjects.

The Constitution specifies furthermore that the Supreme Court can exercise original jurisdiction in cases involving ambassadors, public ministers, and consuls and those cases in which a state is a party. Over the course of our nation's history, it has exercised its original jurisdiction very infrequently. Today, virtually all of the Court's business is in exercising appellate jurisdiction.

Beyond the broad parameters provided by the Constitution, the Court's jurisdiction is relatively vague. In fact, a great deal of what the Supreme Court represents today has developed as a result of the personalities and predispositions of the men and women who have served on the Court, as well as the range of issues with which the Court has had to deal.

One of the key notions that helps us to understand the work of the Supreme Court is **judicial review**. In the case of *Marbury* v. *Madison*, 1 Cranch 137 (1803), the Supreme

Court first asserted its authority to review an act of Congress that appeared to be in conflict with the Constitution. In this case Congress had created a number of federal judgeships, including sixteen circuit court positions and forty-two justice of the peace positions for the District of Columbia, toward the end of the presidency of John Adams. There was a great deal of haste to get the new judges nominated and confirmed before Thomas Jefferson took office, and in the haste twelve of the judicial commissions were not delivered by the Secretary of State John Marshall. By the time Jefferson took office, Marshall had become Chief Justice of the Supreme Court, and an appeal for a **writ of mandamus** had been filed by William Marbury, one of the twelve individuals whose commissions had not been delivered.

There were several dilemmas facing Chief Justice Marshall and the Supreme Court. First, he was of a different political party (the Federalists) than the new President (Democratic-Republicans). Second, as Secretary of State he had been a party to the failure to deliver the commissions. Third, Jefferson openly declared his willingness to disobey any writ of mandamus issued by the Court. In what most constitutional scholars view as a stroke of genius, Chief Justice Marshall held that Marbury had the right to the commission and that the law provided a legal remedy to enforce that right. However, the Court held that Section 13 of the Judiciary Act of 1789, giving the Court the authority to issue writs of mandamus, was unconstitutional in that it altered the jurisdiction of the Court as defined by the Constitution. Therefore, the Court asserted its power of judicial review, but held in this case that it did not have a constitutional basis for action (see Calvi and Coleman 2008:130–33).

In simplest terms, judicial review "is the power of a court to determine whether an act of government is an exercise of constitutional authority and to strike down that act if it adjudges it to be unconstitutional" (Stephens and Rathjen 1980:13). This exercise of authority extends to acts of lower state and federal courts, federal and state legislatures, and executive officers at different levels including those in administrative agencies. This power has been characterized by some observers as the "cornerstone of our constitutional system" (Stephens and Rathjen 1980:13).

The Supreme Court has part of its appellate jurisdiction defined by the Constitution and Congress, but to a large extent the Court establishes much of its own judicial agenda. The two very clear examples that follow illustrate the control the Supreme Court has over its docket.

First, today the vast majority of cases that are appealed to the Court come on **writs of certiorari** (Rehnquist 2001). Certiorari is a discretionary appeal by which the Supreme Court asks the lower court to "send up the record" of the case for review. Under the concept known as the "rule of four," four of the Court's nine justices must vote in favor of the writ to add the case to the docket. Cases that are not accepted are refused without explanation. Even when a case is accepted under this procedure, after the Court has reviewed the record it may vote at a later time not to schedule the case for oral arguments and to drop it from the docket, noting that certiorari was "improvidently granted."

Second, the discretionary nature of Supreme Court appellate processes is demonstrated by the relatively small number of cases decided each year. As I indicated previously, in 2007 the Supreme Court had 9,602 cases on its docket. Out of these cases the

Court disposed of 8,420. However, only 180 cases were decided on the merits, from this number only eighty-six had oral arguments, and seventy-two cases were disposed of by full written opinions during this term. This was down from the 2006 totals of 356 cases decided on the merits. Nevertheless, in 2006 there were seventy-eight cases scheduled for oral argument, and seventy-two cases were disposed of by full written opinions (Pastore and Maguire 2010). These numbers demonstrate something of the fall-off from appeals heard by the U.S. Courts of Appeals to those reaching and finally decided by the U.S. Supreme Court, from both state and federal appellate routes.

Third, the Supreme Court's term does not coincide with either the calendar year or the federal government's fiscal year (which runs from October 1 through September 30). While there is no exact starting *date* for the Court, its term always starts on the same *day*: the first Monday in October. The term typically ends in late June or early July. This meeting schedule was established in the days before buildings were air conditioned, and it allowed the justices to minimize the effects of Washington's notoriously humid summers. Today, the justices may continue in residence in Washington, but frequently they travel, complete personal (that is, non-Court) legal writing of books and law review articles, and give speeches at law schools and professional conferences.

Another interesting facet of the U.S. Supreme Court is the comparatively small number of people who have served on the Court. The general trend is for most members of the Court to serve relatively long terms. The longest occurred in modern times, when Associate Justice William O. Douglas served thirty-six years, from 1939 until his retirement for health reasons in 1975. Since George Washington appointed the first six justices to the Supreme Court, there have only been seventeen Chief Justices (three of whom previously had been Associate Justices), and ninety-nine Associate Justices.

TABLE 11.3	Current Justices of the U.S. Supreme Court		
Name of Justice	Home State	Appointing President	Took oath of office on
Chief Justice			
John G. Roberts, Jr.	Maryland	George W. Bush	9/3/2005
Associate Justices			
Antonin Scalia	Virginia	Ronald Reagan	9/26/1986
Anthony M. Kennedy	California	Ronald Reagan	2/18/1988
Clarence Thomas	Georgia	George H.W. Bush	10/23/1991
Ruth Bader Ginsburg	New York	Bill Clinton	8/10/1993
Stephen G. Breyer	Mass.	Bill Clinton	8/3/1994
Samuel A. Alito, Jr.	New Jersey	George W. Bush	1/31/2006
Sonia Sotomayor	New York	Barack Obama	8/8/2009
Elena Kagan	New York	Barack Obama	8/10/2010

Source: U.S. Supreme Court (2010).

Of this number only two—Thurgood Marshall and Clarence Thomas—have been African-Americans and four—Sandra Day O'Connor, Ruth Bader Ginsburg, and Sonia Sotomayor, and Elena Kagan—have been women (U.S. Supreme Court 2010). Table 11.3 contains information on the current members of the Supreme Court.

Finally, as I mentioned briefly in a previous section, while the Supreme Court is the "court of last resort," it is not necessarily the final word on some issues. For example, during and after the Civil War Congress had imposed certain taxes on income based on the principle of uniformity, or equal percentages owed by each individual. In the case of *Pollock v. Farmers' Loan & Trust Co.*, 157 U.S. 429 (1895), the Supreme Court ruled such personal income taxes invalid since the Constitution provided that taxes must be levied among the states based on their populations rather than uniformly nationwide. The result was that Congress passed, and on February 3, 1913, thirty-six states ratified, the Sixteenth Amendment that provided that "Congress shall have power to lay and collect taxes on incomes, for whatever source derived, without apportionment among the several States, and without regard to any census or enumeration."

As part of the "checks and balances" element of our government, Congress can attempt to legislate away Supreme Court rulings, and the Executive branch may ignore or choose not to enforce the Court's rulings. However, over two hundred years of history has added a great deal of symbolic authority and legitimacy to most Supreme Court decisions.

JUDGES AND JUSTICES OF APPELLATE COURTS

The titles "judges" or "justices" are applied to different jurists serving on appellate courts. Most of the labels have developed through legal custom, and no difference in importance is implied when we use different titles. Nevertheless, in the federal court system and in many state systems, the members of the intermediate appellate courts are called judges. By contrast, those members of the judiciary who serve on the courts of last resort typically are called justices.

In Chapter 4 I discussed the different methods by which judges are chosen in the United States. However, it is important to briefly review that discussion in the context of appellate court judges.

First, as I have mentioned in several places, Article III federal judges are appointed by the President of the United States and confirmed by the United States Senate. This is true for judges in trial courts and appellate courts as well. Second, once these judges are confirmed they have life tenure, and they only can be removed from office through the process of impeachment. As Carp and Stidham (2001) have written, federal judges represent a very elite group within an elite group of the total body of judges in the United States. In fact, we might say that for federal appellate judges this is doubly true. Most of these judges are men from prominent families who graduated from prestigious law schools and who have had successful legal careers. They are not a true cross-sectional representation of the American public by any stretch of the imagination.

State appellate court judicial positions also have been dominated by white males, since these courts tend to have judges drawn from the upper strata of the legal profession. Nevertheless, in recent years state appellate courts have seen increasing numbers of females and minority group members serving as judges, and as more females and minorities enter the practice of law it is likely that more of them will find their way onto state appellate court benches (Alozie 1990; Brown 1998).

Many state appellate court judges and justices, like their federal counterparts, come to the bench through the appointment process. Often these are interim appointments that result from a vacancy on a court. Occasionally state appellate courts can serve as a stepping stone for appointment to the federal bench. At other times these courts serve as positions capping off a long legal career.

Unlike federal judges, most state appointments are interim appointments, and these judges and justices must run in partisan or non-partisan elections or in retention elections through a merit selection process. Table 11.4 shows the different ways state appellate court judges are selected in the United States and their terms of office.

Whether we are considering federal or state appellate judges and justices, a few points are worth repeating. First, to a substantial extent these are positions occupied by white males. In fact, until Jimmy Carter became President in 1977, fewer than 2 percent of the federal district judgeships were held by women. President Carter began a trend that largely has been carried on by his successors: Nearly 15 percent of his appointments to the district court bench were women, and 21 percent were minorities. During Bill Clinton's presidency, nearly half of his district court appointments were either women or minorities, and George W. Bush continued this trend by having women and minorities constitute one-third of his district court appointees. Additionally, for President Clinton one-third of his Courts of Appeals appointments were women, and he appointed more minority judges to appellate court positions than any other president in the nation's history (U.S. Department of State 2008). Therefore, in both federal and state courts we are seeing increasing numbers of women and minorities coming to the appellate benches, but their numbers still are comparatively small.

Second, appointment or election to an intermediate appellate court position is one of the most certain ways eventually to obtain a position on a court of last resort. Not all state or U.S. Supreme Court justices have served on intermediate appellate courts, but in recent years a significant number of intermediate appellate judges have found themselves appointed to positions on the highest courts in their states or at the federal level. In fact, all nine of the current justices of the U.S. Supreme Court—including John Roberts, the current Chief Justice—were federal appellate court judges before being nominated to be members of the Court. Four of the justices (Ginsburg, Roberts, Scalia, and Thomas) served on the Court of Appeals for the District of Columbia Circuit.

Finally, the judges on appellate courts are called on to decide relatively complex and technical points of law. Therefore, this is not a place for on-the-job training. There may be an occasional exception, but most of the judges serving on appellate courts have been law school professors or have had long legal and judicial careers before they

TABLE 11.4	Selection Methods for State Appellate Court Judges	
State	**Method**	**Term**
Alabama Supreme Court Court of Appeals	Partisan election	6 years
Alaska Supreme Court Court of Appeals	Gubernatorial appointment from judicial nominating commission	10 years 8 years
Arizona Supreme Court Court of Appeals	Gubernatorial appointment from judicial nominating commission	6 years
Arkansas Supreme Court Court of Appeals	Partisan election	8 years
California Supreme Court Court of Appeals	Unopposed retention election	12 years
Colorado Supreme Court Court of Appeals	Gubernatorial appointment from judicial nominating commission	10 years 8 years
Connecticut Supreme Court Appellate Court	Legislative appointment	8 years
Delaware Supreme Court	Gubernatorial appointment from judicial nominating commission with consent of state senate	12 years
Florida Supreme Court District Court of Appeals	Gubernatorial appointment from judicial nominating commission	6 years
Georgia Supreme Court Court of Appeals	Nonpartisan election	6 years
Hawaii Supreme Court Intermediate Court of Appeals	Gubernatorial appointment from judicial nominating commission with consent of senate	10 years
Idaho Supreme Court Court of Appeals	Nonpartisan election	6 years

TABLE 11.4	*Continued*	
State	**Method**	**Term**

Illinois
    Supreme Court
    Appellate Court
	Partisan election	10 years

Indiana
    Supreme Court
    Court of Appeals
    Tax Court
	Gubernatorial appointment from judicial nominating commission	Initial=2 years
		Retention=10 years

Iowa
    Supreme Court
    Court of Appeals
	Gubernatorial appointment from judicial nominating commission	8 years
		6 years

Kansas
    Supreme Court
    Court of Appeals
	Gubernatorial appointment from judicial nominating commission	6 years
		4 years

Kentucky
    Supreme Court
    Court of Appeals
	Nonpartisan election	8 years

Louisiana
    Supreme Court
    Court of Appeals
	Nonpartisan election	10 years

Maine Supreme Judicial Court	Gubernatorial appointment	7 years

Maryland
    Court of Appeals
    Court of Special Appeals
	Gubernatorial appointment from judicial nominating commission with consent of senate	10 years

Massachusetts
    Supreme Judicial Court
    Appeals Court
	Gubernatorial appointment from judicial nominating commission with approval by Governor's council	Age 70

Michigan
    Supreme Court
    Court of Appeals
	Nonpartisan election	8 years
		6 years

Minnesota
    Supreme Court
    Court of Appeals
	Nonpartisan election	6 years

Mississippi Supreme Court	Partisan election	8 years

Continued

TABLE 11.4	Continued	
State	**Method**	**Term**

Missouri
  Supreme Court
  Court of Appeals
	Gubernatorial appointment from judicial nominating commission	12 years

Montana Supreme Court	Nonpartisan election	8 years

Nebraska
  Supreme Court
  Court of Appeals
	Gubernatorial appointment from judicial nominating commission	More than 3 years for first election, 6 years thereafter

Nevada Supreme Court	Nonpartisan election	6 years
New Hampshire Supreme Court	Gubernatorial appointment with approval of elected executive council	Age 70

New Jersey
  Supreme Court
 	
  Appellate Division of
  Superior Court
	Gubernatorial appointment with consent of senate
	
	Chief Justice appointment of Superior Court judge
		7 years, followed by tenure

New Mexico
  Supreme Court
  Court of Appeals
	Partisan election	8 years

New York
  Court of Appeals
  Appellate Division of Supreme
    Court
  Appellate Terms of Supreme Court
	Gubernatorial appointment
	
	SCA appointment from lists of Supreme Court justices
		14 years
		5 or duration
		
		5 or duration

North Carolina
  Supreme Court
  Court of Appeals
	Partisan election	8 years

North Dakota Supreme Court	Nonpartisan election	10 years

Ohio
  Supreme Court
  Court of Appeals
	Nonpartisan election	6 years

Oklahoma
  Supreme Court
  Court of Criminal Appeals
  Court of Appeals
	Retention election	6 years

Oregon
  Supreme Court
  Court of Appeals
	Nonpartisan election	6 years

TABLE 11.4	*Continued*	
State	**Method**	**Term**

Pennsylvania
  Supreme Court
  Superior Court
  Commonwealth Court
	Partisan election	10 years

Rhode Island Supreme Court	Legislative election	Life

South Carolina
  Supreme Court
  Court of Appeals
	Legislative election	10 years
		6 years

South Dakota Supreme Court	Retention election	8 years

Tennessee
  Supreme Court
  Court of Appeals
  Court of Criminal Appeals
	Partisan election
	Retention election
		8 years

Texas
  Supreme Court
  Court of Criminal Appeals
  Court of Appeals
	Partisan election	6 years

Utah
  Supreme Court
  Court of Appeals
	Gubernatorial appointment from judicial nominating commission with consent of senate	Initial = 3 years
		Retention = 10 years

Vermont Supreme Court	Gubernatorial appointment from judicial nominating commission with consent of senate	6 years

Virginia
  Supreme Court
  Court of Appeals
	Legislative appointment	12 years
		6 years

Washington
  Supreme Court
  Court of Appeals
	Nonpartisan election	6 years

West Virginia Supreme Court of Appeals	Partisan election	12 years
Wisconsin Supreme Court of Appeals	Partisan election	12 years
Wyoming Supreme Court	Gubernatorial appointment from judicial nominating commission	8 years

Source: Rottman and Strickland (2006).

are chosen to sit on an appellate-level court. They have had a period of public scrutiny and testing, and most are very well qualified to occupy these crucial positions.

APPELLATE COURT DECISION MAKING

One of the major factors that distinguishes appellate courts from trial courts (or courts of original jurisdiction) is the manner in which cases are decided. Unlike many European nations, in the United States trials are presided over by a single judge. Many European nations use panels of judges in trial courts, sometimes combining professionally trained judges and lay judges (or "assessors") who serve as both judges and juries.

In appellate courts in the United States, cases are decided by groups of judges. This pattern of interaction results in these courts being referred to as **collegial courts**. Some appellate courts divide the workload among small groups or panels drawn from the court's total membership. This is the syscdtem often employed in intermediate appellate courts such as the U.S. Courts of Appeals, where most cases are decided by three judge panels. Occasionally, especially in particularly important or controversial cases, the entire group of judges will sit together to hear and decide a case. This is known as an ***en banc*** hearing. The United States Supreme Court hears all of its cases *en banc*, and this typically is the pattern for state supreme courts as well (Marvell 1989).

I have noted elsewhere that only a small percentage of civil and criminal cases are ever appealed. In order to have a basis for an appeal several ingredients must be present. First, there must have been an error of law. These types of errors normally involve some procedural issue arising during the conduct of the trial. They may raise constitutional or statutory issues that need to be decided or clarified. Simply receiving an adverse verdict is not sufficient grounds for appeal. Second, in virtually all instances the appropriate attorney must raise an objection or call the court's attention to the potential error prior to or during the trial.

Third, after the trial and an adverse verdict an appeal must be filed within a specified time period. Lack of **timeliness of** the **appeal** may result in some cases being dismissed by appellate courts. Fourth, there may be other procedural obstacles that prevent appellate courts from accepting or deciding cases. For instance, if the case originated in a state trial court, in most instances the criminal defendant must complete the entire state appellate route first, before any appeals can be filed in federal courts. This doctrine is known as **exhaustion of state remedies**, and it is one way federal courts can refuse cases, and thus exercise control over their caseloads. Additionally, based on Article III, Section 2 of the Constitution the federal appellate courts are precluded from issuing **advisory opinions,** and they will not rule on hypothetical issues. This is the so-called **case or controversy rule** (see Melone and Karnes 2008:121–23). Most state appellate courts are bound by similar rules. In simplest terms, this means that there must be a real issue at dispute and there must be opposing parties who have competing and exclusive interests at stake.

Finally, the party filing the appeal (the defendant in criminal cases) must have the economic resources to undertake the appeals process. The U.S. Supreme Court has affirmed a constitutional right for first-level appeals (*Griffin* v. *Illinois*, 351 U.S. 12

[1956]; *Mayer* v. *City of Chicago*, 404 U.S. 189 [1971]), but beyond that someone must provide funding to carry the appeal forward. At times criminal defendants are fortunate enough to have groups such as the American Civil Liberties Union take on their cases because of the unique circumstances or nature of the issue being appealed. Quite often convicted offenders in death penalty cases are able to find groups to sponsor their appeals. Once these considerations are addressed, an appeal may be filed.

WORKLOADS OF APPELLATE COURTS

The workloads of appellate courts are much smaller than those of the trial courts. As a result of the limitations to the appeals process I have discussed, only a small percentage of cases ever make it to appellate court dockets. Nevertheless, the appellate courts handle a substantial number of cases, and their dockets seem to grow every year. Thus, the question remaining seems to be: how can appellate courts address the issue of their increasing caseloads?

Marvell (1989:282) notes that the volume of appeals has roughly doubled "every decade since World War II." In response to this unrelenting increase, state appellate courts have approached their increasing caseloads with the following solutions:

- adding judges
- creating or expanding intermediate appellate courts
- deciding cases in panels
- employing law clerks and staff attorneys
- deciding more cases without opinion or with unpublished and memorandum opinions
- curtailing oral arguments
- using summary judgments

This section examines the first three of these procedures and briefly touches on the fourth. For an in-depth treatment of all seven of these responses to growth in state appellate court caseloads, see Marvell (1989).

ADDING JUDGES

As appellate caseloads increase, an obvious response is to increase the number of appellate court judges and, indeed, this is the approach taken by some state intermediate appellate courts. However, two factors limit the broad-scale effectiveness of this solution. First, state supreme courts have been reluctant to enlarge the numbers of justices, and nine seems to be the practical limit. Second, unlike some intermediate appellate courts, many state supreme courts hear cases *en banc*. Therefore, increasing the number of justices from five to seven, or from seven to nine in no way improves the courts' capacity to hear or decide cases. In fact, increasing the numbers of judges on courts of last resort potentially could slow down the decision making process. More judges might mean longer oral arguments as well as more ways decisions could be split. This might require greater amounts of time to develop voting coalitions and to reach a consensus. As a result, since 1968 only six states have increased the number of judges on their courts of last resort (Marvell 1989:284).

INTERMEDIATE APPELLATE COURTS

The greatest impact, in response to state appellate caseload growth, has come from the creation of intermediate appellate courts. Additionally, some state court systems have shifted certain appellate responsibilities from state supreme courts to existing intermediate appellate courts. Between 1974 and 1984 fifteen states created intermediate appellate courts, and eleven more expanded the jurisdictions of their intermediate appellate courts. The result of this approach has been a leveling-off of state supreme court caseloads and a tremendous increase in filings with intermediate appellate courts. Since intermediate appellate courts have been able to help states respond to increasing numbers of cases appealed, currently thirty-nine states have one or two intermediate appellate courts as part of their state court systems (Rottman and Strickland 2006).

PANEL DECISION MAKING

In addition to the creation of intermediate appellate courts, an increasing number of states are deciding appellate cases in panels of three to six judges. Marvell (1989:285) found that in the mid-1980s thirteen state supreme courts were hearing some cases in panels, and nearly all state intermediate appellate courts utilized a panel hearing system. Panel hearings allow judges and justices to divide the caseload among small groups while reserving *en banc* hearings for exceptional cases. Not only is this a more efficient system for routine cases, but also the size of some intermediate appellate courts may make *en banc* hearings impractical.

LAW CLERKS AND STAFF ATTORNEYS

State and federal appellate courts increasingly are turning to **law clerks** and **staff attorneys** to help judges handle larger caseloads. As Marvell (1989:286) observed: "Law clerks and staff attorneys perform similar duties. Their overall function is to supply information to the judges by analyzing the parties' arguments and researching the record and law books." Law clerks and staff attorneys can do library and on-line case and statute research that appellate court judges may not have time to do themselves.

This approach, and the others we have examined, can have both positive and negative outcomes. On the positive side, support attorney positions do not require legislative creation, like judges' positions do. Therefore, these positions are easier to establish and less expensive than creating new judgeships. On the negative side, support attorneys may cause "staff usurpation and bureaucratization of the judiciary" when judges have more than three attorney aides each" (Marvell 1989:286). In the end, law clerks and staff attorneys may increase the quality of the opinions that judges write, but not necessarily the quantity (Marvell 1989:289).

OTHER SOLUTIONS

Each of the other solutions listed previously has met with limited application and often minimal success. For instance, Marvell (1989:287) maintains that one way appellate court judges can save time is through deciding cases without written opinions or, alternately, through limiting opinion publication. Most attorneys are opposed to such changes, and many judges seem unenthusiastic about altering their current opinion-writing practices. A few states have tried these options, but they often have abandoned such types of appellate court practices.

THE MECHANISMS FOR APPEAL

While there are a number of ways that convicted criminal offenders can file appeals, the most common mechanisms fit into the categories of **mandatory** or **automatic appeals** on one hand, and **discretionary appeals** on the other hand. Mandatory appeals involve those cases in which the courts are obligated to review the decisions once a conviction has resulted and an appeal has been filed.[2] Del Carmen (1991:414) says that "these appeals are given to defendants upon request, meaning that if the defendant asks the appellate court to review the case, the court must do so." In some instances state statutes provide for mandatory appeals, but often they result from either state or federal constitutional provisions. In 2004, state courts of intermediate appeals disposed of 127,973 mandatory appeals, and state supreme courts disposed of another 24,631 (Schauffler et al. 2005).

By contrast, in 2004 there were 30,578 state intermediate courts of appeals discretionary petitions and another 57,349 heard by state supreme courts (Schauffler et al. 2005). In the case of discretionary appeals, "The defendant asks the appellate court for review but that court has the option to accept or reject the appeal" (del Carmen 1991:414). The appellate numbers from 2004 show that intermediate appellate courts at the state level primarily handle mandatory appeals (by about four to one) and state courts of last resort primarily handle discretionary petitions (by about two to one). This approach allows the state supreme courts to have more control over their own dockets than other appellate courts might have.

Even after state appeals have been exhausted, convicted offenders—especially those who may be serving long prison sentences or facing the death penalty—have the opportunity to ask for federal post-conviction relief (this is often called **collateral relief**). The process involves moving cases from the state courts into the federal courts, and the two most common mechanisms for federal post-conviction relief are **writs of habeas corpus** and **civil rights actions**. Writs of habeas corpus (this term means "having the body" or "you have the body") are normally filed in federal district courts, and they ask that the state be required to come forward and to demonstrate why a prison inmate's incarceration is lawful and justified. Since habeas corpus petitions challenge the very idea of incarceration, if prison inmates are successful in their habeas corpus claims, they may win the right to a new trial or have their convictions reversed, resulting in their freedom. For this reason post-conviction remedies involving habeas corpus petitions often have been called "turn 'em loose suits."

Perhaps one of the more famous examples of a habeas corpus claim was the case of *Gideon v. Wainwright*, 373 U.S. 335 (1963). In this case, Clarence Early Gideon had been convicted of felony theft in the State of Florida and had been tried without the assistance of counsel (which he had asked for but had been denied by the trial court judge). After his conviction and incarceration he filed a writ of habeas corpus with the federal courts, and eventually his appeal reached the United States Supreme Court. In its opinion, the Court held for the first time that the right to counsel provided for in the Constitution's Sixth Amendment applied to indigent state felony defendants who were charged with something other than a capital crime. Gideon eventually was retried with the assistance of an attorney and acquitted. The story of this case is told in Anthony Lewis's book *Gideon's Trumpet*.

Habeas corpus petitions were the primary mechanism of post-conviction appeals for many state prison inmates up until the 1970s, when civil rights actions increased substantially. Since 1996, largely as a result of congressional limitations on appeals by prison inmates, habeas corpus appeals once again have increased in number and civil rights claims have decreased (see, for example, Mays and Winfree 2009:304–06; Scalia 2002). Table 11.5 shows the numbers of habeas corpus writs and civil rights actions filed by federal and state inmates for the decade 1991 to 2000.

Civil rights actions can arise under a number of federal statutes, but the most common cases are appealed on the basis of the **Civil Rights Act of 1871** (more commonly known by its statutory citation 42 United States Code, Section 1983). **Section 1983 suits** can be directed at police officers for violations of suspects' civil rights. They also can be aimed at corrections officials for maintaining unconstitutional conditions of confinement in prisons and jails (Mays and Olszta 1989; Mays and Taggart 1988).

TABLE 11.5 Habeas Corpus and Civil Rights Petitions Filed by Federal and State Inmates, 1991–2000				
	Federal Inmates		State Inmates	
Year	Habeas corpus	Civil rights	Habeas corpus	Civil rights
1991	2,112	999	10,325	25,043
1992	1,507	910	11,296	29,645
1993	1,467	915	11,574	33,018
1994	1,441	1,140	11,908	37,925
1995	1,343	1,110	13,627	40,569
1996	1,703	1,219	14,726	39,996
1997	1,902	974	19,956	27,658
1998	2,321	983	18,838	25,478
1999	3,590	962	20,493	24,732
2000	3,870	1,041	21,345	24,463

Source: Scalia (2002:2).

Unlike writs of habeas corpus, civil rights actions filed by prison inmates do not challenge the basis of their incarceration, but instead raise issues about the conditions under which inmates are confined (Mays and Winfree 2009). Under federal law, civil rights actions can be either criminal or civil. They can address the ways the police have treated suspects (that is, unnecessary or excessive use of force), and as civil matters they ask for equitable remedies or monetary damages.

THE OUTCOMES OF APPEALS

The most fundamental question we can ask is: Once an accused offender has been convicted and has filed an appeal, what happens? Based on the data presented earlier in this chapter, it appears that the simple answer is: not much. Relatively few appeals make it past the first level of screening, and fewer still result in the outcome desired by the person filing the appeal. For example, by one estimate appeals are successful in 10 percent to 20 percent of the cases filed (see Kamisar et al. 2008). Furthermore, the success rate of post-conviction appeals (both habeas corpus and civil rights) is even worse. Only around 2 percent to 4 percent of these cases result in relief being granted (Collins 1993; Kamisar et al. 2008). Therefore, while the public may notice highly publicized cases of inmates winning lawsuits against a state, or shudder at the idea of persons wrongfully convicted, the reality of the situation is that most of the people convicted of crimes in the United States receive the sentence originally imposed by the judge and they serve their period of probation or prison sentence with no further action being taken by the courts. While access to the courts is a constitutionally guaranteed right, in most instances for convicted offenders this right has only symbolic importance.

SUMMARY

Very few people ever have direct contact with appellate courts in the United States. Nevertheless, the state and federal appellate courts perform very important functions in the judicial process. In the federal system—and in most state systems—there are two levels of appellate courts. First, there are the intermediate appellate courts. These courts handle the first-level appeals from trial courts in an effort to correct errors of law that may have occurred in civil or criminal cases. Relatively few cases are appealed, even when errors may have taken place, and of those that are appealed only a small percentage ever goes beyond the intermediate appellate courts.

Second, there are appellate courts of last resort. Often these tribunals are called "supreme courts," and in most instances they have the final say over appellate matters. Interestingly enough, state courts of last resort frequently transact their business with virtually no publicity, positive or negative. Occasionally, as has happened in a handful of states over the past few years, the justices of state supreme courts rule on some issue like the death penalty that galvanizes public opinion. However, in most instances the judges who sit on state appellate benches labor in relative freedom from attention. Some of these judges will go on to serve on the federal bench, but for most, a state appellate judgeship will be the pinnacle of their legal careers.

Within the federal judiciary there is an extensive Courts of Appeals system that covers all of the states, U.S. territories, and the District of Columbia. These courts handle the majority of federal appeals, and while they are federal courts, they are organized around clusters of state boundaries. Therefore, except for the Courts of Appeals for the District of Columbia and the Federal Circuit, the judges serving on federal courts of appeals come from the region over which their court has jurisdiction. The purpose of such an arrangement is to keep these judges in close contact with the sensibilities and sentiments of the citizens of their states and the different regions of the country.

Undoubtedly, the U.S. Supreme Court is the most visible of the nation's appellate courts. The Court's decisions regularly are reported in newspapers and in local and national television newscasts. Nevertheless, most people know little to nothing about the members of the Court or the types of cases they decide. Relatively few citizens know the number of Supreme Court justices, who the chief justice is, nor the names of most of the associate justices. Occasionally, a case such as *Roe* v. *Wade*, 410 U.S. 113 (1973)—dealing with a controversial issue like abortion—will attract national attention to the Court's business. Also, when a vacancy occurs on the Court the public will become aware of potential nominees through the national news media.

The judges and justices who sit on the nation's appellate court benches come to their positions in a variety of ways. Some work their way up through years of trial court service, and others are appointed from positions of prosecuting attorney or they have been attorneys in private practice. States employ several methods for choosing appellate judges, but typically there are fewer methods of selection for these judges than there are for trial court judges. Most of the state and federal appellate judges in the United States reach the bench initially by appointment. For some it may be an interim appointment followed by partisan election or retention ballot. For others (especially federal judges) appointment is the exclusive method for choosing appellate judges.

Whatever the method utilized for selecting appellate judges, one thing is clear: while these judges may not be household names for most citizens, the work they perform is very important. We entrust into the hands of appellate judges the responsibility for deciding whether errors have occurred in the trial courts. If there have been errors, these judges have the duty to craft remedies designed to correct the errors. Normally, to adequately fulfill such an awesome responsibility requires that the individual have practiced law for a considerable length of time. This certainly is not a place for on-the-job training or for novices in the law.

In the federal judicial system and most state systems, the appellate courts decide criminal and civil matters. Some states, notably Oklahoma and Texas, have separate appellate courts for criminal and civil cases. Most of the appellate work of courts in the United States involves appeals from civil trials, and a great deal of the trial court work in this country is civil as well. For criminal cases, the U.S. Supreme Court has guaranteed a constitutional right of first appeal along with the right to counsel for such appeals. Beyond that point, appeals are discretionary and must be funded by the person filing the appeal or some sponsoring organization. Prison or jail terms and potentially substantial fines may be at stake in criminal cases. In civil cases, appeals may be based on errors of law or on the basis of the amount of money awarded in damages. All of these situations have strong emotional and practical dimensions for the people involved in the cases.

QUESTIONS FOR CRITICAL THINKING

1. What are some of the features that distinguish appellate courts from trial courts?

2. What would be the purpose of having two levels of appellate courts? Does your state have one or two levels of appellate courts? How many judges are on these courts? Can you find a state court web page (if one exists) listing the names of your state's appellate judges?

3. How are appellate court judges selected in your state (both initially and for a regular term of office)? Is the selection method the same for the intermediate court of appeals (if one exists) as for the court of last resort?

4. In your state, are the terms for appellate judges the same or longer than those for trial judges? If they are longer, why do you suppose this is the case?

5. Why would death penalty cases warrant an automatic appeal? Does this seem to be a reasonable procedure, or does it simply add unnecessary delay in carrying out a sentence?

6. In which federal court of appeals circuit is your state located? Where does this court meet? How many judges from your state sit on this court of appeals? You probably will have to do some digging to find the answers to these questions, but many of the answers are found on the U.S. Courts website [http://www.uscourts.gov].

7. From Table 11.3 create a list of the nine current justices of the U.S. Supreme Court, then try to find the following: (a) what is each justice's age, (b) what position did the justice hold prior to being appointed to the Supreme Court, (c) which law school did the justice attend, and (d) how do scholars characterize the justice's political philosophy (liberal, conservative, or moderate)?

8. What do we mean by the power of judicial review? What kinds of actions are courts (like the Supreme Court) authorized to review? Where does such a power come from?

9. If the Supreme Court's power largely is symbolic, what makes most people (even the President of the United States) obey the Court's rulings?

10. Why would federal courts require exhaustion of state remedies before accepting an appeal? Who benefits from such a legal principle? Why?

11. Why is adding more appellate judges typically not an effective way to deal with more appeals?

12. As a recent law school graduate, why might you accept a position as a law clerk for a federal appellate judge? Explain.

RECOMMENDED READINGS

Barnum, David G. (1993). *The Supreme Court & American Democracy.* New York: St. Martin's Press. This book focuses on the role of the U.S. Supreme Court, and it illustrates something of the Court's importance in deciding major social issues in the United States. Barnum highlights three essential points in his book. First, law and the political process are inseparable in any system of government, and especially so in the United States. Second, judges not only interpret the law, but in the process are responsible for making law as well (by saying what the Constitution and state and federal statutes mean). Third, the decisions that judges make have implications for policy creation and implementation. Many of the chapters in this book deal with specific cases decided by the Supreme Court, but three chapters in particular deal with federal courts and the appellate process: Chapter 2, "The Organization and Jurisdiction of American Courts"; Chapter 3, "The Appellate Process"; and Chapter 4, "Supreme Court Decision Making."

Baum, Lawrence (2006). *The Supreme Court*, 9th ed. Washington, DC: CQ Press. Baum's book is frequently used for political science courses on the Supreme Court, and in some ways it remains one of the principal texts and reference materials on the Supreme Court. Of particular importance are his discussions on the history of the Supreme Court along with who the justices have been and the process for choosing justices. He deals with the ways in which the Court goes about choosing and deciding cases and addresses the "policy outputs" by the Court. He closes by analyzing the ways in which the Court has had an impact on society.

Carp, Robert A., and Ronald Stidham (2001). *The Federal Courts*, 4th ed. Washington, DC: CQ Press. These authors have written extensively on courts in the United States, and some of their other works are cited elsewhere in this text. However, this particular volume is most directly related to the material within this chapter. They examine the broad sweep of the federal courts—including how these courts are organized and how they have developed over time—as well as the judges and justices who serve on the federal courts. Of particular interest is the chapter on decision making in collegial courts.

Rehnquist, William H. (2001). *The Supreme Court*. New York: Alfred A. Knopf. This book originally was written when Rehnquist was an Associate Justice on the Supreme Court, and it was revised after he became Chief Justice. He examines a number of the significant historical cases decided by the Supreme Court (he devotes a whole chapter to *Marbury v. Madison*) as well as some of the significant justices who have served on the Court. The book provides a unique insider's view of how the Court works, and he spends one chapter on how the Court chooses its cases (based on writs of certiorari) and another on the processes of oral arguments.

Sheldon, Charles H. (1992). *The Washington High Court: A Biographical History of the State Supreme Court, 1889–1991*. Pullman, WA: Washington State University Press. Relatively few books are written on state appellate courts, and even fewer are written specifically on state supreme courts. Sheldon's book is interesting because he looks at the justices who served on the Washington Supreme Court from its creation until 1991. In some ways he helps us understand how a state supreme court works by providing insight into the individuals who were the key actors on this court.

KEY TERMS

advisory opinions
case or controversy rule
circuit riding
Civil Rights Act of 1871
civil rights actions
collateral relief
collegial courts
courts of last resort

discretionary appeals
en banc
exhaustion of state
    remedies
intermediate appellate
    courts
judicial review
law clerks

mandatory (automatic)
    appeals
Section 1983 suits
staff attorneys
timeliness of appeal
writs of certiorari
writs of habeas corpus
writ of mandamus

REFERENCES

Alozie, Nicholas O. (1990). Distribution of Women and Minority Judges: The Effects of Judicial Selection Methods. *Social Science Quarterly* 71(2): 315–25.

Barclay, Scott (1998). Keeping Their Distance: Appellate Courts and Local Communities. *Judicature* 82(1): 35–43, 45.

Brown, Robert L. (1998). From Whence Cometh Our State Appellate Judges: Popular Election Versus the Missouri Plan. *University of Arkansas at Little Rock Law Journal* 20 (Winter): 313–24.

Bureau of Justice Statistics (1981). *Dictionary of Criminal Justice Data Terminology*, 2nd ed. Washington, DC: U.S. Department of Justice.

Calvi, James V., and Susan Coleman (2008). *American Law and Legal Systems*, 6th ed. Upper Saddle River, NJ: Pearson/Prentice Hall.

Carp, Robert A., and Ronald Stidham (2001). *The Federal Courts*, 4th ed. Washington, DC: CQ Press.

CBSnews.com (2000). Illinois Suspends Death Penalty. http://www.cbsnews.com/stories/2000/01/31/national/main155090.shtml.

Collins, William C. (1993). *Correctional Law for the Correctional Officer*. Laurel, MD: American Correctional Association.

del Carmen, Rolando (1991). *Criminal Procedure: Law and Practice*. Pacific Grove, CA: Brooks/Cole Publishing Co.

Furman v. *Georgia*, 408 U.S. 238 (1972).

Gideon v. *Wainwright*, 373 U.S. 335 (1963).

Gregg v. *Georgia*, 428 U.S. 153, 1976).

Griffin v. *Illinois*, 351 U.S. 12 (1956).

Grisham, John (2006). *The Innocent Man: Murder and Injustice in a Small Town*. New York: Doubleday.

Griswold v. Connecticut, 381 U.S. 479 (1965).

Kamisar, Yale, Wayne R. LaFave, Jerold H. Israel, Nancy J. King, and Orin S. Kerr (2008). *Basic Criminal Procedure*, 12th edition. Eagan, MN: West/Thomson Reuter.

Lewis, Anthony (1964). *Gideon's Trumpet*. New York: Random House.

Marbury v. *Madison*, 1 Cranch 137 (1803).

Marvell, Thomas (1989). State Appellate Court Responses to Caseload Growth. *Judicature* 72(2): 282–91.

Mayer v. *City of Chicago*, 404 U.S. 189 (1971).

Mays, G. Larry, and Michelle Olszta (1989). Prison Litigation: From the 1960s to the 1990s. *Criminal Justice Policy Review* 3(3): 279–98.

Mays, G. Larry, and William A. Taggart (1988). The Implementation of Court-Ordered Prison Reform. In *Research in Law and Policy Studies*, Vol. 2, ed. Stuart S. Nagel, 179–98. Greenwich, CT: JAI Press.

Mays, G. Larry, and L. Thomas Winfree, Jr. (2009) *Essentials of Corrections*, 4th ed. Belmont, CA: Wadsworth Publishing Co.

Melone, Albert P., and Allan Karnes (2008). *The American Legal System: Perspectives, Politics, Processes, and Policies* 2nd ed. Lanham, MD: Rowman & Littlefield Publishers.

New York State Unified Court System (2009). http://www.courts.state.ny.us/.

Kathleen Maguire, ed. (2010). *Sourcebook of Criminal Justice Statistics* [online]. http://www.albany.edu/sourcebook/pdf/t5672008.pdf.

Pollock v. Farmers' Loan & Trust Co., 157 U.S. 429 (1895).

Rehnquist, William H. (2001). *The Supreme Court*. New York: Alfred A. Knopf.

Reid, Traciel V. (1999). The Politicization of Retention Elections. *Judicature* 83(2): 68–77.

Roe v. *Wade*, 410 U.S. 113 (1973).

Rottman, David B., and Shauna M. Strickland (2006). *State Court Organization 2004*. Washington, DC: Bureau of Justice Statistics, U.S. Department of Justice.

Scalia, John (2002). *Prisoner Petitions Filed in U.S. District Courts, 2000*. Washington, DC: Bureau of Justice Statistics, U.S. Department of Justice.

Schauffler, Richard Y., Neal B. Kauder, Robert C. LaFountain, William E. Raftery, Shauna M. Strickland, and Brenda G. Otto (2005). *State Court Caseload Statistics, 2005*. Washington, DC: U.S. Department of Justice.

Stephens, Otis H., and Gregory J. Rathjen (1980). *The Supreme Court and the Allocation of Constitutional Power*. San Francisco: W. H. Freeman and Co.

U.S. Department of State (2008). Federal Judges. http://www.america.gov/st/usg-english/2008/May/20080522224217eaifas0.5669672.html.

U.S. Supreme Court (2010). Members of the Supreme Court of the United States. http://www.supremecourtus.gov/about/members.pdf.

Vote 2010: Group Targets Three Iowa Supreme Court Justices. http://www.kcrg.com/news/local/Vote-2010-Group-Targets-Three-Iowa-Supreme-Court-Justices—104909434.html.

Wheeler, Russell R., and Cynthia Harrison (1994). *Creating the Federal Judicial System*, 2nd ed. Washington, DC: Federal Judicial Center.

ENDNOTES

[1] The states of Alabama, Oklahoma, and Tennessee have separate intermediate appellate courts for civil and criminal appeals.

[2] For some automatic appeals, such as those involving death penalty cases, the defendant may not even have to file an appeal. The state will automatically undertake appellate review of the case.

**PART
FIVE**

ISSUES FACING
THE COURTS

12

Addressing the Problems and Crafting Solutions

Photo source: AP Images

INTRODUCTION

As we prepare to enter the second decade of the twenty-first century, it is clear that courts in the United States face a number of major challenges. Some of these are lingering and historical issues. They have been with us for decades and they are likely to persist. Other issues are unique to our present time period. In this chapter we will explore several of these concerns. As a warning, this list is by no means exhaustive, and many judges, attorneys, and legal scholars would add quite a few more dilemmas to the ones mentioned here. For the sake of brevity I will confine these discussions to the particular concerns that have consistently been raised in the literature on courts. By the time you have reached this point in the book, you probably have questions and concerns of your own about the future of the courts and the nature of the judicial process in the United States. Welcome to the vineyard in which many of us labor.

RESOURCE ISSUES

One of the historical and yet lingering issues facing courts in the United States is that of having sufficient resources to administer justice in a reasonable, fair, and dignified way. By resources I primarily mean meeting three types of needs within the courts: a sufficient number of well-trained and well-qualified judges, adequate support staffs, and acceptable physical plants (offices and courtrooms).

To get some idea of the challenges faced by courts, all we have to do is look at their relative budgetary allocations compared with the other components of the criminal justice system. For example, in 2003 (the most recent year for which full employment and expenditure data are available) the United States spent a total of $185 billion for all justice system activities—this includes police, courts, and corrections services at all levels. Of that total, only $42 billion (about 23 percent of the total) was allocated for judicial and legal services, compared with $89 billion for police protection and $63 billion for correctional services. To break down the expenditure numbers another way, 26 percent of the federal government's justice expenditures went to fund judicial or legal operations. For the the states, 24 percent of justice expenditures were allocated for the judicial/legal category, and for local governments it was about 19 percent (Hughes 2006:3).

Employment data also show something of the disparity among the various components of the justice system in this country. In March of 2003, the total number of justice system personnel working for all levels of government in the United States was 2,361,193. The largest group of employees—1,118, 936 (or just over 50 percent)—worked in the various law enforcement agencies around the nation. The next largest group—748,250 (or nearly 32 percent) were employed in corrections. Finally, the judicial/legal area employed 494,007 (or just about 21 percent) of the justice system personnel (Hughes 2006:6). Interestingly, judicial/legal expenditures outpaced the other two segments in spending increases from 1977 to 2003, but this area still lags behind law enforcement and corrections in overall expenditures and employment totals. Tables 12.1, 12.2, and 12.3 show the expenditure growth in justice systems at the federal state and local levels from 1982 to 2003.

TABLE 12.1	Federal Justice System Expenditures, 1982–2003*			
Year	Police	Judicial/legal	Corrections	Total
1982	$2,527	$1,390	$541	$4,458
1987	$4,231	$2,271	$994	$7,496
1992	$7,400	$7,377	$2,642	$17,423
1997	$12,518	$10,651	$3,896	$27,065
2000	$13,999	$9,353	$4,467	$27,820
2001	$15,014	$10,230	$5,199	$30,443
2002	$17,626	$11,013	$5,707	$34,346
2003	$20,422	$9,356	$5,545	$35,323

*Note: Expenditures are recorded in millions.
Source: Hughes (2006:3).

TABLE 12.2	State Justice System Expenditures, 1982–2003*			
Year	Police	Judicial/legal	Corrections	Total
1982	$2,833	$2,748	$6,020	$11,602
1987	$4,067	$4,339	$11,691	$20,157
1992	$5,593	$7,723	$20,439	$33,755
1997	$7,501	$9,803	$29,141	$46,444
2000	$9,787	$13,249	$35,129	$58,165
2001	$10,497	$14,444	$38,432	$63,372
2002	$11,081	$15,365	$39,062	$65,508
2003	$11,144	$15,782	$39,187	$66,114

Note: Expenditures are recorded in millions.
Source: Hughes (2006:3).

TABLE 12.3	Local Justice System Expenditures, 1982–2003*			
Year	Police	Judicial/legal	Corrections	Total
1982	$14,172	$3,784	$3,011	$20,968
1987	$21,089	$6,230	$5,947	$33,265
1992	$29,659	$10,052	$10,404	$50,115
1997	$40,976	$13,101	$13,007	$67,083
2000	$48,219	$14,842	$15,934	$78,995
2001	$50,718	$15,938	$16,721	$83,377
2002	$55,086	$17,042	$18,358	$90,485
2003	$57,503	$17,718	$18,656	$93,877

Note: Expenditures are recorded in millions.
Source: Hughes (2006:3).

I should hasten to add that spending for the courts and related functions, while substantially lower than that for other justice agencies, may be proportionately justified relative to the functions that are performed. In fact, all justice agencies at all levels of government probably would argue that they are understaffed and underfunded. However, if the three branches of our governmental system truly are coequal, then employment and expenditure figures for the judiciary are substantially smaller than those of the two executive branch agencies (police and corrections) within the justice system.

JUDICIAL INDEPENDENCE

Questions about **judicial independence** are also lingering considerations for the courts as they carry out their operations. This area is of such a concern that the American

Judicature Society, one of the nation's major court-reform advocates, has made it one of their top priorities. In fact, in 1997 "The American Judicature Society created the Center for Judicial Independence...in response to an increase in unfair criticism and effort to remove from the bench judges who have issued unpopular rulings" (American Judicature Society 2009a). Judicial independence actually is an umbrella under which there are a cluster of related issues.

BUDGETS

For example, as noted elsewhere in this text, the courts are not really masters of their own budgets. Typically, someone will submit a budget request on the part of the state or federal court systems. The Chief Justice of the United States Supreme Court does this annually for the federal courts, and in most states either the chief justice of the state supreme court or the director of the administrative office of courts (on behalf of the judicial branch) will submit the budget request. However, this request normally goes to the president or governor to be included in the budget package to the appropriate legislative body. In the end, however, the legislature decides how much each agency—including the courts—will receive in funding. Not only do legislative bodies decide the annual appropriations for the courts, but they also decide on the number of judgeships authorized and the amount of office and courtroom space the courts may be given.

COURT JURISDICTION

The question of judicial independence has several other dimensions as well. For example, legislatures can expand or contract the subject matter jurisdictions of the courts. They decide that courts can hear certain kinds of cases and not hear others. They can determine that some cases go to one type of court, while others will be assigned to another. As one brief example of this, in some states traffic cases involving drivers under the age of 18 go to the juvenile courts. However, in other states, all traffic cases go to the limited jurisdiction courts—such as magistrate or municipal courts—irrespective of the age of the driver. Thus, the courts often do not have complete authority in regard to establishing their own jurisdictions either.

ELECTIONS

One of the most serious and persistent challenges to judicial independence comes in the form of judicial elections. As I mentioned in Chapter 4, quite a few states still elect some or all of their judges, oftentimes running under a particular political party label, and this leaves open the possibility that a judge might be defeated in the next election as a result of an unpopular decision (see Lubet 1998; Reid 1999).

Federal judges are insulated from most of these kinds of pressures, but state and local judges that must stand for reelection can be keenly aware of public sentiment before and during political campaigns. Furthermore, in states with judges who are elected in either partisan or nonpartisan elections, there is a concern that candidates for the office of judge may feel somewhat obligated to campaign contributors. In some cases major contributors are attorneys or law firms that might appear before the newly elected or reelected judges. The same might hold true for major corporate contributors. Most judges probably are not swayed by the influence of campaign contributions, but there certainly can be questions about the degree to which such contributions affect the independence of the judiciary.

MANAGEMENT CONCERNS

An old saying in the study of court operations and organization is that "justice delayed is justice denied." As a result of concerns over delays in the administration of justice, many court systems around the United States have moved in the direction of establishing the position of court manager or court administrator. In fact, some states now have elaborate administrative mechanisms to facilitate the smooth flow of cases through the courts. The heavy demands on the courts to solve an endless variety of social problems have necessitated a more administrative, and some would say more bureaucratic, approach to assisting judges and support personnel in carrying out their day-to-day adjudicative responsibilities.

In one of the earliest books on the newly emerging field of court administration, David Saari (1982) said that in most instances it has not been the case that courts in the United States have been poorly managed, so much as that they have not been managed at all. Therefore, over the past three decades **court management** or **court administration** has become a major area of growth. Currently, every state court system, as well as the federal courts, has an administrative arm. In most instances these agencies are called the **administrative office of courts** (AOC). However, the court administration movement, which began in the 1930s, now has found its way into many of the trial court operations around the country as well. Court managers or court administrators—these terms are used somewhat interchangeably—are professionally trained management personnel who are responsible for a range of functions that keep the courts operating smoothly. Most court managers are appointed by the chief judge of the particular jurisdiction or by a panel of judges, and these individuals serve at the pleasure of the appointing judges.

The range of functions typically performed by court managers includes budgeting, personnel management for the courts' support employees, jury management, and case scheduling. In most local court settings, court managers function alongside elected court clerks, and there can be some degree of conflict between these two parties over who has the primary responsibility for performing certain functions, especially in jury management and case scheduling (see especially Mays and Taggart 1986).

Within the typical trial court setting, successful court managers must become politically skilled in order to navigate the potential conflicts in duties between their offices and those of the judges and court clerks. If they fail to develop political astuteness, they often leave their positions after a relatively short tenure. Those who stay have learned to use the power extended to them by the appointing judges, and they reach political compromises with the elected court clerks over who will exercise the primary responsibility in disputed areas. The passage of time and the utility of the position have demonstrated to most judges and court clerks the importance of having professionally trained court managers, and in most large and many smaller court jurisdictions throughout the United States the office of court administrator has become a regular fixture of the judicial process.

PRO SE LITIGATION AND ACCESS TO THE COURTS

Another issue frequently raised by judicial scholars is the increasing volume of ***pro se* litigation**, and concerns over access to the courts in general. In simplest terms, *pro se* litigation occurs any time an individual (or small business, for that matter) decides to forego legal representation and takes the case to court acting as his or her own attorney. I already have briefly mentioned the process of *pro se* representation in criminal cases in Chapter 7, but in this section I discuss it further in the civil context along with the complications it may bring.

Much like the issue of judicial independence, *pro se* litigation has become the focus of court reform groups like the American Judicature Society, largely because of the impact this process can have on the efficient administration of justice (American Judicature Society 2009b). As we approach the discussion of this subject, put yourself in the place of a judge, prosecuting attorney, or court administrator and consider how and why having people represent themselves in court might complicate the smooth processing and flow of cases.

In Chapter 3 I discussed the concept of the courtroom work group. As part of that discussion I noted that there are several common goals that unite courtroom work groups, and key among these goals are: doing justice, maintaining group cohesion, disposing of the caseload, and reducing uncertainty (see Eisenstein and Jacob 1977:25). When it comes to *pro se* representation, having individuals act as their own attorneys easily can upset achievement of the goals of maintaining group cohesion, efficiently disposing of cases, and reducing uncertainty.

Pro se litigation or representation can introduce a great deal of uncertainty into the judicial process when you have individuals who are not trained in the law trying to act as their own attorneys (see Box 12.1). In such situations laypersons may object to questioning or procedures in situations where there is no basis for objection. By the same token, they may fail to object in circumstances where an attorney would be expected to. All of this can put the other members of the courtroom work group on edge, and it may take much longer to process a case than normally would be the situation. Thus, while we allow individuals to serve as their own lawyers in virtually any case in which they want to, doing so interrupts the smooth flow of cases to which members of the courtroom work group have become accustomed.

BOX 12.1

In the News: Pro Se Litigation

In a tight economy, people who have to go to court to press a civil claim are deciding to save the fees associated with hiring an attorney, and increasingly they are acting as their own lawyers. In fact, Gibbs (2008) says that "The number of people serving as their own lawyers is on the rise across the country, and the cases are no longer limited to uncontested divorces and small claims. Even people embroiled in child custody cases, potentially devastating lawsuits and bankruptcies are representing themselves, legal experts say." Glater (2009) notes that "Reliable numbers for people representing themselves in noncriminal cases are hard to come by. Nationally there is no tracking system, and each state's court system follows its own rules." However, recent numbers from California indicate that the number of plaintiffs coming to court without an attorney has risen by 22 percent, and the number of defendants acting *pro se* has increased by 36 percent. Similarly, in the family courts of New York almost 95 percent of the parties in paternity and child support cases came to court without a lawyer.

So what is the big deal with *pro se* litigation? As Glater (2009) acknowledges, "Judges complain that people miss deadlines, fail to bring the right documents or evidence and are simply unprepared for legal proceedings. Such mistakes make it more likely they will fare poorly—no matter the merit of their cases." Simply put, *pro se* litigation introduces an element of uncertainty into what is normally a fairly well established and predictable process. It also places citizens into the role of acting as attorneys in an environment where they have not been trained in the law and they may not fully understand the rules of the game.

Sources: Gibbs (2008); Glater (2009).

ALTERNATIVE DISPUTE RESOLUTION

Although the processes known as **alternative dispute resolution** (or ADR) have been available for some time, their expansion really occurred beginning in the 1970s as a substitute for the frequently lengthy and expensive process of adjudication (see Calvi and Coleman 2008; Vago 2009). Largely developed as a result of substantial delays in civil litigation, ADR has become institutionalized in many court systems, and now some cases (like divorces) may be forced into ADR proceedings before the courts will accept them. In this section I will examine some of the most common forms of ADR and provide examples of how these processes work and the situations in which they are most likely to be found.

There are a variety of reasons for employing alternative dispute resolution mechanisms within our justice system today. Among the more compelling reasons are:

1. A quicker disposition of routine cases.
2. Lower expenses to the parties involved.
3. Reduction of the number of "outside" parties who have to be involved in resolving the dispute.
4. Less congestion and expense for the courts.

Since ADR procedures bypass the normal court system, they can bring about a quicker resolution for most disputes. The less formal nature of ADR means that many of the time-consuming steps that are typically associated with civil litigation can be omitted or abbreviated, and this results in moving cases along much more rapidly. The process may feel less foreign to the parties involved, and it is likely to be a more casual process. The end result, of course, is that the parties involved in the dispute will save time and money, and the courts will have fewer cases with which to deal. Ultimately, this should save taxpayers money as well.

There are several types of ADR currently found around the United States. The most common include **negotiation**, **mediation**, and **arbitration**, but there are hybrid forms of ADR that include so-called **rent-a-judge** programs, **med-arb**, and **minitrials** (Calvi and Coleman 2008:76–78; Vago 2009:276–84). In the remainder of this section I examine these approaches to ADR and the strengths and weaknesses of each.

NEGOTIATION

Negotiation is the simplest form of alternative dispute resolution and, in fact, some people would not even consider it as an alternative to adjudication. Vago (2009: 276) says that "A basic requirement for successful negotiation is the desire of both parties to settle a dispute without escalation." In the process of negotiating, the two disputing parties sit down in face-to-face discussions and try to resolve their differences. No third parties are involved in most of the negotiation processes, and much of the outcome may depend on the skill of each of the parties in presenting and arguing their points. Typically, a compromise is reached that allows both parties to feel like they have gained something as a result of the process. However, if the effort is viewed as a **zero-sum game** (that is, what one side wins the other side loses), then the process of negotiation is less likely to be successful.

MEDIATION

Mediation takes alternative dispute resolution to the next level: It introduces a third-party mediator who intervenes between the two disputing sides. The mediator's responsibility is not to make a decision about who is right and who is wrong, or whose cause is more just. Instead, the mediator tries to help the two parties come to a resolution that both can agree upon. Prior to the start of the process to resolve the dispute, the mediator will craft an agreement to which both sides must subscribe. Vago (2009:277) says that "Mediation begins with an agreement. It is nonadversarial, and the basic tenet is cooperation rather than competition. The role of the mediator in the dispute is that of a guide, a facilitator, and a catalyst."

Mediators are not required to have any type of specialized training, although on occasions they may be attorneys. Although it is not a hard-and-fast requirement, both parties generally will agree to the choice of a particular mediator, and the process often begins with the mediator meeting with each of the disputants separately. This allows the mediator to establish common areas of agreement and the actual basis for the disagreement. After meeting with the parties separately, the mediator normally will bring both sides together to try and crystallize the nature of the disagreement and to craft an acceptable solution. Because the process is well designed for it, the most common type of case seen by a mediator is a divorce. Again, mediation, like negotiation, depends on compromises, and the final resolution typically will be one recommended—but not imposed—by the mediator. If mediation is not successful, then the dispute may be taken to the more formal process of arbitration.

ARBITRATION

As ADR options move from negotiation to mediation to arbitration they become increasingly formal. In fact, arbitration processes may be governed by state laws, and the American Arbitration Association can provide a list of registered arbitrators in an area as well as rules and procedures governing arbitration sessions. With arbitration, the arbitrator is the third party involved in the process, and this individual ultimately will make the decision that settles the dispute rather than helping the two sides reach their own resolution. In this process, the "Disputants agree beforehand both to the intervention of a neutral third party and to the finality of his or her decisions" (Vago 2009: 279). This means that the arbitrator functions somewhat like a judge.

There are several types of cases that involve arbitration today. For example, arbitration might be used in organized labor and management disputes. Arbitration can help resolve labor contract disputes between the two parties and help avert litigation or a costly strike. Additionally, professional athletes who are involved in contract negotiations may submit their disputes to a salary arbitrator. Many automobile manufacturers have inserted into their sales contacts a clause that says if there is a dispute between the consumer (the automobile buyer) and the manufacturer—for example, over a mechanical flaw that a dealer cannot seem to fix or resolve—then the case will go to arbitration. Finally, credit card companies and other credit-issuing agencies (such as banks) often use arbitration to settle disputes with customers in default.

While negotiation, mediation, and arbitration are the three primary forms of ADR, several new procedures or options also have emerged. In the next section we will examine what have been called the hybrid forms of ADR.

HYBRID ADR OPTIONS

In 1976, largely as a result of the backlog of civil cases in its state courts, California pioneered the program that eventually came to be called "rent-a-judge" (Lacayo and Seufert 1988). Two Los Angeles County attorneys discovered "that an obscure 1872 California law authorizes litigants to have any civil case heard by hired referees, who need not be judges or even lawyers" ("Law: Rent-a-Judge" 1981). With over 220,000 civil cases filed in Los Angeles County every year, judges, attorneys, and civil litigants were looking for much speedier ways of processing their cases.

By some estimates, up to 70 percent of the cases involved in the rent-a-judge process have been personal injury cases largely resulting from traffic accidents. However, other types of cases—such as contract disputes, labor disagreements, malpractice suits, and family law cases—have been disposed of in this manner as well. With the rent-a-judge approach, the disputing parties would agree to hire an attorney or a retired judge to conduct a bench trial to resolve their dispute. A variety of different facilities have been utilized as "courtrooms," and a much quicker and less costly (to both the parties and the public) disposition can be reached. Rather than waiting two or three years to get a case set for trial, the rent-a-judge approach often can dispose of cases within a few months. Box 12.2 provides additional information on this program.

BOX 12.2
In the News: Can You Really Rent a Judge?

Retired California judges, as well as those in other states, have found that they can draw their retirement from the state and have a lucrative retirement business serving as "rent-a-judges." While they can earn over $500 per day hearing state court cases on an as-needed basis, they can make up to $10,000 per day hearing private civil disputes. In 2002 the chief justice of the California Supreme Court gave retired judges an ultimatum: hear state cases as needed or hear private cases, but not both. As might be expected, quite a few of the state's nearly four hundred retired judges chose the more profitable private option.

However, the fundamental question in regards to this type of "private justice" is why parties would choose to go this route. The simple answer is related to the old saying that "time is money," and in this regard privately adjudicated claims can be handled much more quickly—typically in months instead of years—saving both sides substantial litigation costs.

Nevertheless, there are a number of critics of these so-called "private justice programs," and many of the criticisms center around two issues. First, most of these court proceedings are conducted in secret. In fact, that is precisely what a great number of the disputants want. Such proceedings essentially shut out the press and the public, so little is known about the settlements and the consequences such settlements may have. Second, private justice "is available only to those who can afford to hire a judge" and, thus, it discriminates against the less well-to-do in society. What we have, some claim, is a mechanism for justice much like our system of health care: one system exists for the haves, and another exists for the have nots.

Source: Kasindorf (2003); Lacayo and Seufert (1988); "Law: Rent-a-Judge" (1981).

Another ADR hybrid is the system that has come to be called med-arb. As should be apparent, this process is a combination of mediation and arbitration. First, the dispute is taken to a mediator for resolution. If some or all of the issues cannot be resolved, the case moves on to arbitration with same person serving as mediator and arbitrator. As Vago (2009:281) notes, this process "has been used often in contract negotiation disputes between public employers and their unionized employees."

Finally, there are minitrials. In some ways this approach resembles that of the rent-a-judge option. The disputes are distilled to their basic elements, both sides are limited in the numbers and types of motions they can file, and the attorneys are given a restricted amount of time in which to argue their cases. The judge or arbitrator in such situations might then advise the parties as to the likely outcome if the case were to proceed further. Such an advisory opinion may help the parties to see what they stand to gain or lose if they cannot settle the case and, thus, they are faced with adjudication.

When ADR options first became viable alternatives to full-blown trials, many attorneys opposed them on the grounds that this would short circuit the justice process as well as cut into their earning potential. Today, however, there are lawyers and even whole law firms that specialize in alternative dispute resolution and they publicly advertise their services in this arena. Thus, while there are still some detractors and skeptics of ADR, for the most part it has become a firmly entrenched element in the American system of justice.

ISSUES OF GENDER AND RACE

Beginning in the 1960s, concerns started to be raised by social scientists and some in the legal profession that the courts did not dispense justice in a fair and totally even-handed fashion when it came to questions of gender and race (see, for example, Gabbidon 2009; Reiman 2006; Van Wormer and Bartollas 2007). While the discriminatory application of the law to certain groups can work both ways—either for or against a particular group—questions about the unequal application of the law and the resulting injustice remain.

GENDER ISSUES

Gender issues really cut along two dimensions in the judicial process. First, consideration must be given to the way women are treated by the courts as victims, offenders, plaintiffs, defendants, and witnesses. Second, the issue of the position of women in the administration of justice—particularly in the roles of attorneys and judges—also must be addressed. I consider both of these in this section.

Women as Victims

In terms of the situation in which women are victims, there have been concerns expressed particularly in regard to two sets of circumstances. First, when women have suffered from sexual assaults, concern has been expressed about the possibility of the victim being twice-victimized: once by the offender and a second time by the justice system. In order to deal with this consideration a number of changes in case processing have occurred since the 1970s. Some police departments now utilize female officers to investigate sexual assaults when there is a female victim. Additionally, officers may receive training on how to be more sensitive when processing cases of females who have been raped. Prosecuting attorneys' offices in some jurisdictions now employ victims' advocates who are specially trained to deal with a variety of crime victims who have suffered some sort of trauma. Finally, quite a few jurisdictions in the United States now have enacted what are called **rape shield laws**. These laws prevent defense attorneys from questioning victims about or making reference to the victim's prior sexual history with the accused person or with anyone else. Box 12.3 provides information on rape shield laws in Canada.

A quick look at some of the figures released by the United States Bureau of the Census shows that in 2002 females eighteen years of age and older constituted slightly over half of the nation's population (51.5 percent). By contrast, for the same year females constituted only 17 percent of those convicted of all felonies and 11 percent of those convicted of violent felonies (Durose and Langan 2004:6). Why are there such disparities in the numbers of women convicted of felonies in comparison to their male

BOX 12.3
Rape Shield Laws in Canada

In 1983 the Criminal Code of Canada was amended to include a rape shield law that had an absolute prohibition against questioning victims about their prior sexual history. The Supreme Court of Canada struck down that law, and in 1992 Parliament enacted a new provision that greatly restricted the lines of questioning to which victims of sexual assault could be exposed, but it did not provide for an absolute prohibition of such questioning.

Rape shield laws are designed to address two particular concerns of rape victims and victims' advocacy groups. The rape shield law primarily was created to keep victims of sexual assault from being cross-examined in court as to their past sexual histories. In addition, the law is intended to prevent the publication of the names or other personal information concerning victims.

Today in Canada a victim's sexual history may be admitted into evidence if it is relevant to the present case and if doing so does not contribute to prejudice in the administration of justice. This allows some questioning by defense attorneys who represent offenders accused of sexual assaults, while maintaining the privacy and dignity of the victim. Is this a foolproof method? Most observers would suggest that it is probably not, but it may serve as the best solution currently available.

Source: Tang (1998).

counterparts? Are they less inclined to engage in criminal activity, or are there forces at work within the criminal justice system that offset these numbers? These numbers warrant a closer look at the ways female offenders are processed by the courts at the stages of prosecution, adjudication, and sentencing.

Women as Offenders

In terms of filing criminal charges against women, 2008 arrest statistics from the Federal Bureau of Investigation demonstrate that nationwide women constitute roughly 1.99 million or slightly less than one-third of the persons arrested (Federal Bureau of Investigation 2010). Obviously this has an impact on the prosecution of criminal cases as well. Two explanations have been offered for this substantial underrepresentation of females in the nation's arrest and prosecution statistics. First, some people maintain that either by biology or by culture, women are simply less criminally inclined than men. Second, however, there has been a strong argument made that the justice system is much less punitive and much more forgiving toward women accused of most crimes. This is often called the **chivalry hypothesis**, and as I discussed earlier in the text, it suggests that agents of the justice system act in ways that show leniency toward accused female offenders (Mays and Ruddell 2008:165; Smith, Visher, and Davidson 1984; Visher 1983).

There also is the likelihood that the justice system can act in ways that are much more punitive toward female offenders. This is known as **paternalism** perspective, and it suggests that when females commit crimes normally associated with males, or they commit crimes in a more male-like fashion, then the justice system should respond in a way to protect society from these female offenders and to protect the women from themselves. Thus, in the prosecution of women accused of committing crimes, it is entirely likely that they will be treated either more leniently or more harshly than their male counterparts for a variety of reasons.

When it comes to adjudication, again women may be treated differently from men. Judges and juries may be more sympathetic to female offenders, at least in cases where their crimes are consistent with female stereotypes. This has become apparent in states that have moved to the use of sentencing guidelines. Without guided sentences, judges traditionally have had a great deal of discretion in deciding which sentences to impose. However, in the jurisdictions that have implemented sentencing guidelines the disparities among convicted offenders have decreased, as sentencing guidelines do not take into account the offender's gender. This especially has been the case for male–female differences in sentences (Nagel and Johnson 1994).

Women as Judges and Attorneys

In addition to women appearing in the courts as victims and defendants in criminal cases and as plaintiffs or defendants in civil cases, they also participate in the judicial process as judges and attorneys. For most of our nation's history, women have been substantially underrepresented in the practice of law. Lentz (2009:445) notes that the first woman admitted to the practice of law in the United States was in Iowa in 1869. Some states specifically excluded women from being licensed to practice law, and the United States Supreme Court, in the case of *Bradwell v. Illinois*, 83 U.S. 130 (1872), "ruled that practicing law was not a privilege under the U.S. Constitution, and states could restrict licensure to males" (Lentz 2009:445). The result was that most women were systematically—and legally—excluded from university-level legal studies and from the practice of law in their communities.

As a result of not being allowed to practice law, women also were foreclosed from public service as judges. For example, "in 1969 there were just over 8,000 women attorneys and only about 200 female judges" in the United States (Lentz 2009:446). While there has been progress in this area, the numbers for women continue to lag behind those of men. "By the 1980s it was estimated that there were over 500 women sitting as judges on state courts and by the early 1990s that number had more than doubled," but the percentage of women judges nationwide still remains small (Lentz 2009:447).

Currently, women comprise over one-fourth of the judgeships on state courts of last resort, roughly 20 percent of the federal district court judgeships, 20 percent of federal appellate judgeships, and three of the current associate justices of the United States Supreme Court are women. Most of the increases in the numbers of female judges have come as a result of the significant increases in the percentage of female law school students and the number of women entering the practice of law. In fact, the American Bar Association (2010a) reports that the percentage of licensed female attorneys in the U.S. grew from 8 percent in 1980 to 20 percent in 1991 and 27 percent in 2000. In addition, in the 2007–08 academic year women comprised 47 percent of the roughly 142,000 law students in the country. That number has been hovering at just under one-half of the total law school enrollment for nearly twenty years (American Bar Association 2010a; USLaw.com 2009).

The exclusion of women from participation in the judicial process has gone beyond their participation as judges and attorneys, however. For instance, even after women gained the right to vote in 1920, some states still systematically excluded them from jury service based on their supposed emotional frailty (Lentz 2009:446). Today no state routinely excludes women from jury service, and the United States Supreme Court, in the case of *J.E.B. v. Alabama Ex Rel. T.B.*, 511 U.S. 127 (1994), has said "the Equal Protection Clause [of the Constitution] forbids intentional discrimination on the basis of gender, just as it prohibits discrimination on the basis of race." Thus, in the process of jury selection, peremptory challenges cannot be used to exclude all females (or all males, for that matter), and "gender, like race, is an unconstitutional proxy for juror competence and impartiality" (511 U.S. 127).

RACE AND JUSTICE

Just as concern over gender remains a consideration in the justice apparatus of the United States, the issue of race (and ethnicity) also must be addressed. Again, as with gender, race or ethnicity is a two-dimensional concern dealing with the way minorities are treated within the justice system and with the numbers of minorities serving as attorneys and judges within the courts.

Minorities as Defendants

Race particularly has been raised as an issue in regard to the disproportionate number of minorities who are arrested and prosecuted in our nation's courts. As an example, in

2004, 38 percent of the people convicted of all felonies in state courts were black. Even more startling is the fact that 46 percent of the state felons convicted of drug charges, and 55 percent convicted of weapons charges, were black. Durose and Langan (2007:2) note that "Whites were 82% of adults in the U.S. population compared to 59% of persons convicted of a felony. Blacks were 12% of the adult population, but 38% of convicted felons." The reasons behind such discrepancies are varied and complex. For example, for any number of reasons it is possible that minorities simply commit more crimes and thus are more likely to be targeted and apprehended by the police as well as prosecuted.

It is equally likely that the policies of the criminal justice system disproportionately affect minorities, particularly those policies that are aimed at controlling drugs. An illustration of this is the so-called 100:1 conversion factor for crack cocaine versus powder cocaine built into the federal laws (see Box 12.4). What this means is that one gram of crack cocaine can result in the same sentence as one hundred grams of powder cocaine, even though the drugs are chemically indistinguishable. The result of this policy is that blacks, who are more likely to possess and sell crack cocaine rather than powder cocaine, are often punished more severely than their white counterparts in the drug trade. In 2007, the U.S. Supreme Court ruled that such a legal inconsistency is not constitutionally justifiable (see *Kimbrough v. United States*, 552 U.S. 85 [2007]).

BOX 12.4

In the News: Crack Cocaine Versus Powder Cocaine

For some time, critics of the 1986 federal drug law have argued that the legal distinction between the penalty for crack (or rock) cocaine violations and the penalty for powder cocaine violations were unjustified. In essence, the law imposed the same penalty for 1 gram of crack cocaine as it did for 100 grams of powder cocaine (the so-called 100-to-1 disparity). While the two forms of the drug cannot be chemically distinguished, Congress decided in the early 1980s to tack a more severe punishment on those accused of involvement with crack cocaine in comparison with those who were arrested for the powder version of the drug. The result was that the application of the law had a racially disparate effect: minorities were much more likely to be involved with crack than with powder cocaine and, thus, much more likely to receive severe criminal penalties.

In 2007, the United States Supreme Court, in a 7-2 decision, supported the view of the trial court judge that the existing distinction created a "disproportionate and unjust effect" (*Kimbrough v. United States*, 552 U.S. 85). The Court affirmed the sentencing decision of the federal trial court judge that had departed downward from the sentence prescribed by the U.S. Sentencing Guidelines. Therefore, after more than two decades of maintaining this legal distinction, the federal drug laws must now treat all forms of cocaine the same.

Sources: Legal Information Institute (2010); Mikkelson (2007).

Not only are blacks convicted of all crimes at disproportionate rates relative to whites, but also this disproportionality shows up in our prison populations. On June 30, 2007, there were 2,090,800 people held in state and federal prisons and local jails in the United States. Of this number, 882,000 were black (814,000 males and 67,600 females) along with 443,000 who were Hispanic (410,900 males and 32,100 females). These two groups taken together represent nearly two-thirds (63.38 percent) of the nation's prison and jail populations (Sabol and Couture 2008:7). Clearly minorities are disproportionately represented in the population of persons processed by the courts and those sentenced to serve time at the local, state, and federal levels.

Minorities as Judges and Attorneys

Just as is the case with women, minorities are substantially underrepresented in the practice of law and on the benches of the nation's courts. For instance, the American Bar Association (2010a) notes that in 1990 blacks comprised 3.3 percent of the licensed attorneys in the United States, and by 2000 this had only grown to 4.2 percent. Hispanics represented the next largest minority group; they constituted 2.5 percent of U.S. attorneys in 1990, and in 2000 they were 3.4 percent of the attorney population. For the 2007–2008 academic year all minority groups accounted for about one in five (22.4 percent) of the nation's law school enrollment.

When the numbers of minorities practicing law are small, this is also reflected in the presence of minorities on the benches of courts in the United States. For instance, the American Bar Association (2010b) has found that nationwide there are approximately 1,144 minority judges sitting in state courts. Of this group, 665 (58.1 percent) are African American, 320 (28 percent) are Hispanic, 122 (10.7 percent) are Asian American or Pacific Islanders, 13 (1.1 percent) are Native American, and 24 (2.1 percent) represent other racial/ethnic groups. These numbers translate into the following percentages: 9.7 percent of state supreme court judges are minorities, 10.6 percent of the judges serving on intermediate appellate courts are minorities, and 9 percent of general trial court judges are minorities. The numbers for federal courts are not any better: Out of nearly 1,300 federal judges only 8 percent are African American, 11 judges are Asian American, and only 1 is Native American (Tobias 2009). As a nation we have a long way to go in order to have the justice system actors reflect the nation's population.

THE USE OF SCIENTIFIC EVIDENCE

The "science" of identifying criminal offenders emerged in the late 1800s when Alphonse Bertillon, who was the chief of France's Judicial Identification Service, devised a method for measuring and classifying the physical characteristics of convicted criminals. This technique, which came to be called the Bertillon method, "utilized measurements of an individual's size, coloring, and markings" and "took into account physical and verbal characteristics" (Mays, Purcell, and Winfree 1992:112; see also Purcell, Winfree, and Mays 1994). While considered cutting-edge science in its day, the Bertillon method was far from precise as an identification technique.

The modern use of scientific evidence within the courts probably can be traced to the introduction of fingerprinting and similar identification procedures, particularly around the first part of the twentieth century. However, since the beginning of the 1980s, the use of emerging technologies in the identification and apprehension of criminal suspects has expanded tremendously. This leaves the courts with the dilemma of assessing these new technologies and determining the degree to which innovative scientific procedures should be admitted as reliable evidence in courts.

While I could discuss a variety of different types of scientific evidence, I will confine my discussion to the use of DNA testing. In 1985 Dr. Alec J. Jeffreys of England introduced a genetic engineering process that he called "**DNA fingerprinting**." This technique was designed to unravel the DNA (deoxyribonucleic acid) molecule that contains each person's unique genetic characteristics. The first criminal case that employed this technique was a multiple murder and rape case from central England. "Criminal investigators, trying to determine if a suspect was indeed the killer, asked Jeffreys in 1987 to apply his DNA technique. The man who confessed was shown to be innocent, and after 'blooding' by 4,500 men in the Midlands, a suspect was identified by police investigations; his identity as the killer was confirmed by DNA fingerprinting" (Mays et al. 1992:113).

While DNA testing is by no means the only new scientific analytical procedure available to the courts, it has received a great deal of publicity, and it illustrates the kinds of procedures courts must go through to establish the validity and reliability of new scientific technologies. This procedure now has been widely accepted as a reliable indicator of a suspect's involvement in criminal activity, and as you will see in the next section, it has played a major role in overturning the sentences of a number of people who have been wrongfully convicted of very serious crimes.

One of the ironies of the increasing use of scientific evidence in courts is that juries may now expect it even in routine cases. This is what some have called the "CSI effect," and in the absence of overwhelming scientific evidence like DNA, prosecutors may have a more difficult time convincing jurors of guilt beyond a reasonable doubt.

WRONGFUL CONVICTIONS

Given the involvement of human beings in the judicial process, and our inherent frailties, the likelihood of a wrongful conviction always will exist in criminal cases. However, national attention has been focused on this issue in the past twenty years, largely as the result of more widespread use of DNA testing and several well-publicized death row cases involving wrongfully accused and convicted individuals (see Grisham 2006; Scheck, Neufeld, and Dwyer 2000). It is important to note at this juncture that wrongful convictions do not involve only death penalty cases. A number of wrongfully convicted people have been found guilty of non-capital crimes as well.

The problems posed by wrongful convictions are many. For example, it has been observed that

> Such cases are troubling for advocates of both the crime control and due process models. For those who believe in crime control, the fact that an innocent person has been imprisoned means that the guilty party is still in the community and could be committing further crimes. Persons who support the due process model,

by contrast, are horrified by the prosecution, conviction, and sentencing of an innocent person. Members of either group probably would agree that these convictions shape our perceptions of justice, or injustice (Mays and Ruddell 2008:187).

Based on the potentially devastating consequences of wrongful convictions, it is critical to review some of the key reasons they occur.

Scholars who have examined the topic of wrongful convictions have discovered several consistent reasons for these miscarriages of justice. The most commonly mentioned themes are: eyewitness misidentification, false confessions, jailhouse snitch testimony, misleading forensic science, prosecutorial misconduct, and ineffective assistance of counsel. I discuss each of these briefly.

EYEWITNESS MISIDENTIFICATION

Most people assume that eyewitness identification of crime suspects is the "gold standard" in courts. However, within the past decade or so serious doubts have been cast on the accuracy of many eyewitness accounts regarding the identification of suspects. In fact, one group of scholars has said that eyewitness misidentification is the primary cause of wrongful convictions (Huff, Rattner, and Sagarin 1996). There are any number of reasons for this, but most of the problems seem traceable to police identification procedures. Police officers typically show eyewitnesses photographs of potential suspects, or they hold physical lineups that include the suspect or suspects. The presumption on the part of the eyewitnesses is that the suspect is included in the grouping somewhere, and they often pick out the person who looks most like the perpetrator of the crime. In some ways there is a psychological compulsion to find the guilty party, and thus, without acting maliciously, eyewitnesses feel the need to identify someone. There also is a whole body of research dealing with cross-racial misidentification as well as the stresses associated with being a crime victim (of rape or robbery, for instance) and the likelihood that this can cause an incorrect identification (see, for example, Huff 2002; Rutledge 2001).

FALSE CONFESSIONS

The idea of a false confession seems puzzling to most people. Frequently we hear the question asked: If someone did not commit a crime, why would that person confess? Often the answer is that coercive interrogation techniques might be used by the police, in combination with a mental disability, and the suspect being under the influence of drugs or alcohol. In fact, police investigators are trained in the use of deceptive interrogation techniques at seminars offered around the country. The courts have sanctioned some of these techniques, such as telling suspects that a codefendant has given police information implicating the person being questioned in the crime, or in telling the suspect that his or her fingerprints or shoe prints were found at the scene of the crime, but that does not mean these practices have ceased altogether.

JAILHOUSE SNITCHES

Frequently, suspects recant their initial confessions, but by that time the damage already may have been done. How often this occurs is not fully known, but the

Innocence Project (2007) discovered that over one-fourth "of the first 130 people exon-erated by DNA evidence had made false confessions" (Mays and Ruddell 2008:192). Another troubling source of wrongful convictions is the testimony provided by **jail-house snitches**. In simplest terms, jailhouse snitches are inmates who may share a cell with the suspected or accused person, and they may be solicited by law enforce-ment authorities to engage the suspect in conversations trying to elicit incriminat-ing statements. Sometimes the statements turn out to be true, but occasionally these statements are totally fabricated by the snitches in order to receive leniency in their own cases, abbreviated sentences, or some other type of compensation. Blitstein (2009:73) says that using informants or snitches in criminal cases "leaves innocents behind bars, puts informants at mortal risk, renders justice opaque and actually leads to more crimes."

There have even been cases where snitches almost have created a business for themselves informing to authorities on multiple cases (see Grisham 2006). In situa-tions where all or part of a case rests on the testimony of a jailhouse snitch, it behooves the courts to insist on corroborating evidence in order to minimize the likelihood that the testimony of another accused criminal is not completely fabricated.

MISLEADING FORENSIC SCIENCE

In the previous section I discussed the use of scientific evidence in courts, with par-ticular emphasis on DNA evidence. It is important to note the significant role that DNA testing has played in establishing guilt or innocence in a substantial number of cases. However, any time a new scientific technique emerges and is applied to the analysis of evidence, there are always questions about reliability and validity. This means that the fundamental question is whether the analysis and attendant testimony from experts should be admissible in court. In Chapter 7 I discussed the use of expert witnesses, and some of these witnesses have been identified as sources of wrongful convictions. The problems arise from three particular areas of concern.

First, there are "scientific" techniques that have been labeled pseudo-science or "junk science." Some of these include the analysis of strands of hair by criminalistics experts (see Grisham 2006), bite marks, lip prints, tool marks, as well as the use of polygraph examination results. Many of these techniques at best have not sufficiently established their credibility to allow their use in courts, and at worst some of them have been discredited entirely.

Second, there have been problems associated with certain crime laboratories around the country. Perhaps the most dramatic example to date has been that of the Houston, Texas, Police Department Crime Laboratory (Bromwich 2006). However, the Houston crime laboratory is not the only one that has been plagued with troubles. Other crime labs have been accused of losing, misanalyzing, or contaminating evidence, and some (like the Los Angeles Police Department Crime Lab) have found themselves so backlogged that they cannot analyze critical evidence in a timely manner (see Mays and Ruddell 2008:195–99).

Third, there also have been documented cases of crime lab technicians creating completely fraudulent reports. There have been cases where criminalistics experts have testified using truthful analyses, but they have exaggerated the degree of trustworthiness of the results. In the end, any and all of these factors can contribute to wrongful convictions of innocent persons.

PROSECUTORIAL MISCONDUCT

Another factor that leads to some wrongful convictions is prosecutorial misconduct. The United States Supreme Court has addressed this issue in the case of *Miller v. Pate*, 386 U.S. 1 (1967), "where the prosecutor concealed from the jury in a murder case the fact that a pair of undershorts with red stains on it, a crucial piece of evidence, were stained not by blood, but by paint" (Gershman 2009:321). In overturning the conviction in that case, Associate Supreme Court Justice Potter Stewart, writing for the majority, said, "More than 30 years ago, this Court held that the Fourteenth Amendment cannot tolerate a state criminal conviction obtained by the knowing use of false evidence. There has been no deviation from that established principle. There can be no retreat from that principle here" (386 U.S. 7). Box 12.5 provides further insights into the Court's ruling in this case.

BOX 12.5

In Their Own Words: Prosecutorial Misconduct

In the Supreme Court case of *Miller v. Pate*, Justice Potter Stewart made several comments relating to the obvious misrepresentation of evidence by the prosecuting attorney. In that case a young girl had been raped and murdered, and a key piece of evidence was a pair of men's underwear that appeared to be stained with blood. However, as Justice Stewart noted:

> Such was the state of the evidence with respect to People's Exhibit 3 [the pair of men's underwear] as the case went to the jury. And such was the state of the record as the judgment of conviction was reviewed by the Supreme Court of Illinois. The "blood stained shorts" clearly played a vital part in the case for the prosecution. They were an important link in the chain of circumstantial evidence against the petitioner, and, in the context of the revolting crime with which he was charged, their gruesomely emotional impact upon the jury was incalculable (386 U.S. 4–5).

> The record of the petitioner's trial reflects the prosecution's consistent and repeated misrepresentation that People's Exhibit 3 was, indeed, "a garment heavily stained with blood." The prosecution's whole theory with respect to the exhibit depended upon that misrepresentation. For the theory was that the victim's assailant had discarded the shorts because they were stained with blood. A pair of paint-stained shorts, found in an abandoned building a mile away from the scene of the crime, was virtually valueless as evidence against the petitioner. The prosecution deliberately misrepresented the truth (386 U.S. 6).

Source: Miller v. Pate 386 U.S. 1 (1967).

BOX 12.6

In Their Own Words: Marvin Zalman on Wrongful Convictions

The rising number of exonerations puts pressure on the criminal justice system. Innocence projects are appealing cases under statutes that allow review where new evidence, including DNA, has become available. Prosecutors feel the greatest pressure. Attorneys for wrongly convicted prisoners will request that prosecutors join them in asking courts to dismiss convictions on the grounds of justice, putting prosecutors in a tough spot. A few reform prosecutors who came to office on platforms critical of their predecessors are more willing to join such motions. Other prosecutors may agree and join such motions, understanding that such errors make their offices look bad. Another response will be to join or at least to not oppose such motions, but to issue public statements that the prosecutors do not necessarily agree that the defendant was actually innocent. These statements may genuinely reflect a belief that the evidence is equivocal or may be token responses designed to keep up unit morale and possibly make lawsuits difficult, although prosecutors have absolute immunity for actions taken regarding core functions.

If prosecutors oppose the motions, they face humiliation if they are granted by judges with prejudice. If the ruling of judges allows the possibility of retrials, prosecutors are then faced with the tough choice of the cost of a new trial and the difficulty of getting witnesses years after the crime. In some instances prosecutors will seek to obtain a guilty plea to a lesser crime with an agreement that the defendant will be released. For actually innocent defendants seeking to end the pressures of imprisonment, this means that they are free but with the permanent mark of a past conviction. As for the judicial process, the greatest pressure exists among appellate courts, which may have to resolve difficult questions on habeas corpus and other collateral appeals. In sum, the growing awareness of wrongful conviction is forcing the judicial system to rethink a very old question in new ways.

Source: Marvin Zalman is professor of criminal justice at Wayne State University. Professor Zalman has written extensively on criminal procedure, and his recent focus has been on the issue of wrongful convictions.

INEFFECTIVE COUNSEL

The final element associated with some wrongful convictions is the ineffective assistance of counsel.   In most cases, concern over ineffective assistance of counsel arises when there is an indigent defendant and a court-appointed attorney. Newspapers around the country occasionally carry stories of defendants convicted in cases where their attorneys slept through part of the trial or where the lawyers were intoxicated. Most situations are not that dramatic, but there have been situations such as the one represented in the Supreme Court case of *United States v. Cronic*, 466 U.S 648 (1984). In that case, the trial court appointed the defendant a young attorney who primarily practiced real estate law and only gave him 25 days to prepare for trial. The real question in this case was whether the defendant was adequately represented by his appointed attorney. In writing for the majority, Justice John Paul Stevens, in rejecting the claim of ineffective assistance of counsel, said, "The criteria used by the Court of Appeals do not demonstrate that counsel failed to function in any meaningful sense as the Government's adversary. Respondent can therefore make out a claim of ineffective assistance only by pointing to specific errors made by trial counsel. In this Court, respondent's present counsel argues that the record would support such an attack…" (466 U.S. 666). The problem is that the average person is not sufficiently trained to know when an attorney has acted in an incompetent manner, let alone being able to prove incompetence. Nevertheless, on appeal convicted offenders must demonstrate that their lawyers failed to do something that would be expected of a competent attorney, and that such an action had an adverse effect in their case. This may be difficult to prove in many situations, but there still are documented cases of ineffective attorneys who have contributed to wrongful convictions.

ADJUDICATING NON-TRADITIONAL ISSUES: THE CASE OF TERRORISM

While many aspects of the law and the judicial process seem firmly established, occasionally new issues arise that cause the courts to rethink the ways in which they do business. Such is the case with all of the individuals being held by the United States government at the detention facility at Guantanamo Bay, Cuba. The question facing the president and members of the executive branch is where to try these individuals. The dilemma confronting the courts in the United States is whether, and to what degree, our laws apply to suspects apprehended overseas in conjunction with the nation's war on terrorism.

Ever since the United States began its engagement in Afghanistan along with the invasion of Iraq, we have had in custody a group of people classified as "enemy combatants." This designation is unique, because it places these people outside of the normal designation of "prisoners of war" and outside of the rights that U.S. citizens have under the Constitution. If they were prisoners of war, then a whole set of international laws and guidelines—such as the Geneva Convention—would come into play. As it stands, however, as enemy combatants they exist in a state of legal limbo. This means that for the last several years legal battles have been fought over whether the Guantanamo Bay detainees have access to U.S. courts through mechanisms such as writs of habeas corpus or not.

The most definitive ruling to date on this issue came in the case of *Hamdan v. Rumsfeld*, 548 U.S. 557 (2006). In this case, the executive branch (the president, acting through the secretary of defense) had established "military tribunals" for the purpose of trying the enemy combatants detained at Guantanamo Bay. Part of the Supreme Court's decision here addressed the issue of whether Congress had the power to prevent the Supreme Court from hearing these cases before the military tribunals had the opportunity to act. In a 5–3 ruling the Court said that it had jurisdiction to hear such cases, and that the military tribunals that had been established violated both the Uniform Code of Military Justice (which governs military trials such as court martials) as well as the Geneva Convention.

While we have not heard the last of these terrorism-related cases, "As the federal courts continue to address the issues surrounding enemy combatants…we will begin to get better definitions concerning the executive branch's powers to carry out its duties in responding to threats, both foreign and domestic. For the time being, however, concerns have been expressed—particularly by due process advocates—over the degree to which the Constitution applies to the war on terror" (Mays and Ruddell 2008:306).

SUMMARY

As living, social institutions, courts will always face problems and challenges. Some of the dilemmas discussed in this chapter are chronic and persistent concerns. Others are of more recent vintage. Nevertheless, understanding the nature of these problems helps us understand the potential solutions that must be crafted.

Among the most persistent problems faced by courts are those involving resources. Court caseloads seem to grow each year, and the demand for judges, juries, courtrooms, and court-appointed defense attorneys grows along with them. The local, state, and federal governments in this country will continue to struggle to meet the resource demands of the courts. By the same token, the courts will struggle to make the case that their particular needs are especially worthy of consideration.

Judicial independence is another of our persistent court concerns. How can we both keep judges independent of extraneous influences and at the same time hold them accountable as public servants? The whole issue of electing judges and the potential influence of campaign contributions to judges running for office continues to confound court reform organizations like the American Judicature Society. Nevertheless, local and state governments often hold jealously to their long-established traditions of electing judges.

The area of court management is one where promises and actual solutions seem to have emerged. Since the 1970s, there has been a clear trend to develop or expand the management capacities of state court organizations along with those of local trial courts. Increasingly, the day-to-day budgetary and personnel operations of courts are placed in the hands of highly educated, professional court administrators.

Pro se litigation, and its impact on court operations, is an issue somewhat out of the public's view. Nevertheless, courts—and especially the courts of limited jurisdiction—are confronted daily with individuals who represent themselves in pressing their claims. While this may be less expensive than hiring an attorney, *pro se* cases may not proceed as smoothly as those in which experienced litigators participate. Therefore, as long as citizens are allowed to represent themselves in court, the courts must make allowances for this and structure proceedings in ways to permit cases to be handled expeditiously.

Early in their introduction, alternative dispute resolution mechanisms were often resisted by the traditional members of the courtroom work group. Now, however, they have been embraced by judges and attorneys as ways to process some cases quickly, thus saving the congested courts both time and money. The trend in ADR seems to be more cases handled and more different mechanisms for handling the types of cases most amenable to alternatives to adjudication.

Issues of race and gender in the judicial process seem to be among the most politically sensitive. The courts need to be aware of situations where there is disparate handling of cases involving women as well as minorities. In addition, as a society we should remove the structural barriers to the full participation by females and minorities in the administration of justice in this country.

Concerns over the use of scientific evidence along with wrongful convictions seem to be linked. There are a number of reasons for wrongful convictions that were detailed in this chapter, but within our justice system we must be particularly careful of the misuses of new and emerging scientific techniques that are being applied to the solution of crimes and the identification of criminal suspects.

Finally, the war on terrorism has opened up new vistas in the judicial process. When, and to what degree, do the laws of the United States apply to individuals that we have apprehended in foreign countries? Do the traditional court structures and legal procedures apply, or should new legal mechanisms be crafted? What rights should we extend to so-called enemy combatants? The area awaits further resolution.

QUESTIONS FOR CRITICAL THINKING

1. What do we mean when we say that courts are not masters of their own fates? Can you think of situations and circumstances in which the courts have their agendas set for them by other agencies and organizations?

2. The Founding Fathers of our nation characterized the courts as the "least dangerous branch of government" since they wielded neither "the purse nor the sword." Does this say something about the importance of courts? Has the image of courts changed since the founding of our country? Explain.

3. As a nation, should we be troubled by the popular election of judges? Does it matter that law firms and other types of businesses give campaign contributions to judges before whom they may appear in future cases?

4. Have you ever thought about a career in court administration? Did you know that this was a career option? What can you find out about these jobs on the Internet? What do they pay, and what are the qualifications that are expected? You might check with your state's administrative office of courts (AOC) to get answers.

5. If you were a lower court judge, how would you feel about citizens representing themselves in court? Would this make you apprehensive? Would you feel obligated to assist, and would this affect your obligation toward neutrality in a case?

6. Look through your local telephone book, or do a Yellow Pages web search based on "alternative dispute resolution." Are you surprised at the number of "hits" that you get?

7. If you own a new or relatively new automobile, look in the owner's manual to see if there is a provision for arbitration if you have a dispute with the manufacturer. Does this segment of the manual spell out your rights? Who seems to be in the position of power in this arrangement? Does such a provision prevent you from filing a lawsuit, or make it more difficult to do so?

8. What do we mean when we say that courts act in ways demonstrating chivalry? How about paternalism?

9. How do you explain the relatively small number of judges who are women or minorities in this country? Are these groups just not interested in serving as judges, or is something else at work? Explain.

10. How good is eyewitness testimony? What kinds of factors influence our perceptions of events?

11. Some people have estimated that between 1 percent and 2 percent of the criminal cases disposed of by courts each year result in wrongful convictions. How satisfied should we be with a 98 percent or 99 percent accuracy rate? Look at some of the numbers presented in the book and determine exactly how many cases a 1–2 percent error rate represents.

12. When it comes to dealing with terrorism suspects that we have apprehended in foreign countries (not those arrested in the U.S.), which courts should have jurisdiction? Civilian courts in the U.S.? Military courts? An international court of some type? Explain your answer.

RECOMMENDED READINGS

Free, Marvin D., Jr., ed. (2003). *Racial Issues in Criminal Justice: The Case of African Americans.* Westport, CT: Praeger Publishing Co. This volume contains fourteen original essays that deal with the problems encountered by African Americans in the criminal justice system. The three primary themes are: the role of race in our society, how the criminal justice system responds to crime and how this affects African Americans, and how we can arrive at solutions to the unequal treatment of minorities within our justice apparatus.

Grisham, John (2006). *The Innocent Man: Murder and Injustice in a Small Town.* New York: Doubleday. John Grisham is mostly known for his fiction works dealing with attorneys and the practice of law. However, in this book he takes on a true-life case of a young man growing up in the small town of Ada, Oklahoma, who is accused of a brutal rape and murder. Eventually, Ron Williamson is convicted of the crimes and sentenced to be executed. In fact, he comes within days of death. A group of journalists and law school students begin a campaign to have his conviction overturned and to have him released from prison. This is one of those books that affirms the old adage that "truth is stranger than fiction."

Merlo, Alida, and Joycelyn M. Pollock, eds. (2006). *Women, Law, and Social Control.* Boston: Allyn & Bacon. This is a book of readings by a number of scholars who reflect on the roles that women play in the criminal justice system. Of particular interest are the two issues that were addressed in this chapter: women as offenders in the system and women as agents of justice.

Scheck, Barry, Peter Neufeld, and Jim Dwyer (2000). *Actual Innocence*. New York: Doubleday. Scheck and Neufeld are the cofounders of the Innocence Project based at Cardozo School of Law. Scheck is perhaps best known as one of the members of the O. J. Simpson "dream team," and he handled the presentation of the DNA evidence to the jury in the Simpson case. In this book Scheck and his coauthors examine a number of cases handled by the Innocence Project where wrongfully convicted persons have been sentenced to prison, and some have been condemned to die.

KEY TERMS

administrative office of courts

alternative dispute resolution

arbitration

chivalry hypothesis

court administration

court management

DNA fingerprinting

jailhouse snitches

judicial independence

med-arb

mediation

minitrials

negotiation

paternalism

pro se litigation

rape shield laws

rent-a-judge

zero-sum game

REFERENCES

American Bar Association (2010a). Lawyer Demographics. http://new.abanet.org/marketresearch/PublicDocuments/Lawyer_Demographics.pdf.

American Bar Association (2010b). National Database on Judicial Diversity in State Courts. http://apps.americanbar.org/abanet.jd/national.cfm.

American Judicature Society (2009a). Judicial Independence Home Page. http://www.ajs.org/cji/default.asp.

American Judicature Society (2009b). Pro Se Forum Home Page. http://www.ajs.org/prose/home.asp.

Blitstein, Ryan (2009). The Inside Dope on Snitching. *Miller-McCune* 2(6):73–74.

Bradwell v. Illinois, 83 U.S. 130 (1872).

Bromwich, Michael (2006). *Fifth Report of the Independent Investigator for the Houston Police Department Crime Laboratory and Property Room*. http://www.hpdlabinvestigation.org.

Calvi, James V., and Susan Coleman (2008). *American Law and Legal Systems*, 6th ed. Upper Saddle River, NJ: Pearson/Prentice Hall.

Durose, Matthew R., and Patrick A. Langan (2004). *Felony Sentences in State Courts, 2002*. Washington, DC: Bureau of Justice Statistics, U.S. Department of Justice.

Durose, Matthew R., and Patrick A. Langan (2007). *Felony Sentences in State Courts, 2004*. Washington, DC: Bureau of Justice Statistics, U.S. Department of Justice.

Eisenstein, James, and Herbert Jacob (1977). *Felony Justice: An Organizational Analysis of Criminal Courts*. Boston: Little, Brown and Co.

Federal Bureau of Investigation (2010). *Crime in the United States, 2008*. http://www2.fbi.gov/ucr/cius2008/data/table_33.html.

Free, Marvin D., Jr., ed. (2003). *Racial Issues in Criminal Justice: The Case of African Americans*. Westport, CT: Praeger Publishing Co.

Gabbidon, Shaun L. (2009). *Race and Crime*, 2nd ed. Thousand Oaks, CA: Sage Publications.

Gershman, Bennett L. (2009). Why Prosecutors Misbehave. In *Courts and Justice*, 4th ed., ed. G. Larry Mays and Peter R. Gregware, 321–31. Long Grove, IL: Waveland Press.

Gibbs, Margery A. (2008). More Americans Serving as Their Own Lawyers. Wisconsin Law Blog. http://wis-injury.com/blog/2008/11/more-americans-serving-as-their-own-lawyers.html.

Glater, Jonathan D. (2009). In a Downturn, More Act as Their Own Lawyers. *NYTimes.com*. http://www.nytimes.com/2009/04/10/business/10lawyer.html:_r=2&hp+8pagewanted+1&hp.

Grisham, John (2006). *The Innocent Man: Murder and Injustice in a Small Town*. New York: Doubleday.

Hamdan v. Rumsfeld, 548 U.S. 557 (2006).

Huff, C. Ronald (2002). Wrongful Conviction and Public Policy. *Criminology* 40(1): 1–18.

Huff, C. Ronald, Arye Rattner, and Edward Sagarin (1996). *Convicted but Innocent: Wrongful Conviction and Public Policy*. Thousand Oaks, CA: Sage Publications.

Hughes, Kristen A. (2006). *Justice Expenditure and Employment in the United States, 2003*. Washington, DC: Bureau of Justice Statistics, U.S. Department of Justice.

Innocence Project (2007). *Police and Prosecutorial Misconduct*. http://www.innocenceproject.org/understand/Government-Misconduct.php.

J.E.B. v. Alabama Ex Rel. T.B., 511 U.S. 127 (1994).

Kasindorf, Martin (2003). Rent-a-Judges Forced Out of California Courts. *USA Today* [Online]. http://www.usatoday.com/news/nation/2003–04-24-rentajudge-usat_x.htm.

Kimbrough v. United States, 552 U.S. 85 (2007).

Lacayo, Richard, and Nancy Seufert (1988). Law: Tell It to the Rent-a-Judge. *Time* [Online]. http://www.time.com/time/magazine/article/0,9171,968299,00.html.

"Law: Rent-a-Judge" (1981). *Time* [Online]. http://www.time.com/time/magazine/article/0,9171,952989,00.html.

Legal Information Institute (2010). *Kimbrough v. United States* (No. 06–6330). Cornell University Law School. http://www.law.cornell.edu/supct/html/06–6330.ZS.html.

Lentz, Susan (2009). Making a Difference: An Overview of Gender and the Courts. In *Courts and Justice*, 4th ed., ed. G. Larry Mays and Peter R. Gregware, 443–64. Long Grove, IL: Waveland Press.

Lubet, Steven (1998). Judicial Discipline and Judicial Independence. *Law and Contemporary Problems* 61(3): 59–74.

Mays, G. Larry, Noreen Purcell, and L. Thomas, Winfree, Jr. (1992). DNA (Deoxyribonucleic Acid) Evidence, Criminal Law, and Felony Prosecutions: Issues and Prospects. *The Justice System Journal* 16(1): 111–22.

Mays, G. Larry, and Rick Ruddell (2008). *Making Sense of Criminal Justice*. New York: Oxford University Press.

Mays, G. Larry, and William A. Taggart (1986). Court Clerks, Court Administrators, and Judges: Conflict in Managing the Courts. *Journal of Criminal Justice* 14(1): 1–7.

Mikkelson, Randall (2007). Supreme Court Allows Lighter Crack Cocaine Terms. Reuters, December 10. http://www.reuters.com/article/idUSN1119916620071210.

Miller v. Pate, 386 U.S. 1 (1967).

Nagel, Ilene H., and Barry L. Johnson (1994). The Role of Gender in a Structured Sentencing System: Equal Treatment, Policy Choices, and the Sentencing of Female Offenders under the United States Sentencing Guidelines. *Journal of Criminal Law and Criminology* 85(1): 181–221.

Purcell, Noreen, L. Thomas Winfree, Jr., and G. Larry Mays (1994). DNA (Deoxyribonucleic Acid) Evidence and Criminal Trials: An Exploratory Survey of Factors Associated with the Use of "Genetic Fingerprinting" in Felony Prosecutions. *Journal of Criminal Justice* 22(2): 145–57.

Reid, Traciel V. (1999). The Politicization of Retention Elections. *Judicature* 83(2): 68–77.

Reiman, Jeffrey (2006). *The Rich Get Richer and the Poor Get Prison*, 8th ed. Boston: Allyn & Bacon.

Rutledge, John P. (2001). They All Look Alike: The Inaccuracy of Cross-Racial Identifications. *American Journal of Criminal Law* 28(2): 207–28.

Sabol, William J., and Heather Couture (2008). *Prison Inmates at Midyear 2007*. Washington, DC: Bureau of Justice Statistics, U.S. Department of Justice.

Saari, David (1982). *American Court Management*. Westport, CT: Quorum Books.

Scheck, Barry, Peter Neufeld, and Jim Dwyer (2000). *Actual Innocence*. New York: Doubleday.

Smith, David, Christy A. Visher, and L. A. Davidson (1984). Equity and Discretionary Justice: The Influence of Race on Police Arrest Decisions. *Journal of Criminal Law and Criminology* 75:234–59.

Tang, Kwong-leung (1998). Rape Law Reform in Canada: The Success and Limitation of Legislation. *International Journal of Offender Therapy and Comparative Criminology* 42(3): 258–70.

Tobias, Carl (2009). Diversity on the Federal Bench. *The National Law Journal*, October 12. http://www.law.com/jsp/nlj/PubArticleNLJ.jsp?id=1202434429480&hbxlogin=1.

United States v. Cronic, 466 U.S 648 (1984).

USLaw.com (2009). Women and the Law. http://www.uslaw.com/library/article/ABAWomenJustice.html.

Vago, Steven (2009). *Law & Society*, 9th ed. Upper Saddle River, NJ: Pearson/Prentice Hall.

Van Wormer, Katherine, and Clemens Bartollas (2007). *Women and the Criminal Justice System*, 2nd ed. Upper Saddle River, NJ: Pearson/Prentice Hall.

Visher, Christy A. (1983). Gender, Police Arrest Decisions, and Notions of Chivalry. *Criminology* 21:5–28.

APPENDIX: THE CONSTITUTION OF THE UNITED STATES AND AMENDMENTS

PREAMBLE

We the People of the United States, in order to form a more perfect Union, establish Justice, insure domestic Tranquility, provide for the common defense, promote the general Welfare, and secure the Blessings of Liberty to ourselves and our Posterity, do ordain and establish this Constitution for the United States of America.

ARTICLE I
SECTION 1

All legislative Powers herein granted shall be vested in a Congress of the United States, which shall consist of a Senate and House of Representatives.

SECTION 2

The House of Representatives shall be composed of Members chosen every second Year by the People of the several States, and the Electors in each State shall have the Qualifications requisite for electors of the most numerous Branch of the State Legislature.

No Person shall be a Representative who shall not have attained to the Age of twenty five Years, and been seven Years a Citizen of the United States, and who shall not, when elected, be an inhabitant of that State in which he shall be chosen.

Representatives and direct Taxes shall be apportioned among the several States which may be included within this Union, according to their respective Numbers, which shall be determined by adding to the whole Number of free Persons, including those bound to Service for a Term of Years, and excluding Indians not taxed, three fifths of all other Persons. The actual Enumeration shall be made within three Years after the first meeting of the Congress of the United States, and within every subsequent Term of ten Years, in such Manner as they shall by Law direct. The number of Representatives shall not exceed one for every thirty Thousand, but each State shall have at least one Representative; and until such enumeration shall be made, the State of New Hampshire shall be entitled to chuse three, Massachusetts eight, Rhode Island and Providence Plantations one, Connecticut five, New York six, New Jersey four, Pennsylvania eight, Delaware one, Maryland six, Virginia ten, North Carolina five, South Carolina five, and Georgia three.

When vacancies happen in the Representation from any State, the Executive Authority thereof shall issue Writs of Election to fill such Vacancies.

The House of Representatives shall chuse their Speaker and other Officers; and shall have the sole Power of Impeachment.

SECTION 3

The Senate of the United States shall be composed of two Senators from each State, chosen by the Legislature thereof, for six Years; and each Senator shall have one Vote.

Immediately after they shall be assembled in Consequence of the first Election, they shall be divided as equally as may be into three Classes. The Seats of the Senators of the first Class shall be vacated at the Expiration of the second Year, of the second Class at the Expiration of the fourth Year, and the third Class at the expiration of the sixth Year, so that one third may be chosen every second Year; and if Vacancies happen by Resignation, or otherwise, during the Recess of the Legislature of any State, the Executive thereof may make temporary Appointments until the next meeting of the Legislature, which shall then fill such Vacancies.

No person shall be a Senator who shall not have attained to the Age of thirty Years, and been nine Years a Citizen of the United States, and who shall not, when elected, be an Inhabitant of that State for which he shall be chosen.

The Vice President of the United States shall be President of the Senate, but shall have no Vote, unless they be equally divided.

The Senate shall chuse their other Officers, and also a President pro tempore, in the absence of the Vice President, or when he shall exercise the Office of President of the United States.

The Senate shall have the sole Power to try all Impeachments. When sitting for that Purpose, they shall be on Oath or Affirmation. When the President of the United States is tried, the Chief Justice shall preside: And no Person shall be convicted without the Concurrence of two thirds of the Members present.

Judgment in Cases of Impeachment shall not extend further than to removal from Office, and disqualification to hold and enjoy any Office of honor, Trust or Profit under the United States: but the Party convicted shall nevertheless be liable and subject to Indictment, Trial, Judgment and Punishment, according to Law.

SECTION 4

The Times, Places and Manner of holding Elections for Senators and Representatives, shall be prescribed in each state by the Legislature thereof; but the Congress may at any time by Law make or alter such Regulations, except as to the Place of Chusing Senators.

The Congress shall assemble at least once in every Year, and such Meeting shall be on the first Monday in December, unless they shall by Law appoint a different Day.

SECTION 5

Each House shall be the Judge of the Elections, Returns and Qualifications of its own Members, and a Majority of each shall constitute a Quorum to do Business; but a smaller number may adjourn from day to day, and may be authorized to compel the Attendance of absent Members, in such Manner, and under such Penalties as each House may provide.

Each House may determine the Rules of its Proceedings, punish its Members for disorderly Behavior, and, with the Concurrence of two-thirds, expel a Member.

Each House shall keep a Journal of its Proceedings, and from time to time publish the same, excepting such Parts as may in their Judgment require Secrecy; and the Yeas and Nays of the Members of either House on any question shall, at the desire of one fifth of those Present, be entered on the Journal.

Neither House, during the Session of Congress, shall, without the Consent of the other, adjourn for more than three days, nor to any other Place than that in which the two Houses shall be sitting.

SECTION 6

The Senators and Representatives shall receive a Compensation for their Services, to be ascertained by Law, and paid out of the Treasury of the United States. They shall in all Cases, except Treason, Felony and Breach of the Peace, be privileged from Arrest during their Attendance at the Session of their respective Houses, and in going to and returning from the same; and for any Speech or Debate in either House, they shall not be questioned in any other Place.

No Senator or Representative shall, during the Time for which he was elected, be appointed to any civil Office under the Authority of the United States which shall have been created, or the Emoluments whereof shall have been increased during such time; and no Person holding any Office under the United States, shall be a Member of either House during his Continuance in Office.

SECTION 7

All bills for raising Revenue shall originate in the House of Representatives; but the Senate may propose or concur with Amendments as on other Bills.

Every Bill which shall have passed the House of Representatives and the Senate, shall, before it become a Law, be presented to the President of the United States; If he approve he shall sign it, but if not he shall return it, with his Objections to that House in which it shall have originated, who shall enter the Objections at large on their Journal, and proceed to reconsider it. If after such Reconsideration two thirds of that House shall agree to pass the Bill, it shall be sent, together with the Objections, to the other House, by which it shall likewise be reconsidered, and if approved by two thirds of that House, it shall become a Law. But in all such Cases the Votes of both Houses shall be determined by Yeas and Nays, and the Names of the Persons voting for and against the Bill shall be entered on the Journal of each House respectively. If any Bill shall not be returned by the President within ten Days (Sundays excepted) after it shall have been presented to him, the Same shall be a Law, in like Manner as if he had signed it, unless the Congress by their Adjournment prevent its Return, in which Case it shall not be a Law.

Every Order, Resolution, or Vote to which the Concurrence of the Senate and House of Representatives may be necessary (except on a question of Adjournment) shall be presented to the President of the United States; and before the Same shall take Effect, shall be approved by him, or being disapproved by him, shall be repassed by two thirds of the Senate and House of Representatives, according to the Rules and Limitations prescribed in the case of a Bill.

SECTION 8

The Congress shall have Power To lay and collect Taxes, Duties, Imposts and Excises, to pay the Debts and provide for the common Defence and general Welfare of the United States; but all duties, Imposts and Excises shall be uniform throughout the United States;

To borrow money on the credit of the United States;

To regulate Commerce with foreign Nations, and among the several States, and with the Indian Tribes;

To establish a uniform Rule of Naturalization, and uniform Laws on the subject of Bankruptcies throughout the United States;

To coin Money, regulate the Value thereof, and of foreign Coin, and fix the Standard of Weights and Measures;

To provide for the Punishment of counterfeiting the Securities and current Coin of the United States;

To establish Post Offices and Post Roads;

To promote the Progress of Science and useful Arts, by securing for limited Times to Authors and Inventors the exclusive Right to their respective Writings and Discoveries;

To constitute Tribunals inferior to the supreme Court;

To define and punish Piracies and Felonies committed on the high Seas, and Offenses against the Law of Nations;

To declare War, grant Letters of Marque and Reprisal, and make rules concerning Captures on Land and Water;

To raise and support Armies, but no Appropriation of Money to that Use shall be for a longer Term than two Years;

To provide and maintain a Navy;

To make Rules for the Government and Regulation of the land and naval Forces;

To provide for calling forth the Militia to execute the Laws of the Union, suppress Insurrections and repel Invasions;

To provide for organizing, arming, and disciplining the Militia, and for governing such Part of them as may be employed in the Service of the United States, reserving to the States respectively, the Appointment of the Officers, and the Authority of training the Militia according to the discipline prescribed by Congress;

To exercise exclusive Legislation in all Cases whatsoever, over such District (not exceeding ten Miles square) as may, by Cession of particular States, and the acceptance of Congress, become the Seat of the government of the United States, and to exercise like

Authority over all Places purchased by the Consent of the Legislature of the State in which the Same shall be, for the Erection of Forts, Magazines, Arsenals, Dockyards, and other needful Buildings; And

To make all Laws which shall be necessary and proper for carrying into Execution the foregoing powers, and all other Powers vested by this Constitution in the Government of the United States, or in any Department or Officer thereof.

SECTION 9

The Migration or Importation of such Persons as any of the States now existing shall think proper to admit, shall not be prohibited by the Congress prior to the Year one thousand eight hundred and eight, but a tax or duty may be imposed on such Importation, not exceeding ten dollars for each Person.

The privilege of the Writ of Habeas corpus shall not be suspended, unless when in Cases of Rebellion or Invasion the public Safety may require it.

No Bill of Attainder or ex post facto Law shall be passed.

No capitation, or other direct, Tax shall be laid, unless in Proportion to the Census or Enumeration herein before directed to be taken.

No Tax or Duty shall be laid on Articles exported from any State.

No Preference shall be given by any Regulation of Commerce or Revenue to the Ports of one State over those of another: nor shall Vessels bound to, or from, one State, be obliged to enter, clear, or pay Duties in another.

No Money shall be drawn from the Treasury, but in Consequence of Appropriations made by Law; and a regular Statement and Account of Receipts and Expenditures of all public Money shall be published from time to time.

No Title of Nobility shall be granted by the United States: And no Person holding any Office of Profit or Trust under them, shall, without the Consent of the Congress, accept of any present, Emolument, Office, or Title, of any kind whatever, from any King, Prince, or foreign State.

SECTION 10

No State shall enter into any Treaty, Alliance, or Confederation; grant Letters of Marque and Reprisal; coin Money; emit Bills of Credit; make any Thing but gold and silver Coin a Tender in Payment of Debts; pass any Bill of Attainder, ex post facto Law, or Law impairing the Obligation of Contracts, or grant any Title of Nobility.

No State shall, without the Consent of the Congress, lay any Imposts or Duties on Imports or Exports, except what may be absolutely necessary for executing its inspection Laws: and the net Produce of all Duties and Imposts, laid by any State on Imports or Exports, shall be for the Use of the Treasury of the United States; and all such Laws shall be subject to the Revision and Controul of the Congress.

No State shall, without the Consent of Congress, lay any duty of Tonnage, keep Troops, or Ships of War in time of Peace, enter into any Agreement or Compact with another State, or with a foreign Power, or engage in War, unless actually invaded, or in such imminent Danger as will not admit of delay.

ARTICLE II
SECTION 1

The executive Power shall be vested in a President of the United States of America. He shall hold his Office during the Term of four Years, and, together with the Vice-President, chosen for the same term, be elected, as follows:

Each state shall appoint, in such Manner as the Legislature thereof may direct, a Number of Electors, equal to the whole Number of Senators and Representatives to which the State may be entitled in the Congress: but no Senator or Representative, or Person holding an Office of Trust or Profit under the United States, shall be appointed an elector.

The Electors shall meet in their respective States, and vote by Ballot for two persons, of whom one at least shall not be an Inhabitant of the same State with themselves. And they shall make a List of all the Persons voted for, and of the Number of Votes for each; which List they shall sign and certify, and transmit sealed to the Seat of the Government of the United States, directed to the President of the Senate. The President of the Senate shall, in the Presence of the Senate and House of Representatives, open all the Certificates, and the Votes shall then be counted. The Person having the greatest Number of Votes shall be the President, if such Number be a Majority of the whole Number of Electors appointed; and if there be more than one who have such Majority, and have an equal Number of Votes, then the House of Representatives shall immediately chuse by Ballot one of them for President; and if no Person have a Majority, then from the five highest on the List the said House shall in like Manner chuse the President. But in chusing the President, the Votes shall be taken by States, the Representation from each State having one vote; a quorum for this Purpose shall consist of a Member or Members from two-thirds of the States, and a Majority of all the States shall be necessary to a Choice. In every Case, after the Choice of the President, the Person having the greatest Number of Votes of the Electors shall be the Vice President. But if there should remain two or more who have equal Votes, the Senate shall chuse from them by Ballot the Vice-President.

The Congress may determine the Time of chusing the Electors, and the Day on which they shall give their Votes; which Day shall be the same throughout the United States.

No person except a natural born Citizen, or a citizen of the United States, at the time of the Adoption of this Constitution, shall be eligible to the Office of President; neither shall any Person be eligible to that Office who shall not have attained to the Age of thirty five Years, and been fourteen Years a resident within the United States.

In Case of the Removal of the President from Office, or of his Death, Resignation, or Inability to discharge the Powers and Duties of the said Office, the same shall devolve on the Vice President, and the Congress may by Law provide for the Case of Removal, Death, Resignation or Inability, both of the President and Vice President, declaring what Officer shall then act as President, and such Officer shall act accordingly, until the Disability be removed, or a President shall be elected.

The President shall, at stated Times, receive for his Services, a Compensation, which shall neither be increased nor diminished during the Period for which he shall have been elected, and he shall not receive within that Period any other Emolument from the United States, or any of them.

Before he enter on the Execution of his Office, he shall take the following Oath or Affirmation:

"I do solemnly swear (or affirm) that I will faithfully execute the Office of President of the United States, and will to the best of my Ability, preserve, protect and defend the Constitution of the United States."

SECTION 2
The President shall be Commander in Chief of the Army and Navy of the United States, and of the Militia of the several States, when called into the actual Service of the United States; he may require the Opinion, in writing, of the principal Officer in each of the

executive Departments, upon any subject relating to the Duties of their respective Offices, and he shall have Power to Grant Reprieves and Pardons for Offenses against the United States, except in Cases of Impeachment.

He shall have Power, by and with the Advice and Consent of the Senate, to make Treaties, provided two thirds of the Senators present concur; and he shall nominate, and by and with the Advice and Consent of the Senate, shall appoint Ambassadors, other public Ministers and Consuls, Judges of the supreme Court, and all other Officers of the United States, whose Appointments are not herein otherwise provided for, and which shall be established by Law: but the Congress may by Law vest the Appointment of such inferior Officers, as they think proper, in the President alone, in the Courts of Law, or in the Heads of Departments.

The President shall have Power to fill up all Vacancies that may happen during the Recess of the Senate, by granting Commissions which shall expire at the End of their next Session.

SECTION 3
He shall from time to time give to the Congress Information of the State of the Union, and recommend to their Consideration such Measures as he shall judge necessary and expedient; he may, on extraordinary Occasions, convene both Houses, or either of them, and in Case of Disagreement between them, with Respect to the Time of Adjournment, he may adjourn them to such Time as he shall think proper; he shall receive Ambassadors and other public Ministers; he shall take Care that the Laws be faithfully executed, and shall Commission all the Officers of the United States.

SECTION 4
The President, Vice President and all civil Officers of the United States, shall be removed from Office on Impeachment for, and Conviction of, Treason, Bribery, or other high Crimes and Misdemeanors.

ARTICLE III
SECTION 1
The judicial Power of the United States, shall be vested in one supreme Court, and in such inferior Courts as the Congress may from time to time ordain and establish. The Judges, both of the supreme and inferior Courts, shall hold their Offices during good Behavior, and shall, at stated Times, receive for their Services a Compensation which shall not be diminished during their Continuance in Office.

SECTION 2
The judicial Power shall extend to all Cases, in Law and Equity, arising under this Constitution, the Laws of the United States, and Treaties made, or which shall be made, under their Authority; to all Cases affecting Ambassadors, other public Ministers and Consuls; to all Cases of admiralty and maritime Jurisdiction; to Controversies to

which the United States shall be a Party; to Controversies between two or more States; between a State and Citizens of another State; between Citizens of different States; between Citizens of the same State claiming Lands under Grants of different States, and between a State, or the Citizens thereof, and foreign States, Citizens or Subjects.

In all Cases affecting Ambassadors, other public Ministers and Consuls, and those in which a State shall be Party, the Supreme Court shall have original Jurisdiction. In all the other Cases before mentioned, the supreme Court shall have appellate Jurisdiction, both as to Law and Fact, with such Exceptions, and under such Regulations as the Congress shall make.

The Trial of all Crimes, except in cases of Impeachment, shall be by Jury; and such Trial shall be held in the State where the said Crimes shall have been committed; but when not committed within any State, the Trial shall be at such Place or Places as the Congress may by Law have directed.

SECTION 3

Treason against the United States, shall consist only in levying War against them, or in adhering to their Enemies, giving them Aid and Comfort. No Person shall be convicted of Treason unless on the Testimony of two Witnesses to the same overt Act, or on Confession in open Court.

The Congress shall have power to declare the Punishment of Treason, but no Attainder of Treason shall work Corruption of Blood, or Forfeiture except during the Life of the Person attainted.

ARTICLE IV
SECTION 1

Full Faith and Credit shall be given in each State to the public Acts, Records, and judicial Proceedings of every other State. And the Congress may by general Laws prescribe the Manner in which such Acts, Records, and Proceedings shall be proved, and the Effect thereof.

SECTION 2

The Citizens of each State shall be entitled to all Privileges and Immunities of Citizens in the several States.

A Person charged in any State with Treason, Felony, or other Crime, who shall flee from Justice, and be found in another State, shall on demand of the executive Authority of the State from which he fled, be delivered up, to be removed to the State having Jurisdiction of the Crime.

No Person held to Service or Labour in one State, under the Laws thereof, escaping into another, shall, in Consequence of any Law or Regulation therein, be discharged from such Service or Labour, But shall be delivered up on Claim of the Party to whom such Service or Labour may be due.

SECTION 3

New States may be admitted by the Congress into this Union; but no new States shall be formed or erected within the Jurisdiction of any other State; nor any State be formed by the Junction of two or more States, or parts of States, without the Consent of the Legislatures of the States concerned as well as of the Congress.

The Congress shall have Power to dispose of and make all needful Rules and Regulations respecting the Territory or other Property belonging to the United States; and nothing in this Constitution shall be so construed as to Prejudice any claims of the United States, or of any particular State.

SECTION 4

The United States shall guarantee to every State in this Union a Republican Form of Government, and shall protect each of them against Invasion; and on Application of the Legislature, or of the Executive (when the Legislature cannot be convened) against domestic Violence.

ARTICLE V

The Congress, whenever two thirds of both Houses shall deem it necessary, shall propose Amendments to this Constitution, or, on the Application of the Legislatures of two thirds of the several States, shall call a Convention for proposing Amendments, which, in either Case, shall be valid to all Intents and Purposes, as part of this Constitution, when ratified by the Legislatures of three fourths of the several States, or by Conventions in three fourths thereof, as the one or the other Mode of Ratification may be proposed by the Congress; Provided that no Amendment which may be made prior to the Year One thousand eight hundred and eight shall in any Manner affect the first and fourth Clauses in the Ninth Section of the first Article; and that no State, without its Consent, shall be deprived of its equal Suffrage in the Senate.

ARTICLE VI

All Debts contracted and Engagements entered into, before the Adoption of this Constitution, shall be as valid against the United States under this Constitution, as under the Confederation.

This Constitution, and the Laws of the United States which shall be made in Pursuance thereof; and all Treaties made, or which shall be made, under the Authority of the United States, shall be the supreme Law of the Land; and the Judges in every State shall be bound thereby, any Thing in the Constitution or Laws of any State to the Contrary notwithstanding.

The Senators and Representatives before mentioned, and the Members of the several State Legislatures, and all executive and judicial Officers, both of the United States and of the several States, shall be bound by Oath or Affirmation, to support this Constitution; but no religious Test shall ever be required as a Qualification to any Office or public Trust under the United States.

ARTICLE VII

The Ratification of the Conventions of nine States, shall be sufficient for the Establishment of this Constitution between the States so ratifying the Same.

Done in Convention by the Unanimous Consent of the States present the Seventeenth Day of September in the Year of our Lord one thousand seven hundred and Eighty seven and of the Independence of the United States of America the Twelfth. In Witness whereof We have hereunto subscribed our Names.

> Go. Washington—President and deputy from Virginia
> New Hampshire—John Langdon, Nicholas Gilman
> Massachusetts—Nathaniel Gorham, Rufus King
> Connecticut—Wm Saml Johnson, Roger Sherman
> New York—Alexander Hamilton
> New Jersey—Wil Livingston, David Brearly, Wm Paterson, Jona. Dayton
> Pennsylvania—B Franklin, Thomas Mifflin, Robt. Morris, Geo. Clymer, Thos. FitzSimons, Jared Ingersoll, James Wilson, Gouv Morris
> Delaware—Geo. Read, Gunning Bedford jun, John Dickinson, Richard Bassett, Jaco. Broom
> Maryland—James McHenry, Dan of St Thos. Jenifer, Danl. Carroll
> Virginia—John Blair, James Madison Jr.
> North Carolina—Wm Blount, Richd Dobbs Spaight, Hu Williamson
> South Carolina—J. Rutledge, Charles Cotesworth Pinckney, Charles Pinckney, Pierce Butler
> Georgia—William Few, Abr Baldwin
> Attest: William Jackson, Secretary

BILL OF RIGHTS (RATIFIED DECEMBER 15, 1791)
AMENDMENT 1

Congress shall make no law respecting an establishment of religion, or prohibiting the free exercise thereof; or abridging the freedom of speech, or of the press; or the right of the people peaceably to assemble, and to petition the Government for a redress of grievances.

AMENDMENT 2

A well regulated Militia, being necessary to the security of a free State, the right of the people to keep and bear Arms, shall not be infringed.

AMENDMENT 3

No Soldier shall, in time of peace be quartered in any house, without the consent of the Owner, nor in time of war, but in a manner to be prescribed by law.

AMENDMENT 4

The right of the people to be secure in their persons, houses, papers, and effects, against unreasonable searches and seizures, shall not be violated, and no Warrants shall issue, but upon probable cause, supported by Oath or affirmation, and particularly describing the place to be searched, and the persons or things to be seized.

AMENDMENT 5

No person shall be held to answer for a capital, or otherwise infamous crime, unless on a presentment or indictment of a Grand Jury, except in cases arising in the land or naval forces, or in the Militia, when in actual service in time of War or public danger; nor shall any person be subject for the same offense to be twice put in jeopardy of life or limb; nor shall be compelled in any criminal case to be a witness against himself, nor be deprived of life, liberty, or property, without due process of law; nor shall private property be taken for public use, without just compensation.

AMENDMENT 6

In all criminal prosecutions, the accused shall enjoy the right to a speedy and public trial, by an impartial jury of the State and district wherein the crime shall have been committed, which district shall have been previously ascertained by law, and to be informed of the nature and cause of the accusation; to be confronted with the witnesses against him; to have compulsory process for obtaining witnesses in his favor, and to have Assistance of Counsel for his defence.

AMENDMENT 7

In Suits at common law, where the value in controversy shall exceed twenty dollars, the right of trial by jury shall be preserved, and no fact tried by a jury, shall be otherwise re-examined in any Court of the United States, than according to the rules of the common law.

AMENDMENT 8

Excessive bail shall not be required, nor excessive fines imposed, nor cruel and unusual punishments inflicted.

AMENDMENT 9

The enumeration in the Constitution, of certain rights, shall not be construed to deny or disparage others retained by the people.

AMENDMENT 10

The powers not delegated to the United States by the Constitution, nor prohibited by it to the States, are reserved to the States respectively, or to the people.

OTHER AMENDMENTS TO THE CONSTITUTION
AMENDMENT 11 (RATIFIED FEBRUARY 7, 1795)

The Judicial power of the United States shall not be construed to extend to any suit in law or equity, commenced or prosecuted against one of the United States by Citizens of another State, or by Citizens or Subjects of any Foreign State.

AMENDMENT 12 (RATIFIED JUNE 15, 1804)

The Electors shall meet in their respective states and vote by ballot for President and Vice-President, one of whom, at least, shall not be an inhabitant of the same state with themselves; they shall name in their ballots the person voted for as President, and in distinct ballots the person voted for as Vice-President, and they shall make distinct lists of all persons voted for as President, and of all persons voted for as Vice-President, and of the number of votes for each, which lists they shall sign and certify, and transmit sealed to the seat of the government of the United States, directed to the President of the Senate;

The President of the Senate shall, in the presence of the Senate and House of Representatives, open all the certificates and the votes shall then be counted;

The person having the greatest number of votes for President, shall be the President, if such number be a majority of the whole number of Electors appointed; and if no person have such majority, then from the persons having the highest numbers not exceeding three on the list of those voted for as President, the House of Representatives shall choose immediately, by ballot, the President. But in choosing the President, the votes shall be taken by states, the representation from each state having one vote; a quorum for this purpose shall consist of a member or members from two-thirds of the states, and a majority of all the states shall be necessary to a choice. And if the House of Representatives shall not choose a President whenever the right of choice shall devolve upon then, before the fourth day of March next following, then the Vice-President shall act as President, as in the case of the death or other constitutional disability of the President.

The person having the greatest number of votes as Vice-President, shall be the Vice-President, if such number be a majority of the whole number of Electors appointed, and if no person have a majority, then from the two highest numbers on the list, the Senate shall choose the Vice-President; a quorum for the purpose shall consist of two-thirds of the whole number of Senators, and a majority of the whole number shall be necessary to a choice. But no person constitutionally ineligible to the office of President shall be eligible to that of Vice-President of the United States.

AMENDMENT 13 (RATIFIED DECEMBER 6, 1865)

1. Neither slavery nor involuntary servitude, except as a punishment for crime whereof the party shall have been duly convicted, shall exist within the United States, or any place subject to their jurisdiction.
2. Congress shall have power to enforce this article by appropriate legislation.

AMENDMENT 14 (RATIFIED JULY 9, 1868)

1. All persons born or naturalized in the United States, and subject to the jurisdiction thereof, are citizens of the United States and of the State wherein they reside. No State shall make or enforce any law which shall abridge the privileges or immunities of citizens of the United States; nor shall any State deprive any person of life, liberty, or property, without due process of law; nor deny to any person within its jurisdiction the equal protection of the laws.

2. Representatives shall be apportioned among the several States according to their respective numbers, counting the whole number of persons in each State, excluding Indians not taxed. But when the right to vote at any election for the choice of electors for President and Vice President of the United States, Representatives in Congress, the Executive and Judicial officers of a State, or the members of the Legislature thereof, is denied to any of the male inhabitants of such State, being twenty-one years of age, and citizens of the United States, or in any way abridged, except for participation in rebellion, or other crime, the basis of representation therein shall be reduced in the proportion which the number of such male citizens shall bear to the whole number of male citizens twenty-one years of age in such State.

3. No person shall be a Senator or Representative in Congress, or elector of President and Vice-President, or hold any office, civil or military, under the United States, or under any State, who, having previously taken an oath, as a member of Congress, or as an officer of the United States, or as a member of any State legislature, or as an executive or judicial officer of any State, to support the Constitution of the United States, shall have engaged in insurrection or rebellion against the same, or given aid or comfort to the enemies thereof. But Congress may by a vote of two-thirds of each House, remove such disability.

4. The validity of the public debt of the United States, authorized by law, including debts incurred for payment of pensions and bounties for services in suppressing insurrection or rebellion, shall not be questioned. But neither the United States nor any State shall assume or pay any debt or obligation incurred in aid of insurrection or rebellion against the United States, or any claim for the loss or emancipation of any slave; but all such debts, obligations and claims shall be held illegal and void.

5. The Congress shall have power to enforce, by appropriate legislation, the provisions of this article.

AMENDMENT 15 (RATIFIED FEBRUARY 3, 1870)

1. The right of citizens of the United States to vote shall not be denied or abridged by the United States or by any State on account of race, color, or previous condition of servitude.

2. The Congress shall have power to enforce this article by appropriate legislation.

AMENDMENT 16 (RATIFIED FEBRUARY 3, 1913)

The Congress shall have power to lay and collect taxes on incomes, from whatever source derived, without apportionment among the several States, and without regard to any census or enumeration.

AMENDMENT 17 (RATIFIED APRIL 8, 1913)

The Senate of the United States shall be composed of two Senators from each State, elected by the people thereof for six years; and each Senator shall have one vote. The electors in each State shall have the qualifications requisite for electors of the most numerous branch of the State legislatures.

When vacancies happen in the representation of any State in the Senate, the executive authority of such State shall issue writs of election to fill such vacancies: Provided, that the legislature of any State may empower the executive thereof to make temporary appointments until the people fill the vacancies by election as the legislature may direct.

This amendment shall not be so construed as to affect the election or term of any Senator chosen before it becomes valid as part of the Constitution.

AMENDMENT 18 (RATIFIED JANUARY 16, 1919)

1. After one year from the ratification of this article the manufacture, sale, or transportation of intoxicating liquors within, the importation thereof into, or the exportation thereof from the United States and all territory subject to the jurisdiction thereof for beverage purposes is hereby prohibited.

2. The Congress and the several States shall have concurrent power to enforce this article by appropriate legislation.

3. This article shall be inoperative unless it shall have been ratified as an amendment to the Constitution by the legislatures of the several States as provided in the Constitution, within seven years from the date of the submission hereof to the States by the Congress.

AMENDMENT 19 (RATIFIED AUGUST 18, 1920)

The right of citizens of the United States to vote shall not be denied or abridged by the United States or by any State on account of sex.

Congress shall have power to enforce this article by appropriate legislation.

AMENDMENT 20 (RATIFIED JANUARY 23, 1933)

1. The terms of the President and Vice President shall end at noon on the 20th day of January, and the terms of Senators and Representatives at noon on the 3d day of January, of the years in which such terms would have ended if this article had not been ratified; and the terms of their successors shall then begin.

2. The Congress shall assemble at least once in every year, and such meeting shall begin at noon on the 3d day of January, unless they shall by law appoint a different day.

3. If, at the time fixed for the beginning of the term of the President, the President elect shall have died, the Vice President elect shall become President. If a President shall not have been chosen before the time fixed for the beginning of his term, or if the President elect shall have failed to qualify, then the Vice President elect shall act as President until a President shall have qualified; and the Congress may by law provide for the case wherein neither a President elect nor a Vice President elect shall have qualified, declaring who shall then act as President, or the manner in which one who is to act shall be selected, and such person shall act accordingly until a President or Vice President shall have qualified.

4. The Congress may by law provide for the case of the death of any of the persons from whom the House of Representatives may choose a President whenever the right of choice shall have devolved upon them, and for the case of the death of any of the persons from whom the Senate may choose a Vice President whenever the right of choice shall have devolved upon them.

5. Sections 1 and 2 shall take effect on the 15th day of October following the ratification of this article.

6. This article shall be inoperative unless it shall have been ratified as an amendment to the Constitution by the legislatures of three-fourths of the several States within seven years from the date of its submission.

AMENDMENT 21 (RATIFIED DECEMBER 5, 1933)

1. The eighteenth article of amendment to the Constitution of the United States is hereby repealed.

2. The transportation or importation into any State, Territory, or possession of the United States for delivery or use therein of intoxicating liquors, in violation of the laws thereof, is hereby prohibited.

3. This article shall be inoperative unless it shall have been ratified as an amendment to the Constitution by conventions in the several States, as provided in the Constitution, within seven years from the date of the submission hereof to the States by the Congress.

AMENDMENT 22 (RATIFIED FEBRAURY 27, 1951)

1. No person shall be elected to the office of the President more than twice, and no person who has held the office of President, or acted as President, for more than two years of a term to which some other person was elected President shall be elected to the office of the President more than once. But this Article shall not apply to any person holding the office of President when this Article was proposed by the Congress, and shall not prevent any person who may be holding the office of President, or acting as President, during the term within which this Article

becomes operative from holding the office of President or acting as President during the remainder of such term.

2. This Article shall be inoperative unless it shall have been ratified as an amendment to the Constitution by the legislatures of three-fourths of the several States within seven years from the date of its submission to the States by the Congress.

AMENDMENT 23 (RATIFIED MARCH 29, 1961)

1. The District constituting the seat of Government of the United States shall appoint in such manner as the Congress may direct: A number of electors of President and Vice President equal to the whole number of Senators and Representatives in Congress to which the District would be entitled if it were a State, but in no event more than the least populous State; they shall be in addition to those appointed by the States, but they shall be considered, for the purposes of the election of President and Vice President, to be electors appointed by a State; and they shall meet in the District and perform such duties as provided by the twelfth article of amendment.

2. The Congress shall have power to enforce this article by appropriate legislation.

AMENDMENT 24 (RATIFIED JANUARY 23, 1964)

1. The right of citizens of the United States to vote in any primary or other election for President or Vice President, for electors for President or Vice President, or for Senator or Representative in Congress, shall not be denied or abridged by the United States or any State by reason of failure to pay any poll tax or other tax.

2. The Congress shall have power to enforce this article by appropriate legislation.

AMENDMENT 25 (RATIFIED FEBRUARY 10, 1967)

1. In case of the removal of the President from office or of his death or resignation, the Vice President shall become President.

2. Whenever there is a vacancy in the office of the Vice President, the President shall nominate a Vice President who shall take office upon confirmation by a majority vote of both Houses of Congress.

3. Whenever the President transmits to the President pro tempore of the Senate and the Speaker of the House of Representatives his written declaration that he is unable to discharge the powers and duties of his office, and until he transmits to them a written declaration to the contrary, such powers and duties shall be discharged by the Vice President as Acting President.

4. Whenever the Vice president and a majority of either the principal officers of the executive departments or of such other body as Congress may by law provide, transmit to the President pro tempore of the Senate and the Speaker of the House of Representatives their written declaration that the President is unable to discharge the powers and duties of his office, the Vice President shall immediately assume the powers and duties of the office as Acting President. Thereafter, when the President transmits to the President pro tempore of the Senate and the Speaker of the House of Representatives his written declaration that no inability exists, he shall resume the powers and duties of his office unless the Vice President and a majority of either the principal officers of the executive department or of such other body as Congress may by law provide, transmit within four days to the President pro tempore of the Senate and the Speaker of the House of Representatives their written declaration that the President is unable to discharge the powers and duties of his office. Thereupon Congress shall decide the issue, assembling within forty eight hours for that purpose if not in session. If the Congress, within twenty one days after receipt of the latter written declaration, or, if Congress is not in session, within twenty one days after Congress is required to assemble, determines by two thirds vote of both Houses that the President is unable to discharge the powers and duties of his office, the Vice President shall continue to discharge the same as Acting President; otherwise, the President shall resume the powers and duties of his office.

AMENDMENT 26 (RATIFIED JULY 1, 1971)

1. The right of citizens of the United States, who are eighteen years of age or older, to vote shall not be denied or abridged by the United States or by any State on account of age.

2. The Congress shall have power to enforce this article by appropriate legislation.

AMENDMENT 27 (RATIFIED MAY 7, 1992)

No law varying the compensation for the services of the Senators and Representatives shall take effect until an election of Representatives shall have intervened.

GLOSSARY

NOTE. Numbers in parentheses indicate the chapter(s) in which the term appears.

active probation (8). Probation involving the occasional, regular presence of a probation officer and a proscribed set of conditions.

actus reus (2). A wrongful act; affirmative action toward the commission of a crime.

administrative law (2). Regulatory law that is generated by regulatory or governmental agencies.

Administrative Office of Courts (6,12). State or federal office that serves the judiciary by providing various administrative, legal, management, and other support services.

admiralty (10). Cases involving maritime or marine law and pertaining to navigation of the sea, ships or shipping, seamen, and transportation by sea.

adversarial justice (1). The legal system in the United States in which one side of a court case "wins" and therefore the other side "loses."

advisory opinions (11). Judicial decisions based on hypothetical cases where no real dispute exists.

affirmative defenses (2). Justifications or excuses in which the defendant alleges that the act committed was not wrong; includes defenses such as self-defense, insanity, necessity, duress, and entrapment.

aggravated assaults (2). Typically felonies, aggravated assaults may involve battery (beating) or assault with a weapon or with the purpose of inflicting severe bodily injury.

aggravating circumstances (8). Factors of the crime which make a more severe punishment from the jury appropriate.

alibi (2). Meaning "elsewhere"; an alibi is not an excuse for a crime, but an assertion that the accused was not present at the commission of the crime.

alternative dispute resolution (12). ADR; a system of providing quicker resolution to cases, lower expense, less congestion in the courts system; ADR is most commonly seen as mediation, arbitration, and negotiation.

American Judicature Society (4). A national organization of judges, lawyers, and others who address issues in the legal system such as judicial independence, ethics, and selection; one of the major advocates of court unification and modernization in the United States.

Anti-Federalists (10). Early American political party opposed to a strong central government and in favor of a weak national judiciary.

arbitration (12). A third party (the arbitrator) functions as an impartial judge over a dispute; commonly used in labor, employment, and credit disputes.

arraignment (7). Official procedure in which defendants in a criminal trial are called before the court and presented with the charges filed against them.

arrest (7). The first step in a criminal trial in which the police formally detain and bring the accused into the criminal justice system.

arson (2). The intentional and willful burning, or attempt to burn, a building or property of another.

assigned counsel system (5). Or appointed counsel; one of the systems by which criminal defendants who cannot afford to pay a lawyer are assigned one for free.

attempts (2). A type of criminal offense in which some overt act has been undertaken, but for some reason (beyond the control of the offender) the total offense was not completed. See also **inchoate offenses**.

automatic appeals (11). See **mandatory appeals**.

bail (7). The process by which defendants secure their release pending court hearings; it may involve the payment of an amount of money set by the court to secure the release of the accused prior to the next court appearance.

bail bondsman (7). Private business person who provides surety, property, or cash as bail for a promise that the accused will appear in court at the appointed date.

bailiffs (6). Personnel who are responsible for security and order in the courtroom.

banishment (2). Casting out of a group with the intent that the solitude or restriction is sufficient punishment for their crime; may involve transportation to some distant location.

barristers (5). In-court lawyers in the English legal system.

bench trial(s) (2,7,9,10). A trial over which a judge alone presides without the presence of a jury.

beyond a reasonable doubt (2). The requirement for weight of evidence in a criminal trial; the highest level possible in the standard of proof or persuasion.

bifurcated hearing (8). Hearings in which the determination of guilt is separated from the punishment decision.

blended sentencing (9). Sentencing structures under which juvenile offenders may be sentenced as adults in the case of serious juvenile crime.

bond (7). Any type of surety (money or property, for example) posted in order to make bail.

breaches of contract (9,10). Cases that frequently arise from landlord/tenant disputes or consumer credit loans; any civil case in which one party alleges that the other has failed to honor the terms of a valid contract.

burden of proof (2). Obligation to shift the evidence from one side to another; in a criminal trial, the burden of proof lies with the prosecutor; may also be called the burden of persuasion.

burglary (2). Unlawful entry of a structure with the intent to commit a felony or theft.

canon law (2). Religious or church-made law.

capital punishment (8). This is the provision under state or federal law for the execution of offenders convicted of certain crimes, especially first degree murder.

case or controversy rule (11). Federal courts are not permitted to hear cases that do not pose actual controversy; they are not allowed to issue rulings in hypothetical cases; see **advisory opinions**.

case screening (5). The process by which prosecutors eliminate the weakest or least important cases from their caseload.

challenges for cause (6). During jury selection, jurors can be challenged (or dismissed) for cause if they express prejudice toward either side in the case.

chancery courts (10). Courts of equity, deciding matters such as trusts, real estate, guardianship, and other similar financial affairs.

change of venue (3,7). A pretrial motion asking for a relocation of a trial in order to avoid impressions on a jury which may have been made by pretrial publicity.

charge to the jury (7). Specific instructions provided by the judge prior to the jury deliberation portion of a trial.

checks–and–balances (1). Coequal branches of government exercising their own unique powers and who are also accountable to other branches of government.

chief judge (4). The judge with the longest tenure, under the age of 65, in a federal court district; these judges are responsible for court administration in addition to their other duties.

chivalry hypothesis (8,12). Evidence that the criminal justice system is much less likely to sanction women than men for criminal activity.

circuit riding (10,11). The judicial practice of hearing oral arguments at multiple locations within a particular jurisdiction, or circuit.

civil death (6). Disqualifying felons from jury service, voting, or other civil liberties as a result of their criminal convictions.

Civil Rights Act of 1871 (11). Most common basis for appeal of cases in which a party alleges deprivation of civil rights by another acting under color of law; see also **Section 1983 suits**.

civil rights actions (11). State or federal suits filed on the basis of violation of an individuals civil rights. See also **Civil Rights Act of 1871** and **Section 1983 suits**.

civil law (2). Law regulating disputes between private parties; may involve divorces, child custody controversies, breaches of contract, and torts.

collateral relief (11). Appealing cases that involve particularly large sentences from the state courts to the federal courts system, usually done through a writ of habeas corpus or a civil rights action.

collegial courts (11). Courts in which groups of judges issue decisions, commonly appearing at the federal appellate level; see also **courts of appellate jurisdiction**.

comity (1). Respect and recognition for the laws and regulations of another, often "sister," legal system, such as the recognition of marriage licenses between city and state governments; deference given by one court system to the jurisdiction and decisions of another.

common law (2). Sometimes called judge-made law; common law is unwritten and built on the legal precedence of letting previous decisions by judges stand as valid on future cases.

community-based sanctions (8). Sanctions that involve placement of convicted offenders into halfway houses, residential treatment centers, or other forms of treatment facility as opposed to incarceration; also may involve probation, parole, and community corrections.

community service (8). Sanctions that involve time spent "serving the community," usually in lieu of jail time; may be a probation add-on.

concurrence (2). Also called nexus, it is the essential connection between the wrongful act and the guilty mind or intent in the commission of a crime.

concurrent jurisdiction (10). The overlap of jurisdiction from multiple legal entities or law enforcement personnel over a case.

concurrent sentences (7,8). The service of multiple jail or prison sentences at the same time.

consecutive sentences (7,8). The service of back-to-back multiple jail or prison sentences.

conspiracy (2). Two or more people entering an agreement to commit a crime; a separate offense from the crime itself and not dependent on the actual commission of the crime.

constitutional courts (10). Federal trial and appellate courts, also called Article III courts, established under Article III of the U.S. Constitution.

constitutional law (2). The highest form of law in the United States, including the U.S. Constitution, and all fifty state constitutions; laws made by any agency or legislative body and judicial decisions must meet the test of constitutionality.

contingency fee (2,10). Fee for legal services based on a percentage of winnings alone and generally not requiring up-front payment.

continuance (3,7). A pretrial motion to postpone a court case until a later date, often to locate other witnesses or give attorneys more time to prepare for the trial.

contract defenders (5). A system of indigent defense in which organizations or private attorneys contract with the court system to provide legal counsel and representation to indigent defendants.

contributory negligence (2). The idea that plaintiffs can contribute to their own injury in a civil case, and may not have access to a 100 percent judgment as a result.

conversion (10). Unauthorized use of another's property in which damage or personal injury occurs.

corporal punishment (2). Physical punishment, such as caning or stoning, as opposed to monetary punishment or loss of liberty (imprisonment).

corpus delicti (2). The "body of the crime." In criminal law the elements that must be proven to establish that a crime has occurred. It included both intent and the wrongful act. See also *mala in se* **offenses** and *mala prohibita* **offenses**.

court administration (12). Services provided by offices or individuals that help in the everyday operations of a court or court system; these services may be provided by professional court administrators, or by elected officials such as recorders or court clerks; see **court administrator(s)** and **court management**.

court administrator(s) (4,6). Individuals trained in law, business administration, or similar disciplines, charged with overseeing the non-adjudicative functions of the courts.

court management (12). Professionally trained management personnel who perform essential non-legal functions of the court, such as budgeting, personnel management, case docketing, and jury scheduling.

court(s) of last resort (1,11). The final court for the appeal of a case based on errors of law; at the federal level, this is the United States Supreme Court.

court clerks (6). Often locally elected officials, they serve to docket cases, summon jurors, and provide courtroom ancillaries (such as court reporters).

court reporters (6). Individuals responsible for maintaining verbatim transcripts of all in-court proceedings.

courtroom work group (3). The group of daily players in a courtroom, including judges, lawyers, bailiffs, and court reporters; may involve other individuals on an occasional basis.

courts of appellate jurisdiction (1). Courts receiving appeals from trial courts based on errors of law.

courts of intermediate appellate jurisdiction (1). Often simply referred to as courts of appeals; these serve below the highest level of appellate courts, the courts of last resort.

courts of limited jurisdiction (9). Lower-level trial courts, sometimes referred to as the "people's courts"; may have jurisdiction over civil cases below a certain dollar amount, and misdemeanor criminal cases.

courts of original jurisdiction (1). General jurisdiction courts, first instance, or trial courts, through which a case enters the legal system.

crimes against persons (2). Crimes in which the victim of the crime is present, such as murder, rape, robbery, or assault.

criminal information (3,7). A formal document prepared by the prosecution and outlining the criminal charges against a defendant.

criminal intent (2). Or *mens rea*, the guilty mind behind the planning or commission of a crime.

criminal law (2). Law focused on crimes against persons or society; cases involve representatives of the government, the prosecutor, representing the people of the jurisdiction.

cross-examination (7). Opportunity for attorneys to question a witness that the other side has called at trial.

customary law (2). Law which results from social norms, mores, and folkways; informal systems of law; see also **khadi justice**.

day fines (8). An equitable economic penalty system in which offenders are given a fine based on their own personal daily income.

defendant (2). The party against whom a lawsuit is brought in both civil and criminal cases.

delinquency (9). Juvenile violations of the law that would be crimes if committed by an adult.

dependency (9). A state of want or need that a child is in through no fault of his or her parents or guardians.

deposition (6). A formal interview of a witness outside of the courtroom during which the witness is under oath and the interview is transcribed.

determinate sentences (8). A fixed, minimum amount of prison time that must be served for a specific crime, minimizing judicial discretion and early parole.

deterrence (7). Punishing a criminal offense to prevent the convicted from repeat criminal acts (specific deterrence) and to discourage others from the same acts (general deterrence).

direct examination (7). The opportunity for attorneys to question witnesses that their side has called at trial.

discovery (3,7). A motion providing an opportunity for each lawyer to review the list of witnesses, potential testimonies, and physical evidence the other side has before a trial begins.

discretionary appeals (11). The types of cases that appellate courts are not bound by law to accept. An example is cases accepted on writs of certiorari by the United States Supreme Court.

diversity of citizenship (10). Rule allowing federal district courts jurisdiction over legal disputes between residents of different states.

DNA fingerprinting (12). Genetic engineering process used to identify each person's unique DNA characteristics.

docket (6). The caseload of a court; includes dates that courtrooms and judges are available.

domestic relations (10). Legal issues centered on marriages and families, including divorce, wills, marriages, paternity disputes, and child custody.

domestic relations courts (9). Specialized courts that handle marriages, divorces, paternity suits, custody disputes, and child support awards.

drug court (9). Specialized courts that incorporate treatments of addiction and rehabilitation to a larger extent than a traditional court, including monitoring the success of the treatment; see also **therapeutic jurisprudence**.

duress (2). Compulsion to commit a crime by another, typically under threat of personal harm or harm against a loved one.

economic sanctions (8). Punishments imposed by courts that have a monetary value; these can include fines along with forfeitures of money and property.

en banc (11). Situations in which an appellate court hears cases with all judges or justices participating, rather than making decisions with panels of judges; see also **collegial courts**.

entrapment (2). An affirmative defense in which the person accused of a crime alleges that the idea for the criminal act originated with law enforcement officials.

equitable relief (2). Decisions rendered by courts in which the objective is to put matters back to their original state before a violation occurred; see also **chancery courts** and **equity**.

equity (1). A branch of law in which decisions are rendered on the basis of what is right; it is said that equity may speak when the law is silent, or when the law would bring about an unjust decision.

exculpatory evidence (3). Evidence that is designed to establish the innocence of an individual; it is evidence that excludes someone from suspicion.

excuses (2). Generally, the types of defenses in which the wrongful act is admitted, but reasons for commission of the act are offered; excuses focus on the blameworthiness of the actor; see also **justifications**.

executive appointment (4). Selection of judges on a temporary or permanent basis by the governor of a state or the President of the United States.

exhaustion of state remedies (11). The principle adhered to by federal courts that litigants must complete all steps involving state court processing before appealing a case to the federal courts.

expert witnesses (6,7). Individuals called to testify in court who possess specialized knowledge or expertise on a particular subject.

eyewitnesses (6,7). Individuals who have personally observed the commission of a crime or an event such as an automobile accident; these witnesses can testify as to their own personal observations and experiences.

false arrest (10). Taking individuals into police custody without sufficient probable cause.

false imprisonment (10). Illegal detention by either law enforcement authorities or private parties.

family courts (9). Tribunals that have jurisdiction over a wide variety of family issues including divorce, child custody, paternity, and probate matters (wills and inheritance).

federalism (1). The notion that different levels of government have different types of responsibilities.

Federalists (10). One of the nation's first political parties; members advocated a strong national government, and prominent Federalists included Alexander Hamilton and John Adams.

fee system (9). The payment of judges (such as justices of the peace) based on the amount of fines and fees they collect.

felonies (2). The most serious category of criminal offenses; felonies normally call for incarceration in a state or federal prison for more than one year.

fines (8). Monetary punishments levied in certain cases; fines typically are imposed in petty misdemeanor or infraction cases such as traffic offenses, although they can be imposed for certain felonies as well.

folkways (2). The basis for customary law in places that typically do not have written criminal codes; see also **mores** and **norms**.

forcible rape (2). As defined by the Uniform Crime Reports, this is the unlawful carnal knowledge (that is, sexual assault) of a female by a male; in many states this now has been revised to more gender-neutral language such as criminal sexual penetration.

forfeiture of property (8). The requirement that goods (vehicles, homes, and other tangible property) that may be the proceeds of a crime be surrendered to the courts or law enforcement authorities.

general jurisdiction courts (1). Courts that are authorized to hear a wide variety of cases including civil and criminal matters.

general trial jurisdiction courts (10). See **general jurisdiction courts**.

going rate (3). The "value" of a case determined by the seriousness of the charge(s), the criminal history of the accused, the nature of the victim, and other related factors.

good time credits (8). The amount of time that may be deducted from a prison inmate's sentence as a result of good behavior and/or participation in rehabilitation programming.

grand jury (7). A body of citizens that meets periodically to review the cases presented by the prosecuting attorney to determine whether there is sufficient probable cause for the cases to continue on to trial.

habitual offender laws (8). Statutes that allow for additional punishment to be imposed for those offenders who have accumulated a sufficient number of felony convictions; in most states these laws come into play when an individual has been convicted of at least three felonies.

half-way houses (8). Non-secure residential placements for certain offenders who have been ordered by the courts to be placed on probation, or as transitional living facilities for offenders on parole who have been released from prison.

hearing officers (4). Individuals designated by the courts or other bodies to hear a limited range of cases; in most instances these individuals will have to have law degrees, although there may be situations where this is not the case; see also **judicial adjuncts** and **referees**.

horizontal overcharging (8). The practice by certain prosecutors to charge criminal defendants with all possible offenses; may be known as "bed-sheeting."

hung jury (6,7). A jury that cannot reach a verdict as a result of a split vote either to convict or acquit.

impeachment (4). The formal process whereby a legislative body (U.S. Congress or state legislature) brings charges against and tries an individual—such as a judge—who has been accused of misconduct in office.

incapacitation (7). The process of incarcerating individuals in order to minimize their criminal opportunities.

inchoate offenses (2). Criminal offenses that for some reasons are incomplete; these include conspiracies, attempts, and solicitations.

indeterminate sentences (8). Criminal sentences that have a minimum and maximum range established by the legislature (for example, one to ten years); these sentences are imposed by judges, but the actual amount of time to be served will be determined by a paroling authority.

indictment (7). A formal accusation of an individual of a crime presented by a grand jury to the appropriate court.

indigent defendants (5). Individuals who are financially unable to hire their own attorneys.

infancy (2). The defense that alleges that the party accused of wrongdoing is below the age of criminal responsibility (age seven under common law).

inferior courts (1). Tribunals that have relatively narrow jurisdictions; they may be authorized to hear civil cases in which the amount in dispute is below a certain dollar value (i.e., small claims) or misdemeanor criminal cases.

informal probation (8). A pre-adjudication diversion process typically used with certain accused delinquent offenders; in most instances, the youngster will have to admit to the charges, then the case will be referred to a less strenuous form of community supervision.

infractions (2,8). Violations of municipal or township ordinances; many of these are traffic offenses, but they may involve other behaviors as well.

initial appearance(s) (7,9). The point at which an accused offender is first brought before a judge; issues such as the charges, representation by counsel, and the amount of bail generally are dealt with at this point.

injunctions (1). A court order requiring that some action be halted.

in limine **motions** (7). Motions that request that courts limit the issues or evidence that may be presented in civil trials.

inquisitional justice (1). The approach to trying cases that has been used in many nations outside of the Anglo-American system of legal influence; under these systems the police, prosecutors, and judges all cooperate in the gathering of evidence; in effect, the defendant must prove innocence rather than the government proving guilt.

insanity (2). The criminal defense that alleges that while the defendant committed the wrongful act, he or she did so with a mental incapacity that nullified the free will that he or she normally would have exercised; if a jury finds a defendant not guilty by reason of insanity, the court normally will order the person confined in some type of mental health treatment facility.

intentional tort (10). Civil harms that result from deliberate acts by a person; these cases require proof that the person that caused the harm (the tortfeasor) acted in a willful way.

interim appointments (4). The authority exercised by governors and the President of the United States to appoint judges (or other officials) to office on a temporary basis until the normal process of filling the vacancy can be exercised.

intermediate appellate courts (11). First-level courts of appeals; where these courts exist, they receive cases that are appealed from general jurisdiction trial courts; often these courts are called the courts of appeals or similar designations.

intermediate sanctions (8). Any type of punishment that exists between traditional probation and incarceration; this can include intensive supervision, non-secure residential placements, community service, and restitution, among others.

intoxication (2). Mental and physical incapacity caused by the ingestion of drugs and/or alcohol to the point of rendering a person incapable of normal functioning.

irrational justice systems (2). Legal systems within which there are relatively few written rules; decisions in cases are based on individual circumstances, and verdicts are handed down by a trial ruler or chief; under such systems there is very little stability or predictability in outcomes; see also **khadi justice**.

jailhouse snitches (12). Informants serving time in jail who are used by law enforcement authorities; these individuals are asked to report on the actions and conversations they have with other jail inmates in order to secure incriminating admissions or confessions.

judicial accountability (4). The notion that judges should be answerable to some group (such as the voters) or other body (such as the state supreme court or judicial conduct commission) for their actions both on and off the bench.

judicial adjuncts (4). Officials who have the duty of assisting judges in the performance of their legal responsibilities; see also **hearing officers** and **referees**.

judicial conduct commissions (4). Governmental bodies normally composed of judges and attorneys (and sometimes private citizens) that must review and potentially sanction judges for their actions; see also **judicial accountability**.

judicial discipline (4). To undertake sanctions against judges when they are found to have committed acts that are prohibited.

judicial independence (4,12). The notion that the judicial branch of government is co-equal to, but separately controlled from, the "political" (executive and legislative) branches of government.

judicial review (1,2,11). First asserted by the U.S. Supreme Court in the case of *Marbury v. Madison*, it claimed for the Court the right to examine and determine the constitutionality of acts of the President and the Congress.

Judiciary Act of 1789 (10). One of the first pieces of legislation passed by the very first session of the United States Congress; it established the nature and functioning of the judicial branch of government, including the number of Supreme Court justices and the types of inferior courts that would exist; it also created the office of United States Marshal for each of the federal court districts.

jurisdiction (1). The legal authority to hear and decide cases by a court; jurisdiction may be constitutionally or statutorily established, and it includes the dimensions of geography, hierarchy, and subject matter.

jury commissioners (6). Elected or appointed officials whose primary responsibility is to assemble a sufficient number of jurors for the cases scheduled by the courts of a particular jurisdiction.

jury nullification (3). Any instance where a jury votes to acquit a defendant, irrespective of the evidence, as a result of the jurors believing that the law is unjust or the sentence disproportionate to the offense.

justice of the peace (9). Judicial office inherited from the English legal tradition; in many states the justices of the peace were not required to possess formal legal training, and often they were paid on the basis of the amount of fines they levied; see also **fee system** and **lay judges**.

justifications (2). Legal defenses that assert that an individual acted in a way that is expected or even preferred by the law; the classic case of justification is self-defense where one life was taken in the protection of another life.

juvenile court (9). Tribunals that have their jurisdictions limited to those individuals under the age of majority (eighteen in most instances); cases may involve delinquency, dependency, and neglect or abuse.

khadi justice (2). A notion articulated by Max Weber based on tribal justice under customary law; the khadi is the chief or tribal leader who also acts as a wise man or judge in disputes between parties.

larceny–theft (2). One of the eight offenses listed in the Part 1 index crimes of the FBI's Uniform Crime Reports; this offense consists of the unlawful taking away of the property of another with the intention of depriving the owner of that property.

law clerks (11). Individuals who serve as assistants, especially to appellate court judges; in most instances law clerks are recent law school graduates who use the clerking opportunity to gain further experience in the law.

law enforcement (1). The responsibility of police agencies to make sure that citizens are obeying the laws that have been enacted by legislative bodies; sometimes used to describe police agencies themselves.

lay judge(s) (4,9). Judges who do not possess law degrees but who, nevertheless, are allowed to serve as jurists in certain courts; see also **justices of the peace** and **magistrates' courts**.

lay witnesses (6). Persons called to testify in a case that do not fall under the designation of an expert witness; see **eyewitnesses**.

legal aid societies (5). Organizations that exist in many cities providing free legal services to indigent clients on a free or reduced-fee basis; in many instances the services are limited to civil matters.

legal clinics (5). Mechanisms designed to give second- and third-year law school students the opportunity to practice their legal skills under the supervision of licensed attorneys.

legal precedence (2). Often associated with the Latin phrase *stare decisis*, meaning "let the decision stand"; this is the practice of courts to decide present cases based on the types of decisions rendered in similar cases in the past.

legality principle (2). There are two key elements to this legal principle: through the publication of statutes, citizens have the right to know what the laws are in advance; additionally, offenses should not be so vague in their meaning that actors in the criminal justice system are left to their own interpretations of the offense; it prohibits the punishment for behaviors on an *ex post facto* (after the fact) basis when no crime originally existed.

legislative courts (10). Under the United States Constitution, these are the so-called Article I courts that can be created (and abolished) by congressional statute; judges in these courts do not enjoy lifetime tenure like those of the Article III courts.

lex talionis (1). Literally, the "law of the claw"; this is the principle of retribution often expressed in the phrase "an eye for an eye, and a tooth for a tooth."

libel (10). A written form of malicious communication designed to defame the character or reputation of another person; see also **slander**.

limited jurisdiction (1). Courts that have a legislatively defined narrow set of cases over which they have authority; see also **courts of limited jurisdiction**.

local legal culture (3,10). The customs that mark the regular pattern of interaction experienced by judges and attorneys who work together on a regular basis in a particular jurisdiction.

long ballot (4). First implemented under the Presidency of Andrew Jackson, this is the approach whereby all offices within a given political entity (city, county, or state) are popularly elected on a regular basis.

magistrates' courts (9). Courts of limited jurisdiction that hear minor civil matters and misdemeanors in criminal cases in some states; under court reorganization schemes these courts often replaced the justice of the peace courts; see also **courts of limited jurisdiction** and **lay judges**.

mala in se **offenses** (2). Acts that are considered wrong because they are bad in and of themselves, even in the absence of statutory law. Typical examples are murder and robbery.

mala prohibita **offenses** (2). Acts that may not be innately wrong, but which are considered wrong as a result of legislation prohibiting them. Examples include seatbelt and motorcycle helmet laws.

mandatory appeals (11). The types of cases that must be reviewed by appellate courts based on either constitutional requirements or statutory law.

mandatory minimum sentences (8). Statutory provisions that require judges to impose certain mandatory prison sentences on offenders convicted of specified offenses.

master list(s) (6,7). These are the complete lists of all persons eligible for jury service within a particular court jurisdiction; from these lists summonses are sent to prospective jurors.

master wheels (6). Mechanisms used to select potential jury members; see also **master list(s)**.

masters (special masters) (4). Individuals appointed by judges to oversee court orders; masters have been utilized in prison litigation and school desegregation cases; see also **judicial adjuncts** and **referees**.

med-arb (12). A hybrid form of alternative dispute resolution in which mediation is first attempted and then, failing successful resolution, the case is scheduled for arbitration; see also **arbitration** and **mediation**.

mediation (12). A form of alternative dispute resolution where a third party (mediator) meets with the two disputing parties in an attempt to reach a negotiated resolution; in most instances mediation is not binding, and the parties can end negotiations and attempt resolution in some other manner.

mediators (4). Neutral third parties who attempt to help two opposing parties arrive at a negotiated settlement in a number of different types of disputes.

mens rea (2). Criminal intent; this expresses the element of the crime that often is described as the guilty mind.

merit selection/Missouri Plan (4). A method of choosing judges that utilizes a committee to select nominees whenever a vacancy occurs; a short list of nominees is submitted to the governor, who then makes an interim appointment; the appointed judge typically must run for office during the next general election and thereafter will run unopposed in a retention election.

minitrials (12). A hybrid form of alternative dispute resolution where all of the elements of the trial exist in abbreviated form and strict time limits are placed on each element of the proceedings.

misdemeanors (2). The least serious criminal offenses; conviction of a misdemeanor may result in a fine or incarceration for up to one in year a local facility such as a jail.

mitigating circumstances (8). Any factor that would reduce the seriousness of a particular criminal offense; for contrast see **aggravating circumstances**.

mores (2). The moral principles under which a group of people live; the basis for customary law; see also **folkways** and **norms**.

motor vehicle theft (2). One of the eight Part 1 index crimes in the FBI's Uniform Crime Reports; the taking and carrying away of any self-contained vehicle such as an automobile, truck, bus, motorcycle, sport utility vehicle, all-terrain vehicle, or snowmobile.

municipal courts (9). Tribunals that are authorized (typically under city charters) to hear violations of city ordinances; see also **courts of inferior jurisdiction** and **infractions**.

murder (homicide) (2). One of the eight Part 1 index crimes in the FBI's Uniform Crime reports; it consists of the willful and unlawful taking of the life of another human being.

natural law (2). The notion that human nature and characteristics are unchanging and, therefore, there is a set of legal standards or guiding principles that supersede laws created by human beings; laws that emanate from a superior, divine being; the Framers of the Constitution called these "inalienable rights."

necessity (2). A legal defense that takes the form of an excuse; the reasoning that an action was required or unavoidable given the circumstances.

neglect (9). In juvenile courts, the charge that parents or guardians willfully and deliberately fail to provide necessities such as food, clothing, shelter, and education for their children or children under their legal custody.

negotiation (12). A form of alternative dispute resolution where the two opposing parties engage in face-to-face discussions in order to resolve their disagreement, without the help of a third party.

nolle prosequi (3). A motion by a prosecuting attorney that indicates the inability or unwillingness to move forward with a criminal case; in simplest terms, "no prosecution."

nolo contendere (7). A plea of no contest; under this plea a criminal defendant does not admit guilt, but does not contest the state's charges; this plea has the practical effect of a guilty plea in that the judge can impose a sentence; tactically, no-contest pleas cannot be used in a civil trial that may follow a criminal trial.

non-negligent manslaughter (2). A less serious form of unlawful death than murder, but one resulting from some cause other than negligence; typically the person who causes a non-negligent manslaughter has acted in a way that is reckless or that exhibits a wanton disregard for the safety of others.

non-partisan elections (4). A method of judicial selection where candidates for the office of judge run without party labels included on the ballot.

norms (2). The typically expected patterns of behavior for any group of people; the basis for customary law within groups that may not have written codes; see also **folkways** and **mores**.

one-shotters (5). Individuals who typically come to court on only one occasion to litigate some issue.

original jurisdiction (9). Exercised by courts that have the authority to hear certain types of cases on an initial basis; see **courts of original jurisdiction**.

order maintenance (1). One of the original functions of police agencies; simply defined, this is keeping the public functioning in an orderly fashion.

panel attorneys (5). These are attorneys appointed in indigent defendant cases that cannot be handled by public defenders as a result of conflicts of interest (for example, when there are multiple indigent codefendants).

parens patriae (9). The legal doctrine that originated in England stating that the king was the "father of the country"; under juvenile law the notion that the judge was to play the role of kindly parent and to act in the best interests of the children coming before the juvenile court.

partisan election (4). A method of choosing judges in which party labels for each candidate appear on the ballot.

paternalism (12). The notion that actors in the juvenile justice system should act as parental figures and decide what is best for youngsters; especially appears in cases where juvenile justice officials act to protect the interests of juvenile females.

peers (6). In a general sense, those individuals who are similar in age and interests to a person; legally, people who are eligible to serve on juries.

peremptory challenges (4,6,7). The basis for eliminating prospective jurors without having to state a particular cause for their exclusion.

petit juries (6). Trial juries; they are smaller (in some instances) and have different functions than grand juries; these juries are the triers of fact in court cases that use juries.

petty misdemeanors (2,8). See **petty offenses**.

petty offenses (9). The least serious misdemeanors; in most instances, these cases call for fines or incarceration of less than six months in a local jail.

plaintiff (2). The person who initiates a civil lawsuit.

plea bargain (7). Negotiations between the defense attorney and the prosecuting attorney over a guilty plea in exchange for leniency through a reduction in the charges, the number of counts, or the recommended sentence.

preliminary hearing(s) (7,9). A type of hearing conducted early in the criminal process to address the charges that have been filed, the issue of representation by counsel, and bail; the primary purpose of a preliminary hearing is to determine whether the state has sufficient probable cause for the case to move forward.

premises liability (10). Responsibility for harms (torts) that can occur within a person's building or on a person's property.

preponderance of the evidence (2). The weight-of-evidence standard utilized in civil cases; defined as just enough evidence to tip the jury's decision making in favor of one party over another.

presentence investigation report (4,7,8). After a jury has determined guilt, the probation department will prepare a presentence investigation report to be presented to the judge; this report contains information on the defendant's criminal history, work or school history, military record (if applicable), family situation, and other variables that would help the judge determine the most appropriate sentence.

preventive detention (7). The use of short-term incarceration prior to a trial in order to prevent the defendant from fleeing the jurisdiction or committing other offenses while on pre-trial release.

probate (9). The types of cases that deal with the resolution of wills and inheritances.

probation (8). Conditional community supervision following adjudication; a sentence imposed by a judge in lieu of incarceration.

pro bono (5). Short for *pro bono publico* or, literally, "for the public good"; the basis under which some attorneys accept cases for no fees or reduced fees for clients who cannot afford to pay for their services.

procedural law (2). "The rules of the game"; the provisions under which courts must operate and the guidelines that must be followed in the application and adjudication of both civil and criminal law.

prosecuting attorney (5). The government official who represents the citizens of the jurisdiction in the criminal law process; may be known as district attorney, state's attorney, commonwealth attorney, or a similar title.

prosecutor (2). See **prosecuting attorney**.

pro se **litigation/proceedings** (9,12). The practice of representing oneself in a civil or criminal trial; the absence of an attorney representing the defendant in a case.

public defender (5). Attorneys paid for by the state to represent indigent defendants.

public order offenses (2). Broadly defined, these are any behaviors that result in a disturbance of the public peace; included in this category are public drunkenness, fighting (sometimes called affray), and disturbing the peace.

public service (1). The types of matters handled by police agencies that do not include law enforcement or order maintenance; public service calls could be classified as "other" matters handled by the police.

Racketeer Influenced and Corrupt Organizations Act (8,10). Federal legislation passed by Congress in 1970 aimed at controlling all forms of organized crime; it provides for prison terms and substantial fines, along with assets forfeitures, for persons convicted of racketeering.

rape shield laws (12). Legislation designed to protect the victims of rape from having to testify about previous (and unrelated) sexual experiences.

referees (4). Individuals employed by the courts to hear certain limited matters; referees may be attorneys, or in some cases they may be retired judges; see also **hearing officers** and **judicial adjuncts**.

rehabilitation (7). Treatment of convicted criminal offenders to address deficiencies that they may experience in order to prevent future violations of the law.

release on recognizance (7). A method of posting bond that requires only a person's word (typically on a signed document) that he or she will return to court on the scheduled date; RORs do not require that money or property be offered as surety.

rent-a-judge (12). A form of alternative dispute resolution permitted in some states whereby the parties can stipulate that they will accept hiring a part time or retired judge to hear a case in order to expedite matters; often used in jurisdictions that have severe backlogs on cases such as those involving personal injury following a traffic accident.

repeat players (5). These are individuals who frequently return to court to litigate routine matters in which they are involved; insurance companies and those involved in the consumer credit business often are repeat players.

residential treatment centers (8). Non-secure facilities for the treatment of convicted offenders, typically within the communities from which they come.

restitution (2). To pay a victim back for losses suffered from either property or personal crimes.

restorative justice (2). A response to criminal behavior that seeks to reestablish the balance between the victim and offender and the offender and society that has been disrupted as a result of crime; it stresses offender accountability, development of personal competencies, and emphasis on public safety.

retribution (7). Punishment for the sake of punishment; retribution looks backwards in that it focuses on the harm done by the offender, in contrast to deterrence or rehabilitation, both of which are forward looking; see also *lex talionis.*

right to counsel (2,5). The procedural right guaranteed to accused criminal offenders under the Sixth Amendment to the U.S. Constitution; originally understood to apply to federal courts and federal cases, but extended to the states in cases such as *Gideon v. Wainwright.*

robbery (2). The taking of anything of value from a person by force or threat of force.

Section 1983 suits (11). The codification of the Civil Rights Act of 1871 protecting individuals from violations by agents of the government acting under color of law.

self-defense (2). A justification defense that allows the use of force (up to and including deadly force) to protect one's life from an imminent threat of bodily harm.

senior judges (4). In the federal system, at the time of retirement, judges can choose to go onto senior status and they can continue to hear cases on a selective basis.

sentencing guidelines (8). A form of sentencing designed to reduce sentence disparities among similar offenses and offenders; some governmental body (often a sentencing commission) determines the appropriate sentences for specific offenses; in most guided sentencing systems the two elements that are considered relevant are the present offense and the offender's criminal history.

separation of powers (1). The principle that state and federal governments divide their responsibilities among three branches—legislative, executive, and judicial—that are separate but equal.

sequestered jury/juries (6,7). The process of confining jury members away from public contact during the process of trying a case and of jury deliberations.

shock incarceration (8). The approach to confining convicted offenders for short periods of time to "give them a taste" of what life behind bars is really like.

slander (10). A form of malicious oral communication that is designed to defame the character or reputation of another person; see also **libel**.

small claims courts (9). Tribunals that have responsibilities for civil cases under a certain dollar value; many times, the litigants represent themselves in these courts; see also **courts of limited jurisdiction**.

solicitation (2). An offense in which one person offers an inducement (usually money) to another person to commit a crime; see also **inchoate offenses**.

solicitors (5). In the British legal system these are lawyers who handle cases outside of the courtroom setting; see also **barristers**.

Speedy Trial Act of 1974 (10). Legislation that mandates that federal authorities must produce an indictment or criminal information within 30 days of an accused federal offender's arrest, and then a trial must be commenced within the next 70 days unless continuance motions are granted.

state attorney general (5). The title used for most of the chief legal officials at the state level; most of these individuals are chosen in partisan elections, and they often handle a variety of criminal and civil matters.

structured sentences (8). The types of sentences that result from the use of sentencing guidelines and other prescriptive forms of sentencing.

subject matter jurisdiction (1). These are the specific types of cases over which courts have legal authority.

substantive law (2). The type of law that defines offenses; the statutes that contain the substantive law provide the different elements that must be proven by the state in order to secure a conviction.

summary probation (8). A type of informal probation in which the convicted offender is not required to be supervised in the community, or where the supervision is relatively limited.

staff attorneys (11). Unlike law clerks, staff attorneys often work for the courts themselves providing a number of legal services that the judges (especially appellate judges) are unable to perform.

status offenses (9). Violations of the law for juveniles that would not be violations if committed by adults; includes such behaviors as truancy, running away, and possession of alcohol.

statutory law (2). The creation of laws by legislative bodies; these laws are systematically codified and published.

tariffs (9). Duties imposed on imported and exported goods.

therapeutic jurisprudence (9). An approach to settling criminal cases that focuses more on the solution of underlying social problems than on the traditional adjudication of legal matters.

timeliness of appeal (11). In all jurisdictions, appeals from adverse verdicts must be filed within certain periods established by statutory guidelines.

tort claims (9). See **torts**.

torts (10). Civil wrongs; torts are offenses against individuals that involve the breach of a legal duty or obligation.

trial *de novo* (7,9). To try a case all over again; typically happens in situations where the initial trial was conducted in a court of limited jurisdiction and the conviction is appealed to a court of general trial jurisdiction.

true bill (7). A formal accusation handed down by a grand jury charging an individual with a crime; often called an indictment.

truth in sentencing (8). The approach to criminal sentencing that requires convicted offenders to serve some substantial portion (often 85%) of the sentence imposed.

typologies of law (2). The different forms that the law can take or different functions performed by law within a society; classification methods for distinguishing the different purposes served by law.

unified court systems (10). Generally, the approach to court organization that limits the jurisdiction to one type of trial court; elimination of specialized courts; see also **courts of general trial jurisdiction**.

United States Attorneys (5). The chief legal authorities for the United States government in each of the federal system's ninety-four court districts.

U.S. magistrate judges (4). Formerly known as United States Commissioners, these judges operate under the supervision of the federal district judges, and they are responsible for duties such as issuing warrants, conducting pretrial hearings, and adjudicating certain federal misdemeanor cases; unlike the federal district judges for whom they work, magistrate judges serve fixed terms of office.

venire(s) (6,7). These are the groups of potential jurors from which juries are selected to try cases; see also **master lists** and **master wheels**.

vertical overcharging (8). The practice by some prosecuting attorneys of charging criminal defendants with offenses higher than may be proven in order to have negotiating room; see also **horizontal overcharging** and **plea bargaining**.

voir dire (4,7). From the French "to speak the truth"; the process of questioning prospective jurors by the attorneys and/or the judge in order to determine their suitability to serve as jurors.

voucher system (5). A mechanism that provides indigent defendants with a voucher (or chit) for a limited amount of money that permits them to secure their own attorney at government expense.

wedding cake model (10). A diagram proposed by Samuel Walker to describe the different amounts of cases at different degrees of seriousness (misdemeanors, less serious felonies, serious felonies, and celebrated cases) and the different ways these cases are processed.

weight of evidence (2). The amount of proof necessary to secure a favorable verdict in either civil or criminal cases.

writs of certiorari (11). Orders from superior appellate courts (such as the U.S. Supreme Court) requiring that a lower court send the record forward on particular cases; it involves a discretionary route of appeal.

writs of habeas corpus (11). Literally "having the body" or "you have the body"; these are show-cause hearings that require the government to demonstrate why a conviction was just and, thus, why the convicted offender is legally incarcerated.

writ of mandamus (11). A court order requiring that individuals (usually government officials) perform a certain task under their authority.

zero-sum game (1,12). The idea from game theory that in contests (such as trials) where there are two opposing parties, whatever one side wins the other side necessarily loses.

TABLE OF CASES

INDEX

413